D0405164

Teaching the Literatures of Early America

Edited by
Carla Mulford

The Modern Language Association of America
New York   1999

© 1999 by The Modern Language Association of America
All rights reserved. Printed in the United States of America

For information about obtaining permission to reprint material from MLA book publications, send your request by mail (see address below), e-mail (permissions@mla.org), or fax (212 477-9863).

Library of Congress Cataloging-in-Publication Data

Teaching the literatures of early America / edited by Carla Mulford.
    p.   cm. — (Options for teaching; 15)
    Includes bibliographical references and index.
    ISBN 0–87352–358–X (cloth) — ISBN 0–87352–359–8 (pbk.)
    1. American literature — Colonial period, ca. 1600–1775 — Study and teaching.   2. American literature — Revolutionary period, 1775–1783 — Study and teaching.   3. United States — History — Revolution, 1775–1783 — Literature and the revolution — Study and teaching.   4. Pluralism (Social sciences) — United States — Study and teaching.   5. American literature — Minority authors — Study and teaching.   6. American literature — 1783–1850 — Study and teaching.   7. Decolonization in literature — Study and teaching.   8. Minorities in literature — Study and teaching.   9. America — Literatures — Study and teaching.   I. Mulford, Carla, 1955–   II. Series.

PS186.T43 1999
810'.7 — dc21   99–047304

ISSN 1079–2562

Cover illustration of the paperback edition: Detail from *Quiviriae Regnum,* by Cornelis De Jode (1568–1600). Antwerp, 1593. Photo courtesy of Edward E. Ayer Collection, The Newberry Library, Chicago.

Published by The Modern Language Association of America
10 Astor Place, New York, New York 10003-6981

Teaching
the Literatures of
Early America

Modern Language Association of America
Options for Teaching
Joseph Gibaldi, Series Editor

For teachers of
early American literature
and for their students

Contents

Part I: Issues, Themes, Methods

Beyond the Boundaries of the Americas

Part II: Selected Courses

Part III: Resources

Acknowledgments

This volume represents the culmination of a long process that began at the 1994 MLA Annual Convention, when I first spoke with Joseph Gibaldi, MLA director of Book Acquisitions and Development, about my interest in publishing a collection of essays on teaching the writings of early America. In the conversations we had since then, Joseph continued to encourage the project, and with goodwill and unflagging interest he saw it through the progressive stages from the initial writing of the proposal for the volume to the conclusion of the volume's second review. I want here to thank him for both his patience and his prodding as the contributors and I addressed the concerns raised by the sometimes perplexingly diverse responses given the project by its various readers all along the way. I also thank the editorial staff at the MLA for their attention to this diverse manuscript. A distinct pleasure in bringing the collection to press was having the opportunity to work with Elizabeth Holland, who managed the project with the interest and concern that every author and editor hopes for.

I would also like to thank the English department staff at Pennsylvania State University, and particularly Pat Gibboney for helping me out with matters relating to the production of the text. Angela Vietto helped me get the manuscript together initially, at a crucial stage in the project, when I faced continued computer glitches in the generation of text. Louis A. Cellucci helped out at a very busy time by proofing the manuscript and reading carefully to assist my preparation of the index. That the volume *has* an index owes much to Louis's efforts.

Yet ultimately credit for the volume belongs with its contributors, who with good humor stayed with the project through the myriad stages of review and revision and whose excellence in teaching enabled them to face the difficult task of writing about teaching. As teachers they have shown us ways to think about and to study the difficult materials of the past. But teaching is a process that also integrally involves students; the varied and interesting responses of our students continually enabled us to find renewed enthusiasm and refreshingly original views of the records of events that happened centuries ago. We thus dedicate this volume to all teachers of early American literature and to their students.

Carla Mulford

Introduction

The teaching of early American literature has long been freighted with the tensions and contradictions inhering in any work that relates to such highly charged issues as the study of European empires in the Americas, of United States nationhood, and of competing racial and ethnic groups on the North American continent. It should come as no surprise, then, that in the last quarter of the twentieth century, an era of shifting geopolitical boundaries and tremendous movements of populations and cultures across the globe (not to mention to and within the United States), scholars and teachers have shown renewed interest in discussing questions central to the functioning of "national" literature. Books and articles abound on questions such as what "American" literature is, what "the literary" is in something defined by a geopolitical space, and how can we teach whatever it is we are calling early American literature. This collection is an indication of the validity of such questions and the rigorous, invigorating, and diverse ways in which scholars and teachers have been addressing the complexities of early materials.

1

Both *early* and *America* are terms that have been under intense scrutiny by scholars, most notably by the literary historian William Spengemann but also by scholars as diverse in their methodologies as Myra Jehlen, Jay Fliegelman, Richard DeProspo, Cathy Davidson, and Annette Kolodny. Early Americanists are questioning the usefulness of the qualifier *early* because of its decided chronological bias in an era when we have been taught to reexamine the constructedness of our conceptions of the past and have been involved in the philosophical critique of the idea of historical representation. We are likewise finding in the term *America* equally as questionable a bias in terms of national identity, in that when most people from the United States say "American," they mean the United States, although the term also historically has been taken to identify the space occupied by Mexico and by Canada in North America and by many different nation-states in South America.

To address the issue of competing narratives about early America and the varieties of definitions possible would take a monograph in itself, of course. Yet it will be useful to identify here what I mean by titling this collection of essays *Teaching the Literatures of Early America*. The words *early* and *America* as descriptors are constructed and comparative terms, surely, but they do help us designate an era that goes roughly from indigenous beginnings, including Native American materials and materials from European contact with peoples of the Americas, to the time of United States nation making, that is, to about 1812, when the United States finalized its political separation from Great Britain (though not from British culture). In general, then, this collection represents the teaching of materials inclusive of Native oral materials and records of Spanish, French, and English colonial contacts through, roughly, the confederation of the Anglo-American states and of what in political culture is called the early Republic. As teachers increase the range of study of colonial groups, it is likely that at some future time a collection like this — or perhaps a revised edition of this collection — will also be able to offer essays on the teaching of Russian, Scandinavian, Dutch, and German writings about the Americas. Many teachers of early American materials are incorporating these materials into the classroom, even though the anthologies currently available do not speak much about the settlement efforts of any of these groups. We can hope that eventually anthologists will begin to consider representing the full range of colonial writing in North America.

Exactly what the literatures from America are is a complicated question. Many scholars still take the literary to represent those writings written with particular artistic-aesthetic, inspirational, or belletristic implications. Notions of what "literature" is will vary from culture to culture, and within any given culture conceptions of "the literary" will vary across time. As this volume attempts to discuss multiple cultures and several decades, it seems appropriate to use the term *literatures* to identify the writings we are teaching, even if some of the materials discussed might not seem particularly "literary" to some who work within particular cultures and who scrutinize specific areas of aesthetic interest. As a whole, the volume represents the varieties of writings scholars and teachers have been examining for the past few decades in their attempt to reconceptualize "American" literature as not merely a function of British culture or a putatively American past, and it offers approaches and methods that are conceptual, topical, national, and generic.

The first section, "Issues, Themes, Methods," is composed of multidisciplinary approaches and then of more narrowly framed examinations, first of the imperial cultures of Spain, France, and England and then of genre studies. This section offers a broad range of approaches to the study of early materials, and it complements the next section, "Selected Courses," where five teachers offer detailed discussions, with the syllabi, of courses they have taught. In the final section, "Resources," teachers can find useful materials, some used by the essay writers, summarized and listed.

"Issues, Themes, Methods" begins with essays addressing broadly conceptual issues in early American studies, with emphasis on introducing new methods and materials for use with students. The complexities of teaching groups traditionally not considered dominant are apparent in the opening essays by James Ruppert and by Amy E. Winans. Treating a number of approaches beginning teachers might take with Native American materials, Ruppert addresses the issues of genre, history, and meaning. Winans shows how teachers might get students to engage the discourse from early African America by examining the concrete circumstances in which Africans' materials reached print during the eighteenth century. Approaches to early American studies by way of gender differentiation interest Sharon M. Harris, whose essay provides a useful glossing of women's writings even as it highlights the teaching of women's writings from the perspectives of feminism and cultural studies. Pattie Cowell's examination of teaching issues in multicultural practice offers a position from which students can be asked to consider the various ways in which they might address Crèvecoeur's historic question, "What is an American?" Carla Mulford discusses some of the means and methods whereby teachers can encourage students to consider the conceptual and ideological problems raised by studies in colonialism.

The following two essays of "Issues, Methods, Themes" treat the writings of imperial Europeans (from Spain, France, and England) and of Anglo-Americans seeking to form their "more perfect union." E. Thomson Shields, Jr., and Dana D. Nelson show ways to discuss the Spanish colonial past as part of American history. Rosalie Murphy Baum suggests how we might fill, with our students, what has been taken by some to be the largest gap in colonial North American culture study: French colonialism.

English and Anglo-American materials — still by far the largest group of materials studied, anthologized, and taught in the United States — are treated in the next essays. David S. Shields turns attention to the writings that came from English people in what are now called the South and the Caribbean. He argues that the tensions in British imperial culture "were manifested most vividly in writings generated by and about the staple colonies," colonies so called because they provided the agricultural staples that would be transformed in England into finished goods. Philip F. Gura discusses the well-known Puritan writings that emanated from England's northern colonies. Frank Shuffelton suggests ways that teachers can examine with students the philosophical, cultural, and linguistic complications of an American Enlightenment culture transmitted in various arenas, from taverns and coffeehouses to books of philosophy in full leather dress.

Nicholas D. Rombes shows how, in teaching early Republican materials and especially in teaching the Federalist and Anti-Federalist debates, we might begin to help students come to terms with the sectional divisions and the differing attitudes toward law and custom that still seem to torment citizens of the United States today.

Genre studies of early materials conclude this section. Teachers who wish to introduce generic interest into existing courses in early American studies as well as those who wish to add an early American component to their existing genre courses in American studies or in literary studies in general will find these essays particularly useful. Their emphasis on Anglo-American materials suggests the continued prominence of Anglo-American voices in United States literary culture. William J. Scheick offers an approach that attempts to deepen students' perspectives on verse from the early era in an incremental way. Joseph Fichtelberg suggests the rich ways in which fiction can be used to underscore the rapidity of cultural change in the era of the early republic. Jeffrey H. Richards examines the many ways in which teachers can approach what are perhaps the most neglected areas of early American genre studies, drama and theater. Writing on early American autobiography, Gregory Eiselein indicates the importance — especially in our own era of talk shows and identity concerns — of having students explore the relation (and the tensions) between self-expression and one's nation or national identity. Kathryn Zabelle Derounian-Stodola shows the vitality of the captivity genre and its important uses not only within Puritan culture but also across cultures.

"Selected Courses" follows the more extended discussions framed in the preceding essays with concrete teaching examples and devices for use in particular course offerings. Russell Reising's treatment of the early American literature survey will provide for teachers new to the field a useful overview of how the survey might be approached using almost any standard anthology. Karen E. Rowe's articulation of her graduate seminar on gender, genre, and culture shows how teachers might construct a set of courses that examine some of the issues scholars today are considering most crucial to the study of early America. José F. Aranda, Jr., suggests a refreshingly comparative approach to the study of Anglo colonialism and Chicano and Chicana writings, beginning with an epigraph taken from a 1960s poem by Richard Olivas that interrogates what we are teaching when we teach the cultural founding of the United States. Like Aranda, Dennis D. Moore shows how we can teach the similarity of cultural tensions in the early American past and the American present by examining, side by side, texts of both periods. The historian Gary L. Hewitt asks students to interrogate the issue of "encounter" in the Americas from 1450 to 1750. The essays and syllabi in this section describe rich, diverse, and wonderfully interesting courses, designed for teachers at the undergraduate and graduate levels who are teaching in a variety of fields and in a number of different kinds of institutions.

The last section, "Resources," should be useful for teachers who wish to review existing literature in the numerous areas represented in this volume as well as teachers who are new to the field and seek a quick survey of secondary materials. Edward J. Gallagher's bibliographic essay provides a thoughtful discussion of available resources for the study of early American literatures.

Part I

Issues, Themes, Methods

Beyond the Boundaries
of the Americas

James Ruppert

The Old Wisdom: Introducing Native American Materials

When one teaches Native American materials in the American literature classroom, three issues should surface. First, an exploration of cultural values and worldviews seems essential. Second, the dynamics of possession, resistance, trade, and war, central to the colonial attempt to define the uniqueness of the American experience, create a focus on the political interaction between Native American and non–Native American societies. Third, Native American oral literary traditions can challenge and illuminate the variety of human creative and literary expression that forms the groundwork of all meaning construction.

Teachers may find that the task of acquainting students with the complex social and cultural milieu of early American literatures can be enlivened by introducing a more thorough knowledge of Native American groups. Yet teaching Native American materials can be a daunting prospect for anyone untrained in the area. When exploration and settlements began, there were over three hundred different cultures and over two hundred different languages. Few people can be considered experts on all cultural groups, especially over spans of hundreds of years. Therefore I present an overview of some of the components necessary for an appreciation of and the successful teaching of Native American oral materials.

Genre

Today most people encounter Native American oral materials in written form. This body of verbal tradition can be divided into oral narratives, oratory, song, and religious expressions. But these groupings are not exclusive, and they often overlap. The categories commonly found in contemporary anthologies, such as fiction, poetry, and drama, may not be very useful in talking about the history of and perception of Native American literatures. Yet they can be valuable when used to contrast non–Native American literatures with Native American genres and goals. Most Native American oral traditions defined their own genres, and most bore only a superficial resemblance to what we call fiction and poetry. A discussion of the genres of poetry and fiction can serve as a starting point for an introduction to Native American literary genres.

While much of the Native American material in print was collected many years ago, most of the oral traditions continue today in some form. Many anthologies place Native American materials at the beginning, as if to imply that these are texts from dead cultures. I use the present tense in this essay to counteract that implication.

Oral narrative might consist of sacred or secular stories. Secular narratives are often told in storytelling sessions with both children and adults present. Sacred narratives are usually told in highly structured ritual contexts. Different cultural traditions limit in different ways who can tell stories and which stories they can tell. Sometimes there are restrictions on the season in which the stories can be told. For example, the Navajos tell traditional narratives only after the first snow has fallen. In some traditions a story is considered sacred or secular depending only on the context of the telling. The Tlingit retain ownership of certain religious or clan narratives while allowing wide dissemination of other narratives. Autobiographical accounts, personal experiences, war stories, hunting stories, and stories of first contact between Natives and non–Natives might be told by anyone. Such personal and historical narratives constitute a significant knowledge base that is able to sustain subsistence living and transfer necessary cultural wisdom.

While Native American oratory may be heard today, much interest has been expressed in the speeches of historical leaders. These orators perfected their skills during a variety of events, such as council meetings, religious presentations, welcomings, petitions, and encounters with other tribes. The highly personal and transitory nature of this form has made it difficult to record, but some traditions have been documented by tribal and nontribal scholars. Many of the speeches of noted orators were recorded at official conferences between Native American and government officials. Such materials must be subjected to scrutiny. For example, the often quoted speech of Chief Seattle was published thirty years after it supposedly took place. Official records of the negotiations bear little resemblance to the contemporary versions of this speech. A more reliable and important example of oratory might be seen in the recorded speeches of Red Jacket, an Iroquois leader whose words deeply influenced political and economic relations for over twenty years. Interesting contemporary examples are included in Nora Dauenhauer and Richard Dauenhauer's *Haa Tuwunaaga Yis*.

Native American songs can also be of a religious or secular nature. In various anthology selections, passages taken range from the religious rituals of the Navajo to the personal songs of the Chippewa. Kenneth Roemer has demonstrated how an examination of the Nightway chant can call into question the conventions of an anthology regarding periodization, authorship, and the power of literature. The personal songs of Sioux or Chippewa people can reveal the interaction between individual and cultural values.

Most often songs have been translated into English with the appearance of poetry. This format downplays the musical dimension and heightens what might be seen by some as a cryptic quality. Chippewa or Sioux personal songs are common anthology selections that must be placed in a cultural context. The Papago elder Chona once commented, "The song is so short because we understand so much" (Underhill 51). While the oral and cultural context of song or chant makes it something quite different from poetry, the emphasis that poetry places on image, pause, and the importance of appreciating each word is also important in understanding Native American song tradition.

The forms of Native American religious expression range from dance dramas staged as public ritual in a Hopi village to the personal vision songs of the Papago; they vary widely, depending on tribal traditions and religions. Religious expression may be a highly formalized series of chants that take years to learn, as with the Navajo, or a personal rite evoking an animal spirit ally, as in many Plains cultures. Expressions from other categories might also be religious, but explicitly religious forms, such as ritual prayers, fit best into this category.

While these categories might prove useful for introducing students to Native American materials, it should be noted that most Native American oral traditions have established their own genres. Oral narratives are often separated into broad groupings — for example, the distant-time stories of the Koyukon Athabaskans. These stories tell of how the world was formed, and they function, as Mircea Eliade has observed, like sacred history. Another grouping is historical narratives that recount events of known people in specific locations, such as the Qanemciq of the Central Yupik Eskimo. Some more-specific narrative genres are categorized by social context such as Navajo Coyote stories, and some by place and time told, such as Alaskan Athabaskan mountain stories. Song and oratorical genres are established by their cultural functions but could also be placed in other broad categories. For example, potlatch oratory also incorporates much historical narrative. An important first step in teaching Native American oral materials is to situate them among other works in an oral tradition.[1]

A Spectrum of Oral Narrative Types

A closer look at the spacious reach of Native American oral narratives helps students establish a context for individual narratives and can reveal the progressive logic and development of specific stories. The figure below shows a way of grouping a body of oral narratives; it has proven useful in assisting students' understanding of the varieties of Native American materials available. On the left we have origin stories, which are about the beginning of things, such as how humans came to be, the origin of death, the origin of the celestial bodies, the functions of the body, the relationship between men and women, and the nature of spiritual power. The world of origin stories is one of creative flux, where the essential nature of things can change.[2] It is usually inhabited by characters who are both animal and human. They are not locked into one fixed form or nature but free to transform at will; they all share a common language and can talk to one another. Stories from this origin era function to found the basic outlines of the world we know today.

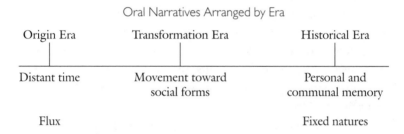

Oral Narratives Arranged by Era

Origin Era	Transformation Era	Historical Era
Distant time	Movement toward social forms	Personal and communal memory
Flux		Fixed natures

Often stories from the origin era do not explain the creation of the world. It is assumed that the world exists, and emphasis falls instead on issues such as the nature of the sun, the creation of humans, the beginning of death and procreation. Unnatural creatures are often eliminated as the world is made safe for human culture.

In stories from the transformation era, the basic outlines of human and animal life are already fixed and stable. Animals and humans have natures that are constant and no longer transform at will; characters act with qualities that are either human or animal. However, the relations among humans, animals, and the spiritual powers of the world have not yet been formalized. Stories from this era establish a reciprocal relation between humans and the animal-spiritual world. They explain how humans should behave toward animals and spiritual powers. When humans think and act in appropriate ways, then humans, animals, and spiritual entities exist in harmony. Often the stories tell of the origin of human social institutions, such as marriage, hunting, and death rituals. A series of covenants and institutions is chronicled that clarifies a human being's place in the world while the narratives delineate the origin of human culture and its values. Stories from this era fall into a variety of Native American genres.

Stories from the historical era are concerned with the actions of named and known people. They may be the experiences of the narrator or of a specific ancestor, relative, or famous person. The narratives may concern hunting, warfare, spiritual activity, or relatives. Their function is to carry on the process of developing and defining the nature of people's experience in the world more than to aggrandize the ego of an individual. In the world of these narratives, human and animal natures are fixed in the forms we recognize today. Transformation is limited to special occasions, and humans must be constantly attentive if they are to experience spiritual power. Ritual and personal vision help connect humans to the spiritual world. But the basic principles and processes that created the world as we perceive it today are still functioning. These stories serve as a modern link to the ancient times.

If considered as a chronological spectrum, clearly the sweep of narratives moves from flux to fixed natures, from the lack of social institutions and cultural values to the creation of them, and from a world hostile to humans and human culture to a world in which humans have a place. Many students might see the origin stories as myths and the historical stories as personal reminiscences and maybe legend. As such, the former would be considered false and the latter possibly true. In Native American communities, however, the distinction is made not between truth and falsehood but between distant time and recent time. The world was different back then; different rules governed the interactions among beings. But the processes, values, and truths of that period are as real as contemporary personal experiences, probably even truer and more real, since they are sacred history and explain the unseen eternal world of spirit. Students might also perceive this chronological presentation as a model of cultural progress from an animal world to human culture or of a fall from an idealized paradise. Neither of these interpretations is accurate. The stories explain the changes in the world in a very nonjudgmental manner, highlighting valuable knowledge. They tell of the natural and foreordained processes of the world without supplying the moral framework of good and evil or the concept of evolution.

Functions of Oral Narratives

My comments so far have attempted to elucidate some literary structures that define oral tradition as seen in Native American materials. But more important for teaching and appreciating these cultural expressions is an understanding of the function of oral materials, especially oral narratives. Western forms such as parables, fables, and fairy tales have been compared to Native American oral narratives. These forms prove to be poor analogues, because they function much differently within their cultures. Native American narratives tend to serve three functions in the community. First, they entertain in ways similar to all oral communication. Second, they instruct listeners in cultural, social, and practical wisdom. Third, the act itself of telling the narratives can create harmony between a community and the sacred processes of the world. Often the act of telling creates healing or hunting luck and promotes proper thinking about the world.

Clearly, these narratives entertain in a fashion understood by all humanity. They have humor, tragedy, suspense, adventure, horror, mystery, and satire. They tell of heroes and monsters, epic journeys, fantastic creatures, strange lands, and familiar relationships. Stories that were not entertaining did not last for hundreds or thousands of years in the oral tradition. Since most storytelling sessions were during the dark winter nights, they brought families, clans, and villages together. While storytelling had other goals, it made life richer and happier.

Many Native American elders emphasize the instructional nature of the stories. Repeatedly they comment that if their children do not hear the stories, they will not turn out to be good, moral people and will not understand their identities as tribal members. The knowledge that is instilled in youngsters throughout their lives in Native

American oral tradition is the knowledge of relations both sacred and practical and of how those relations are arranged and interact with one another. Unquestionably the narratives encode much cultural wisdom. General personal attributes are encouraged, such as being observant, respecting elders, being truthful, avoiding excessive revenge, controlling one's desires, and not being gullible. Vital elements of a worldview are also explored, such as emphasizing the need to seek truth and knowledge in the animal-spiritual world or the importance of obeying spiritual directives over human ones. Since human perception is so limited and the animal-spiritual world so powerful, one must be careful not to take illusion for reality. What appears real to humans can be a misconception based on their lack of proper thinking about culture, society, and the world around them. Discussions of these areas can focus students on the ways that oral literature fulfills many of the same functions as written literature.

While the narratives function to educate the young, their instructional value is not limited to children. Adults and older people listen to the stories, too. Often their understanding of the meaning of a narrative is changed as they grow older. A tale that pleases a child as a simple humorous story about not being gullible may, on mature reflection, reveal wisdom about social relations and spiritual connections. To be successful, oral narratives must resonate on several levels at once. For example, in a well-known Winnebago Trickster tale, Trickster convinces some ducks to dance with their eyes closed while he sings them songs. As they dance by, he grabs them and kills them. One duck opens his eyes and warns the remaining ducks. Consequently, from that day on, these ducks have red eyes. A child might be expected to learn a detail about the natural world and to realize that the ducks were killed because they were gullible. But an adult might think about the ducks' desire to hear Trickster's songs. Many such songs are considered to be full of spirit power. One must earn such a song or have it given by a spirit ally. By seeking a shortcut to spiritual power, the ducks violate the compact between the human and spiritual worlds, and their deaths warn of the folly of such action.

Social wisdom is part of the instructional function. Many stories deal with the execution of social duties, the relationships between kin, the difficulties and responsibilities of marriage, the conflict of loyalty to clan and loyalty to spouse, the necessity of cooperation, and the pitfalls of relying on others. The stories may tell of the origin of a social custom or of the establishment of an institution such as the potlatch or council of elders. When these stories include animal actors, they also forge the bonds of kinship between the human and the animal-spiritual worlds. Through such stories, kinship is extended to the animal world. The essential insight here is that animal and human societies are built similarly.

Many narratives incorporate practical wisdom about techniques for survival and hunting. They may map familiar territory according to personal and clan use or direct the listener to useful locations or sacred sites. Many stories center on accurate observation of the characteristics of animals and natural phenomena. Taken together, all this information instructs the listener in the pragmatic collective experience of ancestors and relatives, knowledge vital to living in a specific area.

A more difficult function to put into English is the idea that the very act of storytelling, whatever its content, serves to keep the community in harmony with the sacred processes of the world. Indeed, for most groups the stories of the distant-time world function like a body of sacred texts that describe sacred history. In some traditions, like the Navajo, the narratives are performed in ceremonies designed to cure individuals and ritually control the disharmonious influences of the world. The Alaska Native elder Catherine Attla, who compares the distant-time stories she was told to the Bible, says, "Long ago, when times were hard, people would appeal for mercy by telling stories. It was their way of praying" (27). While the religious function of the narratives may be highlighted or downplayed, storytelling promotes a connection to a spiritual reality in ways written forms do not. They heal, reestablish spiritual-human balance, and foster hunting luck.

Performance

When we examine song material, it is easy to remember that we are viewing only part of the artistic creation. Some information about a typical context and representative instrumentation can aid appreciation. There are also a number of recordings that can be played in the classroom. But one must also remember that oral narratives written in a book in English are only a partial realization of the story-telling event. Since these stories are performed in a creative interaction with an audience, much of the original will be lost. Videotapes of storytellers can help remind students of the dramatic and interactive quality of the events. Yet videotapes, if they are not in the native language, if they include subtitles, or if they exclude the interaction of an audience, can distort the events. When wrenched out of their context, the stories appear incomplete and confusing. Many elements of an oral tradition influence the recording of a storytelling event. Some stories can be performed only by members of a specific clan, this rule establishing what has been called oral copyright. Other stories can be retold only at a certain time of the year. All these factors distance the reader from the context and the text.

The act of translation of Native American languages into English is monumentally difficult. Dissimilar structures and patterns make it hard to render a fluent recitation in a Native American language into a fluent English version. Many texts published today came from anthropologists not concerned with the literary value of those texts. Many were gathered for linguistic study or for their representation of cultural values rather than for their creative expression. In the last thirty years, collectors and translators of oral materials have been favoring bilingual publications. A bilingual edition allows Native American language speakers the chance to make their own translations. Many recent translations present the text in lines that look like poetry rather than in block prose. This format allows the translator to reproduce something of the breath units of the performance. It also encourages readers to think in terms of drama or poetry. Some scholars have suggested that storytelling might be much closer to these genres than to fiction. A drama or poetry format permits a visual representation of the scene or line groupings that structure the narrative. While these efforts help preserve the oral quality of a taped presentation, they still ignore the role of the audience. Few of the translations in existence come from taped audience-storyteller interactions. The folklorist Barre Toelken found that when a storyteller recites into a tape recorder, what emerges is "a rather full synopsis of characters and incidents," not the fully developed storytelling event (Toelken and Scott 80). Nevertheless, this poetic format allows readers to move closer to the oral event.

Oral Style

Many contemporary translations try to incorporate elements of oral style that previous translations left out. In the past, collectors and translators routinely eliminated facets of oral style in the belief that the English reader required an easy-to-assimilate rendition. For instance, repetition plays a key role in the art of storytelling. It is used for emphasis, to create rhythm and balance, and as an aid to oral composition. Some repetition has ritual and cultural significance; different numbers constitute a completed series for different cultures. The numbers 4 and 5 are probably the most common. Examples are Navajo chants and Cherokee sacred formulas. Marker words are used to separate a structural unit or a scene change. Some words, like *perhaps*, *probably*, and *maybe*, are employed to narrow or expand the distance between the audience and the narrator. With skillful use, such marker words can delineate personal from cultural experience and establish authenticity. Questions often function to modify the tone and the point of view of the narrator. Place references and observations about animals establish important connections between the world of the story and the present world. Code switching, indirect address, and story frames are all used to create the texture of the event, a texture that foregrounds as much cultural meaning as do the characters and the actions. Early translations left out many of these components of dramatic performance. But the more elements of oral style are incorporated into the translation, the greater the obstacles for readers uninitiated in this form of communication and the less likely it is that general readers will find a fluid free translation.

Narrative Expectations for Typical Readers Today

Many readers find the characters in distant-time stories difficult to understand. Frequently these characters can be both animal and human. In the origin era, all creatures share a common nature and a common language. Transformations in attributes and activities come effort-lessly. One moment Raven can fly, and the next he walks. These char-acters often violate a reader's predilection for realism. Many stories are episodic and do not follow realistic expectations of chronology. Moreover, origin-age characters seldom act according to the expecta-tions of modern psychology or to familiar conceptions of the hero. Psychological motivation is often not important in the stories, and the behavior of characters can be obscure. In addition, stories can continue after what appears to be a climax, and plot details may not be neatly resolved. While in contemporary fictional narratives, mean-ing is always tied to plot, in Native American oral narratives plot ex-ists only to introduce a series of what Toelken calls "culturally moral subjects" (Toelken and Scott 86). These subjects encode a nexus of cultural and social values, expectations, questions, and understand-ings. Perhaps one could say that the meaning of a story resides not in its rendition but in the community that embraces it. The audience and the storyteller use the narrative to create a dynamic dialogue among these preexisting subjects. The participants let the story guide the resonances of the culturally moral subjects until the subjects illu-minate one another. Plot and psychological development are second-ary concerns. Even stories that seem etiological are told less to explain the physical origin of things and more to explore cultural and social processes. To think of the stories as the simple science of pretechno-logical peoples is to miss what they have to convey. All this is to say that I often must talk as much about what the stories are not as about what they are.

Finding Meaning

I have found it useful in classes to envision the storytelling event as a map across a narrative terrain. The terrain consists of the diverse cul-turally moral subjects encoded by the story. The storyteller is not re-quired to traverse the field of meaning in the same manner for each telling. The storyteller may choose to traverse one path to emphasize one series of subjects and another path to emphasize another. The choice of narrative path depends on the nature of the audience and on the storyteller's expertise.

It is useful to remember that the general movement in oral narratives is from the fluid origin era to the present nature of things. Frequently that movement proceeds from some point of imbalance or disharmony to some resolution of balance and harmony. The resolution will usually reinforce the wisdom of a cultural value, such as the control of revenge or the importance of listening to the voices of the spirit world. As one explores the motion of the narrative, one's intent should be to understand the oral communal goals of the narrative.

Historic Native American Materials

Early American literatures can be enhanced with more-historical publications, such as speeches, autobiographies, tribal histories, and sermons. Often these provide a fascinating way to look at the confluence of Native American and European values. Many of these texts illustrate a convergence of oral styles and forms with those of a written tradition. Rather than represent a sublimation of the Native American worldview, they reveal how Native American goals can emerge in startling new forms. More than protest or apology, they define identity in innovative terms and emphasize continuance. The works of Samson Occom (1723–92), William Apess (1798–1839), Elias Boudinot (c. 1802–39), and George Copway (1818–69) disclose a complex interface between two competing value systems, two forms of communication, and two worldviews. For example, Apess's "Eulogy on King Philip" (1836) redirects the popular sermon format to subtly challenge colonial representations about Native American life and moral character, while it offers an alternative concept of history.

When works by these writers are coupled with Benjamin Franklin's *Autobiography* or Cotton Mather's writings, some surprising realizations about culture and worldview emerge. Many other interesting couplings can be made; for example, travel journals can be compared with oral narratives that chronicle the first contact between Native American peoples and European explorers. Speeches from Native American orators might be matched with the public political writings commonly used in early American literature classes. Using these materials may take a little more time in preparation, but the rewards are great. The inclusion of such materials strongly enriches students' appreciation of the Native peoples of North America, the history of the interaction between those peoples and European colonists, and of literature itself. By negotiating the intricacies of these materials, teachers and scholars can approach a comprehensive understanding of an enticing period in the cultural history of this continent.

Notes

1. Discussing narrative and dramatic modes, Paul Zolbrod presents a valuable method for approaching Native American materials in his book *Reading the Voice*.
2. Andrew Wiget has a good general discussion of this spectrum in chapter 1, "Oral Narrative," of his book *Native American Literature*.

Appendix
Selected Native American Oral and Written Materials

Apess, William. *On Our Own Ground: The Complete Writings of William Apess, a Pequot.* Ed. Barry O'Connell. Amherst: U of Massachusetts P, 1992.

Attla, Catherine. *K'etetaalkkaanee, the One Who Paddled among the People and Animals.* Fairbanks: Alaska Native Lang. Center, 1990.

Bahr, Donald. *Pima and Papago Ritual Oratory: A Study of Three Texts.* San Francisco: Indian Historian, 1975.

Bierhorst, John. *Four Masterworks of American Indian Literature.* Tucson: U of Arizona P, 1984.

Boudinot, Elias. *An Address to the Whites: Delivered in the First Presbyterian Church on the Twenty-Sixth of May, 1826.* Philadelphia: Geddes, 1826.

Copway, George. *The Life, History, and Travels of Kah-ge-ga-bowh (George Copway).* Albany: Weed, 1847. Rpt. as *The Life, Letters, and Speeches of Kah-ge-ga-bowh, or G. Copway.* New York: Benedict, 1850.

———. *The Traditional History and Characteristic Sketches of the Ojibway Nation.* London: Gilpin, 1850.

Cornplanter, Jesse. *Legends of the Longhouse.* 1938. Iroquois Rpts. Ohswehen: Irografts, 1986.

Dauenhauer, Nora Marks, and Richard Dauenhauer. *Haa Shuka, Our Ancestors: Tlingit Oral Narratives.* Seattle: U of Washington P, 1987.

DeBlois, Albert, ed. *Micmac Texts.* Quebec: Canadian Museum of Civilization, 1990.

Deloria, Ella. *Dakota Texts.* 1932. Pubs. of the Amer. Ethnological Soc. 17. New York: AMS, 1974.

Evers, Larry, and Felipe Molina. *Yaqui Deer Songs / Maso Bwikam: A Native American Poetry.* Sun Tracks 14. Tucson: U of Arizona P, 1987.

Hilbert, Vi, trans. and ed. *Haboo: Native American Stories from the Puget Sound.* Seattle: U of Washington P, 1985.

Jones, Peter. *A History of the Ojebway Indians.* 1861.

Lankford, George E., comp. and ed. *Native American Legends: Southeastern Legends: Tales from the Natchez, Caddo, Chickasaw, and Other Nations.* Little Rock: August House, 1987.

Malotki, Ekkehart. *Hopitutuwutsi: Hopi Tales.* Flagstaff: Museum of Northern Arizona, 1978.

Mattina, Anthony, and Madeline de Sautel, trans. *The Golden Woman: The Colville Narrative of Peter J. Seymour.* Tucson: U of Arizona P, 1985.

Occom, Samson. *A Choice Collection of Hymns and Spiritual Songs Intented [sic] for the Edification of the Sincere Christians of All Denominations.* London: Green, 1774.

———. *A Sermon Preached at the Execution of Moses Paul, an Indian Who Was Executed at New Haven, on the Second of September 1772.* Bennington: Watson, 1772.

Radin, Paul, ed. *Trickster: A Study in American Indian Mythology.* 1956. New York: Schocken, 1972.

Tedlock, Dennis, trans. *Finding the Center: Narrative Poetry of the Zuni Indians*. Lincoln: U of Nebraska P, 1972.

Tukummiq and Tom Lowenstein, trans. *The Things That Were Said of Them: Shaman Stories and Oral Histories of the Tikigaq People Told by Asatchaq*. Berkeley: U of California P, 1992.

Underhill, Ruth. *Singing for Power: The Song Magic of the Papago Indians of Southern Arizona*. 1938. Berkeley: U of California P, 1976.

Underhill, Ruth, Donald Bahr, Baptisto Lopez, José Pancho, and David Lopez. *Rainhouse and Ocean: Speeches for the Papago Year*. Amer. Tribal Religions 4. Flagstaff: Museum of Northern Arizona, 1979.

Vanderwerth, W. C., ed. *Indian Oratory: Famous Speeches by Noted Indian Chieftains*. 1971. Norman: U of Oklahoma P, 1979.

Zolbrod, Paul. *Dine' bahane': The Navajo Creation Story*. Albuquerque: U of New Mexico P, 1984.

Works Cited

Primary Works

Attla, Catherine. *Bakk'aatugh Ts'uhuniy: Stories We Live By*. Fairbanks: Alaska Native Lang. Center, 1989.

Dauenhauer, Nora, and Richard Dauenhauer. *Haa Tuwunaaga Yis, for Healing Our Spirit: Tlingit Oratory*. Seattle: U of Washington P, 1990.

Underhill, Ruth. *Papago Woman*. 1936. New York: Holt, 1979.

Secondary Works

Eliade, Mircea. *Myth and Reality*. New York: Harper, 1963.

Roemer, Kenneth. "The Nightway Questions American Literature." *American Literature* 66 (1994): 817–29.

Toelken, Barre, and Tacheeni Scott. "Poetic Retranslation and the 'Pretty Languages' of Yellowman." *Traditional American Indian Literatures: Texts and Interpretations*. Ed. Karl Kroeber. Lincoln: U of Nebraska P, 1981. 65–116.

Wiget, Andrew. "Oral Narrative." *Native American Literature*. Boston: Twayne, 1985. 1–21.

Zolbrod, Paul. *Reading the Voice: Native American Oral Poetry on the Written Page*. Salt Lake City: U of Utah P, 1995.

Amy E. Winans

Diversity and Difference in African American Writings

Although people from Africa first arrived in North America in the early sixteenth century with the Spanish, the extant record of early black writing begins two centuries later, with Lucy Terry's poem "Bar's Fight." Composed in 1746 but not published until 1855, Terry's poem is generally recognized as the first literary work authored by a person of African descent living in North America. Taken as a first, it can be said to mark the beginning of a varied and growing body of works written by black North Americans.[1] In the years that followed its composition, eighteenth- and early-nineteenth-century African Americans wrote or dictated poetry, slave narratives, Indian captivity narratives, sermons, petitions, freedom-day addresses, letters, criminal narratives, abolitionist tracts, constitutions for mutual aid societies, orations, and much more.

The diversity of these writings is extraordinary, yet they have received little attention from most scholars. In many ways this lack of attention is not surprising, because most early African American texts are strikingly different from later texts, on which the narrative of

African American literary history has traditionally been constructed. Typically, the antebellum slave narrative has been considered the beginning of the African American literary tradition.[2] The overt strategies of protest in this genre and the importance this genre places on an author's writing his or her own narrative (as opposed to using an amanuensis) differ markedly from the discursive strategies and conditions of composition of many earlier texts. Rather than seek to understand early texts on their own terms, many scholars have tended either to ignore them or to evaluate them according to the degree in which they overtly challenge the white-dominant culture and its discursive practices. Yet as scholars such as Phillip Richards and Vincent Carretta have pointed out, many early African American writers shared some assumptions and practices with their white contemporaries—including, for part of the early era, an acceptance of the institution of slavery. Furthermore, many early black texts were dictated to amanuenses, whose precise approaches to shaping the oral narratives remain unclear.

Ironically, then, the very diversity and difference of early African American writing have meant that only a small number of early selections—often the poetry of Phillis Wheatley and, more recently, excerpts from the slave narrative of Olaudah Equiano—have been made available in anthologies and thus in early American literature classrooms. The limited presence of black writers in many early survey courses is particularly troublesome, because it can suggest to students that African Americans and their intellectual activities and writings were relatively unimportant and peripheral to late-eighteenth- and early-nineteenth-century American culture. In fact, this was a signal era in the development of African American culture and writing, an era when many of the first independent African American institutions in the present-day United States were founded and when a substantial free black public emerged for the first time in North America. As I suggest below, we need to include a range of selections in order to help students recognize the variety, complexity, and influence of early African Americans and their writings during this important era.[3]

In both African American literature courses and American literature survey courses, I try to help students understand the varied ways in which African American texts functioned in the cultures of which they were a part. This understanding entails considering the factors that shaped a text's composition, publication, circulation, and consumption. Encouraging students to consider each writer's goals and the ways in which each text was likely to have been used by its readers allows students to recognize the significance of these texts in eighteenth- and early-nineteenth-century culture for people ranging from slaves and servants to presidents. The bulk of class time is spent examining the rhetorical strategies evident in the texts, because the complicated strategies early black writers adopted in the face of an often hostile or apathetic readership indicate the extent to which they were aware of public culture. I ask students to explore ways in which African Americans seem to have adopted, transformed, or rejected the discourse of an era that at best figured them as sentimental objects needing the sympathy and assistance of benevolent white abolitionists and at worst identified them as part of a perpetual underclass whose very humanity was in question.

I've found that it works well both to incorporate a range of early African American texts into my courses, a range illustrative of different genres, authorial situations, and subject matter, and to address issues of literacy, authorship, and readership in our discussions. By approaching texts and their contexts comparatively, students are better able to understand differences across class, region, and individual experience, thereby avoiding broad, erroneous generalizations that can emerge from a more limited consideration of belletristic texts.[4] Although time is limited in survey courses, even adding one or two additional texts to our readings can go a long way toward making possible the comparisons crucial to students' understanding of early culture. By situating texts and writers within the cultural matrix of which they were a part, students learn, for example, that although Wheatley was in many ways a unique writer, she was not isolated, and she was not the only black writer in Boston who publicly questioned slavery. Her connections extended across the Atlantic to the countess of Huntington and, as we know from her letters, extended to her friends Obour Tanner (a free black woman) and Sarah Osborn, who established an evangelical circle in Newport. Further, at the same time that Wheatley's letter to the Mohegan minister Samson Occom questioning slavery was being reprinted in newspapers throughout New England, Massachusetts slaves were circulating petitions challenging slavery's existence in the colony and Caesar Sarter, a former slave, was arguing against slavery in the Massachusetts newspaper the *Essex Journal and Merrimack Packet* (17 Aug. 1774). As we seek to understand what could and could not be published by a slave or former slave, we need to consider the range of activity taking place in revolutionary Boston.[5]

Many teachers now include selections of Wheatley's poetry and letters and excerpts from Equiano's narrative in their survey courses, so I focus here primarily on two types of texts that might be less familiar. First, instructors might wish to consider teaching texts written or dictated by African Americans who inhabited comparatively low social positions and who seem to have lacked the social connections of more widely known and widely published African American writers. I am thinking here particularly of texts such as Briton Hammon's captivity narrative and the criminal narratives dictated by men such as Johnson Green, Peter Mathias, and Joseph Mountain and written by Abraham Johnstone (for a more complete listing of the authors of early criminal narratives, see the appendix to this essay). Many of these texts appear to have been read by audiences that differ significantly from the audiences of the elite genres more commonly included in our anthologies.[6] As some historians have argued, it is likely that criminal narratives were read by people of the "lower sort," particularly by young people who were learning to read, such as poor immigrants and free blacks (Cummins 47). These narratives had a large readership; as William Andrews has noted, they constituted the dominant genre of African American autobiography before 1810. Second, instructors might consider selecting texts written by leaders in the free black community, men who played immensely important roles in improving the quality of free black life in an increasingly hostile setting. These leaders negotiated with sympathetic whites, some of whom were willing to assist in the creation of separate black institutions. Written by the founders of black churches, Masonic lodges, schools, and mutual aid societies, these texts were often directed toward white benefactors but were sometimes directed toward fellow blacks or to a mixed-race audience composed of people of various social positions. Among this body of works are abolitionist writings, sermons, addresses, hymns, and documents associated with mutual aid societies and black churches. Orations and addresses in particular offer valuable insight into the public construction of an African group identity during an era in which blacks' access to rights available to citizens of the new nation was undergoing unpredictable shifts.

Before considering possible approaches to such texts, we should address the distinctive nature of African American authorship and the meanings of literacy for early African Americans. The topics of authorship and literacy are of course relevant to any discussion of early writing, because they elucidate the purpose and contexts of the texts and because they help students recognize how present assumptions about the integrity of individual authorship differ from those of the eighteenth century. This recognition seems to give students greater patience with challenging texts that rely on unfamiliar conventions. Because the writing situations of early black writers are unfamiliar to most students, instructors might wish to address the particularly limited access that African Americans had to literacy during the early era and the role that that limited access began to play in some (not all) arguments against blacks' capacity for independence and freedom. Although writing and print culture in the United States grew increasingly significant during the late eighteenth century, oral culture remained tremendously important, especially for African Americans. Writing was understood as a skill needed for some but certainly not most occupations; many people, including most women and African Americans, could perform their daily activities successfully without needing to write. In fact, throughout much of the early era many people who learned to read — particularly women and blacks — did not learn to write. Although opportunities for formal schooling were quite limited for people of African descent, some schools (often run by abolition societies or by African mutual aid societies) were available in northern cities such as Philadelphia, New York, and Boston. Texts were circulated in published form (ranging from relatively inexpensive broadsides, pamphlets, and almanacs to much more costly bound volumes) or in manuscript form (and in effect "published"). It was not uncommon for materials to be published under pseudonyms or anonymously. Students can be surprised to learn that in contrast to rather strict notions of plagiarism today, early writers borrowed with little restraint from one another without necessarily acknowledging such borrowings. Because today we tend to privilege individual, independent authorship, we overlook many early texts whose authorship does not meet our strict definitions.

Deciding what to include in a syllabus can raise difficult questions. Given the limitations of time, for example, should teachers include dictated texts in their courses? Such texts, which constitute a significant portion of early African American writing, have typically been excluded from American literature anthologies and have been considered inauthentic, less reliable, or less important than texts written independently by African Americans. The questioning of these texts is understandable, given the significant control that whites exercised in their creation. Ironically, though, some dictated texts were among the most widely read of the early era (by both blacks and whites) and thus give us important insight into the reading culture. Not only was John Marrant's captivity narrative dictated, but it was one of the three most popular captivity narratives published during the eighteenth and nineteenth centuries (Potkay and Burr 71).[7] Dictated texts also offer us information (admittedly filtered) about the lives of many African Americans about whom little would otherwise be known; many of their reactions to the white dominant culture differ substantially from the more familiar approaches of the black elite. I include dictated texts in my courses and use them in part as an occasion for discussing authorship more generally. Considering the assumptions reflected in the title of Andrews's exemplary study of early African American autobiography, *To Tell a Free Story*, we examine the question, What in fact is a free story? What conditions shaped or controlled the composition of texts and their publication and thus contribute to our evaluations of whether or not these texts are free stories? In what ways might the author of a dictated text appear less free than one who tells his or her own story?[8] Throughout such discussions I try to help students recognize the implications and limitations of reading early texts for what Desrochers has described as a "'true' black voice of irreconcilable and discernible difference" (43).

Instructors might approach issues of African American authorship from a different angle by considering one of the most famous challenges made to that authorship: the challenge posed to Wheatley and her single published volume of poetry. Students might be asked to examine the documents in her preface that describe her writing situation, particularly the signed testimony of eighteen Boston men who certified her authorship. Inasmuch as the authorship of many African American texts published during the late eighteenth and early nineteenth centuries went unchallenged, instructors might wish to explore with students the grounds on which Wheatley's authorship was questioned. Was she challenged as the second woman in North America to publish a volume of poetry? As a slave? As a person of African descent? Because of the genre in which she wrote? For purposes of comparison, students might also examine Thomas Jefferson's critique of Wheatley, Ignatius Sancho, and Benjamin Banneker in *Notes on the State of Virginia* and consider the type of texts Jefferson turned to for confirmation of black intellectual capability. It sometimes frees up the discussion somewhat if students are reminded that, despite the prominent role that Enlightenment writers like Jefferson play in our courses, the views of such writers do not necessarily represent the (white) eighteenth-century consensus on early black authorship, literacy, or intelligence. We can understand the dangers of making generalizations based on the elite reception of Wheatley's poetry by examining texts written by authors inhabiting relatively lower social positions and writing in different genres. The authorship of the next text I consider appears to have remained unchallenged during the author's day.

Briton Hammon's captivity narrative provides an opportunity not only to illustrate how one might approach a writer whose situation and writing are very different from Wheatley's but also to illustrate how one might introduce early African American writing within an American literature survey more generally. The *Narrative of the Uncommon Sufferings and Surprizing Deliverance of Briton Hammon, a Negro Man* is often the first African American text I discuss, in part because Hammon's prose tends to be more accessible to students than the poetry of Hammon's contemporary Jupiter Hammon. More important, this captivity narrative provides a useful starting point for discussions of types of unfreedom and the connections among genre, readership, and race in early America. Before students read the narrative, we discuss the captivity narrative genre briefly; we review how such narratives are typically marked by a movement from freedom to captivity (a period of spiritual self-examination) to renewed freedom and reintegration into the community. In antebellum American literature survey courses we have already read at least one captivity narrative, usually Mary Rowlandson's.

I sometimes begin our discussion of Briton Hammon's narrative by asking students if and when the narrative persona appears to be free. By beginning with something students assume they know quite a bit about — freedom — we are able to find our way into a very unfamiliar text and era. On the basis of the range of student responses — some students assert that Hammon is never free, some that he is free when he returns home with his master, some that he is free when he works and receives his own wages in Cuba — we discuss different definitions of freedom: intellectual, emotional, physical, legal, political, spiritual, and expressive. Sorting out the different definitions enables us to distinguish between modern and eighteenth-century notions of freedom. We also consider why we assume that Hammon is a slave — and what it meant to be a slave in the eighteenth century. That the word *servant* was sometimes but not always a euphemism for slave has led many to conclude he is a slave, although recently Carretta argued that when Hammon speaks of his "Master," he is in fact referring to his employer and not his owner (24–25). Students need to know that during the era of Hammon's narrative, a variety of states of unfreedom existed in the colonies: during the eighteenth century, approximately half the white immigrant population arrived in the British North American colonies as indentured servants. And not all slaves were black; both Native Americans and, in smaller numbers, whites were enslaved in the Americas (Piersen; Foner). I find it useful to contextualize Hammon's narrative at some length, because students are generally puzzled by the widespread acceptance of servitude and slavery during the eighteenth century.

Examining copies of the original title page of the narrative can also be provocative for students. We discuss the fact that the only mention of Hammon's race is on this page and consider its relative insignificance.[9] The detailed title page suggests a concern with subordination and the position of servitude, not with race. We consider the likely audience of the narrative as a means of pursuing a semester-long conversation about the connections between genre and readership. It is useful to situate the narrative in the context of earlier or roughly contemporaneous captivity narratives such as Rowlandson's, John Marrant's, or Thomas Brown's (written by a young white servant and published in 1760). As John Sekora once noted, Brown's narrative, like Hammon's, was published toward the end of the Seven Years' War, a time when young men of the servant class were increasingly important to the community, given the small number of men who were not away fighting. Clearly the social conditions at the time of the text's original circulation shaped the way the text was read and played a role in the fact that it was published at all. We conclude our discussion by addressing the issue of genre more broadly: we consider the ways in which Hammon's likely status as a slave challenges our understanding of the captivity narrative as a genre. To what extent, that is, do our definitions of this genre depend on the assumption that the subject of the narrative is initially free and is returned to freedom at the conclusion of the narrative? (For a helpful discussion of this issue, see Andrews 42–43.) Exploring such questions can help students understand how the study of African American texts encourages us to reconsider many of the assumptions on which the narrative of American literary history has been based.

Examining the texts of black leaders also encourages us to reconsider how we have approached debates about the nature of citizenship, conduct, and civil society in the new republic, as these debates are reflected in white-authored texts of the era. At the same time that white leaders were puzzling over the nature of citizenship in the new nation and exploring how individual citizens might be united, black leaders such as Prince Hall were directing fellow blacks to consider their conduct in the new nation and encouraging them to "have a fellow feeling for our distres'd brethren of the human race" (76). In fact, the late eighteenth and early nineteenth centuries marked a tremendously important time in the history of African American culture and literature, as newly freed African Americans considered the conflicting meanings of freedom in the new republic and explored the parameters of their expanded autonomy, both private and public. Many recently freed African Americans took new names for themselves, established families, and joined one of the recently established African churches or mutual aid societies. People of African descent increasingly identified themselves and their independent organizations (churches, mutual aid societies, Masonic lodges, and schools) as African.

The growing movement toward a separate group identity did not mean that African Americans were retreating from concerns about their positions in the new republic.[10] Rather, as many of their writings suggest, African Americans were quite concerned about the nature of their positions in the new republic, and indeed many of the discussions of appropriate conduct in these texts are virtually indistinguishable from those directed by white writers toward white citizens. Would Africans who pledged their allegiance to the Constitution, expressed gratitude to white benefactors ranging from Thomas Clarkson to George Washington, and encouraged fellow blacks to be industrious and virtuous find a position as citizens in the new republic? Should they depend primarily on their own organizations for racial uplift? Could they improve their access to the rights of citizenship without the assistance of whites? Finally, should blacks focus their attention on their status in this world or should freedom in the hereafter be their primary concern? Although opinions varied (often according to class positions), many black leaders recognized the importance of the assistance of white benefactors, and their publications reflected this recognition.

Despite the fact that their autonomy in many ways continued to be circumscribed by whites, both friendly and hostile, black leaders continued to explore what being an African in America did and could mean.[11] Some texts displayed a clear focus on black conduct in the here and now. Many abolitionists, both black and white, argued that interest in and support for abolition would occur only when free blacks behaved appropriately (by sending their children to school or apprenticing them to white masters, by expressing gratitude to their white benefactors, and by displaying industry, temperance, and religious devotion) and set an example for enslaved blacks who awaited freedom in states with gradual abolition laws. The black elite was very much aware that the behavior of unruly blacks could not only hinder abolition legislation but also bring about the passage of legislation under which all blacks, regardless of class position, would suffer. Although relationships between members of abolition societies and leaders of the black community were sometimes strained, both white abolitionists and black leaders sought to regulate public and private black behavior. To give students a sense of the ways in which such concerns surfaced, one might ask them to consider Richard Allen's address on the execution of Peter Mathias and John Joyce ("Confessions"). Allen's "Address to the Public, and People of Colour" is just one example of a published text's revealing elite black ministers' concerns with regulating the behavior of free blacks. Students might compare Allen's brief address to that of Johnstone in his *Address of Abraham Johnstone* to get a sense of how blacks of significantly disparate social situations approached the issue of black conduct.

By examining the sermons and orations published during the closing years of the eighteenth century and the early years of the nineteenth, instructors can challenge students to explore the complicated rhetorical strategies of speakers who sought to rally their black listeners and readers without offending or threatening the white benefactors and abolitionists in their audience. Many biblical passages that African American writers quoted and adapted in their works functioned to comfort and thank the often paternalistic white benefactors and at the same time to encourage free and enslaved African Americans to envision a day when their positions in the social order would be transformed. Rather than focus on a single text, I turn to some of the ways a key verse from the Bible was used by a variety of speakers, often to different ends.

According to Albert Raboteau, Psalms 68.31, "princes shall come out of Egypt; Ethiopia shall soon stretch out her hands unto God" (King James Version), is, "without doubt, the most quoted verse in black religious history" (42). Discussing some of the uses of this verse before assigning reading not only heightens students' sensitivity to rhetorical subtleties but also helps them understand the range of meanings evoked when speakers identify themselves as Africans or Ethiopians. Consider how this highly ambiguous verse from Psalms was used by the white minister Samuel Magaw in 1794 when he delivered a sermon in celebration of the opening of the African Church in Philadelphia. For Magaw, the notion of Ethiopia's stretching forth "her hands unto God" entailed black Americans' humbling themselves before God and before the white Christians who had helped them found their church (Nash 128). This verse had far different implications when Allen and Absalom Jones used the same verse at the end of "A Short Address to the Friends of Him Who Hath No Helper" (in Allen and Jones's *Narrative*). There, Allen and Jones conclude a sentimental expression of gratitude toward white abolitionists by explaining that they hope God will add to the ranks of their benefactors *until* "princes shall come forth from Egypt, and Ethiopia shall stretch out her hand unto God" (23). Their statement can appear to be quite humble, yet they are clearly referring to the dawning of a very different day, when blacks would no longer be seeking benefactors but would, instead, be leading the multitudes.

The resonances this verse carried for African American readers may be even clearer to students when they consider Hall's use of it in his 1797 charge to the African Lodge. Hall reminded his audience that although the day was dark "with our African brethren six years ago, in the French West-Indies" that "blessed be God, the scene is changed; they now confess that God hath no respect of persons, and therefore receive them as their friends, and treat them as brothers. Thus doth Ethiopia begin to stretch forth her hand, from a sink of slavery to freedom and equality" (74). Instructors will likely need to remind students that when Hall refers to the change experienced by his "African brethren," he is referring to the long war on the Caribbean island of Saint Dominigue (later renamed Haiti), a war that would lead to the creation of the first independent black republic in the Western hemisphere. Within the context of the reference to the revolution in the West Indies, Hall's comment about Ethiopia's stretching forth "from a sink of slavery to freedom and equality" leaves open the question of the role that African Americans might play in bringing about their own freedom and equality.

As instructors whose courses continue into the early nineteenth century will note, many of the orations given in celebration of the abolition of the slave trade in 1808 draw and build on similar meanings of Ethiopia and Africa.[12] In later addresses one might consider how biblical verses like the one discussed above served as a means of envisioning both an impressive African-Ethiopian past and a hopeful, transformative future. By identifying themselves as Africans, people of African descent living in the United States not only connected themselves to one another but also to Haitians, to ancestors in West Africa, and to Ethiopia. Religious discourse, which was also used in slave rebellions in the South, offered a vision of liberation and hope for blacks throughout the Americas.

The points made in early black texts themselves about African Americans' rights and roles in North America, in addition to the issues an instructor confronts while selecting early black texts for a survey class, call into question the literary historical narrative that positions African Americans and their writing as peripheral. Including a range of African American texts that reflect varying authorial situations allows us to examine our criteria for inclusion more broadly. What quickly becomes clear is that the common major-authors framework of many courses and anthologies — indeed, even those that are multicultural in orientation — tends to narrow our scope in ways that exclude many early texts of women, Native Americans, African Americans, and mixed-race peoples of both sexes. By exploring the conditions of composition, circulation, and reading during the second half of the eighteenth century and the early part of the nineteenth, we can begin to examine our era's continued idealization of the phenomena of single authorship and major authors. Such idealization seems curiously at odds with the cultures we study in early American courses. Bringing issues like these into the classroom encourages students to think critically about what they are learning and how that major-author narrative, if left unchallenged, can continue to exclude very important — indeed, crucial — components of America's multicultural past.

Notes

1. Throughout this essay I focus on works written in English by people of African descent who spent at least part of their lives in the Americas (and whom I refer to as African American or black), thereby omitting discussion of African British writers such as Ignatius Sancho and Quobna Ottobah Cugoano.

2. Indeed, early texts have sometimes been valorized to the extent that they can be understood as precursors to narratives like Frederick Douglass's. In his introduction to *The Classic Slave Narratives*, for example, Henry Louis Gates, Jr., praises Olaudah Equiano's narrative for being "so richly structured that it became the prototype of the nineteenth-century slave narrative" (xiv).

3. See Carretta's anthology *Unchained Voices*; Adam Potkay and Sandra Burr's *Black Atlantic Writers of the Eighteenth Century*; the reprint of Dorothy Porter's *Early Negro Writing, 1760–1840*; and Herbert Aptheker's *A Documentary History of the Negro People in the United States*. Several criminal narratives are available in Daniel Williams's *Pillars of Salt*. See also Dorothy Sterling's *We Are Your Sisters* for several early letters written by black women.

4. If we focus on the black belletristic texts most commonly included in anthologies and do so without offering students a context for these works, we may unknowingly give them the impression that a black community did not exist or that black writing existed only in a subordinate relationship to whites and their writing.

5. See Bruns for a reprinting of the Sarter essay. Instructors seeking additional background on the lives of early blacks in North America to help them contextualize the works and writers I discuss in the following pages should consult James Horton and Lois Horton's *In Hope of Liberty*, William Piersen's *From Africa to America*, and Sidney Kaplan and Emma Nogrady Kaplan's *The Black Presence in the Era of the American Revolution*.

6. Instructors interested in pursing the issue of readership should consult chapter 3 of Shane White's *Somewhat More Independent* for a fascinating discussion of the significant ways in which the portrayal of people of African descent differed in periodicals and almanacs of the late eighteenth century.

7. Venture Smith's slave narrative might also be taught, a fascinating account of a freed African slave turned slave owner. This narrative is particularly useful for exploring African Americans' complex relationship to slavery and also works well as a companion piece to Benjamin Franklin's

autobiography. Consult Desrochers's recent article for a discussion of the ways in which Smith's narrative, dictated to the (white) Connecticut schoolteacher Elisha Niles, reflects aspects of Smith's cultural background from his early years in West Africa.

8. To follow up on these questions, students might be asked to compare a self-authored criminal narrative like Abraham Johnstone's with a dictated criminal narrative like Johnson Green's. Students quickly point to the way in which Johnstone, who denies his guilt, uses religious discourse to defend himself and criticize his accusers, while Green uses it to humble himself before God. Despite these striking differences, students should be encouraged to consider the similarities between the two texts by examining the argument in Johnstone's address to his fellow blacks. It is interesting that he, like Green, seeks to influence the conduct of fellow blacks in part by encouraging the community to assume responsibility for themselves and by encouraging free blacks (especially Christians) to set an example for others.

9. For information in much of this paragraph I am indebted to John Sekora's essay.

10. Instructors might wish to include texts such as "A Charge, Delivered to the African Lodge, June 24, 1797, at Menotomy," by Prince Hall, the founder of the African Lodge in Boston; *A Narrative of the Proceedings of the Black People, during the Late Awful Calamity in Philadelphia in the Year 1793*, by Richard Allen and Absalom Jones, early leaders in the black church movement in Philadelphia; or orations delivered in celebration of the abolition of the slave trade, written by Peter Williams or William Hamilton, leaders in the black community in New York City.

11. In considering questions of national identity, instructors, particularly those who emphasize the transatlantic nature of early writing, may wish to adopt Potkay and Burr's suggestion that some early black writers might be best understood as precursors to those Paul Gilroy has identified as writers of the "black Atlantic."

12. In the appended list of writers, consider the sermons and addresses of Jones, Carman, Parrott, Lawrence, Miller, Hamilton, Peter Williams, Sipkins, and Sidney. Many of these addresses are reprinted in Porter's *Early Negro Writing*.

Appendix
Selected Early African American Writers to 1815

Allen, Richard (1760–1831). *The Life, Experience, and Gospel Labors of the Rt. Rev. Richard Allen to Which Is Annexed the Rise and Progress of the African Methodist Church in the United States.* Boston, 1833.

Allen, Richard, and Absalom Jones. *A Narrative of the Proceedings of the Black People, during the Late Awful Calamity in Philadelphia, in the Year 1793.* Philadelphia, 1794.

Banneker, Benjamin (1731–1806). *Copy of a Letter from Benjamin Banneker to the Secretary of State, with His Answer.* Philadelphia, 1792.

Belinda (?–?). "Petition of an African Slave, to the Legislature of Massachusetts" (1782). In *The American Museum.* Philadelphia, 1787.

Bustill, Cyrus (1732–1806). "An Addrass to the Blacks in Philadelfiea 9thmonth 18th 1787." *William and Mary Quarterly* 29 (1972): 99–108.

Carman, Adam (?–?). *An Oration Delivered on the Fourth Anniversary of the Abolition of the Slave Trade.* New York, 1811.

Cocks, Judith (?–?). Letter (1795), rpt. in Harris.

Coker, Daniel (1780–1835). *A Dialogue between a Virginian and an African Minister.* Baltimore, 1810.

————. *Journal of Daniel Coker, a Descendant of Africa.* Baltimore, 1820.

Collins, Obour (?–?), and Sarah D. Lyna. Letter (1809), rpt. in Sterling.

Cuffe, Paul (1759–1817). *Brief Account of the Settlement and Present Situation of the Colony of Sierra Leone in Africa.* New York, 1812.

————. *Narrative of the Life and Adventures of Paul Cuffe, a Pequot Indian: During Thirty Years at Sea, and in Traveling in Foreign Lands.* Vernon, 1839.

Equiano, Olaudah (1745?–97). *The Interesting Narrative of the Life of Olaudah Equiano.* London, 1789.

Forten, James (1766–1842). *A Series of Letters by a Man of Color.* Philadelphia, 1813.

Fortis, Edmund (1754?–94). *Last Words and Dying Speech of Edmund Fortis, a Negro Man.* Exeter, 1795.

George, David (1743?–c.1810). "An Account of the Life of Mr. David George, from Sierra Leone in Africa; Given by Himself in a Conversation with Brother Rippon of London and Brother Pearce of Birmingham." *Annual Baptist Register, for 1790, 1791, 1792, and Part of 1793.* London, 1793.

Gilbert, Anne Hart (1768–1834). *History of Methodism* (1804). Rpt. in Ferguson.

Gilbert, Anne Hart, and John Gilbert. *Memoir of John Gilbert.* Liverpool, 1835. Rpt. in Ferguson.

Green, Johnson (1757–86). *The Life and Confession of Johnson Green, Who Is to Be Executed This Day, August 17th, 1786, for the Atrocious Crime of Burglary; Together with His Last and Dying Words.* Worcester, 1786.

Gronniosaw, James Albert Ukawsaw (c.1710–72). *A Narrative of the Most Remarkable Particulars in the Life of James Albert Ukawsaw Gronniosaw, an African Prince, As Related by Himself.* Bath, 1772.

Hall, Prince (1735?–1807). *A Charge Delivered to the African Lodge, June 24, 1797, at Menotomy.* Boston, 1797.

———. *A Charge Delivered to the Brethren of the African Lodge on the 25th of June, 1792, at the Hall of Brother William Smith, in Charleston.* Boston, 1792.

Hamilton, William (1773–1836). *An Address to the New York African Society for Mutual Relief.* New York, 1809.

———. *An Oration Delivered in the African Zion Church on the Fourth of July, 1827, in Commemoration of the Abolition of Domestic Slavery in This State.* New York, 1827.

———. *An Oration on the Abolition of the Slave Trade.* New York, 1815.

Hammon, Briton (?–?). *Narrative of the Uncommon Sufferings, and Surprizing Deliverance of Briton Hammon, a Negro Man.* Boston, 1760.

Hammon, Jupiter (1711–c.1800). *An Address to Miss Phillis Wheatly, Ethiopian Poetess.* Hartford, 1778.

———. *An Address to the Negroes in the State of New York.* New York, 1787.

———. *An Evening's Improvement, Showing, the Necessity of Beholding the Lamb of God.* Hartford, n.d.

———. *An Evening Thought, Salvation, by Christ, with Penetential Cries.* 1760.

———. *A Winter Piece: Being a Serious Exhortation, with a Call to the Unconverted: A Short Contemplation on the Death of Jesus Christ.* Hartford, 1781.

Harrison, Ann (?–?). Letter (1811), rpt. in Sterling.

Harrison, Margaret (1743–1811). Letter (1809), rpt. in Sterling.

Haynes, Lemuel (1753–1833). *The Character and Work of a Spiritual Watchman Described: A Sermon Delivered at Hinesburgh, February 23, 1791.* Litchfield, 1791.

———. *The Important Concerns of Ministers, and the People of Their Charge, at the Day of Judgment.* Rutland, 1798.

———. *The Influences of Civil Government on Relief.* Rutland, 1798.

———. *Liberty Further Extended; or, Free Thoughts on the Illegality of Slave-Keeping.* 1776?

———. *Mystery Developed; or, Russell Colvin.* Hartford, 1820.

———. *The Nature and Importance of True Republicanism.* Rutland, 1801.

———. *Universal Salvation, a Very Ancient Doctrine: With Some Account of the Life and Character of Its Author: A Sermon, Delivered at Rutland, West-Parish, in the Year 1805.* Rutland, 1806.

Jea, John (?–?). *The Life, History, and Unparalleled Sufferings of John Jea, the African Preacher.* 1811?

Johnstone, Abraham (?–1797). *The Address of Abraham Johnstone, a Black Man, Who Was Hanged at Woodbury, in the County of Gloucester, and State of New Jersey; To Which Is Added His Dying Confession or Declaration, also a Copy of a Letter to His Wife, Written the Day Previous to His Execution.* Philadelphia, 1797.

Jones, Absalom (1746–1818). *A Thanksgiving Sermon, Preached January 1, 1808, in St. Thomas's, or the African Episcopal Church, Philadelphia: On Account of the Abolition of the African Slave Trade.* Philadelphia, 1808.

Joyce, John (1784?–1808). *Confession of John Joyce, Alias Davis, Who Was Executed on Monday, the 14th of March, 1808.* Philadelphia, 1808.

King, Boston (1760?–1802). "Memoirs of the Life of Boston King, a Black Preacher, Written by Himself, during his Residence at Kingswood-School." *Methodist Magazine for March, 1798.*

Lawrence, George (?–?). *Oration on the Abolition of the Slave Trade.* New York, 1813.

Liele, George (c.1751–1825). "An Account of Several Baptist Churches, Consisting Chiefly of Negro Slaves; Particularly of One at Kingston, in Jamaica; and Another at Savannah in Georgia." *Baptist Annual Register, for 1790, 1791, 1792, and Part of 1793,* by John Rippon, D.D. London, 1793.

Marrant, John (1755–91). *A Journal of the Rev. John Marrant, from August the 18th, 1785, to the 16th of March 1790; to Which Are Added, Two Sermons.* London, 1790.

———. *A Narrative of the Lord's Wonderful Dealings with John Marrant, a Black (Now Going to Preach the Gospel in Nova-Scotia) Born in New York, in North America.* Ed. Rev. W. Aldridge. London, 1785.

Mathias, Peter (1782?–1808). *Confession of Peter Mathias, Alias Mathews, Who Was Executed on Monday, the 14th of March, 1808; for the Murder of Mrs. Sarah Cross.* Ed. Richard Allen. Philadelphia, 1808.

Miller, William (1775–1845). *A Sermon on the Abolition of the Slave Trade.* New York, 1810.

Mountain, Joseph (1758–90). *Sketches of the Life of Joseph Mountain, a Negro Who Was Executed at New-Haven, on the 20th Day of October, 1790, for a Rape, Committed on the 26th Day of May Last.* New Haven, 1790.

Parrott, Russell (1791–1824). *An Address, on the Abolition of the Slave-Trade, Delivered before the Different African Benevolent Societies.* Philadelphia, 1816.

———. *An Oration of the Abolition of the Slave Trade.* Philadelphia, 1814.

———. *An Oration on the Abolition of the Slave Trade.* Philadelphia, 1812.

Powers, Thomas (1776–96). *The Narrative and Confession of Thomas Powers, a Negro, Formerly of Norwich in Connecticut.* Norwich, 1796.

Sarter, Caesar (?–?). "Essay on Slavery." *Essex Journal and Merrimack Packet.* 17 Aug. 1774.

Sidney, Joseph (?–?). *An Oration, Commemorative of the Abolition of the Slave Trade in the United States.* New York, 1809.

Sipkins, Henry (1788?–?). *An Oration on the Abolition of the Slave Trade.* New York, 1809.

Smith, Stephen (1769?–97). *The Life, Last Words, and Dying Speech of Stephen Smith.* Boston, 1797.

Smith, Venture (1729?–1805). *A Narrative of the Life and Adventures of Venture, a Native of Africa.* New London, 1798.

Teasman, John (1754–1815). *An Address, Delivered in the African Episcopal Church, on the 25th March, 1811; before the New-York African Society, for Mutual Relief; Being the First Anniversary of Its Incorporation.* New York, 1811.

Terry (Prince), Lucy (c.1730–1821). "Bar's Fight." *History of Western Massachusetts,* vol. 2. By Josiah Holland. 1855.

Thwaites, Elizabeth Hart (1771–1833). Correspondence and poetry in *A Voice from the West Indies,* by John Horsford. London, 1856. See also Ferguson.

———. *History of Methodism.* 1804.

Wheatley, Phillis (1753?–1784). *The Collected Works of Phillis Wheatley*. Ed. John Shields. New York: Oxford, 1988.

———. *Poems on Various Subjects, Religious and Moral*. London, 1773.

White, George (1764–1836). *A Brief Account of the Life, Experience, Travels, and Gospel Labours of George White, an African*. New York, 1810.

Williams, Frances (c. 1700–c. 1770). "An Ode." *The History of Jamaica*, by Edward Long. London, 1774.

Williams, Peter, Jr. (1780?–1840). *Discourse Delivered in St. Philip's Church, for the Benefit of the Coloured Community of Wilberforce in Upper Canada; on the Fourth of July, 1830*. New York, 1830.

———. *A Discourse Delivered on the Death of Capt. Paul Cuffe, before the New-York African Institution, in the African Methodist Episcopal Zion Church, October 21, 1817*. New York, 1818.

———. *An Oration on the Abolition of the Slave Trade*. New York, 1808.

For additional selections and authors, see Porter's detailed bibliographical essay ("Writings").

Works Cited

Primary Works

Allen, Richard. "Address to the Public, and People of Color." Porter, *Early Negro Writing* 415–17.

———. "Confessions of John Joyce." Porter, *Early Negro Writing* 414–26.

Allen, Richard, and Absalom Jones. *A Narrative of the Proceedings of the Black People, during the Late Awful Calamity in Philadelphia, in the Year 1793*. Porter, *Pamphlets* 3–24.

———. "A Short Address to the Friends of Him Who Hath No Helper." Porter, *Pamphlets* 23.

Aptheker, Herbert, ed. *A Documentary History of the Negro People in the United States*. Vol. 1. New York: Citadel, 1951.

Bruns, Roger, ed. *Am I Not a Man and a Brother? The Antislavery Crusade of Revolutionary America, 1688–1788*. Boston: Chelsea House, 1977.

Carretta, Vincent, ed. *Unchained Voices: An Anthology of Black Authors in the English-Speaking World of the Eighteenth Century*. Lexington: UP of Kentucky, 1996.

Ferguson, Moira, ed. *The Hart Sisters: Early African Caribbean Writers, Evangelicals, and Radicals*. Lincoln: U of Nebraska P, 1993.

Green, Johnson. *The Life and Confession of Johnson Green*. Carretta, *Unchained Voices* 134–41.

Hall, Prince. "A Charge Delivered to the African Lodge, June 24, 1797, at Menotomy." Porter, *Early Negro Writing* 70–78.

Hammon, Briton. *Narrative of the Uncommon Suffering and Surprizing Deliverance of Briton Hammon, a Negro Man*. Carretta, *Unchained Voices* 20–25.

Harris, Sharon M., ed. *American Women Writers to 1800*. New York: Oxford UP, 1996.

Jefferson, Thomas. *Notes on the State of Virginia*. Ed. William Peden. New York: Norton, 1954.

Johnstone, Abraham. *The Address of Abraham Johnstone*. Philadelphia, 1797.

Magaw, Samuel. *A Discourse Delivered July 17, 1794, in the African Church of the City of Philadelphia*. Philadelphia, 1794.

Newman, Richard, ed. *Black Preacher to White America: The Collected Writings of Lemuel Haynes, 1774–1833*. Brooklyn: Carlson, 1990.

Porter, Dorothy, ed. *Early Negro Writing, 1760–1837*. Baltimore: Black Classics, 1995.

——, ed. *Negro Protest Pamphlets*. New York: Arno, 1969.

Potkay, Adam, and Sandra Burr, eds. *Black Atlantic Writers of the Eighteenth Century*. New York: St. Martin's, 1995.

Shields, John, ed. *The Collected Works of Phillis Wheatley*. New York: Oxford UP, 1988.

Sterling, Dorothy, ed. *We Are Your Sisters: Black Women in the Nineteenth Century*. New York: Norton, 1984.

Williams, Daniel, ed. *Pillars of Salt: An Anthology of Early American Criminal Narratives*. Madison: Madison House, 1993.

Secondary Works

Andrews, William L. *To Tell a Free Story: The First Century of Afro-American Autobiography, 1760–1865*. Urbana: U of Illinois P, 1986.

Carretta, Vincent. Introduction. Carretta, *Unchained Voices* 1–16.

Cummins, Eric. "'Anarchia' and the Emerging State." *Radical History* 48 (1990): 33–62.

Desrochers, Robert E., Jr., "'Not Fade Away': The Narrative of Venture Smith, an African American in the Early Republic." *Journal of American History* 84 (1997): 40–66.

Foner, Philip S. *History of Black Americans: From Africa to the Emergence of the Cotton Kingdom*. Westport: Greenwood, 1975.

Gates, Henry Louis, Jr., ed. *The Classic Slave Narratives*. New York: Penguin, 1987.

Gilroy, Paul. *The Black Atlantic: Modernity and Double Consciousness*. Cambridge: Harvard UP, 1993.

Horton, James, and Lois Horton. *In Hope of Liberty: Culture, Community, and Protest among Northern Free Blacks, 1700–1860*. New York: Oxford UP, 1997.

Kaplan, Sidney, and Emma Nogrady Kaplan. *The Black Presence in the Era of the American Revolution*. Amherst: U of Massachusetts P, 1989.

Nash, Gary. *Forging Freedom: The Formation of Philadelphia's Black Community, 1720–1840*. Cambridge: Harvard UP, 1988.

Piersen, William D. *From Africa to America: African American History from the Colonial Era to the Early Republic, 1526–1790*. Boston: Twayne, 1996.

Porter, Dorothy B. "Early American Negro Writings: A Bibliographical Study." *Papers of the Bibliographical Society of America* 39 (1945): 192–268.

Raboteau, Albert J. *A Fire in the Bones: Reflections on African-American Religious History.* Boston: Beacon, 1995.

Richards, Phillip M. "Phillis Wheatley and Literary Americanization." *American Quarterly* 44 (1992): 163–91.

Sekora, John. "Red, White, and Black: Indian Captivities, Colonial Printers, and the Early African-American Narrative." *A Mixed Race: Ethnicity in Early America.* Ed. Frank Shuffelton. New York: Oxford UP, 1993. 92–104.

White, Shane. *Somewhat More Independent: The End of Slavery in New York City, 1770–1810.* Athens: U of Georgia P, 1991.

Sharon M. Harris

Early Women's Texts

Written texts by women in this country begin, at least according to our current state of knowledge,[1] in the early seventeenth century, but women's political and cultural influences begin much earlier and are integral to women's emergence in the literary history of the United States. For indigenous colonial women, texts were created and distributed orally over many generations before being translated into written form. Oral transmission necessarily includes the alteration of texts over time and is necessary to the cultural development and creativity of those texts. Native American women participated in this transmission process through positions of influence in their societies that also shaped national customs and development. The Lady of Cofitachique, for instance, flourished in the early sixteenth century and ruled the area that is now Georgia and South Carolina. Knowledge of the influences of early Hispanic women in the Americas is still more fully developed in colonial Latin American studies than it is in United States literary studies, but the contributions of a few Hispanic women have recently come to light. Like Queen Isabella of Spain,

Doña Ana de Zaldivar y Mendoza of Mexico was instrumental in the late sixteenth century in funding colonizing explorations into the Southwest, and Francisca Hinestrosa is known to have come to the Americas with Hernando de Soto. By the eighteenth century, significant numbers of Hispanic women, including Eulelia de Callis y Fages of California, populated the southwestern United States.

Within European groups settling the area now broadly conceived as the continental United States, women played a significant role in exploration, colonization, and settlement. Early French women pioneered regions throughout the land: the aristocratic Frances Mary Jacqueline La Tour came to New England in 1643, and Judith Giton Royer Manigault left an account of her travel from France to Carolina in 1685. French women involved in spreading Catholicism to the Americas were also early influences. Philippine Duchesne became a frontier missionary in the late eighteenth century, following the lead of Sister Marie Tranchepain, de Saint Augustine, and other women missionaries who had earlier settled in Louisiana. Dutch women, especially from the upper classes, were not only among the earliest settlers but also some of the most business-oriented women of the period; many settled in New Netherland in the mid-seventeenth century, and their influence in the New York region continued to grow throughout the Revolutionary and early federal periods. Letters, account books, and other historical records kept by seventeenth- and eighteenth-century Dutch women, including Maria van Cortlandt van Rensselaer and Alida Schuyler Livingston, are available in translation, and in the eighteenth century Dutch American women artists emerged who wrote primarily in English, including the poet and novelist Ann Eliza Bleecker.

Like their Continental European counterparts, English women in the New World were an extraordinarily active and diverse group. In the mid-1640s Lady Deborah Moody founded a colony on Long Island, and in Maryland during the same period Margaret Brent became the first woman in the colonies to demand the right to vote. By the eighteenth century, Anglo-American women's writings proliferated, and so did their other accomplishments: Elizabeth Timothy of South Carolina, Mary Katherine Goddard of Maryland, and Sarah

Potter Hillhouse of Georgia were newspaper publishers; Jane Colden of New York was a botanist; Martha Daniell Logan of South Carolina was a horticulturalist; Eliza Lucas Pinckney, also of South Carolina, experimented with the uses of indigo; Laetitia Sage Benbridge was recognized as an accomplished miniaturist painter; Bridget Richardson Fletcher gained renown as a hymnist; and Jane Fenn Hoskens was a well-known traveling Quaker minister.

Native American women, like Native American men, were in a uniquely disrupted position in the eighteenth century; as their cultural homelands were being colonized, they sought ways to resist. Two means of attempting to stay the influence of European colonization were to preserve their culture through song and artifact and to act as negotiators between the cultures. Among such eighteenth-century activists were Mary (or Molly) Brant and Coosaponakessa. Brant was a sister of the chief of the Six Nations, Joseph Brant, and a Canienga interpreter who negotiated between the Mohawks and the British; Coosaponakessa (Mary Musgrove Matthews Bosomworth) was a Creek who aided negotiations between several Native American groups and the English in Georgia. Catherine Montour, the spouse of a Seneca chief, also acted as an interpreter in mid-eighteenth-century New York and Pennsylvania.

If Native American women were struggling against the effects of European imperialism and colonization, so too were women from Africa. The vast majority of African women in America in the early period were either slaves transported to the colonies through the Middle Passage or the descendants of those slaves. Although there were few reliable translators of early traditions of African American literature, as there were few for Native American texts, a significant record of the past is available to us, if not great in quantity. Through song and craft, African traditions were perpetuated in this country and intermingled with European customs. Several early African women made remarkable inroads in figuring the presence of African American activism and artistry in the American colonies. Lucy Terry, in the folk ballad, and Phillis Wheatley, in classical form, contributed to the American poetic tradition. Black women filed petitions seeking freedom from slavery, and a few, including Jenny Slew in 1765 and

Elizabeth Freeman in 1781, succeeded; a woman known only as Alice was recognized as an oral historian in Pennsylvania; and Catherine Ferguson of New York founded a Sunday school for African American and Anglo-American children late in the century. Most African American women's contributions are simply referred to in writings by others. By piecing together these accounts, however, we can recognize women such as Jinny Cole, kidnapped in the early eighteenth century and brought to the American colonies. She was enslaved in Rhode Island and Massachusetts until her death seventy years later, yet she was renowned in her community as a storyteller and seamstress (Sheldon 896–98), thus affording us a view of the local artist whose individual works are lost to us but whose influences are immeasurable.

One of the greatest changes in women's experiences during the early period was their access to education. Most young women received their initial education in the home. In tribal societies, this education came in the form of narratives such as the Zuni song "How Women Learned to Grind" that accompanied training in domestic skills. Increasingly for Anglo-American women, and occasionally for African American women, in-home education included learning to read and write. As dame schools and female academies emerged, more young women gained formal, institutional educations. Early teachers, including Sarah Pierce and Susanna Rowson, created their own textbooks to advance the subjects and pedagogical practices available to their students. By the end of the eighteenth century, education was becoming common among middle- and upper-class white women. And increasingly such educations included public speaking. At the Young Ladies Academy of Philadelphia, for instance, graduates were expected to give speeches to a "promiscuous" audience. One young graduate, Priscilla Mason, took the opportunity of the graduation speech to "offer a few thoughts on the vindication of female eloquence" (71) in her 1793 address to the academy. Presented the year after the publication of Mary Wollstonecraft's feminist exposition *A Vindication of the Rights of Woman*, Mason's terminology and ardent assertions in favor of female education — "Our high and mighty Lords (thanks to their arbitrary constitutions) have denied us the means of knowledge, and then reproached us for the want of it" (72) — was a notable contribution to the emerging demand for women's rights that would find full bloom in the nineteenth century.

As women of the middle and upper classes became better educated, their writings expanded in scope and style. One of the most interesting representations of this change is the late-eighteenth-century interest in satirical writings. Most women included only satirical anecdotes in otherwise serious expositions. Judith Sargent Murray, for instance, satirized culturally inculcated sexual differences in "On the Equality of the Sexes" (1790); in a journal intended for her mother to read, young Sarah Eve satirized her minister's propensity for powdered wigs; and Elizabeth Graeme Fergusson satirized the country parson in a poetic parody. Rarer was Elizabeth Magawley, who published in the *American Weekly Mercury* an extended satirization of male writers who depicted women as foolish and unintelligent.

Having reached this understanding of the diversity of women's cultural heritages and historical presence, students more readily examine women's texts as integral to an understanding of early America. A particularly effective way to capture this diversity and to integrate women's texts into our educational process, especially in survey courses, is to focus on narratives by women. Such a focus allows students to recognize the changes in women's status within particular segments of the culture and the multivalent ways in which women contributed to various literary genres, political debates, and societal reformations. Women's roles in society, across all cultures of the early period, were under continual reconsideration, whether because of scientific inscriptions of gender (Harding; Parrish; Samuels; Schiebinger) or changing religious and political attitudes; women's self-reflective consideration of gender polity, therefore, is integral to and as diverse as their narrative explorations of self and culture.

In familiar narratives, such as captivity accounts and religious tracts, women writers explored their individual mortality and morality in relation to greater powers and often in instances of conflict. These texts vary widely: Mary White Rowlandson struggles to locate a moral existence acceptable to her Puritan beliefs while being held captive by indigenous people whom she had been trained to view as inferior; Mary Jemison attempts to explain her assimilation into

Seneca society as a moral choice; the Quaker Sarah Wister records her personal spiritual crises and awakenings; and Abigail Abbot Bailey, who must confront her husband's incestuous abuse of one of their daughters, writes of her moral dilemmas. All these women, like their male counterparts, crafted a delicate balance between individual need and ever-changing cultural and societal norms.

In the emerging novel form of narrative exploration, however, women writers in particular coupled the search for a moral identity with the gender politics of the late eighteenth century. Novelists such as Susanna Rowson, Hannah Webster Foster, Judith Sargent Murray, and Rebecca Rush constructed gender in relation to class, race, ethnicity, and/or nationalism. Rowson's *Charlotte Temple*, for example, presented a conservative perspective in its gender politics that comforted late-eighteenth-century readers and played into the discourse of parental and familial social structures. Like the patriarchal discourses of Thomas Paine (whose *Crisis No. 1* used the good parent–bad parent argument for revolutionary purposes) or George Washington (the father of his country) or the Revolutionary leaders who, in opposition to the tyrannical mother country, became founding fathers, Rowson argues that young women should adhere to parental guidance and that parents should be benevolent and forgiving. Equally of concern for an American audience was her portrayal of the French teacher as the force that leads astray the amiable young Charlotte Temple. At the time Americans were increasingly at odds over their alliance with France, whose society was in perpetual disruption (both because of the violence inherent in those disruptions and because it too closely resembled their own wartime and current political volatility) and which seemed to advocate more liberty for women than the new country wished to perpetuate. The French salons, renowned for their intellectual endeavors and rumored to harbor promiscuous activities, could not be reconciled with an advocacy of republican motherhood. Thus for all of its titillating escapades, *Charlotte Temple* reinforced many dominant-culture attitudes.

Foster's *The Coquette* and Murray's *The Story of Margaretta* present more complex situations and resolutions than does Rowson's earlier novel, if ultimately they resort to similarly resolute conclusions. *The Coquette*'s "fallen" heroine must die for her indiscretions, but the novel exposes the sexual double standard of New England culture and Eliza Wharton remains a sympathetic, if "ruined," character. In *The Story of Magaretta* (*Selected Writings* 153–272) Murray presents a more radical argument: young women can be educated to value themselves and thus to resist the rakes and roués who will attempt to seduce them. If her overall vision is conventional — that marriage and motherhood is the ultimate goal of (white, middle-class) women — her argument that education and self-assertion are the best means of achieving that goal is a significant advancement in figuring women as self-sufficient, intelligent members of society. Rowson, Foster, and Murray focus almost exclusively on middle-class white society; thus Rush's 1812 novel *Kelroy* is particularly useful for exploring representations of class, race, and gender in early American novels. Rather than the typical rake, it is the domineering mother who destroys her daughter's possibilities for marriage and happiness in this novel, forcing the daughter to seek support in friends and her own self-sufficiency. By using the convention of twins (literal and figurative), Rush exposes the different experiences of young women and men in the early federal years. The main character, Helen Cathcart, has a twin brother, Charles — a relationship that suggests an inherent equality. But Charles becomes a lawyer, and his economic independence allows him, unlike his sister, to escape the need to please others for his survival. Whereas Murray argues against the culturally inculcated appearance of differences between the sexes' capabilities, Rush examines the politics of appearances as requisite to women's lives. The attention in these novels to the gap between appearances and reality is a particularly viable focus of discussion for students who have read Benjamin Franklin's *Autobiography*, which also keenly addresses appearances in terms of cultural attitudes.

Race relations on the continent had been problematic since the beginnings of exploration and colonization. Not only were the interactions of various peoples strained by misguided racial attitudes, but the dominant culture had always seen the romantic involvement of people of different races as dangerous, disruptive, and immoral. In 1639, for example, Mary Mandame of Plymouth, Massachusetts, was convicted of a "dalliance" with a Native American man; she was whipped and sentenced to wear a badge of shame on her sleeve. In an 1801 novel, *Female Quixotism*, Tabitha Tenney plays off of the cultural distrust of interracial relationships when she has her main character, Dorcasina Sheldon, unwittingly wrap her "snowy arms" around her African American gardener's "ebony neck." (For an extended discussion of race relations in this novel, see Harris, "Lost Boundaries.") *Kelroy* also addresses important issues of race and class. For instance, the Hammond family's African American servant, Henry, is a free man whom Rush invests with a moral nature and free will to judge right and wrong, even when it means going against his employer's wishes. But the text is also rife with racial stereotypes and ill treatment of the black servant, Sancho. Rush's discourse (including racist terms but also the liberal use of "fellow creature" and "species") illustrates how scientific classifications of race in the eighteenth century were perpetuated through popular culture. Equally problematic but effective in analyses of race and class representations in the early federal period is Rush's depiction of the Gurnet family. An entire chapter is devoted to this once-impoverished family that, when newly endowed with wealth, seeks to cross class boundaries. As the object of satire, the Gurnet family exposes Rush's class biases in ways that are fruitful for discussions of the volatile exchanges over class attitudes and the new political order of a republic versus that of a democracy.

While early novels were most often focused on current social and political debates, by the 1820s novels would increasingly be drawn to historical analyses. The most renowned such novel is Catharine Maria Sedgwick's *Hope Leslie* (1827), which examines the early Puritan culture in terms of gender, race, and political mores. Early women writers' interest in history, however, had long preceded the publication of *Hope Leslie*. Historical narratives were a key means for early women writers to engage the changing culture and women's opportunities in those evolving societies. Gender issues were particularly prevalent in this narrative form. Women were most prolific in the historical-narrative genres of diaries and letter books. Most of the standard anthologies of early American literature and especially Harris's *American Women Writers to 1800* offer representative texts of these forms. But petitions were equally important as sources of historical narratives.

Slave petitions often included autobiographical narratives that, cumulatively, present a significant record of the historical experiences of Africans brought to North America as slaves. "The Petition of an African Slave," published in 1787, recounts the life of "Belinda, an African," who had been kidnapped seventy years earlier and whose petition to the Massachusetts State Legislature asked for her freedom and financial restitution from her master's estate. Other forms of petitions captured significant historical moments as well: in 1733 a group of women merchants published a petition, "We the Widows," to protest the government's failure to treat them comparably to their male colleagues; and Ann Gwinnett of Georgia used the petition as a form of formal protest during the American Revolution to demand that the United States Congress remove a military officer from his command because of asserted improprieties in relation to a duel in which her husband died.

While letters, diaries, and petitions tended to emphasize history in the making, other genres offered women writers a reflective means of engaging history over time and, occasionally, of questioning how history has been constructed, especially to the exclusion of women. Students sometimes believe that such questions only emerged in the late twentieth century, but early women's narratives clearly challenge such "presentist" attitudes. Formal histories, essays, and dramas were vehicles for historical examinations of political orders and their relation to gender.

Formal histories by women began to emerge only in the late eighteenth century. Mercy Otis Warren used the moment of revolution and political reconstruction to offer her opinions on the background to and the consequences of the newly emerging republic. Not unlike Cotton Mather's *Magnalia*, Warren's three-volume *History [. . .] of the American Revolution* (1805) includes admiring accounts of the Revolutionary leaders and political positions she supported during the war. Hannah Adams spearheaded the tradition of scholarly histories by women in the United States. Her major work, *A Summary History of New-England* (1799), moves chronologically from the early seventeenth century through the Revolutionary era. The first woman admitted to the Boston Athenaeum, Adams produced numerous other historical texts, including studies of Christianity, Judaism, and London society, as well as children's history books.

It was Judith Sargent Murray and Mercy Otis Warren, however, who most explicitly linked history writing and gender politics. As the most prolific woman essayist of the eighteenth century, Murray used this narrative form to expose historical biases and to offer new visions of historical accountability. In "On the Equality of the Sexes," Murray argued that woman as the inferior sex was a historical construct, not reality, and noted its contemporary form was deeply linked to early Christian inscriptions of gender difference. Asserting that the creation stories of Genesis do not indict Eve if read in the original "Hebrew tongue," Murray claims that "blind *self love*" (*Selected Writings* 12) causes men to blame Eve and subsequently all women for the fall of humankind. Like Priscilla Mason, Murray argues that the differences between the sexes are not innate but result from men's traditional denial of education to women. She seeks to rectify the inattention to women's accomplishments and cultural contributions in a four-part essay, "Observations on Female Abilities." Beginning with the thirteenth century and moving through Western history to her own times, Murray reinscribed women into international history; interestingly, the shortcoming of the text is its too-brief section on United States women, as if she envisioned "America" as beginning in 1776 and thus being too youthful a landscape to yet write about. What emerges in her history of women, however, is a move from theory (as in "On the Equality of the Sexes") to practice — a scholarly compendium reenvisioning women as integral members of society with particular talents and as longstanding contributors to Western civilization.

Mercy Otis Warren's dramas were, like Murray's essays, an important contribution to the reconstruction of attitudes about women's roles in society.[2] Most of her plays focused on the American Revolution, but in *The Ladies of Castile* Warren moved to early-sixteenth-century Spain to examine earlier struggles for liberty and independence as well as the integral nature of gender constructions to such struggles. In *The Ladies of Castile* Warren also used the past as a means to reinscribe definitions of manhood and womanhood. The "true man," presented in the characterization of Conde Haro and Don Francis, is not hungry for battle; rather, he is ambivalent about the violence of war and enters into such controversies only as a last resort. Further, he is merciful in battle and acts on principle rather than expediency. Alternatively, Warren presented the failure of manhood in Don Pedro, the traitor, and Don Velasco, who seeks complete control over his daughter Donna Louisa, using her as a commodity of exchange and asserting that for her to act on her own will is equivalent to prostituting herself. Because Louisa has been dominated throughout her life, she cannot follow her principles and thus is presented sympathetically but as an example of failed womanhood. Her mirror image is Donna Maria — assertive against Louisa's passivity, a warrior in her own right regarding matters of principle ("I scorn to live upon ignoble terms — / A supple courtier fawning at the feet / Of proud despotic nobles, or of kings"), and it is she rather than Louisa who survives at the play's conclusion.

In her historical dramas, Warren also raised an issue of significance to many women's writings of the period: the eighteenth-century construction of genius to exclude women. As Christine Battersby and others observe, the Enlightenment brought not only a new consideration of women's roles in the polis but also a redefinition of genius as aligned with masculine creativity, and it was integral, as Emory Elliott argues, to the transition of authority from the clergy to "men of letters."[3] In the preface to The Ladies of Castile Warren asserted that the writing of a tragedy "requires judgement, genius, and taste"; though the requisite diffidence of a woman writer is evident in Warren's preface, the issue of genius and artistic abilities is notable at the beginning of the play. Murray more openly challenged the exclusionary sense of genius in "On the Equality of the Sexes" by figuring Genius as female. While most women simply recorded their personal thoughts and opinions of national events in their writings, a few women like Warren and Murray used the nationalist discourse surrounding the "Genius of America" to insert conceptions of female genius into the philosophical construction of creativity that would become the touchstone for artistic achievement in subsequent decades.

Although there is still much work to be done in the consideration of women's writings and their contributions to the cultures of early America, there is a substantial body of scholarship and, equally important, texts now available for classroom use: anthologies, but also full-length texts by diarists (e.g., Drinker, Wister, Moore), poets (Bradstreet, Wheatley, Stockton, and Pattie Cowell's classic collection of pre-Revolutionary poets), and a wide variety of narratives (Andrews's *Journeys in New Worlds*, June Namais's *A Narrative of the Life of Mrs. Mary Jemison*, and *The Selected Writings of Judith Sargent Murray*, to name only a few). Teachers of early American literature, whether focusing solely on women's writings or presenting an integrated landscape of early writings, now have opportunities for offering women's texts as new and invigorating sources for expanding our students' knowledge of the early period.

Notes

The works of the women detailed in this essay and information on their lives are (unless otherwise indicated) available, with further bibliographic references, in Harris, *American Women Writers to 1800*.

1. Among the scholars instrumental in establishing the field of early United States women's studies are Cott, Kerber (*History* and *Women*), Norton (*Mothers* and *Daughters*), and Ulrich (*Wives* and *Tale*) in history; Cowell, Eberwein, Kolodny, Lang, and Davidson in literature; Allen (*Grandmothers* and *Hoop*), Bataille and Sands, Begay, Hungry Wolf, and Katz in Native American studies; and Kaplan, Spillers and Pryse, and Starling in African American studies. Their early research has now been expanded on — in their subsequent works and by a significant number of scholars of early United States women's literature and culture. See, for instance, Braxton, Derounian-Stodola, Foster, Harris, Mulford, and Taves.

2. As Jeffrey Richards astutely demonstrates, Murray's plays also engaged contemporary issues such as the roles of Committees on Safety and of soldiers returning from battle.

3. For extended discussions on the transformation of "genius" in this period, see Battersby, Elliott, and Harris, "Early American Women's Self-Creating Acts."

Works Cited

Primary Works

Adams, Hannah. *A Summary History of New-England*. Boston, 1799.

Foster, Hannah Webster. *The Coquette*. Ed. Cathy N. Davidson. New York: Oxford UP, 1986.

Mason, Priscilla. "The Salutatory Oration, Delivered by Miss Mason." *The*

Rise and Progress of the Young Ladies' Academy of Philadelphia. Philadelphia: Stewart, 1794.

Murray, Judith Sargent. *The Gleaner*. Boston: I. Thomas and E. T. Andrews, 1798. 3 vols. Ed. Nina Baym. Schenectady: Union Coll. P, 1992.

———. *The Selected Writings of Judith Sargent Murray*. Ed. Sharon M. Harris. New York: Oxford UP, 1996.

"The Petition of an African Slave." *American Museum*, June 1787.

Rowson, Susanna Haswell. *Charlotte Temple*. Ed. Cathy N. Davidson. New York: Oxford UP, 1986.

Rush, Rebecca. *Kelroy*. New York: Oxford UP, 1992.

Tenny, Tabitha. *Female Quixotism*. Ed. Jean Nienkamp and Andrea Collins. New York: Oxford UP, 1992.

Warren, Mercy Otis. *History [. . .] of the American Revolution*. 1805. New York: AMS, 1970.

———. *The Ladies of Castile. The Plays and Poems of Mercy Otis Warren*. Ed. Benjamin Franklin V. Delmar: Scholars, 1980.

"We the Widows." *New-York Weekly Journal* (1733).

Secondary Works

Allen, Paula Gunn. *Grandmothers of the Light: A Medicine Woman's Source Book*. Boston: Beacon, 1991.

———. *The Sacred Hoop: Recovering the Feminine in American Literary Traditions*. Boston: Beacon, 1986.

Andrews, William L., ed. *Journey in New Worlds: Early American Women's Narratives*. Madison: U of Wisconsin P, 1990.

Bataille, Gretchen M., and Kathleen M. Sands. *American Indian Women: Telling Their Lives*. Lincoln: U of Nebraska P, 1984.

Battersby, Christine. *Gender and Genius: Toward a Feminist Aesthetics*. London: Women's, 1989.

Begay, Shirley M. *Kinaalda, a Navajo Puberty Ceremony*. Rev. ed. Rough Neck: Navajo Curriculum Ctr., 1983.

Braxton, Joanne M. *Black Women Writing Autobiography: A Tradition within a Tradition*. Philadelphia: Temple UP, 1989.

Cott, Nancy F. *The Bonds of Womanhood: "Woman's Sphere" in New England, 1780–1835*. New Haven: Yale UP, 1977.

Cowell, Pattie. *Women Poets in Pre-Revolutionary America, 1650–1775: An Anthology*. Troy: Whitston, 1981.

Davidson, Cathy N. *Revolution and the Word: The Rise of the Novel in America*. New York: Oxford UP, 1986.

Derounian-Stodola, Kathryn Zabelle, ed. *The Journal and Occasional Writings of Sarah Wister*. Rutherford: Fairleigh Dickinson, 1987.

Elliott, Emory. *Revolutionary Writers: Literature and Authority in the New Republic, 1775–1810*. New York: Oxford UP, 1982.

Foster, Frances Smith. *Written by Herself: Literary Production of African American Women, 1746–1892*. Bloomington: Indiana UP, 1993.

Harding, Sandra. *Whose Science? Whose Knowledge? Thinking from Women's Lives*. Ithaca: Cornell UP, 1991.

Harris, Sharon M. *American Women Writers to 1800: An Anthology*. New York: Oxford UP, 1996.

———. "Early American Women's Self-Creating Acts." *Resources for American Literary Study* 19.2 (1993): 223–45.

———. "Lost Boundaries: The Use of the Carnivalesque in Tabitha Tenney's *Female Quixotism*." *Speaking the Other Self: American Women Writers*. Ed. Jeanne Campbell Reesman. Athens: U of Georgia P, 1997. 213–28.

Hungry Wolf, Beverly. *The Ways of My Grandmothers*. New York: Morrow, 1980.

Kaplan, Sidney. *The Black Presence in the Era of the American Revolution, 1770–1800*. Greenwich: New York Graphic Soc., 1973.

Katz, Jane B., ed. *I Am the Fire of Time: The Voices of Native American Women*. New York: Dutton, 1977.

Kerber, Linda K. *Toward an Intellectual History of Women: Essays*. Chapel Hill: U of North Carolina P, 1997.

———. *Women of the Republic: Intellect and Ideology in Revolutionary America*. New York: Norton, 1986.

Kolodny, Annette. *The Land before Her: Fantasy and Experience of the American Frontiers, 1630–1860*. Chapel Hill: U of North Carolina P, 1984.

Lang, Amy Schrager. *Prophetic Woman: Anne Hutchinson and the Problem of Dissent in the Literature of New England*. Berkeley: U of California P, 1987.

Mulford, Carla J. *Only for the Eye of a Friend: The Poems of Annis Boudinot Stockton*. Charlottesville: UP of Virginia, 1995.

Namais, June, ed. *A Narrative of the Life of Mrs. Mary Jemison*. Norman: U of Oklahoma P, 1992.

Norton, Mary Beth. *Founding Mothers and Fathers: Gendered Power and the Forming of American Society*. New York: Knopf, 1996.

———. *Liberty's Daughters: The Revolutionary Experience of America, 1750–1800*. Boston: Little, 1980.

Parrish, Susan Scott. "The Female Opossum and the Nature of the New World." *William and Mary Quarterly* 54.3 (1997): 475–515.

Richards, Jeffrey. "Patriotic Interrogations: Committees of Safety in Two Early American Plays." Amer. Literature Assn., Baltimore, 25 May 1997.

Samuels, Shirley. *Romances of the Republic: Women, the Family, and Violence in the Literature of the Early American Nation*. New York: Oxford UP, 1996.

Schiebinger, Londa. *Nature's Body: Gender in the Making of Modern Science*. Boston: Beacon, 1993.

Sheldon, George. *History of Deerfield, Massachusetts*. Vol. 2. Greenfield: E. A. Hall, 1895–96.

Spillers, Hortense J., and Marjorie Pryse, eds. *Conjuring: Black Women, Fiction, and Literary Traditions*. Bloomington: Indiana UP, 1985.

Starling, Marion Wilson. *The Slave Narrative: Its Place in American History*. Boston: Hall, 1981.

Taves, Ann, ed. *Religion and Domestic Violence in Early New England: The Memoirs of Abigail Abbot Bailey.* Bloomington: Indiana UP, 1989.

Ulrich, Laurel Thatcher. *Good Wives: Image and Reality in the Lives of Women in Northern New England, 1650–1750.* New York: Oxford UP, 1982.

———. *A Midwife's Tale: The Life of Martha Ballard, Based on Her Diary, 1785–1812.* New York: Knopf, 1990.

Pattie Cowell

Figuring Multicultural Practice in Early American Literature Classrooms

As with most discourses, analyses of early American literature and culture have been framed in figures: frontier, encounter, wilderness, errand, journey, savage, virgin, empty. Whether such figures function as literary tropes or representations of social practices, they can generate productive conversations among teachers and students. Yet given the shape-changing power of image, figures cannot control conversations once they have begun. As a consequence, figures provide an animating and open ground for classroom dialogue, even on emotionally charged issues and materials.

Figures work particularly well to spark multicultural discussion and practice in early American literature classrooms because they provide students of varying personal and educational backgrounds with an intellectual meeting place. Like all of us, students struggle to find constructive approaches to historically distant and potentially volatile materials. The apparently common ground of figures makes a congenial opening. For example, students can approach the complex political relations being negotiated in the literature of the new republic through the figure of family used by many late eighteenth-century writers. This figure allows students at all levels to trace how ideas of family order were translated into republican structure and aesthetic principle.

But figures expose as well as constitute. Because they draw from a richness of shared tradition, they become powerful communal discourses so apparently encompassing that we must listen hard to hear the critique always implied by missing questions and voices. Do all who use the figure of family — common in both senses of the word — have the same construct in mind? Whose families inhabit the figure? To recover the silences, to learn that they are not silences at all, classroom communities can engage a series of generative figures that allow students both to conceptualize and to critique cultural practices.

Multicultural pedagogy in early American studies derives from two overlapping assumptions: that human history in North America and the United States has multicultural origins, however much origin stories work to conceal them, and that multicultural practice is not so much about individual identity as it is about engaging complex selves with others. From elaborate contemporary narratives of encounter and obsessive Puritan prescriptions for family and communal governance to the later, more distanced reflections of Crèvecoeur and Tocqueville, early North American residents and visitors addressed multicultural questions.

Beginning with an assumption of multicultural origins obviates the need for presenting or defending multicultural study as anachronistic. The literary evidence of early North Americans' concern with multicultural practice is overwhelming: essays containing painstaking rationales for European relations with Indians and for slavery, novels that seem to function as conduct books describing appropriate gender behaviors, legal documents assigning political rights to the propertied, African American petitions for freedom, treatises about women's education, even the rapidly changing substance of children's reading. The questions raised by twentieth-century readers may differ from those raised by early Americans and indicate our different locations in time and space, but they are not new.

———

The examples and discussions that follow sketch a few of the figures that could structure a variety of early American literature courses, from the introductory survey to the graduate seminar. Multicultural practice can inform genre courses, thematic textual groupings, historical overviews, cultural studies approaches, and formalist analyses. My organization is figural rather than chronological, but the suggestions are easily rearranged. Assignments can be adjusted for the level of student experience by increasing or decreasing students' autonomy in their design. Beginning students should have more materials provided for them; more advanced students should be encouraged to explore broader textual resources, perhaps investigating eighteenth-century periodical literature on microfilm or locating an otherwise inaccessible document in the Early American Imprints collection. The availability of manuscript materials will depend largely on a college or university's location and individual instructor's resources, but questions of publication and access can themselves become course content.

A crucial (perhaps luckily) irresolvable issue for multicultural practice is the definition of multiculturalism itself. Forging a group operational definition — mapping the terrain — will often be a subtext for entire courses, because students are unlikely to agree. That very disagreement makes definitions a useful place to start discussion. Because multiculturalism is a media term associated in our time almost entirely with race, it may be important to make multiculturalism more "multi." Early assignments need careful structuring to highlight issues of (at least) gender, class, ethnicity, religion, and sexuality as well as race.

Adapting an exercise from Gregory Jay, I sometimes pursue definitions by asking students to write brief essays of cultural identity. In effect, they draw themselves on the multicultural map. I encourage them to define *cultural identity* as they wish, but I specify that the essays will be public: I place them on reserve in the library or post them to a class Web page and make them the text for an hour or so of class discussion. The assignment isn't due until three or four weeks into the semester, allowing students time to become more familiar with one another, to establish what the appropriate group trust level will be, and to gather a quantity of shared reading and talk. My white students struggle most with the assignment. Some claim to have no cultural identity; others grapple with an awareness of white privilege. All who genuinely engage the assignment come to the shock of self-recognition that is a necessary prerequisite for recognizing others. Students in classes that had initially seemed homogeneous discover identities that are not necessarily written on their bodies. As they learn who is present, they also begin to notice who is absent. This heightened understanding of the class social text makes students less naive readers of literary texts as well. The transitions from initial assignments in early American texts to student essays and back to the early texts have been revealing. The texts become more immediate, the cultural stakes higher.

Assignments from works such as Crèvecoeur's *Letters from an American Farmer* or Jefferson's *Notes on the State of Virginia* are also useful for discussing definition, because they both construct and undercut American myths of community. Crèvecoeur's "What Is an American?" begs for extended discussion of the intersections of class, religion, region, and race. Later letters contrast the naive observations of Letter III with painfully graphic illustrations of the brutalities of slavery and the chaos of revolution. Jefferson's discussion of origins, slavery, agrarian ideals, law, and region works to much the same end. If the ostensible purpose of including a version of Chief Logan's speech is to celebrate Native American oratory, Jefferson's larger purpose is to vindicate American "nature." Enlightenment assumptions about nature, human nature, and social good explode Crèvecoeur's early melting-pot metaphor: native and newcomer still face each other warily; frontier folk and natives have their functions, but only in the service of an urban elite; religious communities become not so much tolerant of others as secularized and, increasingly, irrelevant. An epistolary journey takes Crèvecoeur's narrator from a kind of naive pluralism into a more complex and more painful sense of community. Jefferson's responses to François de Marbois's queries attempt a scientific study of community but always within a political and cultural agenda.

What Crèvecoeur and Jefferson leave out of their communities is as significant as what they include. Placing them in a classroom conversation with a contemporary like Ann Eliza Bleecker adds gender to their definitions of culture. Bleecker's "Lines Written in the Retreat from Burgoyne" and "On Reading Dryden's Virgil," her responses to the deaths of daughter and mother as the family flees the British in 1777, or her fictionalized captivity narrative *History of Maria Kittle* use Crèvecoeur's journey motif to different ends. The dislocations caused by the Revolution and by confrontation with Native Americans reinforce for Bleecker her vulnerability. Grief, anger, and resignation take on gendered meanings that one can amplify, and sometimes contradict, by adding other voices to the classroom conversation: Judith Sargent Murray's essay "On the Equality of the Sexes," for example, or Phillis Wheatley's letter to Samson Occom, or Thomas Paine's "Occasional Letter on the Female Sex," or Sally Wister's girlhood journal of the Revolution, or Belinda's "Petition of an African Slave." In concert, works such as these undercut naive figures of community. As students fill in the outlines of a national origin story, they also ask whose revolution it was.

Resources from Jonathan Ned Katz's *Gay/Lesbian Almanac* and from Martin Duberman, Martha Vicinus, and George Chauncey's *Hidden from History: Reclaiming the Gay and Lesbian Past* stretch figures of community again, adding sexual cultures to classroom definitions of early North American multiculturalism. Or one can explore a useful counterpoint by juxtaposing Médéric-Louis-Elie Moreau de St. Méry and Charles Brockden Brown. Moreau's *American Journey, 1793–1798* records his shock at American women's "unlimited liberty" and their willingness to find "unnatural pleasures with persons of their own sex" (285–86). One of Brown's untitled short fictions explores a romantic friendship between two characters, Sophia and Jessica, that may have been the precursor for the loving relationship between Constantia and Sophie in *Ormond*. The distance between Moreau's disgust and Brown's acceptance is filled with anxiety. Can a new nation survive such disruptions in dominant social patterns? How are we to order relations within a national community?

The classroom conversation outlined here could take many other forms, but the point is to complicate narrow or naive definitions of multicultural community. One consequence of fully developing these definitions is that it allows students to find the conjunctions between and within individual identities. All communities occupy fault lines. Different class-based, racial, or ethnic affiliations may fragment a gender community. Sexual difference may diversify a community otherwise coherent in racial or class identifications. The point in multicultural classroom practice is not to tidy up the interlocking, overlapping, contentious communities that call themselves American.

In advanced classes, it is sometimes useful to supplement early American texts with recent analyses of cultural difference. For beginning students, I introduce these materials through lecture and discussion. I have presented Diane Ravitch's "Multiculturalism: E Pluribus Plures," a vigorous defense of cultural pluralism, with Frances Aparicio's "On Multiculturalism and Privilege: A Latina Perspective," an equally vigorous critique of pluralism. Ravitch bases her defense on a concept of "universalism," arguing that "particularistic multiculturalism" will destroy "a richer common culture" (340, 342–43). Aparicio reminds readers that simple juxtapositions of racial, gender, or class cultures do not describe their interactions: "Our emphasis on multiculturalism, for example, when defined merely as diversity or as tolerance for difference, bypasses the differentials of power among groups that in fact keep some in dominant positions and others in subordinate roles" (576). Abdul JanMohamed and David Lloyd's "Toward a Theory of Minority Discourse" or Chandra Talpade Mohanty's "On Race and Voice: Challenges for Liberal Education in the 1990s" can be as effective as Aparicio's essay and with much the same conclusions. All three critiques add power relations to discussions of multiculturalism, much as Clifford Geertz does in his recipe for elephant and rabbit stew ("take one elephant and one rabbit . . ."): cultural elephants need have no fear of losing their savor in the recipe (333–34). While such an equal-opportunity recipe provides neither equality nor opportunity, it does provide a useful illustration of Aparicio's critique. One student was so caught by it that she structured her final research project around the figure of a new multicultural recipe.

As students explore ways to integrate frameworks of race, class, gender, and sexuality with the literary texts they are reading, the figure of borders sometimes seems indispensable — borders contested, avoided, and inhabited, borders on land, between peoples, within the self. Gloria Anzaldúa's *Borderlands / La Frontera*, Renato Rosaldo's *Culture and Truth*, June Jordan's "Report from the Bahamas," and Trinh T. Minh-ha's *Woman, Native, Other* provide recent analyses of the figure, embedded in narratives of personal experience and genre-bending that students often find both baffling and compelling. Anzaldúa and Trinh confront readers with our often unexamined genre expectations and insist that we read their narratives of difference differently. Preparing students for these books, or selections from them, can open the discussion of genre so crucial to understanding the literariness of early texts.

Given the constant shape-changing of the geopolitical and geo-social landscape during the periods of European exploration and colonization, the border figure is easily adapted to early American literature classrooms. The theological border between Massachusetts Bay and Rhode Island and the regional border between Pennsylvania and Maryland use a figure with dozens of applications. What does Prince Hall's petition to the Massachusetts Bay General Court, for example, have to say about the thin and permeable border between African American slaves and free blacks? How should we conceive the borders created by conflicting stories of cultural origin? Or the religious borders that divide Puritan and Quaker, Calvinist and antinomian, Protestant and Catholic? Or the gendered border between public and private voices marked by Abigail Adams's epistolary plea to husband John to "Remember the Ladies" (905)? Or the racist borders highlighted by Olaudah Equiano's call to "nominal Christians" to answer for the institution of slavery (58)? These borderlands can be destructive, violent, filled with fear. And they can be generative, sites of self-discovery and new knowledge. Most often, they will be all these things, a circumstance students often find startling as they grapple with the pain and wonder so prominent in early texts.

It's fortunate for literature that borderlands are inhabited by stories as well as people. The familiar figure of storytelling evokes some deceptively simple questions that serve multicultural classroom practice. Who is telling the story? Whose story is told? Or even more simply, Who can speak? The ethical dimension of these questions unfolds in the early American classroom from the very first assignments. As we present Native American texts, both multicultural practice and responsible literary history insist that we discuss how the texts come to us. How do interpretive approaches to Chief Powhatan's 1609 speech recognize that our only version is recorded by John Smith? Does it matter that Chief Logan's 1774 address to a peace council comes through Thomas Jefferson? Is an as-told-to slave narrative authored by the speaker or the writer? If a folk song comes to us in multiple versions, which is more authentic, and does authenticity matter? How do we *read* oral literatures that are mediated by speakers from other cultures and presented outside their performative contexts? How do readers and teachers choose between using corrupted texts or none at all?

Any of these questions can animate lengthy and important classroom discussions that, finally, are about agency. Who gets to tell the story, and what does that mean about the context of social relations, about voice, authorship, audience, literacy, intertextuality, and textual access? Such questions gather power and complexity from the interdependent assumptions that a speaker's cultural location shapes access to knowledge(s) and that though individuals can learn about "others" they cannot transcend their locations (Alcoff 98). At this point the ethical dimension of storytelling gives way to the epistemological. What do we know? What can we know? What must we acknowledge that we cannot know? What are an individual's responsibilities to speak and to be silent?

The texts and examples that support discussions of these questions abound. Anne Hutchinson's decision to speak for herself and the consequences. The credence given to a Hopi account of the 1680

Pueblo revolt as compared with Antonio de Otermín's epistolary description of the same event. Silences in transcripts of the Salem witchcraft trials. Elizabeth Ashbridge's autobiographical account of the relation between religious conversion and domestic abuse. The authority and safety of Benjamin Franklin's "Remarks Concerning the Savages of America" and their connection with the prominence of the author. Sarah Knight's condescending depiction of the rural people she encounters on her 1704 journey from Boston to New York. The mediation of Jupiter Hammon's published sermons and poems by white "friends," possibly the Lloyd family that owned him. The manuscript circles that both circulated and contained Susanna Wright's protofeminist verse epistle "To Miss Eliz^a Norris — at Fairhill."

The discussions of agency this catalog highlights become especially interesting when class conversations turn to the gender and race-switching common in the ubiquitous "anonymous." The voluminous early modern print culture exchange attacking and defending "woman," the *querelle des femmes*, makes an instructive case in point. Much (though not all) of the renaissance and seventeenth-century *querelle* was conducted by men who assumed female voices when it was convenient for their arguments. Though students are disturbed by the vehemence of the *querelle* and often surprised that a "woman question" has been part of literature for so long, they readily grasp the significance of the connection between ethos and authority, between the apparent speaking voice and credibility.

An equally fascinating case, one that can be treated more quickly than the prolific documents relating to the *querelle*, is the much-reprinted "The Maid's Soliloquy." Detailing the persona's ambivalence about marriage, "The Maid's Soliloquy" was first published in England in the *Gentleman's Magazine* (Jan. 1747) and then reprinted in other English periodicals. The earliest North American publication was in the *New York Evening Post* (Dec. 1747). At least four other North American printings followed, in the *South Carolina Gazette* (4 Mar. 1751), the *New American Magazine* (Feb. 1758), the *Newport Mercury* (2 May 1763), and *Philo Copernicus . . . The American Calendar* (Philadelphia, 1772), a 1773 almanac. Do we read the poem differently when it appears pseudonymously ascribed to "Horatio" (as it did in the *Post*) and when it is said to be "Written by a lady in this Province" (as the *Gazette* claimed)? Is the poem more "American" when we learn from J. A. Leo Lemay that it was probably written by the New Jersey politician Lewis Morris?[1] What is the relation between the cultural identities of authors and their texts? between storytellers and credibility?

Figures permeate human discourse, often (perhaps usually) below the level of conscious examination. This essay is no exception to the rule; it relies on fault lines and maps and conversations to describe multicultural practice in early American literature classrooms. When we look at figures directly, push them to disclose the sources of their power, they become telling pedagogical tools. I have asked classes to develop research projects that explore one or more text(s) in relation to the figure of cultural exchange. Two or three weeks after the assignment is explained, I take a few minutes of class time for students to discuss their chosen texts. Then I ask them to list texts that would not work for the assignment. Much to their surprise, we have yet to find one.

Note

1. The information about "The Maid's Soliloquy" summarized here illustrates scholarly conversation at its most generous. While preparing the third edition of *The Heath Anthology of American Literature*, Carla Mulford learned from John Shawcross that the poem was first printed in the *Gentleman's Magazine*. She then wrote to J. A. Leo Lemay, whose *Calendar of American Poetry in the Colonial Newspapers and Magazines and in the Major English Magazines through 1765* is a standard index for early Americanists to poems printed in the English colonies and who maintains a master list of updates on poems indexed in the volume. Lemay confirmed in October 1996 that the poem was written by Lewis Morris and that it is available in manuscript in the Robert Morris papers at Rutgers University Library, New Brunswick, New Jersey. Mulford shared this information with me, and I included it with other printings of the poem assembled in my research on colonial women poets.

Works Cited

Primary Works

Most of the primary selections I refer to can be found in familiar anthologies, such as *The Heath Anthology of American Literature*, 3rd. ed.;

The Harper American Literature, 2nd. ed.; *The Norton Anthology of American Literature*, 5th. ed.; or *American Women Writers to 1800*. I chose the text locations cited here for their availability.

Adams, Abigail. Letter to John Adams. 31 Mar. 1776. *Heath* 1: 905.

American Women Writers to 1800. Ed. Sharon M. Harris. New York: Oxford UP, 1996.

Ashbridge, Elizabeth. *Some Account of the [. . .] Life of Elizabeth Ashbridge [. . .]*. 1755. Excerpted in *Heath* 1: 605–16.

Belinda. "Petition of an African Slave." *American Women Writers* 253–55.

Bleecker, Ann Eliza. *The Posthumous Works of Ann Eliza Bleecker [. . .]*. Ed. Margaretta V. Faugeres. New York: Swords, 1793.

Brown, Charles Brockden. *The Life of Charles Brockden Brown, Together with Selections [. . .]*. Ed. William Dunlap. Philadelphia: Parke, 1815.

"The Coming of the Spanish and the Pueblo Revolt (Hopi)." *Heath* 1: 492–95.

Crèvecoeur, J. Hector St. John de. *Letters from an American Farmer*. 1782, 1793. Ed. Albert E. Stone. New York: Penguin, 1981.

Equiano, Olaudah. 1789. *The Interesting Narrative of the Life of Olaudah Equiano*. Ed. Robert J. Allison. Boston: Bedford, 1995.

Franklin, Benjamin. "Remarks concerning the Savages of America." 1784. *Norton* 1: 516–20.

Hall, Prince. "To the Honorable Council and House of Representatives for the State of Massachusetts-Bay in General Court Assembled January 13th, 1777." *Heath* 1: 1010–11.

Hammon, Jupiter. Poetry. *Harper* 1: 472–75.

The Harper American Literature. Ed. Donald McQuade et al. 2nd ed. New York: Harper, 1994.

The Heath Anthology of American Literature. Ed. Paul Lauter et al. 3rd ed. Lexington: Heath, 1998.

Jefferson, Thomas. *Notes on the State of Virginia*. 1787. *Thomas Jefferson: Writings*. Ed. Merrill Peterson. New York: Lib. of America, 1984. 123–325.

Knight, Sarah. *The Journal of Madam Knight*. 1704–05. Ed. Sargent Bush, Jr. *Journeys in New Worlds: Early American Women's Narratives*. Ed. William L. Andrews. Madison: U of Wisconsin P, 1990. 87–116.

Logan. Speech at the End of Lord Dunmore's War. *Harper* 1: 501–02.

"The Maid's Soliloquy." *Heath* 1: 711–12.

Moreau de St. Méry, Médéric-Louis-Elie. *Moreau de St. Méry's American Journey, 1793–1798*. Trans. and ed. Kenneth Roberts and Anna M. Roberts. Garden City: Doubleday, 1947.

Murray, Judith Sargent. "On the Equality of the Sexes." *American Women Writers* 149–56.

The Norton Anthology of American Literature. Ed. Nina Baym et al. 5th ed. New York: Norton, 1998.

Otermín, Antonio de. "Letter on the Pueblo Revolt of 1680." *Heath* 1: 483–91.

Paine, Thomas. "An Occasional Letter on the Female Sex." *Harper* 1: 611–14.

Powhatan. Letter to Captain John Smith. [c. 1609]. *Harper* 1: 100.

Wheatley, Phillis. Letter to Samson Occom. 11 Feb. 1774. *Heath* 1: 1112.

Wister, Sally. Journal. Excerpted in *American Women Writers* 300–02.

Wright, Susanna. "To Miss Eliz\^a Norris — at Fairhill." "Susanna Wright's Verse Epistle on the Status of Women in Eighteenth-Century America." By Pattie Cowell. *Signs* 6 (1981): 795–800.

Secondary Works

Alcoff, Linda. "The Problem of Speaking for Others." *Cultural Critique* 20 (Winter 1991–92): 5–32. Rev. in *Who Can Speak? Authority and Critical Identity*. Ed. Judith Roof and Robyn Wiegman. Urbana: U of Illinois P, 1995. 97–119.

Anzaldúa, Gloria. *Borderlands / La Frontera: The New Mestiza*. San Francisco: Aunt Lute, 1987.

Aparicio, Frances R. "On Multiculturalism and Privilege: A Latina Perspective." *American Quarterly* 46 (1994): 575–88.

Duberman, Martin, Martha Vicinus, and George Chauncey, Jr., eds. *Hidden from History: Reclaiming the Gay and Lesbian Past*. New York: NAL, 1989.

Geertz, Clifford. "History and Anthropology." *New Literary History* 21 (1990): 321–35.

JanMohamed, Abdul, and David Lloyd. "Toward a Theory of Minority Discourse." *Cultural Critique* 6 (Spring 1987): 5–12.

Jay, Gregory. "Taking Multiculturalism Personally: Ethnos and Ethos in the Classroom." *American Literary History* 6 (1994): 613–32.

Jordan, June. "Report from the Bahamas." 1982. Rpt. in *Moving towards Home: Political Essays*. London: Virago, 1989. 137–46.

Katz, Jonathan Ned. *Gay/Lesbian Almanac: A New Documentary*. New York: Harper, 1983.

Lemay, J. A. Leo. *Calendar of American Poetry in the Colonial Newspapers and Magazines and in the Major English Magazines through 1765*. Worcester: Amer. Antiquarian Soc., 1972.

Mohanty, Chandra Talpade. "On Race and Voice: Challenges for Liberal Education in the 1990s." *Cultural Critique* 14 (Winter 1989–90): 179–208.

Ravitch, Diane. "Multiculturalism: E Pluribus Plures." *American Scholar* 59 (Summer 1990): 337–54.

Rosaldo, Renato. *Culture and Truth: The Remaking of Social Analysis*. Boston: Beacon, 1989.

Trinh T. Minh-Ha. *Woman, Native, Other: Writing Postcoloniality and Feminism*. Bloomington: Indiana UP, 1989.

Carla Mulford

Resisting Colonialism

Students often discover to their surprise that they enjoy learning and talking about colonialism in early America. The way most students respond to the materials and the issues makes clear that they find the conceptual and political questions quite open and interesting, indeed provocative. I discuss elsewhere the scope of materials I use to teach early American literatures.[1] Instead of considering particular materials, this essay concentrates on the concepts and methods one might raise and employ in the discussion of colonialism.[2] Courses in colonialism require a high degree of intellectual and spoken self-consciousness from both teachers and students: the word *colonialism* has an expansive meaning that goes well beyond the idea of "planting" colonies (the somewhat innocuous-sounding expression common in the American colonial era), and its meaning for us today is freighted with a burdened history of strife dating back in recorded Western history at least to the times of Greek and Roman conquests.

In the classroom, when first addressing the era of European colonization in the Americas, I tend to talk about historical matters from a comparative European colonial perspective. Students sometimes wonder why we begin with European studies, when we are, after all, "supposed" to be talking about "American" writings. This is a good question, and it allows us to discuss Europe's problems as they became registered in the landscape of South and North America and to examine the technological impulses of the early modern era and the ways in which the new technology, like the new science, assisted Europeans' movements around the globe. It is an opportunity to discuss, too, how we have sometimes unquestioningly accepted nationalism, as if the geopolitical state we now call the United States was always and almost inherently a particularly exceptional entity. It is useful to remind students that the construction of "the United States" was a late development in the process of colonization of the Americas and that our attitudes about it now are deeply drawn from the conceptualization of high nationalism that emerged in the later nineteenth century (Kammen). By employing a comparative studies approach and by centering discussion directly on colonialism as both a practice historically implemented by peoples who usually did not question its implications for indigenous peoples and a process that might describe relations between people (not necessarily from the historical past), we of course create the potential for serious intellectual and emotional disagreement. It is important to me to enable students to discuss issues critically important to us all while also allowing disagreement to occur. Students are expected to remain as civil as possible with one another and to accept open disagreement as part of the terrain of colonialism. I prefer for students to understand that, at least in my class, no one "wins" in disagreements; indeed, if the effect of self-consciousness has been clear enough, no one wants particularly to win.[3]

My colonialism courses are framed conceptually by two emphases, first, that students remain aware that colonial materials and the cultures they reproduce are more complicated than we might imagine (students sometimes naively or nostalgically assume that life was somehow simpler in the past), and second, that students consider that we might ourselves today be implicated in colonial processes. After some time, students come to understand the first point, that colonialism is much more complicated than they might initially have imagined. The second issue, our own participation today in colonial processes, is more difficult because it is theoretical and ideological. Some scholars today call the method *critical pedagogy,* although such terms never can clearly describe what goes on in any particular classroom situation.[4] In this essay, I first treat some issues related to language and the social construction of reality (then and now). Then, in a discussion of "frontiering," I turn to methods that can encourage students to view colonialism as a process of exchange between peoples, a process that we need to differentiate within and across regions and across time. I discuss one instance in early American history that has been especially interesting for my students. (The instances will vary, of course, depending on the students and the teacher's special expertise.) And I conclude by suggesting some ways we can help students grapple with colonialist and ideological concerns in our own time.

Means and Methods for Examining Colonialism

The European written archive provides us with wonderful examples of the long history of Europeans' intellectual and critically complex awareness of colonialism and its effects. Even in the earliest years of contact in the Americas, Europeans described their colonial endeavors in terms ranging from martial and religious "conquest" to the more innocent-sounding "planting" of colonies. One way into the discussion about issues in colonialism is to examine a well-known text not specifically associated with colonial matters for instances of what we might today identify as colonialist discourse. Samuel Johnson's *Dictionary of the English Language* (1755) can be a remarkably useful and interesting tool for this task, prepared as it was when a shift in systems of exchange values (particularly, the development of a capital-based monetary system) assisted the instauration of Western literary traditions still evident today (Hart; see also DeMaria; Forbes; Hudson; O'Brien; Reddick, "Johnson," *Making*).

Johnson's *Dictionary* is an excellent example of the intellectual and political disciplinary practices then being inscribed. As reflected in Johnson's dictionary, people in the eighteenth century continued unquestioningly to use the Latin meanings of words related to colonial endeavors without any concern for what colonization meant to peoples whose lands were being taken over. Students are interested to see that the word *colonialism* is not found in Johnson's *Dictionary,* though the noun *Colony* and the infinitive verb form *To Colonize* are. (In English, *colonialism* seems to have been used most during the era of Britain's high colonialism, an era called by some historians the second British empire, in India during the nineteenth century.) The first question we can ask, then, is whether people in Johnson's day were aware of what it "meant" (given our perspective today that colonialism has mostly been detrimental to indigenous populations) to colonize other lands and peoples. To Johnson, who himself abhorred people who came from colonies and who was clearly aligning his dictionary project with the tradition of classical learning associated with imperial Greece and Rome, a *colony* was "a body of people drawn from the mother-country to inhabit some distant place" or "the country [so] planted; a plantation." Johnson's definition for the infinitive is even more revealing of the assumptions held by many people of his era. *To Colonize* meant "to plant with inhabitants; to settle with new planters; to plant with colonies." The inhabitants already on the lands thus "planted," then, would seem to have been absent from their lands, absent even from Johnson's history, because they didn't come from the metropole, the "mother-country," to inhabit their spaces. They already were there, but evidently absent, in the representation given them by the lexicographer interested in educating general readers in the authority of classical tradition (DeMaria). A second and related question to address with students is the extent to which, among learned English people, Johnson's representations might have been commonplace and unquestioned "truths" about what constituted civility (literate learning and the metropolis) and savagery (oral traditions and country and woods life).

Published in a pivotal moment when the first British empire was starting to crack and crumble from economic instability caused by colonial processes, Johnson's dictionary definitions provide us a fine glimpse of the ways in which colonialism can mask its intents and effects under the guise of "enlightenment" or even, sometimes, "sympathy" for the lands and peoples colonized. The dictionary works to imply that colonies are good and that the "planting" always occurs as if on empty space, without harm, and in peace. If Johnson's examples don't strike us today as peaceful — among others, he uses *Bacon's Holy War* and the example of the tension between planting for "the propagation of the Christian faith" as opposed to the finding of "gold and silver, and temporal profit and glory" — the impression nonetheless is that English colonies were founded according to what was then called "God's Providence," even though the colonies might then have been running amok as a result of people's improvidence. For Johnson, as for many who considered themselves humanists interested in learning about the world, the planting of colonies was effected by the colonizers' marking the lands taken and the peoples conquered with a certain sort of "civility" that set these lands and people apart as the colonizers' "own," because it was inhabited by colonists from the "mother-country." These are characteristic assumptions of the eighteenth century, and they reveal a form of nationalistic universalism that can be a good starting point for discussing colonialism and examining our own conceptual blind spots about colonial American materials. One went from *here* to *there*, from the center to the periphery, the metropole to the country, the mother-country to the colony, Christian lands to "heathen" places, to bring a part of that strange world under the colonizer's gaze, domain, and dominion. Of course, even in Johnson's day, as in centuries before, these assumptions were questioned. By examining the *Dictionary*, we can see, in part, the ways in which colonial processes empty "history" of some of its content, on the basis of assumptions about one's more sophisticated culture. As I try to show students, and as I try to suggest toward the end of this essay, we might still be operating under these assumptions today.

The example of Johnson's *Dictionary* can work well to show students how language usage and "historical" representations work to enforce certain ways of being in the world for members of a dominant group. Is it inaccurate to suggest that colonialism does not occur in societies that have no explicit term for the practice as we understand it today? Colonialism discursively expressed indeed can be said to be a function of high nationalism, which developed, for varieties of reasons, in the nineteenth century. Students can often in quite sophisticated ways pick up this point because they have done relevant work in other courses and usually have a better knowledge of the nineteenth- and twentieth-century past than of this earlier era. So Johnson's dictionary works well to suggest to students the richness of the archive of early materials representing a perspective derived from the position of the colonial power and lacking self-consciousness about colonialism. Encouraged to find examples of such works in their own day, students will often cite films like *Pocahontas* and *Dances with Wolves*, pointing to problems in the films' replication of colonial stories from a "colonialist" perspective.

Conceptually, it is useful to consider colonialism as manifest in language and linguistic constructions of peoples and places. By looking at how actions and peoples are normatively discussed by the dominant group, students become aware that language, far from being "empty" of meaning, is freighted with cultural constraints they usually haven't before considered. Often in discussions about language and the ways in which words construct our perception of the world, students will bring up examples having to do with the "savage" as opposed to the "civil" society. Here it can be useful to let students know that, from some of the earliest points of contact, writers were aware of the social constructedness of language; I often have them read a selection from Montaigne's *Of Cannibals* and point them to passages in Shakespeare's *Tempest* (especially those involving Caliban). For teachers interested in having students make the association, from the start of the class, with current practices today, also asking students to find examples in current language and/or cultural practices can assist the discussion. If students have trouble thinking critically about residual effects of colonialism in our current language systems, my tendency is to select an example or two for their consideration. What area of society are we describing, I'll ask, if we use the term "Third World," and what sorts of social formations are we examining if we talk about societies as "primitive"? We discuss the cultural impulses and assumptions evident in any society that would instaurate its own cultural identity by talking about other peoples and spaces as Third World or primitive, and we look at examples of what might be indicated by these terms. Students usually end up raising examples drawn from cities in their home state of Pennsylvania.[5] Some of the more interesting discussions have suggested the extent to which supposed Third World experiences occur in major cities and also on reservations of Native peoples within the United States. We acknowledge that people who live in the so-called Third World on some other continent might view the United States as an evil empire too.

The point about language and colonial processes provides a crucial first step to students' understanding of the ways in which we are still participating in historically informed cultural processes. Some students don't care to think of culture (and themselves) this way, and they resist being implicated in colonialist processes that offend them. These students prefer to think of contemporary society as much more informed and "free" than that of, say, the fifteenth century. Here the example of Montaigne works well, as Montaigne certainly critiques the colonial processes even as his writings are strikingly implicated in precisely that process. Some students find that studies in language and in colonialism provide them a means by which they can begin to think about and describe the complex and contradictory images about life in the United States. For these students especially, the discovery of a way to discuss complexities they have observed (but have had no words to describe) can be quite exhilarating. The point about language is one that we tend to keep alive all semester, as discussion of the varieties of forms of colonialism across time are taking place.

After we make points about the importance of language to colonial processes, the stage of discussion that seems most useful to take up next is a historical one that differentiates forms of colonialism across time. Historically constituted, colonialism in the areas we now call the Americas can be said to have two eras, characterized by two key means and methods.[6] A first era resulted from a military or martial or political situation, often assisted by religious imposition, when dominant European powers were competing over territories and peoples. This will be apparent to students who read primary or secondary works by Columbus or Cabeza de Vaca, Villagrá or Coronado, Cartier or Brébeuf. A second era of colonialism involves the dynamics of market capitalism primarily, where the relations between towns and rural areas and then between the federal government and the territories that were changing status to states of the union were driven by and dependent on the dynamics of the market for maintaining social stability. Here, an economic rather than a military-political relation (with the economic relation mystified by increasingly stratified social boundaries assisting a cultural attitude about "individualism") ensured the cooperation of contingent groups. Certainly the terms suggest the constellation of occurrences in what we now call the early modern era (roughly, the contact era to what Anglo-Americans called the early Republic) and the modern era (which United States citizens have been taught to call the "industrial" era), or the era of colonialism and the era of high nationalism.

Just as certainly, the terms and the bipolar breakdown into martial versus economic colonialism do not account for the differing problems within local systems. Clearly, neither formulation can be exclusively accurate. In the early era of colonialism, the English have been said to have been less martial than the Spanish, for instance, and the French involved primarily in missionary conversion *seem* historically to have been the most peaceful colonists. (By the way, students enjoy debating whether missionary work is colonialist.) Likewise, in the era of economic colonialism, the United States government was directly involved in martial colonialism against Native American nations as settlers willing to pledge allegiance to the United States system pushed westward, southward, eastward, and northward. Despite its obvious shortcomings, however, I have found this formulation useful, for it gives students a way to look at colonialism from different vantage points. That is, it enables them to come to terms with aspects of history that they may otherwise merge together because of lack of familiarity with historical circumstances that their teachers might take for granted.

For students new to issues in colonialism, it can be difficult to learn about language and historical processes in a nuanced way. That is, the study of colonialism can lead students, especially those new to the field, to polarize the view of the world. While a certain amount of simplification can work to create for students a reasonably accurate "narrative" of the historical past, as I've suggested above, oversimplification can occur especially at the outset of study, when students can sometimes think of Europeans as all colonizers and thus all "bad" and indigenous populations as all "good" — and it is best dispelled then. Thus I attempt to get students early on in any course dealing with colonialism to recognize that power among peoples rarely works solely on a colonizer-over-colonized, dominant-over-subject-group model. Instead, students should see power in any contact and settlement situation as being relational and proportional to numbers, arms, and qualities of peoples involved. During any period of contact between one group that is technologically empowered and another that is not, a liminal era of cultural interplay emerges, as described in the ethnographic work of scholars like James Clifford, Nicholas Thomas, Richard White, Daniel Usner, James Merrell, Mechal Sobel, and many others who have worked in cultural anthropology and Native American, African American, and European colonial studies. My goal is that students come to terms early with this complexity and nuance. Otherwise, they can reduce the colonial era so that many of the most interesting materials lose their resilience and complexity. One of the easiest ways to emphasize not locating power simply with nation, race, or class is to have them read, if studying English colonialism, the few extant letters of Richard Frethorne, an indentured servant, alongside writings by John Smith and Edward Maria Wingfield. Students of French colonialism might examine the materials from the *Jesuit Relations*, especially those of Brébeuf and Le Jeune, or they might consider the multiple constructions of "the other" evident in John Williams's account of his captivity among French-allied Abenakis. Students of Spanish colonialism might read Cabeza de Vaca's narrative or they might do an intensive reading of Columbus's first narrative about his voyage. To assume that those from Europe always had power and those whose lands were being settled by aliens were always defeated can deny the real complexity of living on the borders of contact.

Sometimes, to make the point more clear, I employ a paradigm adapted from cultural historians who discuss borders as having varieties of implications. If students can be encouraged to think of frontier borders as occurring in at least four dimensions — political, military, cultural, and ethnic — they can begin to see the complexities that can result when differing peoples meet one another for the first time, or across time.[7] Frontiers can be considered political if they are drawn by a presumably "dominant" power, such as the border between Portugal and Spain, drawn by a pope, or if they are agreed on by two presumable powers of state, as in the varieties of treaties drawn up between indigenous peoples and European monarchs or their representatives. In the latter instance, even "political" frontiers are problematized because Native American representatives at treaty parties between Native American groups and Europeans often were not given power or favor by their communities, of course. Frontiers are military when they are marked by armed groups. Forts, in other words, can mark military boundaries. Frontiers are cultural when two groups, even from within the same "political" or "ethnic" category, adopt differing ritual customs, usually related to religious practice and food. Thus, for instance, most Europeans who settled here, as most Native people, had cultural boundaries that produced clashes within the group and against other groups. Finally, frontiers have ethnic dimensions, as when differing groups, such as Irish, Scotch-Irish, and Scots settled in spaces considered inappropriate by people from the English mainland. Ethnic frontiers also occurred in many areas when synethnic groups emerged as a result of forced captivity or selective intermarriage. Surely, complications of racial and ethnic dispersal arose from the very start, so that peoples conceived historically as both dominant and nondominant engaged lived experiences usefully designated as *bordering*, where individuals from both parts are to some extent "other."

I hope students will attempt to grapple with the overall point that, in the absence of technological might, presumably overpowered peoples in nontechnologically driven cultural economies can come to terms with their situations through varieties of approaches to frontiers. In accommodating themselves to settlers who came to their lands to live and work, indigenous peoples were not *necessarily* colonized. In figuring out how to work with and for European peoples who captured them and brought them to strange lands, Africans were not *necessarily* colonized, either. To be sure, the actions of Europeans against Native American and African peoples were palpably ugly and indescribably brutal. Yet the primitivizing and nostalgic longing for some "pure" Native American or African person in some past and idyllic, precontact moment is just as palpably cruel in its sentimentalism and its conservationist effects. Such essentialism that leaves aboriginal peoples timelessly "pure" denies the processes of change that occur in all social formations and in the environment,[8] and it confines them within a system that constructs them as ever dominated and thus necessarily powerless.

Reading the Colonial Archive

Perhaps the most difficult problem in examining materials from the colonial American past is that the archive is dominated by documents written by those who came and settled here rather than those whose lives and lands have been ancestrally indicated across time by Europeans' written records and by their own oral cultural retention. As I suggest elsewhere, so long as we construct any "past" according to materials inscribed rather than orally transmitted, we can be said to be participating in a colonial project that creates in literacy an empowering arsenal and devalues oral traditions ("*Huehuetlatolli*"). Admitting this failing in the study of written history, though, it is not appropriate simply to dismiss the record of the past because it might be linguistically skewed in favor of those who came and colonized or settled here in the Americas. Indeed, the revisionist work of the 1970s, 1980s, and 1990s treats us to multiple sets of ways in which we can begin to think about colonialism without necessarily replicating the bias of the colonizing position. By attempting to read the colonial archive while also resisting the implications of colonialism, students can begin to come to terms with some biases that have occurred historically and some that persist today. Resisting colonialism is a difficult and probably never-ending process.

Teachers interested in the issue of colonialism — whether the imperialism of the early Americas (the purview of this essay) or, say,

England's cultural imperialism in Ireland or world imperialism by media-driven cultures — will want to work with materials and eras they know best. By way of illustration, let me suggest only one example (because of space limitations) from the Spanish colonial era using Gaspar Pérez de Villagrá's *History of New Mexico*.[9] I have selected the Villagrá example because it represents the image of the sort of repressive military colonialism (the first form of colonialism codified above) combined with religious efforts. My students tend to react negatively to colonialism that seems repressive and militarized, but they judge such colonialism particularly harshly when it seems to have been assisted by religious impulses and practices.[10]

Villagrá's *History of New Mexico* (*Historia de la Nueva México*, 1610) is a triumphal poetic narrative, written in classical epic tradition, of Juan de Oñate's expedition into New Mexico in 1598. Himself probably a member of the new creole (synethnic, Spanish and Native) culture emergent after the initial era of Spanish settlement, Villagrá employs high epic style evocative of the high drama that the entry into New Mexico held in the eyes of Spanish imperial powers interested in securing the lands, peoples, and potential mineral wealth of southwestern North America. Like the longer epic poems of what literary scholars have called the Spanish Golden Age, Villagrá's poem treats both a historical and religious subject after the manner of Vergil and Lucan, as redirected into Christian triumphs by Renaissance writers like Ariosto and Tasso. The *History of New Mexico*, in other words, affiliates itself with a long-admired classical, written tradition — and the Spanish-language interpreters of that tradition — such that the scenes, events, and peoples discussed are perhaps closer to their written originals than the experiences Villagrá purports to record. On the simplest level of linguistic colonialism, then, this is a colonial epic of high merit from the vantage point of the student of Europe's role in America. An epic written by a someone who was himself probably mixed in racial background, its very form provides a useful example of the multiple forms of bordering on frontiers that I have mentioned in the preceding section.

The *History of New Mexico* also provides intriguing glimpses into

Native receptions of alien peoples. Oñate's expedition into New Mexico occurred just over fifty years after Coronado's (bloody) expeditionary force first entered the area (1540–42). Coronado established Spain's claim to a wide expanse of the Southwest, but the encounters there seem to have left Native peoples with much distrust of Europeans and their ways. Other expeditions followed (Sánchez Chamuscado, 1581; Beltrán and Espejo, 1582), but the Spanish groups retreated from what they considered hostile indigenous peoples and inhospitable living conditions; they also experienced extreme tensions within their own groups. The Oñate expedition became a focal point of Spain's attempted conquest of the area, and the group seems to have enacted — as Cortés and his group seem to have done before — ritual conquest dramas evocative of the *Reconquista* era centuries earlier, when peoples from territories of what we now call Spain and Portugal drove Africans and non-Hispanic peoples out of peninsular Europe to reconquer what they considered their homeland.

When Oñate and his men and missionaries entered new areas inhabited by Native peoples they had not before met, they would use what were for them familiar characters and props, including banners that offered images of "Our Lady of the Remedies."[11] Attempting to capture Native peoples according to a spectacle known in Spain and New Spain, Oñate would seem to have understood the importance of ritual drama in the lives of both Spanish and Native peoples. Yet the drama was now accepted everywhere, and it was redirected sometimes according to a Native scripting that transformed this drama of Christian imperialism into one of Native supernaturalism. In the view of one historian (Gutiérrez 50–51), pueblo ritual seems to have reincorporated Oñate's drama and made it into a drama whereby Pueblo people might become holy by uniting with the Spanish, the presumed "Children of the Sun."[12]

As Oñate and his men approached the pueblo, Villagrá reports, the people came out bearing gifts such as mantles (probably blankets), and they (men and women) sought the sexual attentions of the men and women of the expeditionary group. According to Villagrá, the expedition "went through all the towns" contented (142), even though their conquest was "much marred / Through not knowing the language of these folk / And telling them our intentions" (143). The Spanish record indicates that the intruders saw Native men make sexual advances to young boys, men, and women from the Spanish and mestizo entourage and that the Spanish group seems to have responded with disgust. They commented about the willingness of women to couple with the Spanish men. The expeditionary force evidently seems to have unknowingly taken advantage of Pueblo peoples' gifting rituals by moving easily from town to town, accepting wares and foods and sexual gratification. But they seem not to have understood that what the Puebloans offered as gifts were offered not as tribute but as an exchange between superior peoples and holy people. According to Gutiérrez, for the Native peoples of this area, it was common for men and women to want to give their bodies to persons they deemed holy. The Spanish expeditionary force offered all the trappings of holiness. As superior people, the Pueblo peoples assumed the holy ones would meet them with similar desires.

As this example indicates, colonialism is a process of exchange that has more than two sides. We might read from the side of the supposed colonist that the men were successfully taking over for Spain the lands of the peoples who lived in the pueblos. We might read from the side of the supposed colonized, who assumed theirs was a free-will offering of goods and persons to holy persons, that they successfully brought supernatural powers to their lineages by coupling with the strange persons who came in their way. And if we accept Gutiérrez's historical interpretation of the circumstances, we can read Villagrá's text knowing that both sides evidently used the experiences of the contact moment to enact crucially important ritual dramas about their places in the world and the world of the supernatural.

Power inhered in the Spanish forces' swords, of course, but, for Native people, power might also have inhered in the ways in which one conducted oneself during a ritual coupling with a holy person. The easy assumption that students might have about colonialism — that takeover was always inflicted by aggressive, martial men or mystifying religious people on an unwilling Native population — is reasonably called into question in instances like this one, where, in the absence of a mediating language, both Spanish expeditionary people and Native might have assumed power was accruing to each separate group during the "colonial" exchange.

Colonial Retentions, Colonial Resistances

When students talk about colonialism in history, they sometimes retain the impression that it all happened long ago and in some faraway place. It is true that in treating any historical cultural moment, we engage a discourse of alterity that verifies our own being in time by drawing conclusions about others' existences at some other time. Yet when we discuss historical phenomena we make history. The history thus told tends to invoke a story line that itself reproduces a normative power arrangement in behalf of an already ongoing and authorized "text" of history—that Europeans came to areas now called the Americas and took over lands and peoples against their wills, killing some, enslaving others, and leaving a mess that we all must somehow deal with now. In such a narrative, some elements of the past thus discussed get silenced, while other elements are brought forward for discussion. That is, as Michel-Rolph Trouillot suggests in a different context, just as the producers of the colonial story *in* the past lived *in*equalities, so the story *of* that past yields *un*equal historical power. In selecting, emending, adapting, erasing, we tell stories that seem to be about others but stories that are also abundantly about ourselves. The struggle we all face is how we tell the story with some degree of self-consciousness about not reproducing that colonial narrative.

How we talk about *what* stories can serve as an index of the extent to which colonial processes are resisted and/or reproduced. In language and in actual lived circumstances, colonialism remains in our day, and it is intimately connected to our cultural constructions of what is "just" and "unjust," "appropriate" and unacceptable to members of a putatively free nation such as the United States. At some point in the semester, frequently toward the beginning, I usually introduce some instance of what could be called an issue in colonialism in our own day. Often it's an instance taken from an informative and growing newspaper called *Indian Country Today,* published twice per

month (and available electronically and by mail nationally) for First
Nations readers by Native Americans living in the Pine Ridge and
Dakota areas. The stories I have used cover topics including casino
gambling conflicts, takeovers of ports and highways through or ac-
cessing reservation spaces, and Native American repatriation of sacred objects. It can be instructive to compare the coverage of a Native-
centered event or issue by a well-known newspaper such as the *New
York Times* with the coverage accorded it in *Indian Country Today*.[13] I
also select newspaper articles about other continents and cultures.
One semester, my example was taken from the *New York Times* reports, beginning 20 January 1997, on ritual slaves in Ghana. In
southeastern Ghana, according to reports, ritual slavery of young
women, who begin their slavery as virgins, continues despite the constitution's barring of slavery in Ghana. Known as *trocosi*, or "slaves of
the gods," in the Ewe language, young women are given to Ghanian
priests as appeasements for the misdoings of relatives. Like people in
many African nations and many in Ghana itself, we Westerners might
question the practice, but it is accepted among rural farm people, reports say, in parts of Ghana. Is it colonialist to wish to stop such ritual
bondage? I ask my students. Are such Ghanian priests "colonialist"?
Who shall deem what is correct and just action for people in Ghana
when the constitution in Ghana prevents slavery yet the practice
continues?

Colonialism has occurred throughout time and in all geographic
areas. In early American literature courses, we have tended to consider colonialism primarily as a historical era in which European
peoples, employing instruments of technological benefit (the astro-
labe) and harm (armaments), moved onto a continent about which
they knew nothing and conquered and killed immense numbers of
peoples. Yet colonialism, not just a historical event, is a complicated
process, one that has occurred historically and still does (in concept,
if not in fact) in many different places and under various guises. Let
me return to a point I made at the outset of this essay: there is a great
need for self-consciousness especially in projects that treat contemporary or historical materials and that might seem to be ethnographic in
their attempts to situate arguments into ongoing debates about Euro-

pean cultures in contact with indigenous peoples. Our debates today are freighted with multiple histories of racial discord and can reproduce a power differential among people without our even reflecting on what we're doing. As Michel de Certeau has said about any process of history creation, we could be said, as teachers of colonialism, to be creating an "intelligibility [. . .] established through a relation with the other" and contingent on a "process of selection between what can be *understood* and what must be *forgotten* in order to obtain the representation of a present" that is knowable (2, 4). In this present, however we tell the story, we are deeply, profoundly entangled in colonial processes that we can only partially assess because we are ourselves — whoever we are and whatever intellectual and ideological place we teach from — complicit in the cultural construction and its narration.[14]

Notes

1. See "*Huehuetlatolli*," "Recovering," and "Seated amid the Rainbow." Typically, I use the survey anthology for which I prepared the early materials, *The Heath Anthology of American Literature*, which goes up to the American Civil War era. I am preparing an anthology of readings solely in early American literature for Oxford University Press, *Early American Literatures*.

2. My comments derive from experience teaching colonial materials — roughly from the point of European contact with indigenous peoples of the Americas through the era of the early Republic — as a faculty member in an English department, a history department, and an American studies program. They are based too on readings in the fields of comparative colonial cultural history, environmental studies, and cultural anthropology, in addition to wide reading in more traditional materials of early American literature and history. While my comments in this essay pertain specifically to pre-1800 materials, I have also found the methods described useful for my course in nineteenth-century studies, Exiled in the Land of the Free: Native Nations and U.S. Indian Policy, 1737–1887. The title comes from a collection edited by Oren Lyons, *Exiled in the Land of the Free: Democracy, Indian Nations, and the U.S. Constitution*. The dates run from the infamous Walking Purchase of 1737 to what many consider to be the United States government's final blow against Native sovereignty, the Dawes Acts, which concluded in 1887.

3. The advent of electronic communication affords us wonderful teaching opportunities. I can send electronic mail to most of the students who have offered particularly insightful or crucial remarks, made comments

painful to others to hear, or received discomfiting comments. This personal contact can dispel classroom anxiety about discussing difficult matters. Many colleagues accomplish some of the same goals by setting up electronic discussion groups among students. This is another successful, viable option for teachers who cannot provide this sort of personal attention because they have larger classes, heavy teaching loads, or other duties.

4. There are numerous essays and books about this method. A good source for understanding the many different ways such issues can be (and have been) approached is Kincheloe and Steinberg.

5. In Pennsylvania the two major cities have had nicknames for some time: Philadelphia has long been called the City of Brotherly Love, and Pittsburgh, once a major steel-manufacturing site, for most of the twentieth century was called Steel City, USA. Ironically, from the vantage point of central Pennsylvania, students can see how the local news media continue to represent Philadelphia negatively, thus replicating the historical attitude toward and representation of Philadelphia common in the central and western areas of the state in colonial times. It creates a wonderful example of how, whether we know it or not, we continue to participate in centuries-old colonial processes. Knowing the history of the state in which one teaches can be a good tool for helping students come to terms with colonial processes and the ways that the historical circumstances are imperceptibly repeated today.

6. It is difficult to recall how I came upon the following formulation, but I believe I must have adapted it from writers on nationalism and colonialism, perhaps with particular regard to Britain and Irish nationalism.

7. The point is adapted from cultural anthropology and discussed in a clear way by Francis Jennings (*Founders*).

8. Describing an entirely different circumstance, Nicholas Thomas aptly points out, "Aboriginal people are caught between the attribution of unchanging essences (with the implication of an inability to change) and the reproach of inauthenticity" (*Colonialism's Culture* 30). I make a similar point in "Seated amid the Rainbow." This point seems to me crucial to an understanding of the process of colonialism.

9. I offer other teaching examples elsewhere ("*Huehuetlatolli*," "Seated," and "Recovering").

10. I sometimes think this attitude expresses (in its anti–Spanish colonialism bias) a historical perspective common in the nineteenth-century era of high nationalism, which, as Michael Kammen has shown, was an era of distinct Anglophilia.

11. This information is documented in various sources, but the very best source on these matters, in my view, is Ramón Gutiérrez, *When Jesus Came* (46–66), which my explanation below (and my teaching) draws from. See also Trexler.

12. As one might expect, the Pueblo have called Gutiérrez's view into question, but it nonetheless serves as a meaningful means of examining the

multiple viewpoints from which we can consider issues in colonialism with our students. Indeed, discussing the reasons why some Pueblo peoples might censure views like Gutiérrez's would prove a fruitful method for exploring the problem of who tells which stories about which people from the colonial past.

13. Student projects of this sort have been really insightful. A pre-med student prepared a highly sophisticated analysis of the coverage of what the mass media called the "Navajo disease" and what local experts instead called "Four Corners disease" that afflicted tourists and Native Americans alike in 1992. This viral epidemic was caused by dust particles carrying viral contaminants from rodents in the Four Corners area of the Southwest. The student found corrective information being offered by Native American doctors and medicine men to Native American people, whereas the mass media frequently (though, happily, not exclusively) portrayed Native Americans as dubious of Western medicine. Most mass-media reports implied that the problem was located racially among the Navajo (Diné) peoples, whereas the virus spread to tourists and non–Native peoples generally as much as it did among Native Americans.

14. On the issue of ongoing complicity, see the sources Clifford cites in his section on "culture collecting" (231–36). I take the point that we are all always entangled in colonial enterprises from recent anthropological work, but especially from Thomas (*Entangled*).

Works Cited

Primary Works

Johnson, Samuel. *A Dictionary of the English Language*. London: Strahan, 1755.

Villagrá, Gaspar Pérez de. *Historia de la Nueva México, 1610*. Trans. and ed. Miguel Encinias, Alfred Rodriguez, and Joseph P. Sanchez. Albuquerque: U of New Mexico P, 1992.

Secondary Works

Certeau, Michel de. *The Writing of History*. Trans. Tom Conley. New York: Columbia UP, 1988.

Clifford, James. *The Predicament of Culture: Twentieth-Century Ethnography, Literature, and Art*. Cambridge: Harvard UP, 1988.

DeMaria, Robert, Jr. *Johnson's* Dictionary *and the Language of Learning*. Chapel Hill: U of North Carolina P, 1986.

Forbes, Alexander M. "Johnson, Blackstone, and the Tradition of Natural Law." *Mosaic* 27 (1994): 81–98.

Gutiérrez, Ramón. *When Jesus Came, the Corn Mothers Went Away: Marriage, Sexuality, and Power in New Mexico, 1500–1846*. Stanford: Stanford UP, 1991.

Hart, Kevin. "Economic Acts: Johnson in Scotland." *Eighteenth-Century Life* 16 (1992): 94–110.

Hudson, Nicholas. "The Nature of Johnson's Conservatism." *ELH* 64 (1997): 925–43.

Jennings, Francis. *The Founders of America*. New York: Norton, 1993.

Kammen, Michael. *Mystic Chords of Memory: The Transformation of Tradition in American Culture*. New York: Vintage, 1991.

Kincheloe, Joe, and Shirley Steinberg. *Changing Multiculturalism*. Buckingham, Eng.: Open UP, 1997.

Lyons, Oren, et al. *Exiled in the Land of the Free: Democracy, Indian Nations, and the U.S. Constitution*. Santa Fe: Clear Light, 1992.

Merrell, James. *The Indians' New World: Catawbas and Their Neighbors from European Contact through the Era of Removal*. Chapel Hill: U of North Carolina P for the Inst. of Early Amer. History and Culture, 1989.

Mulford, Carla. "*Huehuetlatolli*, Early American Studies, and the Problem of History." *Early American Literature* 30 (1995): 145–51.

———. "Recovering the Colonial, Beginning Again: On Teaching American Writings to 1800." *Heath Anthology of American Literature Newsletter* 11 (1994): 2–8. <http://www.georgetown.edu/tamlit/essays/colonial.html>.

———. "Seated amid the Rainbow: On Teaching American Writings to 1800." *American Literature* 65 (1993): 342–48.

O'Brien, Karen. "Johnson's View of the Scottish Enlightenment in *A Journey to the Western Islands of Scotland*." *Age of Johnson* 4 (1991): 59–82.

Reddick, Allen. "Johnson beyond Jacobitism: Signs of Polemic in the *Dictionary* and the *Life of Milton*." *ELH* 64 (1997): 983–1005.

———. *The Making of Johnson's Dictionary, 1746–1773*. Rev. ed. Cambridge: Cambridge UP, 1996.

Sobel, Mechal. *The World They Made Together: Black and White Values in Eighteenth-Century Virginia*. Princeton: Princeton UP, 1987.

Thomas, Nicholas. *Colonialism's Culture: Anthropology, Travel, and Government*. Princeton: Princeton UP, 1994.

———. *Entangled Objects: Exchange, Material Culture, and Colonialism in the Pacific*. Cambridge: Harvard UP, 1991.

Trexler, Richard C. *Sex and Conquest: Gendered Violence, Political Order, and the European Conquest of the Americas*. Ithaca: Cornell UP, 1995.

Trouillot, Michel-Rolph. *Silencing the Past: Power and the Production of History*. Boston: Beacon P, 1995.

Usner, Daniel H., Jr. *Indians, Settlers, and Slaves in a Frontier Exchange Economy*. Chapel Hill: Univ. of North Carolina P for the Inst. of Early Amer. History and Culture, 1992.

White, Richard. *The Middle Ground: Indians, Empires, and Republics in the Great Lakes Region, 1650–1815*. Cambridge: Cambridge UP, 1991.

Spanish and French Colonial Writings

E. Thomson Shields, Jr., and Dana D. Nelson

Colonial Spanish Writings

Why should someone teach colonial Spanish texts in a course on early American literature? The answer requires reconsideration of what is traditionally meant by *early America*. While most children in the United States learn about Spanish conquistadores like Juan Ponce de León, Hernando de Soto, and Francisco Vázquez de Coronado in grade school, courses on colonial American culture and literature from elementary to graduate levels primarily emphasize the United States's British colonial heritage. The actions of solitary Spanish colonial figures, but not Spanish settlement and culture, occupy a space in the national psyche — for instance, Ponce de León's search for the fountain of youth, Soto's "discovery" of the Mississippi River, and Vázquez de Coronado's search for the seven cities of gold. We habitually emphasize British colonial settlement at the expense of richer and more challenging understanding of the colonial context out of which United States culture and literature emerged. We cannot appreciate or fully understand the United States's colonial Spanish heritage if we

believe these early Spanish forays were nothing more than that—
exploratory entrances without any lasting cultural significance.

In fact, Hispanic culture has a longer continuous history in what
is now the United States than British culture. Starting with the first
permanent settlement in Saint Augustine, Florida, in 1565, then continuing with the founding of New Mexico in 1598, Texas in 1683,
Arizona in 1687, and California in 1769, large portions of the United
States have older Hispanic American than Anglo-American histories.
In New Mexico and Texas, some Hispanics continue to own land that
their families have held since the seventeenth and eighteenth centuries, as long as some families of British heritage have owned properties in places like Virginia and Massachusetts.

Extended histories such as these have extended cultures to match,
including written cultures. Christopher Columbus's 1493 letter describing what he had found across "the Ocean Sea" began a tradition
of Spanish-language literature about the New World. As early as
1542, a first-person Spanish-language account of events in what is
now the United States became available with the publication of Alvar
Núñez Cabeza de Vaca's *Relación* (*Account*). In 1610 Gaspar Pérez de
Villagrá's epic poem *Historia de la Nueva México* was published; it was
one of the first publications concerning the settlement of and one of
the first pieces of belles lettres by someone who had lived in what is
now the United States. Many other Spanish works from or about that
region were written during the sixteenth, seventeenth, and eighteenth centuries. Teachers of early American literature can use these
works as rich pieces of literature in and of themselves. Also, studying
these works develops a picture of the various cultures of colonial
North America. Students find that reading colonial North American
Spanish literature offers a broad historical, cultural, and religious context in which to consider United States literary and cultural heritages.[1]

In our surveys, we have time to cover only a few Spanish writers—especially because we include writers from other non-British traditions. We make the effort to include Spanish works because
studying writers like Columbus, Núñez Cabeza de Vaca, and Pérez de
Villagrá helps convey the complexity of colonial projects and of
United States national formation better than concentrating solely on

English-language works does.[2] Thankfully, many of these materials are becoming more widely available in American literature anthologies. Many are also available in affordable paperback editions (wherever possible, we cite good paperback editions available for classroom use). Most teachers of early American literature, including us, are just beginning to experiment with multicultural, multilingual approaches to the subject. But we believe that by teaching such materials, discovering their possibilities with the help of our students, teachers come to understand them better. Teachers — using the skills of literary interpretation that they already possess and picking up the context for these works as they go along — will help bring these works into the tradition of early American literature.[3]

Columbus

Of all the writers of Spanish-language works about the New World, Christopher Columbus is most familiar as a historical icon. However, Columbus is less well known as a writer. Studying even short excerpts from Columbus's writings can emphasize the value of using primary texts as a check on received wisdom — about Columbus as the "discoverer" of America; about Columbus the visionary who knew that the earth was round, not flat; about Columbus the gentle humanitarian. Traditional (and often erroneous) ideas of who Columbus was and what he did result in part from how his works were translated and transmitted. Few of Columbus's own manuscripts still exist; instead, they come to us published, transcribed, or translated by someone else.[4] Starting an early American survey course with Columbus's writings can be particularly useful because the bibliographic and thematic issues they raise reappear throughout early American literature.

The log book from Admiral Columbus's first voyage highlights these provocative issues. The original log has disappeared; instead, all we have is a combination of summary and transcription by Bartolomé de las Casas. From the very outset, reading "Columbus" in his log foregrounds important literary questions — questions of quotation, transmission, translation, and context. When students read from las Casas's digest, they must attend to switches between first person (direct quotation) and third person (las Casas's summary). For example, las Casas tells the story of first sighting land on the night of 11 October 1492 in the third person:

> A sailor named Rodrigo de Triana saw this land first, although the Admiral, at the tenth hour of the night, while he was on the sterncastle, saw a light, although it was something so faint that he did not wish to affirm that it was land. But he called Pero Gutiérrez, the steward of the king's dais, and told him that there seemed to be a light, and for him to look: and thus he did and saw it. (Columbus 59)

Students recognize from this passage and others like it that we only get Columbus's story mediated by someone else. Las Casas both promoted Columbus's ventures as a means for extending Christianity and founded the *leyenda negra*, the Black Legend, revealing how many of the Spanish explorers and settlers abused the native populations of the Americas. Thus, when las Casas quotes Columbus directly, readers have to ask why he believed these words and not others were important enough to quote.

Columbus's log also raises the question of translation. The interesting aspect for students is that the question of translation is not limited simply to non-Spanish-speaking readers of the log. Columbus raises issues of translation in detailing his interactions with the native peoples. Consider the following passages from las Casas's version of the log, direct quotations from Columbus. The first comes from Sunday, 14 October 1492:

> I soon saw two or three [villages], as well as people, who all came to the beach calling to us and giving thanks to God [. . . and who] when they saw I did not care to go ashore, threw themselves into the sea swimming and came to us, and we understood that they were asking us if we had come from the heavens. (73–75)

Then, five days later, on Friday, 19 October:

> In the morning I want to go forward so far that I can find the town and see or talk with this king of whom these men give the following details: he is the lord of all these nearby islands

and he goes about dressed and wearing much gold on his person. Although I do not give much credit to what they say, from not understanding them well and also from recognizing that they are so poor in gold that any little bit that the king may wear seems much to them. (101–03)

Columbus seems to claim perfect understanding of the natives of the Caribbean islands yet, at infrequent intervals, admits to not understanding their languages (how could he—he has been in the islands only a few days). Recognizing such discrepancies helps students guard against assuming a translation is an exact reproduction of the original communication.

Even so, just because a work can be taught only in translation does not mean it should be omitted from the classroom: translation was a major literary form by which people of the sixteenth, seventeenth, and eighteenth centuries came to know about the New World. Columbus's letter concerning his first voyage exists in two different original languages, Spanish and Latin (known as the letters to Santangel and to Sánchez, respectively). It was translated and published in several versions, including a metrical one in Italian. Many colonial Spanish works had similarly wide distribution, particularly through collections of narratives such as Giovanni Battista Ramusio's Italian *Navigazioni e viaggi* (1550–74) and Richard Hakluyt's English *Divers Voyages* (1582). Recognizing what can be safely transmitted from one language to another, such as structure and imagery, and what cannot, such as exact words, is interesting for students.

But Columbus's writings come from his experiences in the Caribbean, not North America. Their importance for early American literature surveys, when America is defined as what is now the United States, is their place as a beginning, as the first idea of the New World to which all later European writers had to respond. Though Columbus may never have realized that he had discovered not a land mass at the easternmost edge of Asia but an entirely different continent, he still created the first widely promulgated portrait of this region for Europeans—a picture of the Americas as a terrestrial paradise; as a land filled with gold and spices, the riches Europeans wanted from Asia; and as a land filled with people lacking religion, just waiting to become Christians. The questions his writings raised, of how to perceive the land, its resources, and its people, run throughout early American literature.

Núñez Cabeza de Vaca

Some of the first writers to respond to Columbus's portrait as it applied to North America were part of the conquistadores' expeditions to explore it and, it was assumed, to settle new lands. One was Alvar Núñez Cabeza de Vaca, an officer in the expedition led by the *adelantado* Pánfilo de Narváez.[5] Students find Núñez's *Relación* (or, sometimes, *Naufragios*, that is, "shipwrecks")[6] at turns fascinating, infuriating, and illuminating. Its novel-like quality, along with its unusual view of conquest and colonialism, may explain why this narrative has received perhaps the most critical attention of all the works recovered from the United States's colonial Spanish heritage.[7]

Núñez's story can be divided into two parts, the stranding of the expedition and the ultimate survival of only four expedition members. The first part begins in 1527, when Narváez sets sail from Spain with five ships and six hundred men for la Florida. Finally arriving near Tampa Bay in the spring of 1528, Narváez sends the ships ahead and leads his group northward by land, a strategy Núñez advises against. As Núñez fears, the ships are never seen again. The party — reduced by illness, exhaustion, and mounting Native American retributions for their treatment by the Spaniards — eventually reaches the Florida panhandle. They build rafts, hoping to follow the Gulf coast to Mexico. But in the gulf, Núñez's raft is separated from Narváez's and eventually lands in present-day Texas, near Galveston.

In the second part of the story, the surviving Spaniards are saved, then enslaved, by local Indians. During his three years among the coastal Indians, Núñez acculturates to native ways so successfully that he eventually escapes, finds three other survivors, and travels westward in search of Spanish settlements. The four men — three Spaniards and one African slave, Esteban — survive by acting as faith healers among the Native Americans of the region, performing ceremonies that result in miraculous cures. Crossing what is now Texas with help from native guides, the four men finally meet a group of

Spanish soldiers in northern Mexico in 1536, marking their return "home." But even their return to the culture they left behind eight years before is difficult, for the soldiers are capturing Native Americans as slaves, a practice Núñez now finds abhorrent.

Núñez's *Relación* works well in class in several ways. First, it forestalls students from romanticizing Native Americans and from seeing them as either simple savages or simple victims. The first half of the story tells the traditional tale of European conquerors trying to conquer the seemingly primitive indigenous peoples. However, in the second half, after Núñez lands on shore and has to balance European beliefs with Native American cultural practices, the traditional conquest ideal comes under question. Here, Native Americans are portrayed as slave masters and friends, as saviors, equals, and followers. They are not a people easily categorized.

Second, Núñez's story provides a moving record of one man's intense transformation in a different land, from a conquistador to someone who learns to identify with Native Americans while still valuing his identity as a Spaniard and a Catholic. Núñez's text conveys a range of possible reactions to intercultural contact, offering alternatives to the domination model. Thus the narrative questions what it means to be American. Students find Núñez's postexpedition identity — caught somewhere between and outside European and Native American cultures — a fascinating topic for discussion. For such reasons, Juan Bruce-Novoa highlights *La relación* as a key American text articulating two important aspects of the "American dream": "the ideal of a life forever remaking itself in the process of the adventure, never limited by national borders or monolingual territories" and the fact that in America "the immigrant ceased to be a foreigner and was never able to return to his place of origin" (17). *La relación* encourages students to consider post-"discovery" Americanness as a process of transformation — at turns violent, fearful, resisted, mystified, and embraced — but always inevitable for both indigenous and settler peoples. In this sense, Americanness does not descend only from British colonists but is a dynamic that characterizes experiences across the Americas.

Núñez's story works well alongside other works that came out of sixteenth-century Spanish expeditions in North America. The best known of these expeditions are those in the 1540s led by Hernando de Soto and by Francisco Vázquez de Coronado. The Soto narratives tell about the conquistador's exploits from the Florida peninsula to the Mississippi River and beyond. Unlike Narváez, Soto purposely leaves his ships because he has not found the riches he feels he needs for success; ultimately, he dies along the Mississippi River, leaving the survivors to build boats and sail downriver to Mexico. Several survivors of the expedition recorded their experiences, the most significant of which, the *Relaçam verdadeira* (*True Relation*), was written by the anonymous Portuguese Gentleman of Elvas.[8] And a lengthy narrative of the expedition, *La Florida del Inca*, was written in 1605 by a half-Incan, half-Spanish writer known as the Inca Garcilaso de la Vega. These two narratives contrast how a participant describes events (here, portraying Soto as a tragic figure) with how someone not involved describes the same events (in this case as an epic hero).[9]

The Coronado expedition ranged through the Southwest, going from what is today New Mexico as far west as the Grand Canyon and as far east as Kansas. Pedro de Castañeda, one of Coronado's men, details Coronado's fruitless search for cities of gold; his narrative also reveals what happens to Esteban, Núñez Cabeza de Vaca's fellow survivor. Juxtaposing Castañeda's and Núñez's narratives allows students to compare portraits of the first African American to be featured in American literature. Núñez portrays Esteban as a secondary character who behaves as the Spanish survivors do, while Castañeda portrays Esteban as greedy and self-serving. Spanish exploration narratives from the sixteenth century allow for classroom discussion of how interactions among European, Native American, and even African cultures helped define — and complicate — what we mean by *American*.

Villagrá

As Spanish culture in North America moved from initial encounters to settlement, the northern reaches of Spain's American empire began to take on increasingly regionalized identities. Like colonial British North America, colonial Spanish North America was not a monolithic whole but a group of different colonies, each with a particular identity and history. La Florida covered the southeastern United States, from the Florida peninsula north to some vague point (anywhere from South Carolina to Canada) and west from the Atlantic to the Mississippi River. California extended from Baja California north to at least Cape Mendicino. Nuevo México included the present state of New Mexico and lands throughout the southwestern United States, from the Colorado River in the west to the Mississippi River in the east. Tejas was a vague area north of the Rio Grande. Pensacola was formed out of the southwestern sections of la Florida, centering on the Florida panhandle. And the Mississippi River region was identified only by the Spanish name for the river, Río del Espíritu Santo.

As each territory was settled, people described how the regions created a permanent Spanish presence, documenting the processes in letters, legal documents, and reports to religious or governmental superiors back in Europe, as well as in books, prose narratives, and even poems. Among the most interesting of these works is Gaspar Pérez de Villagrá's epic poem *Historia de la Nueva México*. Published in 1610, Villagrá's poem recounts Juan de Oñate's 1595 to 1601 mission to settle Nuevo México, including the uprising and eventual defeat of the Acoma Pueblo Indians. As an introduction to Oñate's exploits, Villagrá gives the region's history of Spanish exploration and of the peoples living in the area.

That Villagrá's work is a poem allows students to see that the writing of history and of literature are not essentially different. It is worth asking students to consider how the epic form guides Villagrá's portrayal of events like Oñate's attack on Acoma Pueblo. From canto 18 through the end of the poem, Villagrá accords the Acoma people surprising stature, reflecting the epic requirement that the hero's opponents be estimable adversaries. When Villagrá depicts the Acoma rebellion as one to recapture liberty in the face of enslavement, students hear a startling anticipation of Patrick Henry in Gicombo, the Acoma leader who urges his compatriots to commit suicide in the face of sure defeat: "Do you not see that we have now arrived / At that last sorrow and that final point / Where we all must, without our liberty, / Live out our sorry lives as infamous wretches?" (273).[10]

Despite the intelligence, eloquence, and family loyalty Villagrá accords the Acoma Pueblo peoples — perhaps even because of it — the text celebrates Oñate's stunning force in quelling the rebellion. The narrative lingers on the effects of violence on the bodies of the Pueblos, who are repeatedly compared to animals. José Rabasa summarizes this effect by stating that the *Historia de la Nueva México* portrays "an aesthetic of colonial violence" that justifies war against Native Americans and that the poem's aesthetic force comes from "the use of grotesque images that rob indigenous peoples of all dignity even in death" (110). However, by giving voice to the Acomas, depicting them as worthy and equal opponents, Villagrá creates a curious interpretive ambivalence. Though he tries to justify the violent conquest of Nuevo México's peoples, students, schooled in the value of liberty, can't help but appreciate the human dignity of the Acomas' fight for freedom from colonial rule.

Similar ambivalences arguably characterize many writings of Spanish settlement, stemming perhaps in part from the philosophy of *fe y oro* ("faith and gold"), which taught that the main purpose of conquest was to spread the Christian faith, for which God would provide resources — gold. How writers weigh the terms of this philosophy determines their outlook on the Spanish project of settlement. Do riches gained or never found demonstrate God's pleasure or displeasure? Does the desire for riches and power overpower the first imperative, Christian settlements and conversions?

Innumerable texts grapple with these questions. From la Florida, Gonzalo Solís de Merás's late-sixteenth-century *Memorial* describes the 1565 founding of St. Augustine as led by Pedro Menéndez de Avilés. Franciscan friar Alonso de Escobedo's early-seventeenth-century epic poem "La Florida" provides an interesting religious contrast to Villagrá's military epic.[11] Other works by Franciscan missionaries in la Florida include Luís Gerónimo de Oré's *The Martyrs of Florida* (c. 1617), telling of the various missionaries who served in the northern reaches of la Florida from Georgia to Virginia. And Juan de Paiva's late-seventeenth-century "Origin of the Game of Ball That the Apalache and Yustagan Indians Have Been Playing since Pagan Times until the Year of 1676" records the Native American oral story of how the ball game, a practice with religious significance, came into existence, to show why the game ought to be outlawed. And in 1722 Andrés Gonzales de Barcía Carballido y Zuñiga published his *Chronological History*, the first comprehensive history dedicated solely to the enterprise of la Florida.

In Nuevo México Juan de Montoya's *Account of the Discovery of New Mexico and Many Other Provinces and Cities Newly Found* [. . .] (1601) provides a contemporary counterpart to Villagrá's version of Oñate's ventures. Alonso de Benavides's *Memorial* (1630) tells of Franciscan efforts to evangelize the Native Americans of Nuevo México. Various documents tell the story of the 1680 Pueblo revolt, the only successful revolt by indigenous peoples against European colonization in the Americas,[12] while the next governor, Diego de Vargas, tells the story of Spain's reconquest of Nuevo México under his command.[13]

The variety of works beyond those suggested above is endless. There are folk plays from Nuevo México and Tejas. There are letters by Native Americans from la Florida. There are exploration narratives of California, Pensacola, and the Mississippi River Valley. Some of these works have been brought together in annotated literary bibliographies (see esp. Fernández and Shields). As the literature of colonial Spanish North America becomes more accessible, those of us who teach early American literature surveys will have greater opportunities to discover with our students the many ties between the United States's cultural heritage and its colonial Hispanic past.

Notes

1. There are many ways to define American literature. We have chosen to limit our remarks to places now within the borders of the United States as a way of connecting a specific element of the colonial past to a specific part of the present. Of course, Spanish explorers, settlers, and writers had no concept of such a place as the United States. For that reason, other geographic and cultural stances would be equally as interesting to use, especially those that put Spanish writings from what is now the

United States into the context of wider Spanish exploration and coloni-zation. For example, one might look at the literature of la Florida as part of the literature of the colonial Spanish Caribbean, or one might look at the literature of Nuevo México as part of the colonial Mexican literary tradition. Each such approach has its value and its complications.

2. We use what are taken as the "correct" versions of Spanish surnames — for example, Soto rather than de Soto, Núñez or Núñez Cabeza de Vaca rather than Cabeza de Vaca. However, many sources use the more tradi-tional names, a practice that in most settings, especially the classroom, does not need to be discouraged.

3. For more information than the brief historical overview given here, David J. Weber's *The Spanish Frontier in North America* is very good. It is the most recent overview history in the tradition sometimes called "Spanish Borderlands" studies. Weber includes an excellent bibliography of primary and secondary sources.

4. Columbus wrote several texts about his 1492, 1493, 1498, and 1502 voyages, though no writings by Columbus concerning his second voy-age still exist. All of Columbus's letters and some by other members of his expeditions are available in Jane.

5. Most North American conquistadores had the title of *adelantado*, usually translated as *governor* but different from our contemporary definition. An *adelantado* was an entrepreneur who used his own money to settle a land and in return received the rights to serve as military and civil gover-nor of a region.

6. *Naufragios* was the running title given the work when it was published in 1555 along with a third-person account of Núñez's later endeavors in South America. The recent University of California Press edition renders *Naufragios* as *Castaways*.

7. Two good translations of Núñez's work have been recently published, one from Arte Público Press in Houston, and one from the University of California Press. Both work well in the classroom, providing good intro-ductory essays and bibliographies.

8. Written in Portuguese by a Portuguese member of a Spanish expedition, the *Relaçam verdadeira* points out the truly multilingual nature of early American literature.

9. Both Soto narratives are in the two-volume *The De Soto Chronicles* (Clay-ton, Knight, and Moore), available in hardcover and paperback.

10. Gilberto Espinoza's 1933 prose translation comes even closer to Patrick Henry's line "Give me liberty or give me death." In this version, Gi-combo says, "we have reached the final point where, without liberty, it is better that we were dead" (250). In fact, comparing strategically chosen passages from these two translations allows students to consider the cul-tural forces influencing translation and to discuss the difficult issue that faces translators of poetry — whether one should strive primarily for meaning or be accountable to form. The issue of translation can thus be discussed even if the teacher cannot read the original Spanish.

11. To date, only one incomplete prose translation of Escobedo's poem has been published, *Pirates, Indians and Spaniards: Father Escobedo's "La Florida."* The only Spanish-language edition of the poem is a doctoral dissertation by Alexandra Sununu.

12. Many of these documents can be found in Hackett.

13. These writings are available in several different volumes that are being published by the University of New Mexico Press, including Kessell and Hendricks, and in Espinosa.

Works Cited

Primary Works

Barcía Carballido y Zuñiga, Andrés Gonzales de. *Barcía's Chronological History of the Continent of Florida [. . .] from the Year 1512, in Which Juan Ponce de Leon Discovered Florida until the Year 1722.* Trans. Anthony Kerrigan. Introd. Herbert E. Bolton. Gainesville: U of Florida P, 1951.

Benavides, Alonso de. *Fray Alonso de Benavides' Revised Memorial of 1634.* Ed. and trans. Frederick W. Hodge, George P. Hammond, and Agapito Rey. Coronado Cuarto Centennial Publications 4. Albuquerque: U of New Mexico P, 1945.

———. *The Memorial of Fray Alonso de Benavides, 1630.* Trans. Mrs. Edward E. Ayer. Ed. Frederick Webb Hodge and Charles Fletcher Lummis. Chicago: n.p., 1916; Albuquerque: Horn, 1965.

Castañeda, Pedro de. *The Journey of Coronado.* Trans. and ed. George Parker Winship. San Francisco: Grabhorn, 1933; New York: Dover, 1990.

Clayton, Lawrence A., Vernon James Knight, Jr., and Edward C. Moore, eds. *The De Soto Chronicles: The Expedition of Hernando de Soto to North America in 1539–1543.* 2 vols. Tuscaloosa: U of Alabama P, 1993.

Columbus, Christopher. *The Diario of Christopher Columbus's First Voyage to America, 1492–1493.* Abstracted by Bartolomé de las Casas. Ed. and trans. Oliver Dunn and James E. Kelly. Norman: U of Oklahoma P, 1989.

Escobedo, Alonso de. "La Florida." *Estudio y edición anotada de "La Florida" de Alonso Gregorio de Escobedo, O. F. M.* 3 vols. Ed. Alexandra Sununu. Diss. City U of New York, 1993. 2 vols. Ann Arbor: UMI, 1993. 9325153.

———. *Pirates, Indians, and Spaniards: Father Escobedo's "La Florida."* Trans. A. F. Falcones. Ed. James W. Covington. St. Petersburg: Great Outdoors, 1963.

Elvas, Gentleman of. *The Account by a Gentleman from Elvas.* Clayton, Knight, and Moore 1: 19–219.

Espinosa, J. Manuel, ed. and trans. *The Pueblo Indian Revolt of 1696 and the Franciscan Missions in New Mexico: Letters of the Missionaries and Related Documents.* Norman: U of Oklahoma P, 1988.

Hackett, Charles Wilson, ed. *Revolt of the Pueblo Indians of New Mexico and Otermín's Attempted Reconquest, 1680–1682.* 2 vols. Trans. Charmion Clair Shelby. Coronado Cuarto Centennial Publications 8 and 9. Albuquerque: U of New Mexico P, 1942.

Hakluyt, Richard. *Divers Voyages Touching the Discouerie of America and the Ilands Adiacent unto the Same, Made First of All by our Englishmen and Afterwards by the Frenchmen and Britons. And Certaine Notes of Aduertisements and Obseruations, Necessarie for Such as Shall Heereafter Make the Like Attempt. With Two Mappes Annexed Heereunto for the Plainer Understanding of the Whole Matter.* London: Woodcocke, 1582. Ed. John Winter Jones. First Series 7. London: Hakluyt Soc., 1850. New York: Franklin, n.d.

Jane, Cecil, ed. and trans. *The Four Voyages of Columbus.* 2 vols. in 1. New York: Dover, 1988. 2 vols. Second Series 65, 70. London: Hakluyt Soc., 1929–1932.

Kessell, John L., and Rick Hendricks, eds. *By Force of Arms: The Journals of don Diego de Vargas, New Mexico, 1691–93.* Albuquerque: U of New Mexico P, 1992.

la Vega, Garcilaso de, el Inca. *La Florida.* Trans. Charmion Shelby. Ed. David Bost. Clayton, Knight, and Moore 2: 25–559.

Montoya, Juan de. *Account of the Discovery of New Mexico and Many Other Provinces and Cities Newly Found, Sent from the Indies to Spain and Thence to Rome. New Mexico in 1602: Juan de Montoya's Relation of the Discovery of New Mexico.* Ed. George P. Hammond and Agapito Rey. Albuquerque: Quivira Soc., 1938; New York: Arno, 1967. 37–75.

Núñez Cabeza de Vaca, Alvar. *The Account: Alvar Núñez Cabeza de Vaca's Relación.* Trans. Martin A. Favata and José B. Fernández. Houston: Arte Público, 1993.

———. *Castaways.* Trans. Frances M. López-Morillas. Ed. Enrique Pupo-Walker. Berkeley: U of California P, 1993.

Oré, Luís Gerónimo de. *The Martyrs of Florida (1513–1616).* Trans. Maynard Geiger. Franciscan Studies 18. New York: Wagner, 1936.

Paiva, Juan de. "Origin of the Game of Ball That the Apalache and Yustagan Indians Have Been Playing since Pagan Times until the Year of 1676." Trans. John H. Hann. *Apalachee: The Land between the Rivers.* Ripley P. Bullen Monographs in Anthropology and History 7. Gainesville: U of Florida P–Florida State Museum, 1988. 331–53.

Ramusio, Giovanni Battista. *Navigazioni e viaggi.* 1550–74. 6 vols. Ed. Marica Milanesi. Torino: Einaudi, 1978.

Solís de Merás, Gonzalo. *Pedro Menéndez de Avilés: Adelantado, Governor, and Captain-General of Florida: Memorial by Gonzalo Solís de Merás.* Trans. Jeannette Thurber Connor. Publications of the Florida Historical Soc. 3. Deland: Florida State Historical Soc., 1923.

Villagrá, Gaspar Pérez de. *Historia de la Nueva México, 1610.* Trans. and ed. Miguel Encinias, Alfred Rodríguez, and Joseph P. Sánchez. Albuquerque: U of New Mexico P, 1992.

———. *History of New Mexico by Gaspar Pérez de Villagrá, Alcalá, 1610.* Trans. Gilberto Espinosa. Ed. Frederick W. Hodge. Quivira Soc. Publications 4. Los Angeles: Quivira Soc., 1933.

Secondary Works

Bruce-Novoa, Juan. "Shipwrecked in the Seas of Signification: Cabeza de Vaca's *Relación* and Chicano Literature." *Reconstructing a Chicano/a Literary Heritage: Hispanic Colonial Literature of the Southwest*. Ed. María Herrera-Sobek. Tucson: U of Arizona P, 1993. 3–23.

Fernández, José B. "Hispanic Literature: The Colonial Period." *Recovering the US Literary Heritage*. Ed. Ramón Gutiérrez and Genaro Padilla. Houston: Arte Público, 1993. 253–64.

Rabasa, José. "Aesthetics of Colonial Violence: The Massacre of the Acoma in Gaspar de Villagra's *Historia de la Nueva México*." *College Literature* 20.3 (1993): 96–114.

Shields, E. Thomson, Jr. "Beyond the Anthology: Sources for Teaching Sixteenth- and Seventeenth-Century Colonial Spanish Literature of North America." *Heath Anthology Newsletter* 12 (Fall 1994): 2–11. 3 Mar. 1999. <http://www.georgetown.edu/tamlit/newsletter/12/shields.html #section1>.

Weber, David J. *The Spanish Frontier in North America*. New Haven: Yale UP, 1992.

Rosalie Murphy Baum

Early French North American Writings

With James Axtell, I believe that the "largest gap" in our study of early North American literature is "the full story of French experience, not only in Canada but also in the Great Lakes and the Ohio, Mississippi, and Missouri valleys" (*Beyond 1492* 213). French texts can introduce students to new forms of consciousness, new ideas and images, in the imagining and interpreting of America and can make each English North American work we now read a more complex experience, intellectually and aesthetically. Students become intensely involved in past events as they begin to view history as a multiplicity of histories (texts) and realize "that there is no such thing as a *single* correct view of any object under study but [. . .] *many* correct views, each requiring its own style of representation" (White, *Tropics* 47). In addition, when introduced to the complexities of America's early multinational history,[1] students are fascinated by the parallels between the early American experience and the ethnic, national, and religious conflicts many countries are experiencing today.

In this essay I first examine several areas in which a knowledge of

French North American literature can significantly affect our understanding of the diversity of the early American consciousness and experience. I then consider some of the questions we must answer as we determine the nature and scope of survey courses in early American literature. Finally, I describe a few of the ways in which French North American literature can be added to early American survey courses currently focused on English colonial literature.

There are many areas in which the juxtaposition of English and French colonial writings — by authors like Jean Ribault (also Ribaut, Ribauld), René de Laudonnière, Jacques Cartier, Samuel de Champlain, René Robert Cavelier Sieur de La Salle, and Jacques Marquette — changes the narrative now offered by the Anglo-American selections in anthologies of American literature. For example, students aware of issues of territorial possession only between the English and Natives discover the complexity of the concept of ownership among the European powers. They are introduced to the argument of fifteenth-century jurists that medieval canonical law gave the pope jurisdiction over territorial claims in heathen areas and are bemused by Spain's claim, sanctioned by the pope, to exclusive possession of the Americas as a result of Columbus's first voyage. Because Anglo-American accounts suggest that territorial struggles in the New World were decided primarily by military might, students are surprised that fear of damnation was the greatest concern of Breton and Norman fishermen and merchants entering Spain's territories. They learn that France was the first country to challenge papal authority and argue that possession of a heathen region should be determined by occupation, not simply discovery, of the region.

Familiar with the pattern of English empire — the line of settlement up and down the eastern seaboard — students now discover the "riverine" pattern of the French empire (Eccles, *France* 147), the corridors of forts, missionary posts, and settlements embracing the Saint Lawrence River, the Great Lakes, and the Mississippi Valley. They learn that during the seventeenth and eighteenth centuries the French could travel from the Saint Lawrence Valley south to the Gulf of Mexico, north to Hudson Bay, or west to the Rocky Mountains — using birchbark canoes and stopping at trading and missionary posts or

settlements. (The phrase "New France" refers to all French possessions in North America, defined by royal charter in 1627 as land from
the Atlantic Ocean to the Great Lakes and from Florida to the Arctic
Circle.) An awareness that the colonial period began in the Minnesota area in the late 1660s and in the Illinois area in the early 1670s
further corrects the impression that colonization occurred only on the
eastern coast. The belief that the western expansion of the English
was hampered by the wildness of the country or unfriendly Natives is
complicated by the discovery of French efforts in the seventeenth and
eighteenth centuries to strengthen their corridors to prevent English
expansion. In addition, the realization that Fort Caroline, a French
Huguenot colony, was destroyed by the Spanish in 1565 and that
Port Royal was destroyed by the English in 1613 (thus delaying the
settlement of Acadia) corrects the impression, created by most literary
anthologies, that the conflicts of the early period were primarily between English settlers and Natives.

French North American literature also helps students recognize
that while the Indians were obstacles to the English, they were neces-
sities to the French: the French required the goodwill of the Natives
because of the vast area over which they had stretched their posts and
settlements, because of their emphasis on the fur trade, and because
of their commitment to converting the Natives.[2] Students who have
read about "white Indians," primarily English Puritans who were kidnapped and adopted into Native tribes, now learn about French *cou-
reurs de bois*, that is, "Indianized" Frenchmen, entrepreneurs who
exulted in the freedom and independence of a style of life that blended
French and Native ways. They meet "Indianized" French missionaries (primarily Jesuits) who practiced a "cultural relativism, without [
. . .] succumbing to ethical neutrality" (Axtell, *European* 69–70),
adopting the food, dress, technology, language, and customs of the
Natives while retaining many of the values of Catholicism and French
culture. They discover that in the 1660s Jean Baptiste Colbert, the
minister appointed to reorganize the French colonial empire, urged
that Natives be integrated into French culture and encouraged
intermarriage.[3]

But there are many other areas in which French voices complicate or clarify our understanding of the early period of American exploration, conquest, and settlement.[4] For example, students can explore the different attitudes toward converting the Natives by juxtaposing the sporadic attempts of the English with the sustained efforts of the Recollects (a branch of the Franciscans) and Jesuits. They can consider Eccles's argument that the French had two frontiers, a geographical one to be settled and "a religious frontier of the mind" (*Canadian Frontier* 7). Students, seeking usually silent voices, can discover one of the forgotten roles of women in the New World, as religious leaders and educators, by reading the letters of the Ursuline nun Marie de l'Incarnation (Marie Guyart Martin), which describe almost forty years of life in Quebec in the seventeenth century.[5] They can be encouraged to rethink, with historians like Lawrence Henry Gipson, the causes of the Revolutionary War, noting that the events of the 1770s were precipitated in large part by events of the 1760s, especially the Great War for the Empire (also known as the Seven Years' War or French and Indian War), which removed French pressure from the interior and north and necessitated greater economic support for the British Empire.[6]

In deciding which works to include in survey courses, especially given the many authors writing in different languages, however, we need to consider a number of questions. The following are a few I like to discuss with students: Should early American literature be primarily, or only, a literature of settlement, as it has been in the past? Or, like recent anthologies and critics such as William Spengemann, are we going to recognize the "poetics of adventure" (*Adventurous Muse* 3) of the early period and argue that even "the development of modern literature cannot be explained apart from the writings of the New World discoverers, explorers" (1) as well as settlers? If we focus on settlement literature as the "beginning" of American literature, we will have no literature in English from the sixteenth century; only Spain and France had settlements in North America then. What will we consider a settlement? Must it contain women and children? Must the women be married or can they be Ursuline nuns? Must the settlements be successful, what many anthologies call "permanent" settlements? If they must be permanent, does that mean that we support a literature of conquest? For example, because the Spanish destroyed Fort Caroline, would we not read René de Laudonnière's *Notable History of Florida*?

But the main question students like to address when we consider adding French North American literature to courses in early American literature is whether translations belong in literature courses. Almost everyone tends to agree that translations represent a significant loss, not simply in subtleties of style but even in structure and meaning. With translations, our knowledge and aesthetic experience are partial — even misleading.

However, there are persuasive arguments for including translations of early French North American works in courses. Even if English has become the dominant language in the United States today, America's founding heritage is multilingual. Thus, it is seriously misrepresentative — in terms of national identity and national language — to teach early American courses in which only English North American works are included. What that offers the student is the *English* experience, the *English* identity, the *English* language (with its unique character), not the early *American* experience, as William Spengemann has persuasively argued (*Mirror*).[7]

Perhaps the misrepresentation of the American experience as being only English is least defensible when we consider the Natives, whose literature we do not have. The "heart of colonial writings, even when not explicitly mentioned," "colonized or indomitable" (Adorno 181), the Native should be described, interpreted, by as many voices as possible. The English notion of "otherness" should not — alone — be allowed to represent the Native. We are more likely to define European-Native similarities and differences and to learn about the diversity of the Natives if we also embrace French, Spanish, Portuguese, Dutch, Swedish, and Russian perspectives.

Another reason to reconsider our usual reservations about teaching literature in translation is that the writers of the early period did not have the sense of linguistic or cultural nationalism that we have today. Interest in the New World created an enthusiastic reading public throughout Europe, and literary, philosophical, and scientific works were often published simultaneously in two, three, or even four languages (Echeverria 53). A complex international scene sometimes led men of one country to explore under the flag of another and to write an account of their voyages in the sponsor's language or to arrange for immediate translation for the sponsor. For example, Giovanni da Verrazzano's Italian narrative of his voyage of 1524 was immediately translated into French (with addenda) for his patron, the French king. Jean Ribault's 1563 *The Whole and True Discovery of Terra Florida* (later rewritten as *The True and Last Discouerie of Florida*) was written while he was in England seeking the support of Queen Elizabeth; no French manuscript exists, and some scholars speculate that the account was originally written in English. Pierre Esprit Radisson's first four narratives were written in English, the second two in French, reflecting his shift of allegiance from France to England. Louis-Armand de Lom d'Arce, baron de Lahontan's *New Voyages to North-America* (1703) was first published in French, then translated and expanded into an English edition for the duke of Devonshire (a version preferred by Reuben Gold Thwaites). Thus, just as we try to avoid applying critical tastes today to earlier works but instead determine the historical and aesthetic value of a work by its rhetorical effectiveness in its own period, we need to suspend our bias against translation, given the different linguistic expectations of the early period.

Two approaches I have found successful in adding the French consciousness and experience to courses in early American literature are to plan one section or more around French writers and to integrate French and (established) English writers. The examples of both approaches below, given the constraints of space, are only a beginning.

Recalling George M. Wrong's view that the work of Marc Lescarbot, Samuel de Champlain, and Gabriel Sagard is unequaled among authors of the early period, I have used these authors to show students the quality and range of the French literary accomplishment. Wrong describes Lescarbot, in *Nova Francia*, as "Rousseau before Rousseau" (xiii), offering a vision of a New World of freedom and equality to replace the corrupt Old World; Champlain, in his *Voyages*, as a more realistic thinker, planning the spread of the French culture and religion in a great French empire; and Sagard, in his *Long Journey*, as a deeply religious lay brother in the Recollects who fears that European institutions and customs will corrupt the Natives, whose lives are natural, simple, socialistic, unselfish.

Another kind of grouping of French authors I have found effective encourages students to read varying accounts of the same or related events.[8] For example, through the very different narratives of Jean Ribault, René de Laudonnière, Nicolas Le Challeux, Jacques Le Moyne de Morgues, and Dominique de Gourgues, a class can examine a number of attempts to make a meaningful story out of the environmental considerations, cultural negotiations, and violent events that characterized the first two French settlements in Florida, Charlesfort (1562) and Fort Caroline (1564–65), the latter destroyed by the Spanish.[9] Ribault's account of Charlesfort is rhapsodic. Le Challeux's begins with the idyllic and concludes with the horrifying; Laudonnière's attempts to establish the heroic but establishes the disastrous. Le Moyne's, originally published in Latin, is valuable for its artwork. Gourgues's offers an extravagant account of the later (1568), revengeful slaughter of the Spanish at San Mateo. Reading this multiplicity of texts, students experience the cacophony of voices and recapture something of the "web of negotiations taking place" (Adorno 173) in one of the most violent colonial episodes between the French (in this case, Huguenots) and Spanish, as individual students or small groups argue the perspectives of different writers.

Another very effective clustering of narratives — because of differences in substance and tone — focuses on René Robert Cavelier Sieur de La Salle, whom the historian Francis Parkman considered the greatest of French explorers for his attempts to create a new France in the West, and the Recollect friar Louis Hennepin, whom Percy G. Adams calls "the greatest of geographical liars" (46). La Salle clearly inspired great admiration and loyalty as well as great envy and hatred — as accounts of his efforts by his brother Jean Cavelier, his loyal lieutenant Henri de Tonty (also Tonti), and others reveal.[10] Perhaps most entertaining to students are the discrepancies among the accounts of La Salle, Tonty, and Hennepin. The pompous Hennepin lifts whole passages from Zenobius Membré's eyewitness journal and also brags, fourteen years after La Salle's death, that he had descended the Mississippi to its mouth two years before La Salle. Such clustering discourages monolithic views of history and vividly reminds students that narratives of the New World reflect each author's intentions, aspirations, and capacities.

A fourth successful grouping is created by the students themselves, who browse through Thwaites's *Jesuit Relations and Allied Documents* and choose readings that particularly interest them.[11] The *Relations*, in 73 volumes, consists of reports (originally in French or Latin) from the Jesuit missions compiled by the Jesuit superior at Quebec from 1611 to 1768. Some students become absorbed in reports of the progress and difficulties, accomplishments and failures of Jesuits in their everyday activities; others are fascinated by the descriptions of Native beliefs, customs, and life; many are attracted to the accounts of Iroquois warfare and of Jesuit captivity or martyrdom. The letters of Marie de l'Incarnation — a French nun who, at Paul Le Jeune's request, helped to establish a school for children in Quebec — are an excellent complement to such a unit, adding the voice of an intelligent, practical, and deeply religious woman to the Jesuit accounts of life in the Saint Lawrence area.

The second approach — juxtaposing (established) English and French writers — can have several purposes: to illustrate different attitudes, assumptions, and beliefs among the English and French; to reveal different conventions and forms within established genres;[12] to provide a context for reading currently established English-language texts; and to compare authorial visions. Again, the constraints of space allow only a few examples.

French writers offer accounts of the Natives very different from those by canonical authors like William Bradford or Mary Rowlandson. The differences in attitudes toward and assumptions and beliefs about the Natives among the English and French writers destroy forever the notion of Europeans' having a monolithic response to the Natives. Cartier's detailed accounts of his dealings with the Iroquois chief Donnacona (1535–36) constitute the best example I have read of the attempts of Europeans and Natives to communicate: a dialogue of gesture, custom, and word, largely incomprehensible to

both yet the basis of decisive, even tragic actions.[13] Conversely, Le
Jeune's "On the Means of Converting the Savages" (1634) and Jean
de Brébeuf's "Instructions for the Fathers of Our Society Who Shall
Be Sent to the Hurons" (1637) reveal an impressive awareness of Native values and assumptions and are notable for their insistence on
"sincere affection" (Brébeuf 118) and respect for the Natives. Champlain's frustrations in his efforts to organize forest warfare for the Hurons, Algonquins, and Montagnais and to teach them military tactics
are amusing—and clear—comments on what happens between perplexingly different cultures, even when they are united against a common enemy. Narratives that contribute richly to the concept of the
"bon sauvage" include those of the Parisian lawyer and writer Marc
Lescarbot, the Recollect Gabriel Sagard, and the military leader baron
de Lahontan.

The limitations of our definitions of genres become clear when
we examine the French experience or juxtapose English and French
texts, as with the captivity narrative, for example. Once introduced to
Rowlandson's account as the paradigmatic form, students can discover that most seventeenth- and eighteenth-century captivity narratives, even many Puritan accounts, involve contact with the French.
They learn that the Puritan captivity narrative is formally very different when the enemy is not the Natives or the wilderness but the
French and Catholicism (as in the narratives of John Williams and
Hannah Swarton, with their critiques of Catholic customs, rituals,
and theological positions) and that Jesuit captivity narratives, which
seldom mention the English or address theological issues, are very
different from Puritan narratives. Students are first amazed, then puzzled by the attitudes of Jesuits like Isaac Jogues, captured in 1642 by
the Mohawks; Pierre Millet, a captive of the Oneidas from 1689 to
1694; and Claude Allouez, a particularly persistent missionary
among the Hurons and Algonquins. They struggle with the Jesuits'
acceptance of suffering, torture, and martyrdom, and they are fascinated by the Jesuits' intermingling of their lives with the Natives' in
what would appear to be a cultural relativism if not for the Jesuits' intense efforts to be worthy of their own religious beliefs and goals. A
particularly interesting juxtaposition that complicates many of our
generalizations about the genre of the captivity narrative is the

account of the Puritan John Gyles, kidnapped at the age of nine, and of the Catholic Pierre Esprit Radisson, kidnapped at sixteen.[14]

French texts can also offer a significant context for reading established English-language texts. Passages from Verrazzano, Champlain, and Lescarbot complement a reading of Bradford's *History of Plymouth Plantation:* Champlain's 1605 description of Plymouth's moderate temperature and mild winters (71), compared with Bradford's descriptions of the Puritans' arrival in winter, reminds us of the subjectivity of European images of their new world; Champlain's and Lescarbot's descriptions of the Nausets some fourteen years before the Pilgrims arrive offer a context (since the Natives themselves are silent) for considering the "*mutuality* of discovery and acculturation" (Axtell, *Beyond 1492* 26); Verrazzano's description of the Natives' rescue of one of his drowning men glosses Bradford's accounts of the "proud and very profane young man" (66) and of John Howland. The "theatrical" in the Europeans' new world, found in Thomas Morton's description of the Maypole celebration and Bradford's very different account, becomes a more central, even cross-cultural experience in the context of the drama of Chief Donnacona's men, described by Cartier, and in Marc Lescarbot's réception, *The Theatre of Neptune in New France* (1606), perhaps the first play written by a European in North America, a play starring both Europeans and Natives.

Finally, the juxtaposition of authorial visions of English and French writers reminds us that "man is an animal suspended in webs of significance he himself has spun" (Geertz 5). A reading of Bradford's *History of Plymouth Plantation* and Marie de l'Incarnation's letters, the latter an epistolary account of the settling of a colony, reveals two deeply religious and practical leaders who could hardly be more different; however, both authors' accounts begin in hope and conclude somewhat despondently. Such comparisons clarify each author's philosophy and narrative strategies, reminding us that descriptions of historical events "display the coherence, integrity, fullness, and closure of an image of life that is and can only be imaginary" (White, *Content* 24).

It may be difficult now to obtain classroom texts for some of the readings suggested in this essay (although all are available in English).

But interest in multiple (and varied) accounts of the early period and delight in reading works that have not yet received the imprimatur of an anthology easily motivate students to read selections placed on reserve. In fact, a surprising number of my students will — on their own — work to uncover more texts they believe should be included in the canon, and I often have students prepare as a writing assignment an anthology entry of an early author not yet anthologized. Students also enjoy background reading in the compelling works of James Axtell, John Bakeless, W. J. Eccles, Gary B. Nash, and Evelyn Page.

In rejecting a canon of early American literature focused on English writings and thinking instead of a multinational and multilingual literature that includes different ways of seeing and describing, students and faculty members recognize that "documents describing past symbolic actions are not innocent, transparent texts; they were written by authors with various intentions and strategies" (Hunt 14). They reconsider established literary patterns of representation and discover new genres and rhetorical strategies among the diverse writers making sense of unknown lands, unfamiliar people, and their own new selves.

Notes

1. The designation *nation* is considered a misnomer before the eighteenth century by scholars who emphasize the deep sectional divergences within countries and note that exploration and colonization were financed by geographical or religious sections of countries (see, e.g., Davies 45–54; Hudson 247–64).

2. Some scholars argue that too great an emphasis on the fur trade model of French occupation has led archaeologists to neglect other areas, such as villages, farmsteads, and industrial sites, that could provide more sophisticated models of the French presence (see Walthall).

3. See Axtell, *European*, and Nash for detailed discussions of the differences in English and French attitudes toward the Natives. Nash points out that not until the eighteenth century did writers like Robert Beverley and William Byrd wish the English had urged intermarriage with the Natives (106).

4. Knowledge of early French North American literature also contributes to an understanding of later literature by, for example, George Washington Cable, Kate Chopin, Willa Cather, and Louis Hémon.

5. There are works by other French nuns, like Jeanne-Françoise Juchereau de la Ferté (1650–1723), Marie-Andrée Regnard Duplessis (1687–

1760), Marie Morin (1649–1730), Véronique Cuillerier, and Catherine Porlier, but I am unaware of English translations.

6. Thanks to John Nott, an independent historian-scholar, for discussions in this area.

7. For a work in English by an English immigrant describing French settlement, students can turn to Frances Brooke's *History of Emily Montague* (1769) — often called the first Canadian novel in English and the first example of New World fiction.

8. Evelyn Page identifies the writers mentioned in this paragraph as creators of "the first of the clusters of settlement narratives which were to become characteristic of habitation" (85).

9. Among the Spanish, Francisco Lopez de Mendoza Grajales, Gonzalo Solís de Merás, and Bartolomé Barrientos wrote versions of the attack on Fort Caroline, praising Pedro Menéndez de Avilés's destruction of the French Huguenots.

10. In 1922 Isaac Joslin Cox edited two volumes that include accounts of La Salle's journeys by Henri de Tonty, Louis Hennepin, Chrétien LeClercq, Zenobius Membré, Anastasius Douay, Jean Cavelier, Henri Joutel, and La Salle himself.

11. Similar units can evolve around Richard Hakluyt's *The Principal Navigations & Discoveries of the English Nation*. For example, volume 8 includes Verrazzano, Cartier, Sir Francis Roberval, Laudonnière, and John Alphonse of Xanctoigne. See also David B. Quinn's five volumes.

12. Among the better-known French writers, we also discover genres not anthologized at the present time in English selections: for example, Lahontan's "Conference" or "Dialogue" with Adario, a Huron chief; Charlevoix's epistolary journal to the duchess of Lesdiguières; and Lescarbot's réception, *The Theatre of Neptune in New France*.

13. Ramsay Cook offers an excellent discussion of the authenticity and authorship of Cartier's *Voyages* in his introduction to the University of Toronto edition.

14. Radisson's distress at killing three of his Iroquois captors to escape with an Algonquin is an important comment on Hannah Dustan's dramatic escape in Cotton Mather, *Magnalia Christi Americana*, book 7.

Works Cited

Primary Works

Allouez, Claude. *Journal*. Thwaites, *Jesuit Relations* 50: 249–311; 51: 21–69; 54: 197–214.

Barrientos, Bartolomé. *Pedro Menéndez de Avilés, Founder of Florida*. Trans. Anthony Kerrigan. Gainesville: U of Florida P, 1965.

Bradford, William. *History of Plymouth Plantation*. Ed. Samuel Eliot Morison. New York: Knopf, 1952. Mod. Lib. Coll. Ed., 1981.

Brébeuf, Jean de. "Instructions for the Fathers of Our Society Who Shall Be Sent to the Hurons." Thwaites, *Jesuit Relations* 12: 117–23.

Brooke, Frances. *History of Emily Montague*. Toronto: McClelland, 1995.

Cartier, Jacques. *The Voyages of Jacques Cartier*. Trans. Henry Percival Biggar. Toronto: U of Toronto P, 1993.

Champlain, Samuel de. *Of Savages*. Champlain, *Works* 83–189.

———. *The Voyages, 1613* Champlain, *Works* 204–469.

———. *The Works of Samuel de Champlain*. Trans. Henry Percival Biggar. Vol. 1. Toronto: Champlain Soc., 1922.

Charlevoix, Pierre [François-Xavier] de. *Journal of a Voyage to North-America*. 2 vols. Ann Arbor: Univ. Microfilms, 1966.

Cox, Isaac Joslin, ed. *The Journeys of René Robert Cavelier Sieur de La Salle*. 2 vols. New York: Allerton, 1922.

Gorgues, Dominique de. "The Fourth Voyage of the Frenchmen into Florida." Hakluyt 9: 100–12.

Gyles, John. "Memoirs of Odd Adventures, Strange Deliverances, etc." Vaughan and Clark 91–131.

Hennepin, Louis. "Account of a Voyage down the Mississippi." *A Description of Louisiana*. Ann Arbor: Univ. Microfilms, 1966. 343–59.

Jogues, Isaac. "Narrative." *Held Captive by Indians: Selected Narratives, 1642–1836*. Ed. Richard VanDerBeets. Knoxville: U of Tennessee P, 1973. 4–40.

Laudonnière, René [Goulaine de]. *Three Voyages*. Trans. and ed. Charles E. Bennett. Gainesville: UP of Florida, 1975.

Lahontan, baron de. *New Voyages to North-America*. 1703 ed. Ed. Reuben Gold Thwaites. 2 vols. Chicago: McClurg, 1905.

La Salle, René Robert Cavelier, Sieur de. *The Journeys of René Robert Cavelier Sieur de La Salle*. Ed. Isaac Joslin Cox. 2 vols. New York: Allerton, 1922.

Le Challeux, Nicolas. "A True and Perfect Description of the Last Voyage, or Navigation, Attempted by Capitaine John Rybaut." Lorant 88–116.

Le Jeune, Paul. "On the Means of Converting the Savages." Trans. John Cutler Covert. Thwaites, *Jesuit Relations* 6: 145–55.

Le Moyne de Morgues, Jacques. "The Narrative." Lorant 33–87.

Lescarbot, Marc. *Nova Francia; or, The Description of That Part of New France, Which Is One Continent with Virginia*. Trans. P. E. London: Bishop, 1609.

———. *The Theatre of Neptune in New France*. Trans. Harriette Taber Richardson. Boston: Riverside, 1927.

Marie de l'Incarnation. *Word from New France: The Selected Letters of Marie de l'Incarnation*. Trans. and ed. Joyce Marshall. Toronto: Oxford UP, 1967.

Marquette, Jacques. *Voyages*. Thwaites, *Jesuit Relations* 59: 87–211.

Mather, Cotton. "Article XXV. A Notable Exploit [. . .]." *Magnalia Christi Americana*. Vol. 7. Hartford: Andrus, 1820.

Mendoza Grajalas, Francisco Lopez de. *Relation of the Journey of Pedro Menéndez de Avilés in Florida*. Old South Leaflets, Gen. Ser., vol. 4, no. 89. Boston, 1897.

Millet [Milet], Pierre. Letter. Thwaites, *Jesuit Relations* 64: 66–107.

Morton, Thomas. *New English Canaan*. New York: Arno, 1972.

Radisson, Pierre Esprit. *The Explorations of Pierre Esprit Radisson*. Ed. Arthur T. Adams. Minneapolis: Ross, 1961.

Ribault, Jean. *The True and Last Discouerie of Florida. Divers Voyages Touching the Discovery of America*. Trans. and ed. Richard Hakluyt. New York: Franklin, n.d. 91–115.

Rowlandson, Mary. "A True History of the Captivity and Restoration of Mrs. Mary Rowlandson." *Journeys in New Worlds*. Ed. William L. Andrews. Madison: U of Wisconsin P, 1990. 27–65.

Sagard, Gabriel. *Sagard's Long Journey to the Country of the Hurons*. Trans. H. H. Langton. Ed. George M. Wrong. New York: Greenwood, 1968.

Solís de Merás, Gonzalo. *Pedro Menéndez de Avilés: Memorial*. Trans. Jeannette Thurber Connor. Gainesville: UP of Florida, 1964.

Swarton, Hannah. "'A Narrative of Hannah Swarton Containing Wonderful Passages Relating to Her Captivity and Deliverance,' Related by Cotton Mather." Vaughan and Clark. 145–57.

Verrazzano, Giovanni da. *The Voyages of Giovanni da Verrazzano: 1524–1528*. Trans. Susan Tarrow. Ed. Lawrence C. Wroth. New Haven: Yale UP, 1970.

Williams, John. *The Redeemed Captive*. Ed. Edward W. Clark. Amherst: U of Massachusetts P, 1976.

Secondary Works

Adams, Percy G. *Travelers and Travel Liars: 1660–1800*. Berkeley: U of California P, 1962. Rev. ed. New York: Dover, 1980.

Adorno, Rolena. "New Perspectives in Colonial Spanish American Literary Studies." *Journal of the Southwest* 32.2 (1990): 173–91.

Axtell, James. *Beyond 1492: Encounters in Colonial North America*. New York: Oxford UP, 1992.

———. *The European and the Indian: Essays in the Ethnohistory of Colonial North America*. New York: Oxford UP, 1981.

Bakeless, John. *The Eyes of Discovery: The Pageant of North America as Seen by the First Explorers*. New York: Dover, 1950.

Cook, Ramsay. "Donnacona Discovers Europe: Rereading Jacques Cartier's Voyages." *The Voyages of Jacques Cartier*. Toronto: U of Toronto P, 1993. ix–xli.

Davies, K. G. *The North Atlantic World in the Seventeenth Century*. Vol. 4. *Europe and the World in the Age of Expansion*. Minneapolis: U of Minnesota P, 1974.

Eccles, W. J. *The Canadian Frontier: 1534–1760*. New York: Holt, Rinehart, 1969.

———. *France in America*. New York: Harper, 1972. Rev. ed. East Lansing: Michigan State UP, 1990.

Echeverria, Durand. *Mirage in the West: A History of the French Image of American Society to 1815*. New York: Octagon, 1966.

Geertz, Clifford. *The Interpretation of Culture*. New York: Basic, 1973.

Gipson, Lawrence Henry. "The American Revolution as an Aftermath of the Great War for the Empire, 1754–1765." *Political Science Quarterly* 65.1 (1950): 86–104.

——. *The Coming of the Revolution: 1763–1775*. New York: Harper, 1954.

Hakluyt, Richard, ed. *The Principal Navigations Voyages Traffiques and Discoveries of the English Nation*. 12 vols. New York: AMS, 1965.

Hudson, Nicholas. "From 'Nation' to 'Race': The Origin of Racial Classification in Eighteenth-Century Thought." *Eighteenth-Century Studies* 29.3 (1996): 247–64.

Hunt, Lynn. "Introduction: History, Culture, and Text." *The New Cultural History*. Ed. Hunt. Berkeley: U of California P, 1989. 1–22.

Lorant, Stefan, ed. *The New World: The First Pictures of America*. New York: Duell, 1946.

Nash, Gary B. *Red, White, and Black: The Peoples of Early America*. 2nd ed. Englewood Cliffs: Prentice, 1974.

Page, Evelyn. *American Genesis: Pre-colonial Writing in the North*. Boston: Gambit, 1973.

Parkman, Francis. Preface. *La Salle and the Discovery of the Great West*. Vols. 5–6. *The Works of Francis Parkman*. Boston: Little, 1897–98.

Quinn, David B. *America from Concept to Discovery. Early Exploration of North America*. 5 vols. New York: Arno, 1979.

Spengemann, William C. *The Adventurous Muse: The Poetics of American Fiction, 1789–1900*. New Haven: Yale UP, 1977.

——. *A Mirror for Americanists: Reflections on the Idea of American Literature*. Hanover: UP of New England, 1989.

Thwaites, Reuben Gold. *France in America: 1497–1763*. New York: Harper, 1905. New York: Cooper Square, 1968.

——. Introduction. *New Voyages to North-America by the Baron de Lahontan*. Chicago: McClurg, 1905. ix–xlix.

——, ed. *The Jesuit Relations and Allied Documents*. 72 vols. New York: Pageant, 1959.

Vaughan, Alden, and Edward W. Clark, eds. *Puritans among the Indians*. Cambridge: Belknap, 1981.

Walthall, John A. *French Colonial Archaeology: The Illinois Country and the Western Great Lakes*. Urbana: U of Illinois P, 1991.

White, Hayden. *The Content of the Form: Narrative Discourse and Historical Representation*. Baltimore: Johns Hopkins UP, 1987.

——. *Tropics of Discourse: Essays in Cultural Criticism*. Baltimore: Johns Hopkins UP, 1978.

Wrong, George M. Introduction. *Sagard's Long Journey to the Country of the Hurons*. By Father Gabriel Sagard. New York: Greenwood, 1968. xiii–xviii.

British Colonial and
Postcolonial Writings

David S. Shields

The Literature of England's Staple Colonies

During the seventeenth century the Acts of Trade and Navigation legislated a commercial system that protected trade in certain "enumerated" goods, promoting the production in America of agricultural staples that would be traded for finished English goods. Maryland, Virginia, the Carolinas, and British East Florida with the British West Indies reorganized their economies into staples monocultures, dependent on a slave labor force and concentrating wealth in the hands of a small class of planters, merchants, and placemen. Their economies, social organization, cultural mythology, and manners were remarkably similar to one another and differed markedly from those of Canada, New England, and the middle colonies. To understand British American literature, we must remember that the staple colonies were the empire's great engines of wealth, so that they dominated British imaginings about America.

The central tensions of British imperial culture were manifested most vividly in writings by and about the staple colonies. Until very recently the anthologies used to teach American literature covered

these writings inadequately, requiring instructors to compile anthologies from primary sources. For those inclined to do that, I provide
certain titles not found in current anthologies that illuminate the literature and culture of the staple colonies. But Myra Jehlen and Michael
Warner's *The English Literatures of America* and the expanded third
edition of the *Heath Anthology* (Lauter) now supply useful samplings
of imperial literature. Even the more traditional collections contain
selections that allow a limited exploration of the literature of the
staple colonies. For instance, Captain John Smith's *A Description of
New England* is widely excerpted. This tract summarized Smith's experience and thinking on colonial enterprise. Excerpts that can serve
as a good starting point for an examination of imperialism include
Smith's commendation of the Dutch as the model for English colonial enterprise (1: 330–31) and his ridicule of Spanish-inspired
quests for gold (1: 348); also worth exploring are Smith's praises of
Spain's energy in exploration and colonization (1: 348–49). Smith repeatedly claimed that America was not so much a garden of Eden as
a fertile land that could be remade into a garden if settlers labored to
improve it, and that claim announced the central problem of the imperial enterprise: Who will do the work? Smith's descriptions of Virginia in *The General Historie* and *A Map of Virginia* display the
characteristic inclination of British imperialists to view territory with
an eye to potential commodity.

The fancifulness of British imperial visions of New World wealth
can be humorously underscored by reading the description of the first
of the "merchantable commodities" touted by Thomas Hariot in *A
Briefe and True Report of the New Found Land of Virginia* (Jehlen and
Warner 68). "Silke of grasse or grasse Silke" was nothing more than
marsh grass imagined as a cash crop by early Virginia colonists. Wish-
ful thinking made gold and goods visible everywhere. One episode
that never fails to communicate the sharpness of colonists' hunger for
wealth to current readers is Smith's account in *The Proceedings of the
English Colonie in Virginia* of the gold fever that seized Jamestown
after a settler discovered mica flakes on the banks of the James River
(1: 218–19). (Bring a chunk of mica to class to show how little it resembles gold.) The spectacle of aristocratic reprobates with pockets

stuffed with shiny sand feeding on jimsonweed because they were too greedy to leave their sandbanks dramatizes the ludicrously extreme wish for wealth driving British colonial enterprise.

In certain respects Smith's writings did not foretell the staple colonies that would come into being. His political egalitarianism, derived from his reading of the philosopher Sir Robert Bruce Cotton, did not anticipate the hierarchical world of the plantocracy — an expression of the Stuart Restoration (Lemay, *American Dream,* 192–94). Smith's vision of a countryside of self-made English yeomen has, at best, an ironic resonance in lands that would soon be partially vacated of their indigenous groups and occupied by enslaved Africans. His preoccupation with the productive powers of the land scanted the importance of trade at a time when trade began to dominate thinking about the British "empire of the seas."

One must look to later texts — such as Richard Lewis's "To Mr. Samuel Hastings [. . .] on his launching the Maryland-Merchant" (1729–30), James Kirkpatrick's *The Sea-Piece* (1750), or James Sterling's paean to the projector of the Northwest Passage and future governor of North Carolina, *An Epistle to the Hon. Arthur Dobbs* (1752), to find provincial celebrations of maritime commerce and visions of how the exchange of goods transforms the globe (Lemay, *Men,* 133–37, 274–80; Shields, *Oracles,* 26–29). These works inaugurated America's literature of commercial heroism; they proposed the merchant as the hero of the modern age. Students can easily grasp the outcome of this literary project: the late-twentieth-century media's creation of cults of personality around Lee Iacocca, Ted Turner, and Bill Gates, for instance, repeats this early modern rhetoric. Indeed, a random read-through of a current issue of *Forbes* magazine can quickly acquaint a classroom with the reigning vision of commercial heroism. An instructor might present these paeans to enterprise with the many objections raised by Alexander Pope and Samuel Johnson to the celebration of persons absorbed in furthering their worldly self-interest.

Anthologies that include Ebenezer Cook's *The Sot-Weed Factor* afford an opportunity to examine problems arising from the commercial mystique attaching to the staple colonies. The tobacco factor's misadventures burlesque metropolitan myths surrounding the New World, both positive and negative. His hunger for fortune is colored with all the credulousness that commercial greed and metropolitan condescension can provide. Maryland appears as an earthly Tartarus whose crudity and discommodity exaggerate every anti-imperial slander aimed at America during the seventeenth century by Englishmen trying to prevent emigration. This caricature of Maryland lends itself to all sorts of uses in the classroom. It dramatizes the problem of publicity: If reputation is everything, then how does one counter a bad report? You take its language and imagery and blow it up until it is a flagrant fiction incredible even to the dull-witted. This fantasy Maryland becomes disassociated with peoples' conceptions of the actual place. A good parallel case is the South. The media-made Dixie of greedy crackers, lazy hillbillies, fox chases, hard-drinking carouses, hard-used belles, and courthouse brawls—the Dixie of *Hee-Haw* and *The Dukes of Hazzard*—operates at a fanciful remove from the actualities of southern life and thus diminishes one's trepidations about southern violence, anti-intellectualism, cupidity, and sexism. (Not that the South has a monopoly of these vices.) One can then point out that all of these Dixie images appeared first in Cook's poem. A West Indian analogue is Ned Ward's *A Voyage to Jamaica* (also in Jehlen and Warner). Henry Brooke's 1703 "The New Metamorphosis" supplies a humorous gloss on the weight of the metropolitan expectations on commercial adventurers in its story of failed enterprise.

Attempts by British Americans to project in positive terms the ideals of the agricultural civilization of the staple colonies culminated in a trilogy of New World staple georgics composed after mid-century. They have only recently begun to be anthologized. All dress the creation of the plantation culture in a Vergilian heroism. Charles Woodmason's "Indico" (1757) described the problems attending the cultivation of the dye plant in South Carolina. Fragments of the work were published during Woodmason's lifetime in the *South Carolina Gazette*. It was followed in 1764 by James Grainger's celebrated georgic *The Sugar-Cane*. This elaborate poem attempted to inculcate the ideal of humanity among the plantocracy while celebrating the productions of the sugar islands for an imperial audience. Portions of the fourth book, "The Genius of Africa," have been included in the third edition of volume 1 of the *Heath Anthology* and Jehlen and Warner's *The British Literatures of America* because of its extraordinarily precise delineation of the material circumstances and culture of African slaves on the islands. The last of the staple georgics, George Ogilvie's *Carolina; or, The Planter* (1776), served both as paean to the creation of rice culture in South Carolina and elegy to the imperial civilization that the American Revolution destroyed. It is noteworthy for a nascent ecological consciousness; it argues that nature will exact retribution for the depredations wrought by planters on the land.

The staple georgics permit two sorts of classroom approaches. They invite discussions of the relation of material culture to intellectual culture. They also show students the ways empires warranted conquest and dominion with ethical myths. Great Britain's fantasy of being the new Roman Empire, bestowing the "arts of peace" (including agriculture) on uncivil peoples and lands, is readily apprehendible, and it reveals the political significance of neoclassicism. They also suggest how the neoclassical myth suffered stress when tied to a culture dependent on slavery. Both Grainger and Ogilvie must erect on that myth a secondary myth, elaborated comprehensively in Samuel Martin's *Essay on Plantership* (1765), celebrating the planter's "humanity" and benevolent patriarchal stewardship of people and nature.

William Byrd's writings are those most frequently used to exemplify the ideals of the plantocracy. His 15 June 1731 letter to John Boyle remains the classic depiction of plantation life as utopian in its virtuous simplicity: "We live in all the innocence of the patriarchs, under our vines and our fig-trees, surrounded with our flocks and our herds" (2: 443–45). Read against his *Histories of the Dividing Line,* the letter reveals the rhetorical character of his representations of plantation living. The *Histories* treats the motives of Virginia colonization, the moral probity of the planter class, and the project of civility with irony. Close attention to the tensions inscribed in the many comparisons in the works reveals a self-understanding so complex that any attribution of simplicity or integrity to it are specious. One can also learn something about the different communities of discourse in which the plantocracy operated. The "public" history is a transatlantic document suffused with imperial mythology and concerned with mastery over territory, the imperative to "improve" holdings, and the character of authority faced with uncontrollable persons (lubberly Carolinians, Native Americans). The "secret" history, directed to his circle of friends in Virginia, registers the permissive raillery of elite masculine sociability that playfully dislocates the defining distinctions of provincial life (civility/crudity; faith/faithlessness; love/lust).

While the *Histories* is notable for the invisibility of African slaves, it gives ample notice to Native Americans and women. Indeed, the treatment of women in the *Histories* has proved provocative for feminist commentary. "The Female Creed," Byrd's courtship letters written under cognomens to various ladies, and the sexual episodes recounted in the diaries provide a rich field for mapping the desires, resentments, fantasies, and frustrations that troubled the conversation between the sexes. To identify the formulaic elements of Byrd's treatment of women, one can have the class read Felicity Nussbaum's *The Brink of All We Hate* for a survey of conventional antifeminist slanders and a letter-writing manual that lays out the conventions of gallantry. Another Virginian work that supplies a more concentrated view of elite manners and motives in courtship is Robert Bolling's journal of his failed romance with Anne Miller, published as *Robert Bolling Woos Anne Miller*. Bolling's sardonic wit and his various courtship poems supply a uniquely detailed picture of the conflict between the elite practice of dynastic marriage and the competing ideal of companionate marriage based on mutual affection. Women's views of courtship are more difficult to locate. Perhaps the most elaborate source is the series of poems composed by "a lady" documenting a thwarted transatlantic romance. Originally appearing in the *Barbados Gazette,* they were featured prominently in *Caribbeana* (1741), Samuel Keimer's two-volume London collection of the paper's finest pieces.

The most astute observer of woman's place in the imperial scheme and the social order of the staple colonies was Aphra Behn, a native of Martinique and a pioneer public woman of letters in England. Her play "The Widow Ranter," treats Bacon's Rebellion in

Virginia, not as a vindication of either Governor William Berkeley or Nathaniel Bacon (indeed they probably serve as pretexts for a meditation on Monmouth's Rebellion in England, a matter too hot to handle directly on stage), but as an exploration of power and authority within a market where persons (especially women) are valued as vehicles of commerce. In colonies where marriageable women were scarce, particularly those with sufficient liberty and fortune to act in their own interests, Behn discovered new conditions of exchange, new configurations of love and power sharing. The play is easily taught, so long as one contextualizes women's ownership of property in late-seventeenth-century Anglo-America. Because of the dialogue's distinctly characterized lines, a performance in class by strong readers would bring the persons and positions alive. Acts 1 or 5 would suit best.

Though a Tory in politics, Behn had a Whiggish appreciation of the imperial benefits of trade, perhaps because of her transatlantic heritage. *Commerce* and *improvement* were positive terms in her ethical lexicon. Among residents of the staple colonies, one woman stands as the foremost champion of colonial improvement. Eliza Lucas Pinckney pioneered the cultivation of indigo on the English mainland, adapting French methods used in the islands to the soil conditions of South Carolina, stimulating the Carolina indigo boom of the 1750s. Her letters detailing her agricultural enterprise, collected as *Letterbook of Eliza Lucas Pinckney, 1739–1762,* and her manuscript of devotions, published as *The Journal and Letters of Eliza Lucas,* testify to a woman's will to secure prosperity and establish in her environs civility, domestic order, and grace. The manifold uses of the familiar letter as an instrument of expression for women are well demonstrated in these writings. They have been widely anthologized, particularly in collections of primary sources documenting southern history and culture.

In one respect the teaching of women's participation in the literary world of the staple colonies waits on scholarship. No southern or West Indian equivalent to the rich bodies of salon writing surrounding Elizabeth Graeme Fergusson in Philadelphia, Annis Boudinot Stockton at Princeton (see Mulford), and Sarah Wentworth Morton in Massachusetts is available for study. When Daphne

O'Brien finishes her edition of the writings of Margaret Lowther Page, mistress of Rosewell Plantation and tidewater Virginia's greatest woman of letters, we should be able to appreciate the effort by women in the staple colonies to superintend features of the conversation and conduct of society. Like all belles lettres, that of the *salonnières* made manifest the sharing of pleasure that made society the scene of happiness.

The salon promoted a sociability more civil and "sensible" than that practiced in gentlemen's clubs. In all-male companies, experiments with liberty of expression and conduct were undertaken behind a wall of secrecy and according to private regulation. This liberty was often exploited, so that club talk and club writings became the most extravagant, subversive, and innovative expression of the age. The great masterwork of Anglo-American club literature, Dr. Alexander Hamilton's two-thousand-page *History of the Ancient and Honourable Tuesday Club*, used the proceedings of an Annapolis, Maryland, club as a comic prism to talk about world history, imperial politics, mythology, the republic of letters, and manners (see Micklus). Premised on the third earl of Shaftesbury's discursive principle of "total raillery" — a liberty to subject all matters among friends to trial by humor — Hamilton's *History* mocked the vanity of the provincial world to achieve a playful freedom from the compulsions of business, public work, and domestic life. The many hand-drawn illustrations offer an unusual approach to the humor of the club. The Tuesday Club made explicit its adherence to an ideal of the club as a privileged zone of masculine freedom. Passages touch on all the major issues animating the construction of a masculine world: the dependence of homosociality on a discourse of the female body, the question of the role of shared appetite in the formation of community, the erotics of friendship, the role of laws and forms in regulating interest, and the dependence of the *sensus communis* on humor. An interesting classroom experiment is to form salons and clubs among the students and offer a role-playing protocol derived from an evening's activity at an early American club. The imitation salons and mock clubs could operate according to the rules established by the model club. The distinctions among gossip, sensible conversation, and raillery become readily apparent.

Other people inhabited the staple colonies besides planters, ministers, merchants, and their wives—the elite who enjoyed the leisure to be sociable. Those who occupied the lower social ranks—artisans, tradesmen, laboring men and women, small landholders, tenant farmers, indentured servants, and slaves—often lacked the leisure to write. Have students read microfilmed issues of the *South Carolina Gazette* or *Virginia Gazette* so that they can observe the number of ads for runaway servants or the notices for slave auctions. They quickly see how much the staple colonies depended on the labor of bound persons. First-person narratives of such people are particularly difficult to find outside court depositions. For this reason the late-seventeenth-century testimony of James Revel, *The Poor Unhappy Transported Felon's Sorrowful Account of His Fourteen Years of Transportation at Virginia in America* stands as a singularly valuable document. It portrays a world where slaves and indentured servants labor side by side in miserable conditions and where indentured servants are resented by local landowners because once at liberty they become economic rivals, securing land and competing in local markets with a zeal fired by memories of ill usage.

The religious impetus for Revel's account links it to the most famous of first-person accounts of African American slavery, Olaudah Equiano's widely anthologized *The Interesting Narrative of the Life of Olaudah Equiano; or, Gustavus Vassa, the African* (1789). The complexity of Equiano's narrative, with its elements of spiritual autobiography, commercial success story, and maritime adventure reveals the complexities of identity in transatlantic imperial commerce (Costanzo). The doublings of persona, the transmutations of subjectivity, and the curious combinations of genres and discourses makes *The Narrative* a rich field for the sorts of postcolonial analyses in cultural syncretism and scission found in the writings of subjects of the European empires.

Equiano's narrative is the superlative expression of an exceptional human being. In certain respects it is as unrepresentative of the common circumstances of the life of his race and class as most masterworks are of the world of their authors. Given the paucity of first-person slave narratives from the staple colonies and given the centrality of these conditions in the intellectual and moral history of

the English-speaking world in the eighteenth century, we are forced
to read portraits by Europeans on slavery to understand something
of the human crisis of imperial commerce. James Grainger's fourth
book of *The Sugar-Cane* remains the most detailed English portrait of
New World African slavery. It is useful to read in tandem with texts
on African American material culture, such as John Vlach's *Back of the
Big House* or *The Afro-American Tradition in Decorative Arts*. The actor
John Singleton's verse *A General Description of the West Indian Islands*
(1767) supplies portraits of slave housing, labor, material culture, and
burial practices. The use of torture to compel slaves to perform tasks
is treated at length in *Jamaica: A Poem* (1776), and there is a thor-
oughgoing critique of the treatment and living conditions of slaves in
abolitionist writings by metropolitan critics, such as John Marjoribanks's *Slavery: An Essay in Verse Inscribed to Planters* (1792) and Hannah More's *Slavery: A Poem* (1788). An invariable trope in literary
critiques of slavery was to show the disparity in condition between
those who labor and those who receive the fruits of the labor. The
wealth and luxury of the planter appears as the coerced benefit of the
toils and pains of the African laborers. This point is well conveyed in
the portrait of Charleston supplied by J. Hector St. John de Crèvecoeur in the ninth of the *Letters from an American Farmer*. There the
festivity of the metropolis of slave country is paid for by the misery of
the surrounding countryside. Crèvecoeur, like the abolitionists, inspired pity and sympathy for the slaves by sentimental appeals to the
imagination. He raises the question, How can the culture of the
United States be accommodated to the injustice of the labor system
in the slave states? He invokes an American common sense cherishing
liberty for all and equality of condition to make Charleston (and, by
extension, all the former staple colonies) an alien territory driven by
a white will to luxury rather than by a morality.

Crèvecoeur is certainly characteristic of eighteenth-century
thinkers in making labor a conspicuous issue in determining the morality of American economic and political arrangements. The ethics of
labor is one of the problems most characteristic of the literature of the
staple colonies, and it remains an issue that can connect our world
with theirs. Play devil's advocate by taking up one of the antebellum

southern critiques of northern wage slavery and ask whether in theory slave paternalism might be a less economically brutal form of exploitation.

The most conspicuous flowering of labor theory was occasioned by the founding of Georgia. James Oglethorpe sought to make the territory between South Carolina and Spanish Florida a workhouse in the wild where the able-bodied poor of Great Britain could be habituated to labor far from urban corruptions. In tracts such as his *A New and Accurate Accounte of the Provinces of South Carolina and Georgia* and Benjamin Martyn's *Reasons for Establishing the Colony of Georgia* one encounters the Lockean notion that education in the ways of work can re-create character and redeem the poor from indolence and poverty. Oglethorpe's bootstrap benevolence proved popular with a range of metropolitan reformers and placemen but less so with professional persons and ambitious propertied men who took up residence in the new colony. The Georgia trustees governed from England, and no local legislature served to address residents' concerns. This paternalistic exclusion of Georgians from participation in the government led to the creation of an organized opposition, the "clamorous malcontents," who initiated a literary campaign demystifying Oglethorpe's utopia of labor. *A True and Historical Narrative of the Colony of Georgia* (1741) by Patrick Tailfer and others (anthologized in Radzinowicz) subjects the ideals of Georgia to withering satire and wonders at the morality of a scheme that enables persons to labor only for their own subsistence and not for wealth. The hierarchical presumptions of paternalism stand baldly revealed.

The professional men and planters who composed the clamorous malcontents were not the only ones who held a vision of a civil life and the enrichment of the community. Artisans and persons of the middling sort identified with the rising condition of their communities. Charles Hansford, a blacksmith in tidewater Virginia, celebrated the happiness, glory, virtue, and goodness of his province in "My Country's Worth" (also in Jehlen and Warner). Hansford identified the good order of life with the accomplishment of the Virginia gentry, whose honor and courtesy defined civility. Their conduct supplied a telos for the aspirations of the citizenry.

We cannot dismiss Hansford's esteem for the Virginia gentry as a retrograde expression of a culture of deference. When we consider how many members of this class were installed in the pantheon of "the founders" who have stood as models of probity and civic seriousness throughout most of United States history, we must consider seriously the extent to which virtue, learning, and civility were embodied in them. Jefferson's *Notes on the State of Virginia* (widely available in history collections and some literary anthologies) is the usual text for raising these issues. The text raises many provocative points: Jefferson's disinclination to equate social equality with the spread of virtue among a citizenry; his attribution of differing mental capacity to different races, positing an essentialized racism; his pessimistic assessment of the aggregate effects of public education; his view that slavery results in the moral contamination of the ruling classes; his conviction that religion can result only in intellectual tyranny when established by the coercive power of the state; and his picture of Native Americans as moral agents who govern themselves by manners rather than by formal governments. The paradox of a public intellectual who affirms a social hierarchy while asserting republican ideals of liberty and virtue tells much about the peculiar tensions in the ideology of the South's patriot gentry.

In the end we must determine how useful the ideals of the southern gentry remain. We can identify and judge readily their failures to enact their ideals in practice. Should we judge negatively persons who presumed a right to govern on the basis of superior parts, attainments, learning, and social standing and who attempted to discipline their exercise of power by rigorous codes of duty and honor? Is it a superior way of governing for a ruling class to pretend it is not a ruling class but an epiphenomenon of the citizenry and to abide not by morality or a customary code of duty but by the laws of expediency? This line of questioning permits a very edifying classroom debate.

Works Cited

Primary Works

Behn, Aphra. "The Widow Ranter." Jehlen and Warner 233–91.
Bolling, Robert. *Robert Bolling Woos Anne Miller*. Ed. J. A. Leo Lemay. Charlottesville: UP of Virginia, 1990.

Brooke, Henry. "The New Metamorphosis or Fable of the Bald Eagle." *Civil Tongues and Polite Letters in British America*. Ed. David S. Shields. Chapel Hill: U of North Carolina P, 1997. 81–86.

Byrd, William. *The Correspondence of the Three William Byrds of Westover, 1684–1776*. 3 vols. Ed. Marion Tinling. Charlottesville: UP of Virginia for Virginia Historical Soc., 1977.

———. "The Female Creed." *Another Secret Diary of William Byrd of Westover*. Ed. Maude H. Woodfin and Marion Tinling. Richmond: Dietz, 1942. 453.

———. *Histories of the Dividing Line*. 1728. Ed. Louis B. Wright. Cambridge: Harvard UP, 1966.

Cook, Ebenezer. *The Sot-Weed Factor: or, A Voyage to Maryland*. London, 1707.

Equiano, Olaudah. *The Interesting Narrative of the Life of Olaudah Equiano; or, Gustavus Vassa, the African, Written by Himself*. 1789. Ed. Paul Edwards. 2 vols. London: Dawsons, 1969.

Grainger, James. *The Sugar-Cane, A Poem in Three Books*. London: [J. and R. Dodsley], 1764.

Hamilton, Alexander. *The History of the Ancient and Honourable Tuesday Club*. Ed. Robert Micklus. 3 vols. Chapel Hill: U of North Carolina P, 1990.

Hansford, Charles. "My Country's Worth." *The Poems of Charles Hansford*. Ed. James A. Servies and Carl R. Dolmetsch. Chapel Hill: U of North Carolina P for the Virginia Historical Soc., 1961. 47–68.

Jamaica. A Poem in Three Parts. London: Nicoll, 1777.

Jefferson, Thomas. *Notes on the State of Virginia*. Ed. William Peden. New York: Norton, 1954.

Jehlen, Myra, and Michael Warner. *The English Literatures of America*. New York: Routledge, 1997.

Kirkpatrick, James. *The Sea-Piece: A Narrative, Philosophical and Descriptive Poem*. London: Cooper, 1750.

Lauter, Paul, gen. ed. *The Heath Anthology of American Literature*. 3rd ed. Vol. 1. Lexington: Heath, 1997.

Lewis, Richard. "To Mr. Samuel Hastings, Ship-wright of Philadelphia on His Launching the Maryland-Merchant, a Large Ship Built by Him at Annapolis." *Pennsylvania Gazette* 13 Jan. 1729/30.

Marjoribanks, J[ohn]. *Slavery: An Essay in Verse Inscribed to Planters and Others Concerned in the Sale of Negro Slaves*. Edinburgh, 1792.

Martin, Samuel. *Essay on Plantership Humbly Inscribed to His Excellency George Thomas, Esq.* London: Millar, 1765.

[Martyn, Benjamin.] *Reasons for Establishing the Colony of Georgia*. London: Meadows, 1733. Rpt. in Reese.

More, Hannah. *Slavery: A Poem*. London, 1788.

Ogilvie, George. *Carolina; or, The Planter*. 1776. Ed. David S. Shields. Rpt. of 1791 ed. Spec. issue of *Southern Literary Journal* (1986).

[Oglethorpe, James.] *A New and Accurate Accounte of the Provinces of South-Carolina and Georgia*. Rpt. in Reese.

Pinckney, Eliza Lucas. *The Letterbook of Eliza Lucas Pinckney, 1739–1762*. Ed. Elise Pinckney. Chapel Hill: U of North Carolina P, 1972.

Radzinowicz, Mary Ann, ed. *American Colonial Prose: John Smith to Thomas Jefferson*. Cambridge: Cambridge UP, 1984.

Reese, Trevor, ed. *The Most Delightful Country of the Universe*. Savannah: Beehive, 1972.

Revel, James. *The Poor Unhappy Transported Felon's Sorrowful Account of His Fourteen Years of Transportation at Virginia in America*. Ed. John M. Jennings. *Virginia Magazine of History and Biography* 56 (1948): 180–94.

Singleton, John. *A Description of the West Indies. A Poem in Blank Verse in Four Books*. London, 1767.

Smith, John. *The Works of Captain John Smith*. Ed. Philip L. Barbour. 3 vols. Chapel Hill: U of North Carolina P, 1986.

Sterling, James. *An Epistle to the Hon. Arthur Dobbs, Esq.: In Europe from a Clergyman in America*. Dublin, 1752.

Tailfer, Patrick, et al. *A True and Historical Narrative of the Colony of Georgia by Pat. Tailfer and Others with Comments by the Earl of Egmont*. Ed. Clarence L. Ver Steeg. Athens: U of Georgia P, 1960.

[Ward, Edward "Ned."] "A Trip to Jamaica." *The Second Volume of the Writings of the Author of the London-Spy*. London: How, 1704.

Woodmason, Charles. "Indico: A Colonial Poem on Indigo Culture." Ed. Hennig Cohen. *Agricultural History* 30 (1956): 42–43.

Secondary Works

Costanzo, Angelo. *Surprizing Narrative: Olaudah Equiano and the Beginnings of Black Autobiography*. New York: Greenwood, 1987.

Lemay, J. A. Leo. *The American Dream of Captain John Smith*. Charlottesville: UP of Virginia, 1991.

———. *Men of Letters in Colonial Maryland*. Knoxville: U of Tennessee P, 1972.

Mulford, Carla. *Only for the Eye of a Friend: The Poems of Annis Boudinot Stockton*. Charlottesville: UP of Virginia, 1995.

Nussbaum, Felicity A. *The Brink of All We Hate: English Satires on Women, 1660–1750*. Lexington: UP of Kentucky, 1984.

Shields, David S. *Oracles of Empire: Poetry, Politics, and Commerce in British America, 1690–1750*. Chicago: U of Chicago P, 1990.

Vlach, John Michael. *The Afro-American Tradition in Decorative Arts*. Cleveland: Cleveland Museum of Art, 1978.

———. *Back of the Big House: The Architecture of Plantation Slavery*. Chapel Hill: U of North Carolina P, 1993.

Philip F. Gura

The Literature of Colonial English Puritanism

Some recent historical scholarship contends the Chesapeake was crucial in the formation of early American culture, yet for many early Americanists today the discourse of Puritan New England remains central to scholarship on early American literature. In the decades since Perry Miller described the "New England mind," however, particularly in the wake of the "new" social history and the concomitant emergence of scholarship centering on questions of race, class, and gender by "ideological" critics, the ways scholars interrogate New England Puritan writing have changed. Interesting new questions and concerns raised by recent criticism allow us to revivify the Puritans in ways that Miller's generation never imagined.

Some scholars, for example, particularly historians, debate how well the clerical authors on whom Miller most relied in his exhaustive studies represented the New England population as a whole (Rutman). Others like Charles Hambrick-Stowe and Charles Lloyd Cohen question Miller's unwillingness to examine the more affective dimensions of Puritan theology. Amanda Porterfield and Ivy Schweitzer describe how issues of gender, which Miller never engaged, deeply informed Puritan theology and religious experience. Still others, like Jeffrey Hammond, have enlarged our understanding of the literary dimension of Puritan writings.

Despite such revisionist work, however, Miller's paradigm remains central to scholars' conversations about New England Puritanism, and thus it is still useful to introduce the Puritans through his work, particularly his justly famous essay "Errand into the Wilderness," in which he spells out his understanding of the reasons for Puritan settlement of the New World. There and elsewhere he explains the Puritan mission as linked inextricably to the deteriorating prospects for religious reform in England and, after 1660, to the New Englanders' increasing sense that they too had failed at reform. Against this background students can discuss Governor John Winthrop's "Modell of Christian Charity" and Samuel Danforth's *New England's Errand*, seminal texts for understanding how New Englanders came to view their place in history. The instructor then can complicate students' understanding of the reasons for New England's settlement by introducing the revisionary work of Sacvan Bercovitch, whose adumbration of Miller was formative for ideological critics and has controlled much writing about the Puritans in the 1970s and 1980s. Bercovitch argues that Miller underestimates the progressivist thrust of the jeremiad and its concomitant cooptation of any significant challenge to the dominant, "middle-class" ideology it engendered. By examining the Puritans using both Miller and Bercovitch, students are challenged to reconsider the pieties with which we usually speak of the New England colonists (Bercovitch, *American Jeremiad*).

Having established this dual perspective, the instructor can move in several directions. Students might investigate the relevance to the debate between Miller's and Bercovitch's adherents of William Bradford's understanding of the Pilgrim mission as illustrated in "Of Plymouth Plantation." They might inquire if such first-generation Puritans as Thomas Shepard, in his "Autobiography" (*God's Plot*) or Edward Johnson, in *Wonder-Working Providence*, were as self-consciously "American" as Bercovitch suggests. Or they might consider to what extent Anne Bradstreet's "Dialogue between Old England and New"

(Bradstreet, *Works* 179–88) is a gendered commentary on the Puritan mission (Bradford; Shepard, *God's Plot* 35–80; Johnson). Students also might be encouraged to test Theodore Dwight Bozeman's claim, widely accepted by historians if not by literary critics, that Miller and Bercovitch make too much of the "errand" as a theme in early American culture. To the contrary, Bozeman finds it a rather uncharacteristic trope in Puritan writing, and his conclusions can be tested by further reading of Winthrop's *Journal* or William Hubbard's *General History of New England*. At the least, students thus confront how literary criticism is often determined, for better or worse, by critics' agendas.

Because both Miller's and Bercovitch's rhetorically powerful formulations of New England Puritanism encourage the problematic persistence in scholarship of American exceptionalism and of purported continuities between colonial literature and American Renaissance literature, it is important that students read New England literature in a transatlantic perspective. By engaging, for example, more personal texts that speak to the purpose of the Great Migration — Winthrop's "Christian Experience," say, and Bradstreet's autobiographical "To My Dear Children" — the class can discuss why many literary scholars continue to insist on the primacy of New England ideas from early in the subsequent formation of what Miller termed the American "mind" and Bercovitch, the American "ideology" (Gura, "Study" 305–09). By examining the construction of American exceptionalism, students can see first-hand why many historians of British North America vociferously argue that the New England colonies, like others in the New World, were merely cultural outposts of Britain. Here they also might entertain William Spengemann's provocative notion that even to speak about American literature in this period is fatuous, because the literature in fact was only a version of that written in *English* (*New World*).

To pursue this discussion, teachers can assign readings from the extant conversion narratives of Thomas Shepard's Cambridge church, narratives that Patricia Caldwell considers "the beginnings of American expression," for they alert students to how the rank and file themselves spoke about how English Puritans became "American"

(Shepard, *God's Plot* 149–227; Caldwell). Students can compare the poems in the first edition of Bradstreet's *Tenth Muse* (1650) with those added to the second (1678) or consider whether there is a difference between the early 1630s and the late 1640s in Governor Winthrop's treatment, in his "Journal" (239–41), of his sense of New England's mission. Instructors should contextualize the "missionary" aspect of New England's settlement within the larger frame of English Puritan reform — they can do so economically by summarizing the scholarship of Stephen Foster or Bozeman, both of whom insist that American Puritanism be treated primarily as a variant of English church reform. The class can then compare texts by "American" Puritans that were composed before their authors' migration — Thomas Hooker's *The Danger of Desertion* and Cotton's *God's Promise to His Plantations*, say — to later work by these or other ministers (Shepard's sermon series "The Parable of the Ten Virgins" [c. 1637] is a good choice) to examine settlers' self-consciousness about being in the New World (Foster; Bozeman, *Ancient Lives*; Hooker; Cotton; Shepard, "Parable"). They also can evaluate Bercovitch's widely accepted claim for "the Puritan origins of the American self" (*Puritan Origins*).

Thus charting the Puritans' self-consciousness about being in the New World, students also become aware of the manifold ways the making of a "New" England, the renovation of the Church of England three thousand miles from the center of clerical authority, contributed to the debate over who the Puritans were and what they were doing in America. Reading Winthrop's account of Anne Hutchinson's church trial for heresy (*Short Story*) and Roger Williams's tracts on toleration, students see that, free to organize their spiritual and political lives in accordance with their understanding of Scripture, New Englanders from an early date often disagreed on matters of ecclesiastical and civil polity. Unanimity of doctrine was never the rule, and particularly in first- and second-generation texts, students can consider examples of the varieties of American Puritanism — not, that is, the New England "mind" but various New England "minds."

This is the thrust of revisionary scholars' work, and it is easily demonstrated through comparing the various texts surrounding Hutchinson and Williams with such doctrinal statements as the Cambridge Platform (Gura, *Glimpse*; Delbanco, *Puritan Ordeal*; Knight; Hall, *Antinomian Controversy*; Walker 194–237).

One can use such sources concerning Puritan radicalism, particularly Winthrop's *Short Story* of Hutchinson's trial, many ways, but most important to show how New Englanders understood and responded to the range of possibilities for spiritual and ecclesiastical reform spun from Puritanism's centripetal motion (Winthrop, *Short Story*). As Knight has shown, for example, and as students can explore in the writings of her protagonist, John Cotton, well after the Hutchinsonians' defeat the clergy remained bifurcated into preparationists and spiritists, in ways that indelibly marked the development of New England theology.

Reviewing Puritan radicalism in the colonies is another way the class may engage Spengemann's claims about the necessity to treat all this early writing as the literature of British North America, not as "American" literature (Spengemann, *Mirror* and *New World*). When New England dissent is treated as part and parcel of transatlantic debates over the inherently schismatic nature of Puritanism, and more specifically New England's tacit encouragement of such fragmentation through espousing a congregational polity, the intellectual ferocity of such texts from the 1640s and 1650s as Johnson's *Wonder-Working Providence* becomes explicable. Reminding students of Williams's friendship with John Milton and of Milton's interest in Williams's treatises on liberty of conscience as he considered the same subject further cautions against too parochial a view of what constitutes American literature. Thus, like the personal narratives from the 1630s that indicate the range of opinion about what it meant to go to New England, the polemical literature of later decades engages students in the question of what was at stake for scholars who chose to read the discourse of Puritan New England apart from that of England itself.

After the instructor has complicated students' notions of New England's founding and its subsequent intellectual development (vis-à-vis the emergence of a discourse, if not yet a literature, that we can term "American"), the class can consider how Puritan literature contributed as well to a renovated understanding of the self and its relation to the other. After being introduced to this unit through consideration of what the modernist poet John Berryman, in his "Homage to Mistress Bradstreet," found powerful and convincing in his illustrious predecessor, the class can begin to appreciate the luminosity of the quotidian that marks some of the Puritans' best writing, particularly Bradstreet's and Taylor's verse (Berryman 11–34; Bradstreet, *Works* 144–48; Taylor 309).

If students are fully to appreciate this literature's power, though, the instructor should not divorce aesthetics from theology but engage head-on the religious doctrine that underlies these personal writings. Winthrop's "Christian Experience" and Shepard's "Autobiography" (Shepard, *God's Plot* 35–80), for example, explain how the adherents of the Puritan faith found validated in its inescapable undulations scriptural notions of the impermanence of all earthly things and thus the Bible's counsel to trust all to faith. Students will find Shepard's moving acceptance of the death of his first wife — "But I am the Lord's, and he may do with me what he will" — not a cry of defeat but rather the acknowledgment of someone who has taken his true measure and found the greater glory in God (*God's Plot* 73). Similarly, Anne Bradstreet's "Upon the Burning of Her House," as searching an account as we have of a Puritan's discovery that she should be in the world but not of it, finds the poet thrown back from her self to the rock on which true faith must be built and marks her not so much the ancestor of Emily Dickinson as an exemplary Puritan. As alien to some students as such points of Calvinist doctrine might be, they are the undeniable foundation of Puritan self-expression.

But as both Shepards's and Bradstreet's texts reveal in their demonstration of their authors' continuing regard for the things of this world, students also discover that, though Puritans demanded an acknowledgment of the insignificance of the self in the face of God, they found the ego difficult to subdue. This encouraged a psychological drama whose explication in Puritan literature provides another window on the texts' potential Americanness. Cotton Mather, for example, offers a prime example of this conundrum; for as Mitchell Breitwieser has noted of this exemplary Puritan, Mather simultaneously showed self-effacement and self-aggrandizement as he sought to refashion himself to negotiate the rapid shifts between the seventeenth and eighteenth centuries. Teachers can contrast the optimism of Mather's directions for spiritual busyness in his *Bonifacius* with the piercing self-doubt of his *Diary*, enabling students to see how painful the move from Puritan to Yankee culture was.

Another valuable text for introducing students to the demands New Englanders made on themselves is Mather's "Life of Winthrop." As Bercovitch has shown in his exegesis of this segment of the *Magnalia Christi Americana*, an acceptance of the vanity of earthly wishes could nurture in some settlers a vigorous, forward-looking ethic that had its counterpart in their ministers' postmillennial vision (Bercovitch, *Puritan Origins* and *American Jeremiad* 3–30). Indeed Bercovitch views this ethic as the seed of the middle-class hegemony that most identifies the liberal culture of the United States. Progress — the spiritual growth of the self outlined in Shepard's "Journal" as well as in Jonathan Edwards's "Personal Narrative" and of the Christian community, as detailed in Edwards's *History of the Work of Redemption* — was understood as the proud assumption of one's role, no matter how small, in God's supernal plan (Shepard 81–134; Edwards, *Reader* 281–96, 124–36; Bercovitch, *Puritan Origins* 1–34).

After considering how Puritans vividly renovated their understanding of the self through their theological emphases, students can move to the colonists' depiction of community, particularly in polemical literature like Winthrop's "little speech" on liberty ("Journal" 243–45) and in more explicitly historical accounts like Bradford's *History*. The inescapable tension in Puritan culture between individual and community goals, epitomized in Samuel Sewall's "Diary," caused no small degree of consternation and confusion and demanded frequent rationalization. Students are quick to point out, for example, that the Puritans' much-vaunted ethic of charity was severely compromised by the colonists' treatment of Native Americans and those within communities who practiced magic and were thus condemned as "witches." Admittedly, the literature devoted to categorizing and neutralizing such marginal figures composes the least attractive component of New England Puritan literature, but students still should explore representative texts, if only to ascertain how fragile a bond held together Puritan self and society.

By examining witchcraft, for example, students can discuss not only how the "other" very often was a projection of the Puritans' own fears about themselves but also the problematic relation between "folk" and "high" culture, a subject that recently has become central to consideration of early American culture (Hall, *Worlds* 71–116; Godbeer; Delbanco, *Death*). The New Englanders' reliance on interpreting supernatural wonders and signs and their attempts to control their environment through astrology and white magic, everywhere visible in Sewall's and Mather's diaries and in Increase Mather's *Illustrious Providences*, vividly remind readers that the crime of witchcraft occupied only one pole on the continuum of folk belief and that at best the line between clerical and popular religious belief was blurry. Similarly, reading Cotton Mather's "Wonders" alongside Robert Calef's satirical denunciation of the Salem witch trials alerts students to late-seventeenth-century New England writers' confrontation with not only the pain of their degeneracy but a future whose terms were set more and more by the discourse of the Enlightenment, a fact brought home vividly through a comparison of Cotton Mather's *Christian Philosopher* with Jonathan Edwards's "Images or Shadows of Divine Things." Particularly as the class moves on to early-eighteenth-century Puritanism, then, the instructor should emphasize the constant challenges to the Puritans' understanding of their faith and the accommodations they made in order to presume that they still inhabited the religious world of their fathers.

Alerted to the ways in which popular religious beliefs existed alongside a more formal and complex theology, students can easily move to Indian captivity narratives, which, like witchcraft literature, are enriched by a consideration of their often-gendered language. The captivity accounts by Mary Rowlandson and Hannah Dustan (C. Mather, "Narrative"), for example, are as much about the expectations of Puritan society for these women as about the horrors of existence among the ultimate "other." Even as students find themselves intrigued by the violence described by Rowlandson or John Williams, however, they should be reminded, as Richard Slotkin has demonstrated, that the potential attraction of Native American life is what made these histories truly horrific to their Puritan readers. Eunice Williams, John's daughter, who chose never to return from her captivity, offers a particularly memorable example of the acceptability of Native life for some and demonstrates what writers as far back as Thomas Morton of Merrymount knew: the wilderness was potentially as seductive and attractive as it was terrifying (Demos). Attending to the moving narratives that express such ambivalence, students can address the degree to which the commonly accepted Eurocentric accounts of the Indian wars are more wish fulfillment than fact.

Narratives of witchcraft, the wilderness, and Native Americans, then, vividly demonstrate that precisely when New England Puritans wrote self-consciously about themselves they frequently juxtaposed the self with things different or other. Thus, by the early eighteenth century, even the region of which they were a part, "New England," was increasingly defined by that which *it* was not — specifically, England. Such transitional figures as Cotton Mather, Benjamin Colman, and Sewall, for example, struggled to speak to two audiences and remain relevant to both — that is, to address the concerns of their immediate neighbors as well as the transatlantic community of discourse whose center was London. Their milieu defined by the "club" culture that had developed in various British North American colonies by the 1720s, colonists of the generation after Cotton Mather — what we might term the last Puritan generation — became obsessed not by the self in America but by the self in British America (Shields, esp. 1–12). Whether this attitude hastened the decline of New England Puritanism or was merely a result of its internal tensions is moot. When, however, widespread religious revivals broke out in 1739 in the wake of George Whitefield's initial visit to America, peoples' spiritual lives were revivified not by a new, virile strain of Puritanism but rather by a novel form of pietism nurtured across the Atlantic, one that privileged emotion in a new way and demanded a sensibility as much literary as religious.

Far from being an outdated exercise in filiopiety, then, the study of New England Puritan literature immerses both instructor and students in this complex evolution and thus provides the opportunity to engage some of the most important questions about early America now being framed by historians and literary critics alike. The varied reasons for settling the New World and calling it one's own; the manifold ways in which Europeans came to view themselves, over time, as "Americans"; how an American self might differ, in its self-referentiality as well as in its understanding of others, from the European; how concepts of the other — dissidents, participants in rival religious systems (like witchcraft), or Native Americans — framed colonial identity: these and a host of other topics leap from the pages of New England texts, testament to their undeniable richness as discourse and their continuing centrality to our understanding of early American culture.

Works Cited

Primary Works

Berryman, John. *"Homage to Mistress Bradstreet" and Other Poems*. New York: Noonday, 1970.

Bradford, William. "Of Plymouth Plantation." Gunn 120–37.

Bradstreet, Anne. "To My Dear Children." Heimert and Delbanco 137–41.

———. "Upon the Burning of Her House." Heimert and Delbanco 144–46.

———. *The Works of Anne Bradstreet*. Ed. Jeannine Hensley. Cambridge: Harvard UP, 1967.

Calef, Robert. "More Wonders of the Invisible World." Heimert and Delbanco 347–50.

Colman, Benjamin. "Practical Discourses on the Parable of the Ten Virgins." Heimert and Delbanco 370–78.

Cotton, John. *God's Promise to His Plantations*. Heimert and Delbanco 75–80.

Danforth, Samuel. "New England's Errand into the Wilderness." Gunn 198–208.

Edwards, Jonathan. *A History of the Work of Redemption (Sermon One)*. Edwards, *Reader* 124–36.

———. "Images or Shadows of Divine Things." Edwards, *Reader* 16–21.

———. *A Jonathan Edwards Reader*. Ed. John E. Smith, Harry S. Stout, and Kevin P. Minkema. New Haven: Yale UP, 1995.

Gunn, Giles, ed. *Early American Writing*. New York: Penguin, 1994.

Heimert, Alan, and Andrew Delbanco, eds. *The Puritans in America: A Narrative Anthology*. Cambridge: Harvard UP, 1985.

Hooker, Thomas. *The Danger of Desertion*. Heimert and Delbanco 62–69.

Hubbard, William. *A General History of New England, from the Discovery to MDCLXXX*. C. 1680. Cambridge: Massachusetts Historical Soc., 1815.

Johnson, Edward. Excerpt from *Wonder-Working Providence of Sion's Savior in New England*. Heimert and Delbanco 112–16.

Mather, Cotton. *Bonifacius: An Essay upon the Good*. Ed. David Levin. Cambridge: Harvard UP, 1966.

———. *The Christian Philosopher*. Ed. Winton U. Solberg. Urbana: U of Illinois P, 1994.

———. "Cotton Mather's 'Life of John Winthrop.'" Bercovitch, *Puritan Origins* 187–205.

———. *The Diary of Cotton Mather*. 2 vols. New York: Ungar, 1957.

———. "A Narrative of Hannah Dustan's Notable Deliverance from Captivity." Vaughan and Clark 159–64.

———. "Wonders of the Invisible World." Heimert and Delbanco 337–41.

Mather, Increase. "Illustrious Providences." *Narratives of the Witchcraft Cases*. Ed. George Lincoln Burr. New York: Scribner's, 1914. 1–38.

Rowlandson, Mary. "The Sovereignty and Goodness of God." Vaughan and Clark 29–76.

Sewall, Samuel. "Diary." Gunn 247–53.

Shepard, Thomas. *God's Plot: Puritan Spirituality in Thomas Shepard's Cambridge*. Ed. Michael McGiffert. Amherst: U of Massachusetts P, 1994.

———. "The Parable of the Ten Virgins." Heimert and Delbanco 171–75.

Taylor, Edward. "Poems." Heimert and Delbanco 294–315.

Vaughan, Alden, and Edward W. Clark. *Puritans among the Indians: Accounts of Captivity and Redemption, 1676–1724*. Cambridge: Harvard UP, 1981.

Williams, Roger. "The Bloudy Tenent of Persecution." Heimert and Delbanco 196–200.

Winthrop, John. "Christian Experience." Gunn 113–18.

———. "Journal." *The Heath Anthology of American Literature*. Ed. Paul Lauter. 2nd ed. Vol. 1. Lexington: Heath, 1994. 239–45.

———. "Modell of Christian Charity." Heimert and Delbanco 81–92.

———. "On Arbitrary Government." *Puritan Political Ideas, 1558–1794*. Ed. Edmund S. Morgan. Indianapolis: Bobbs, 1965. 149–60.

———. *Short Story*. Hall, *Antinomian Controversy* 199–310.

Secondary Works

Bercovitch, Sacvan. *The American Jeremiad*. Madison: U of Wisconsin P, 1978.

———. *The Puritan Origins of the American Self*. New Haven: Yale UP, 1975.

Bozeman, Theodore Dwight. "The Puritans' 'Errand into the Wilderness' Reconsidered." *New England Quarterly* 59 (1986): 231–51.

———. *To Live Ancient Lives: The Primitivist Dimension in Puritanism*. Chapel Hill: U of North Carolina P, 1988.

Cohen, Charles Lloyd. *God's Caress: The Psychology of Puritan Religious Experience*. New York: Oxford UP, 1986.

Delbanco, Andrew. *The Death of Satan: How Americans Have Lost the Sense of Evil*. New York: Farrar, 1995.

———. *The Puritan Ordeal*. Cambridge: Harvard UP, 1989.

Demos, John. *The Unredeemed Captive: A Family Story from Early America*. New York: Knopf, 1994.

Foster, Stephen. *The Long Argument: English Puritanism and the Shaping of*

New England Culture, 1570–1700. Chapel Hill: U of North Carolina P, 1991.

Godbeer, Richard. *The Devil's Dominion: Magic and Religion in Early New England*. New York: Cambridge UP, 1992.

Gura, Philip F. *A Glimpse of Sion's Glory: Puritan Radicalism in New England, 1620–1660*. Middletown: Wesleyan UP, 1984.

———. "The Study of Early American Literature, 1966–1987: A *Vade Mecum*." *William and Mary Quarterly* 3rd ser. 45 (1988): 305–41.

Hall, David D. *The Antinomian Controversy, 1636–1638: A Documentary History*. Middletown: Wesleyan UP, 1968.

———. *Worlds of Wonder, Days of Judgment: Popular Religious Belief in Early New England*. New York: Knopf, 1989.

Hambrick-Stowe, Charles. *The Practice of Piety: Puritan Devotional Disciplines in Seventeenth-Century New England*. Chapel Hill: U of North Carolina P, 1982.

Hammond, Jeffrey. *Sinful Self, Saintly Self: The Puritan Poetry of Experience*. Athens: U of Georgia P, 1993.

Knight, Janice. *Orthodoxies in Massachusetts: Rereading American Puritanism*. Cambridge: Harvard UP, 1994.

Miller, Perry. *Errand into the Wilderness*. Cambridge: Harvard UP, 1956.

Porterfield, Amanda. *Female Piety in Puritan New England: The Emergence of Religious Humanism*. New York: Oxford UP, 1992.

Rutman, Darrett B. *American Puritanism: Faith and Practice*. Philadelphia: Lippincott, 1970.

Schweitzer, Ivy. *The Work of Self-Representation: Lyric Poetry in Colonial New England*. Chapel Hill: U of North Carolina P, 1991.

Shields, David S. *Oracles of Empire: Poetry, Politics, and Commerce in British America, 1690–1750*. Chicago: U of Chicago P, 1990.

Slotkin, Richard. *Regeneration through Violence: The Mythology of the American Frontier, 1600–1800*. Middletown: Wesleyan UP, 1973.

Spengemann, William. *A Mirror for Americanists: Reflections on the Idea of American Literature*. Hanover: UP of New England, 1989.

———. *A New World of Words: Redefining Early American Literature*. New Haven: Yale UP, 1994.

Walker, Williston. *The Creeds and Platforms of Congregationalism*. 1925. Boston: Pilgrim, 1960.

Frank Shuffelton

The American Enlightenment and Endless Emancipation

At the first reference to the Enlightenment as a period or a cultural phenomenon, a certain wary look often steals across the eyes of some students, an indication that they think they are supposed to know what the Enlightenment is but that they have only the vaguest notion of it. The Enlightenment is often unfamiliar to our students because it failed to play a major role in several of the important founding narratives of American literature; Perry Miller jumped from Edwards to Emerson, and Vernon Parrington tended to avoid the term in favor of describing the influences of "English Independency and French romantic theory" (x).[1] More important, they are suspicious of the seemingly overenthusiastic and optimistic terms in which enlightened thinkers seem to describe themselves. Rather than sharing Kant's celebration of "man's release from his self-imposed tutelage" and embracing his call to "dare to use your own reason" (463), they have enough sense of history to be instinctively more sympathetic to Max Horkheimer and Theodor Adorno's 1944 claim that "the fully enlightened earth radiates disaster triumphant," even if they have never heard of the Frankfurt School (3). The Age of Reason seems to many of them more like the cant of reason, and when they first read great texts of the American Enlightenment such as Franklin's *Autobiography*, Crèvecoeur's *Letters*, or Jefferson's *Notes on the State of Virginia*, they not infrequently find them boring or even oppressive. "He's so pompous," they say of Franklin; Crèvecoeur's apparent self-contradictions seem to them only insincere or hypocritical, and Jefferson's discussion of racial differences crowds out recognition of anything else he might have to say.

These are surely limited, limiting responses to these texts, but students who respond in this way are right, at least as far as they go. The Enlightenment and its writings are problematic, and we cannot simply pass out copies of Franklin's *Autobiography* as Andrew Carnegie once did in the expectation that it would change people's lives. When students come to recognize Franklin's humor that invites them to laugh at him and themselves, the *Autobiography* becomes a considerably more complex and interesting text. Crèvecoeur and Jefferson are less easily redeemed by humor than Franklin, but they, along with many other participants in the American Enlightenment, begin to appear more interesting when we teachers show that their apparent self-contradictions represent the problems at the heart of the modernity in which we still live. To do this, we need to conceptualize the Enlightenment so as to reaffirm what Horkheimer and Adorno characterized as "the dialectical link between enlightenment and domination, and the dual relationship of progress to cruelty and liberation" (169). The Western apparatus of "reason" can become a specious excuse to reject as inhuman and irrational those who do not fit its standards and to subjugate them under regimes of patriarchy, literacy, and empire. Thus Henry Louis Gates, Jr., argues that the eighteenth century's privileging of the written word as the sign of "the presence of a common humanity" embedded a dominating "racist discourse" in Western thought (*Figures* 14). Enlightened reason can reduce the world to mere systems of observable facts and, as Michel Foucault has pointed out, "cover with its dominating network the inert, grey space of empiricity" (341). Yet at the same time enlightened reason also brought with it scientific and technical discoveries that significantly improved the material possibilities of human life, and it has underwritten that respect for individual men and women that Jürgen Habermas and others describe as the unfinished emancipatory project of the Enlightenment. The notion of a common humanity shared by every individual was a radical idea that informed the American Revolution, the international movement to abolish slavery, and the vindication of the rights of women. *The Age of Reason* is an empty term, deserving of our students' tepid responses, but the Enlightenment dialectic of knowledge and freedom, presented in all its troubled complexity, can seize and enlarge their imaginations.

It is one thing to have a conceptual vision, however, and another to introduce it into the discourse of the classroom. It is necessary to locate the thematic sites on which the Enlightenment operates most clearly in America even as we pay attention to its more cosmopolitan phenomena such as Shaftesburian ethics, Augustan literary norms, or republican political theory. The Enlightenment dialectic between domination and emancipation, knowledge and freedom, perhaps most clearly reveals itself in American writers through three strategies: first, the often difficult and conflicted move to value the humanity, the subjectivity, of those who are "other" than the assumed norm of European males, particularly women, Native Americans, and African Americans; second, the creation of the so-called public sphere, in which the "critical reasoning of private persons on political issues" ushered in new forms of life on every level (Habermas 29); finally, the critique of reason itself, the process of self-examination that made the Enlightenment the first scene of restless modernity. It is crucial in the classroom to recognize each of these Enlightenment strategies as an ongoing process, not necessarily progressive and certainly never complete. In our time we still struggle against racism, new voices continue to demand a place in the national conversation, and we who try to teach the young to reason are most successful when we find ourselves reasoned against. If we are to present the Enlightenment as an argument, we might best succeed by extending that dialectic into the classroom, for ultimately a rational critique of the Enlightenment affirms one of its central and enduring values. How do we do this? Perhaps by engaging the students in a discussion that opens up the complex, often contradictory, sometimes ironic and skeptical world of American Enlightenment writers. It might go like this.

From the moment of first contact between Europe and the New World, the Native Americans posed a challenge to European assumptions about human nature and culture. Once they admitted that Indians were fully human, most European writers found it necessary to label them under the category of "savage" in order to keep their way of life from contaminating "civilization." Even a sympathetic, shrewd ethnographic observer like Roger Williams reduced his Narragansetts to one more set of natural signs, typologically conceived, that a provident deity had set up for the moral edification of European Christians. In spite of Williams's hopes for Christianizing the Indians, the "Wild Americans" are "Natures Sons," and as such they function as an external system of monitory signs for "Sonnes of God" (99). A century later, however, Cadwallader Colden's *History of the Five Indian Nations* (1747) avoided Williams's ethnographic present and inserted the Iroquois into history, albeit a specifically European history. Yet precisely because Colden included them in the history of European imperial conflict, the Five Nations could appear as agents with their own motives and ends. If he still denoted them as barbaric, he also understood them within the categories of European civil life, particularly as "War-like" soldiers and "Polite" diplomats (14). Although Colden offers only a glimpse of what the Iroquois were before the arrival of the Europeans, the place of the Five Nations in the pattern of temporal change that he calls history allows them a freedom to reflect on themselves and the world. No longer mere types of wildness as they were for Williams, they possess a subjectivity that enables them to participate in dialectic engagement with an expanding Atlantic culture.

Caught between contending European powers, Colden's Indians are skilled orators and treaty makers who repeatedly defend their independence with deeds and with speeches that insist on the validity of their view of the world and themselves. When the English try to prevent the Onondaga from talking with M. de la Barre, the French emissary, they reply, "You say we are Subjects to the King of England and the Duke of York, but we say, we are Brethren. We must take care of our selves. Those Arms fixed upon the Post without the Gate, cannot defend us against the Arms of La Barre" (51). When the French try to press aggressively what seems to be an advantage, Garangula, the Onondaga spokesman, replies in no uncertain terms, "We are born free, We neither depend upon Yonnondio nor Corlaer. We may go where we please, and carry with us whom we please, and buy and sell what we please" (55). Whether the pun on "arms" owes to the Onondaga original or the translator, the Five Nations make clear that they are skilled rhetoricians, self-conscious and shrewd about their linguistic strategies. During a ceremony in which the Oneidas released some prisoners, Swerisse, a chief, reminds the English that a captured Oneida woman had not been returned, threatening, "If Corlaer will not hearken to us in this Affair, we shall not hereafter hearken to him in any." When the English commissioners take offense, the other Oneida chiefs reassure them, "What we said of not hearkening any more to Corlaer, was not from the heart, but only by way of Discourse, to make Corlaer more careful to release our People that are Prisoners" (27). Colden's extensive representation of the Indian "way of Discourse" establishes the Five Nations as subjects neither to a European king nor to European culture but as speaking subjects (i.e., subjects in a very different sense) whose self-consciousness about the power of language to shape their world makes them out to be as fundamentally "modern" as the French and English they engage.

Paradoxically, of course, the Five Nations enjoyed the freedom Colden depicts only as long as they could play off the French and English against each other, and when Colden looks for ethical standards by which to measure the Indians, he finds them in the Roman history that underlies his own culture. When a group of aged Mohawks refuse to flee their village during a French-led attack and are killed, they are likened to "Old Roman Senators" who "would rather dye than desert their Houses" (17). Decanesora, the Onondaga leader, "had a great Fluency in speaking, and a graceful Elocution, that would have pleased in any Part of the World. His Person was tall and well made, and his Features, to my thinking, resembled much the Bustos of Cicero" (140). Enclosed within Colden's presumptively universal categories of European discourse, Decanesora, or Teganissorens as he was known to his own people, nevertheless becomes a particularized authoritative voice for Colden, who later comments, "I choose to give an Account of this [conference] from Decanesora's Mouth, [. . .] The Account given of it by the Indians agrees, in all the material Points, with that published by the French, and I am confident it is not less genuine" (152). Decanesora achieves his particularity because of, not despite, Colden's assumed universality of reason among men, which impels Colden to find the signs of reason among those who are culturally other.

Although many writers continued to regard Indians as "savage," American writers most closely identified with Enlightenment values continued Colden's attention to Indian speaking subjects. Frequently Indian speakers demonstrate the power of genuine subjectivity to surprise or challenge, to use their reason in ways that disrupt and free up conventional patterns of thought and behavior. Thus Franklin begins his ironically titled "Remarks concerning the Savages of North America" by dryly commenting, "Savages we call them, because their manners differ from ours, which we think the Perfection of Civility; they think the same of theirs" (969). He concludes his subversion of his own society's confounding of ethics and commerce with Canassetego informing Conrad Weiser of his suspicions that when the white men gathered in church on Sunday "whatever they pretended of Meeting to learn *good things*, the real Purpose was to consult, how to cheat Indians in the Price of Beaver" (974). Crèvecoeur makes Andrew the Hebridean pass through a comically unsettling encounter with a party of Indians at Mr. P. R.'s house before he can be fully initiated in his Americanness (99), and Jefferson in *Notes on the State of Virginia* includes Logan's famous speech as a reproof to European natural historians who theorized about New World degeneracy. Instead of being dominated by the category of reason, these Indians are freed by it into their own speaking particularity.

Yet we should also recognize with our students that, as Adorno and others have charged, reason can also be used as a principle of domination. Jefferson's recognition of Indian reasoning seems to contradict his strictures on African intellectual powers, which attempt to exclude blacks from a putatively reasonable Euro-American civility. Yet if he used reason to underwrite a racist discourse that excluded Africans, he refused to use it to justify slavery, and, more problematically, his denial of reason to those already socially and politically dominated by the institution of slavery would seem to call into question the category of reason itself. His thinking in this instance brings reason under suspicion as a somewhat arbitrary attempt to legitimate an already existing mode of oppression. Jefferson, perhaps above all other writers of the period, foregrounds the problematic Enlightenment dialectic because he is the thinker who most forcefully urges a reasoned emancipatory discourse of equality while at nearly the same time appealing to a notion of "reason" as a strategy to insist on inequalities in his society.

The recognition of reason in others during the American Enlightenment was thus a complex and troubled process, incomplete at best, but a distinguishing mark of the period. The written word was the privileged sign of rationality, and by the end of the eighteenth century women, Indian, and African American writers appeared in print to signify that reason was not a uniquely white or masculine possession. John Marrant, Phillis Wheatley, Mercy Otis Warren, and Judith Sargent Murray benefited from universalizing assumptions of reason in all humans, but at the same time they were enabled by the emergence of a new notion of public life in which reasoning men and women could speak and be heard. Jürgen Habermas's notion of the public sphere has been influential in recent scholarship and criticism of this period, but it has been insufficiently noticed that Habermas restricts the public sphere neither to print culture nor to the discourse of politics and government. The public sphere flourished in the oral culture of taverns and tea tables as well as in the rich manuscript culture of the eighteenth century, and it embraced discourses of aesthetics and belles lettres as well as of science and learning.[2] Cadwallader Colden, for example, who had been so attentive to the public discourse that negotiated the boundary between the Five Nations and the British Empire, was also a notable contributor to the discourse of science. Trained as a physician, Colden turned his attention to natural philosophy in New York, where his account of the flora attracted international attention and engaged him in a widespread correspondence with amateur and professional scientists.

Colden's scientific correspondence brought him into an American network of writers who shared his interests, particularly Alexander Garden of South Carolina, John Mitchell, John Bartram, and Benjamin Franklin. He was apparently the first to suggest the formation of an intercolonial scientific society, proposing in 1728 to William Douglass of Boston "a Voluntary Society for the advancing of Knowledge" (Hindle 60). The idea recurred during the 1740s in his correspondence with Franklin, where Colden supported Bartram's scheme for a philosophical society. The suggestion bore fruit in Franklin's 1743 "Proposal for Promoting Useful Knowledge among the British Plantations in America" that laid the foundations for the American Philosophical Society, which came together in Philadelphia in 1767. This network of early scientists eventually included notable writers such as Bartram's son William, Benjamin Rush, and Jefferson, who eventually became president of the Philosophical Society. Their work aimed to bring the unknown worlds of the American continent — the external world of nature and the internal world of human behavior — under the discipline of reason, to reduce a fearsome (if sometimes sublimely exhilarating) wildness to a web of knowledge. Franklin's writings on electricity, the first volumes of the society's *Transactions*, Rush's *Medical Inquiries and Observations upon the Diseases of the Mind*, William Bartram's *Travels*, and Jefferson's *Notes on the State of Virginia* are all examples of this scientific impulse. But if these texts are all driven in some way by a will to knowledge, they speak in different voices. The scientific public sphere was constituted by speakers and writers who came from diverse positions in society, from the formally trained and politically well-connected Colden to Franklin the upstart tradesman and John Bartram the self-educated farmer. If they sought to speak as equals in knowledge, they did so within the convention of a society of individual participants, a society typically conceived of as one whose transactions would consist of the differently voiced submissions of widely distant members.

The scientific public sphere, in other words, was, like its parallel constructions, a conversation, an attempted realization of a central trope of the enlightened world. Its texts were intended as responses to an ongoing exercise of rational inquiry that characterized a civilization that transcended distinctions between Europe and America and between West and East. (This fantasy of a universal spirit of civilization was behind the eighteenth-century genre of fictional travelers from the Orient who commented on Western culture, for example, Montesquieu's *Persian Letters*, Goldsmith's *Citizen of the World*, and, in a peculiar sense perhaps, Crèvecoeur's *Letters*.) Thus Jefferson wrote his *Notes* in response to a request from a visiting French intellectual, François de Marbois, and aimed to answer the arguments advanced by European natural historians, particularly the comte de Buffon, that all life forms, including human beings, degenerate in mind and body under the American climate. Jefferson's composition of the *Notes* involved him in correspondence with a variety of informants; he submitted a draft of the manuscript for comments from Charles Thomson, the president of the Continental Congress, and after the first, limited publication he sent copies to a selected but wide group of readers. Finally, his finished text resists the apparently simple coherence of narrative but is organized as responses to twenty-three separate queries, offering not a naturalized portrait of Virginia but a collage, a colloquy in effect, of twenty-three voices speaking out of different subject positions.

The conversational ideal is central even to William Bartram, who became for later Romantic readers like Coleridge an archetypal solitary promenader. He begins his *Travels* by acknowledging that he is answering "the request of Dr. Fothergill, of London, to search the Floridas, and the western parts of Carolina and Georgia, for the discovery of rare and useful productions of nature" (29). He encounters a nature informed with the principles of reason, which support both aesthetic and moral insights, including the discovery of a basis in nature for the fundamental ethic of polite conversation. He finds a spring "where the water or element in which [the fish] live and move, is so perfectly clear and transparent, it places them all on an equality with regard to their ability to injure or escape from one another; [. . .] what is really surprising is, that the consciousness of each other's safety, or some other latent cause, should so absolutely alter their conduct, for here is not the least attempt made to injure or disturb one another" (151). This situation corresponds to what Warner calls "the principle of supervision," "a paradoxical kind of discipline" (41) in which speakers encounter conversation "not as a relation between themselves as men, but rather as their own mediation by a potentially limitless discourse" (40). Bartram points out that the fish retain their predatory natures; only their behavior is changed by the transparent medium in which they find themselves. Like Bartram's fish, participants in the open exchange of the public sphere are liberated into a putative equality necessary for the citizens of the political public sphere, the polite conversation of the literary public sphere, and the exchange of knowledge of the scientific public sphere.

Bartram, however, pays as much attention to the people he meets, particularly the Indians, as to the botanical specimens requested by Fothergill, and he fills his text with conversations he takes part in during his journey. More important, the book conversationally engages Fothergill and the scientific community, the Quaker world Bartram comes from, and an American society he is not entirely at ease with. Setting out on his travels in 1773 but not publishing his account until 1791, he is largely silent about the American Revolution, which falls in the interval, but he clearly points his text toward both the concern of the early Republic for a new social order and its desire for a national expansion that will unexpectedly undermine the revolutionary promise of 1776. In his concluding pages he describes the Cherokees as model citizens of the new world: "frank, cheerful, and humane; tenacious of the liberties and natural rights of man; secret, deliberate, and determined in their councils; honest, just, and liberal, and ready always to sacrifice every pleasure and gratification, even their blood, and life itself, to defend their territory and maintain their rights" (381). Yet Indians like the Cherokees are models precisely because "they have been able to resist the continual efforts of the complicated host of vices, that resist the continual efforts of the nations of the old world," and "as moral men they certainly stand in no need of European civilization" (386, 385). Bartram's text is thoroughly of his moment, engaging in conversation contemporary voices calling for the eradication of savagery as well as those like Jefferson who would have the Indians take the next step on the ladder of progress toward civilization. At the same time his self-identification with a world governed by "the simple dictates of natural reason, plain to every one" (388) legitimates his Quakerly evasion of the revolutionary violence that brought about the republic in which he is now a citizen. Above all, Bartram entertains, a century and a half before Adorno, the suspicion of a relation between civilized reason and vice figured as civilized violence.

The polyglossic, conversational ideal underwrites many other important texts of the American Enlightenment, both externally as a rhetoric and internally as a formal principle. As Bakhtin has suggested, that ideal is perhaps fundamental to the increasing popularity of the novel in the eighteenth century, particularly evident in the case of the epistolary novel. And as a text like Judith Sargent Murray's *The Gleaner* suggests, it is connected to strategies of emancipation. *The Gleaner* is a virtual anthology of literary forms, containing a play, novel, and essays, and it supports an important argument for "the female right to that *equality with their brethren, which it is conceived, is assigned to them in the Order of Nature*" (709). Benjamin Franklin, the master of American polyglossia, formed his writing style and strategies upon the multiply voiced *Spectator* and seemed almost to prefer to speak to his public in voices that could not be simply identified as his own. Silence Dogood, the Busybody, Richard Saunders, and Polly Baker all attest to Franklin's affinity for a gallery of voices with which to engage a broad audience, and his ironic strategies in handling these voices enlarged this audience to include those who saw through his mask and those who accepted it, those who might disagree with him personally and those who were his friends. Franklin's polyglossic experiments in textual self-making culminate in the *Autobiography*, where he first speaks as a father to a son, then, in apparent response to requests by Abel James and Benjamin Vaughan, repositions himself both to have an influence "on the Minds of Youth" and to present himself as an example "of the manners and situations of a *rising* people" (1373–74). In the third part he steps forward with "*a great & extensive project*" to reform universal manners by forming a "Society of the *Free and Easy*," and he now places himself in the larger context of "the great Affairs of the World, the Wars, Revolutions, &c. [. . .] carried on and effected by Parties" (1395–96). In each rhetorical self-transformation he adopts a new subject position from which to enact versions of the self conceived for different audiences, successively defined in larger terms as the family, the nation, and "Mankind."

This fluid and dialectic sense of self, however, eventually calls into question the conception of a universal "Mankind," particularly one defined in terms of the category of reason. As Franklin assumes new faces to confront the world, he begins to seem all mask and no center, to be in effect a reasoning process and not a substantial self who possesses reason. At the same time, his shape shifting and trickery, his willingness to recognize the endless possibilities of subjectivity, inescapably aligns reason with interest and will. Franklin is one of the most interesting and important figures of the American Enlightenment because he turns reason back upon itself to reveal its limitations and to mock our misplaced pride of possession. Thus he describes "being becalm'd off Block Island, [when] our People set about catching Cod & haul'd up a great many." Having resolved to maintain a vegetarian diet, he resists taking part in the resulting meal, even though he "had formerly been a great Lover of Fish, & when this came hot out of the Frying Pan, it smelt admirably well." Balanced "between Principle & Inclination," reason loses out to appetite when he notices that some of the fish have smaller ones in their stomachs. "Then, thought I, if you eat one another, I don't see why we mayn't eat you. So I din'd upon Cod very heartily and continued to eat with other People. [. . .] So convenient a thing it is to be a *reasonable Creature*, since it enables one to find or make a Reason for every thing one has a mind to do" (1338–39). Reason is a malleable instrument for Franklin; recognition of its limits brings him into the equality of the human community and prevents him from using it as an exclusive principle. His account of his experiment in acquiring moral perfection constitutes his most profound critique of reason. A master of deadpan comedy, he describes his plan of moral self-engineering, later admitting that a Quaker friend had to prompt him to add humility to his list of virtues, and engages in rationalization after rationalization as his scheme unravels. After many erasures wear holes in his paper record book, he transfers his tables to the "Ivory Leaves of a memorandum Book [. . .] which I could easily wipe out with a wet Sponge" (1389). Although he claims that "the Endeavour made a better and a happier Man than I otherwise should have been" (1391), he admits that he ultimately failed at perfection, particularly in the matter of humility. "For even if I could conceive that I had compleatly overcome it, I should probably be proud of my Humility" (1394). Reason is not to be simply rejected — it has won its partial victory — but a final assessment must judge the victory incomplete. Of course the trick here is that Franklin's remark is precisely the thing a genuinely humble man would say; true humility must deny its presence. Yet Franklin surely knew this and knew that his readers did as well. So here may be the trickster's cleverest deception, and on we students go in an endless interrogation of his motives that turns into an unending interrogation of reason and pride. Our freedom to reason, as Franklin recognized, ultimately demands that we question even ourselves as reasoners, all the while retaining the value of reason as the sign of our freedom.

Engaging our students in a discussion like this means that we can together experience writers like Franklin, Jefferson, and Bartram as participating with us in that shared process of thinking about the world Foucault intends by seeing in the Enlightenment "the discourse of modernity on modernity" (Kelly 141). It means recognizing with Henry Louis Gates, Jr., that if the Enlightenment is the root of modern racist discourse, it also offers "a conceptual grammar of antiracism" ("Critical Remarks" 323). Recovering the overlooked concept of the American Enlightenment means, finally, that we must recognize that the concept of America is not merely exceptional but engages us in dialogue with the larger world of men and women. And that is not boring.

Notes

1. The most important historical study is May; see also Pole; Shuffelton.
2. Michael Warner employs a Habermasian scheme, but restricts his discussion to printed texts and ultimately defines the public sphere in terms of

readership rather than writing. For another view see Shields; see also Calhoun.

Works Cited

Primary Works

Bartram, William. *Travels of William Bartram*. Ed. Mark Van Doren. New York: Macy, 1928.

Colden, Cadwallader. *The History of the Five Indian Nations Depending on the Province of New-York in America*. Ithaca: Cornell UP, 1958.

Crèvecoeur, J. Hector St. John. Letters from an American Farmer *and* Sketches of Eighteenth-Century America. New York: Penguin, 1981.

Franklin, Benjamin. *Writings*. New York: Lib. of America, 1987.

Habermas, Jürgen. *The Structural Transformation of the Public Sphere: An Inquiry into a Category of Bourgeois Society*. Trans. Thomas Burger. Cambridge: MIT P, 1989.

Horkheimer, Max, and Theodor W. Adorno. *Dialectic of Enlightenment*. New York: Continuum, 1994.

Jefferson, Thomas. *Notes on the State of Virginia*. New York: Penguin, 1998.

Kant, Immanuel. "What Is Enlightenment?" *Kant: Selections*. Ed. Lewis White Beck. New York: Macmillan, 1988. 462–67.

Murray, Judith Sargent. *The Gleaner*. Schenectady: Union Coll. P, 1992.

Williams, Roger. *A Key into the Language of North America*. Ed. John J. Teunissen and Evelyn J. Hintz. Detroit: Wayne State UP, 1973.

Secondary Works

Calhoun, Craig, ed. *Habermas and the Public Sphere*. Cambridge: MIT P, 1992.

Foucault, Michel. *The Order of Things: An Archaeology of the Human Sciences*. New York: Random, 1970.

Gates, Henry Louis, Jr. "Critical Remarks." *The Anatomy of Racism*. Ed. David Theo Goldberg. Minneapolis: U of Minnesota P, 1990. 319–32.

———. *Figures in Black: Words, Signs, and the "Racial" Self*. New York: Oxford UP, 1987.

Hindle, Brooke. *The Pursuit of Science in Revolutionary America, 1735–1789*. Chapel Hill: U of North Carolina P, 1958.

Kelly, Michael. *Critique and Power: Recasting the Foucault/Habermas Debate*. Cambridge: MIT P, 1994.

May, Henry F. *The Enlightenment in America*. New York: Oxford UP, 1976.

Parrington, Vernon L. *Main Currents in American Thought: The Colonial Mind, 1620–1800*. New York: Harcourt, 1927.

Pole, J. R. "Enlightenment and the Politics of American Nature." *The Enlightenment in International Context*. Ed. Roy Porter and Mikulas Teich. Cambridge: Cambridge UP, 1981. 192–214.

Shields, David S. "British-American Belles Lettres." *The Cambridge History of*

American Literature. Ed. Sacvan Bercovitch. Vol. 1. New York: Cambridge UP, 1994. 307–44.

Shuffelton, Frank, ed. *The American Enlightenment*. Rochester: U of Rochester P, 1993.

Warner, Michael. *The Letters of the Republic: Publication and the Public Sphere in Eighteenth-Century America*. Cambridge: Harvard UP, 1990.

Nicholas D. Rombes

Federalism and Conflict

What kind of place should the new American republic be? What kinds of values should its citizens share? Can and should everyone's voice be heard in the political process? And how are the entire nation's interests to be represented? Who are "the people" in "We the People"? Studying Federalist and Anti-Federalist writings from 1786 through 1789 allows students to examine various and often conflicting questions, the answers to which still have resiliency today. Examining the conflict helps students see that during a formative and important period in our nation's history consensus was often rare and that the Constitution was produced and ratified in a sometimes contentious environment of debate. Differences between Federalists and Anti-Federalists are important also because they bring to the surface political, social, and cultural assumptions that helped determine the kind of place the United States would become. Depending on the course and on the instructor's course goals, the writings can be fruitfully taught through various lenses (political, philosophical, economic, cultural) or through an integrated approach that treats such writings as a set of often conflicting ideas about power in the United States.

170

Today it might be easy to read the Federalist and Anti-Federalist writings as a collected and distilled body of ideas, yet this reading process tends falsely to suggest a predetermined outcome to the debate. To avoid encouraging such a process, instructors should talk with students about the original conditions of publication. This emphasis on historical context encourages students to view the debates from within, to some extent, by showing there was no guarantee that the Federalist arguments would prevail. By encouraging students to read *against* their knowledge of the outcome, teachers can help them see the debates not simply as dry philosophical discourses on ideal government, but as real arguments whose outcome would affect the daily lives of citizens. I usually provide some brief publication history, noting that the essays that we now know as *The Federalist* first appeared as a series of eighty-five letters to the public in several New York newspapers between October 1787 and May 1788. Written under the pseudonym Publius ("people-lover") by Alexander Hamilton, James Madison, and John Jay, the essays were designed to persuade readers of the need for the new national Constitution. Like the essays that constituted *The Federalist*, Anti-Federalist writings also began appearing in newspapers and in pamphlet form after the proposed Constitution was submitted to the public in 1787. An emphasis on the historical context encourages students to view the debates from within to some extent by showing there was no guarantee that the Federalist arguments would prevail.

Teachers might raise the issue of language and power and note how language not only expresses ideas but also shapes ideas and creates boundaries of discussion. Specifically, the very term *Anti-Federalist* was first used by Federalist writers to stigmatize their opposition with a negative name. I often first ask students to write down their associations with the prefix *anti-* before moving on to a more specific consideration of the associations contemporary readers might have had with the tag (Anti-Federalist suggests anti-Constitution, which might also suggest antipatriotic). Indeed, one historian has noted that during this period the "Antifederalist label itself quickly became a political epithet, implying disloyalty to the country, and it was used to discredit enemies" (Sharp 30). By looking carefully with students at how language that first seems to be merely descriptive is, on closer examination, value-laden, teachers can more clearly show how the very rhetoric of the debate helped shape its outcome.

In addition to helping teachers historicize the ratification debates, discussions of publication history also allow instructors to touch on issues of canon formation, especially if this issue has already been raised in the class. The reason Anti-Federalist writings are traditionally less likely to appear in American literature anthologies than writings from *The Federalist* is not only that they "lost" the argument, so to speak (Joyce Appleby has noted that "nothing weakens a position so much as losing" [221]), but also that their initial publication was not the result of a concerted, organized effort. Instead, their writings were the product of what one writer has called a "loose negative coalition" (Lewis 2). Indeed, an edition of Anti-Federalist writings (Cecelia Kenyon's) did not appear until 1966 (Wood, Introduction vi). Thus Federalist writings are represented by a single, unified "classic text," though they actually make up a large and diverse body, while Anti-Federalist writings are represented as more fragmentary, reactionary, and generally incoherent. One practical way for teachers to provide students with a sense of the original publication contexts of both Federalist and Anti-Federalist writings is to bring in (or ask students to retrieve) a photocopy of a newspaper page from the era with a Federalist or Anti-Federalist essay (available from Charles Evans's Early American Imprint series from American Bibliography). Alternatively, it might be useful to have a general discussion of print culture to illustrate that most Federalist and Anti-Federalist writings appeared in newspapers alongside a variety of other types of writings (news, advertisements, speeches, poems, stories, toasts, and so forth). This can help students think of the debates as part of a larger discursive environment.

Contexts

Although the ideological differences between Federalist and Anti-Federalist writings were often passionately expressed and deeply felt, I have found that students can make better sense of these differences only after having first examined some political and cultural assumptions common to both sides. Most shared certain values about what kind of place the republic should be, although they differed — often significantly — about how to bring that place into existence. Students are better able to grasp the import of the debate over ratification after exploring the complex political, social, and cultural ideological crises that gave rise to the Constitutional Convention.

As many scholars have noted, the existing Articles of Confederation were weak — deliberately so. "The American people," one historian suggests, "deeply suspicious of political power beyond the state and local level, had fatally crippled the Articles of Confederation government by restricting its authority to deal with the problems facing the nation" (Sharp 1). Indeed, Gordon Wood notes an increasing tendency in post-Revolutionary America to view Congress as an instrument necessary only in times of crisis, such as war, and he has pointed to the difficulty of even gathering a quorum during the 1780s (Wood, *Creation* 359). Thus, the Constitutional Convention — which, it is important to note, was initially called "for the sole and express purpose of revising the Articles of Confederation," not to eliminate them — addressed very real threats to the legitimacy of the new nation (*Journals of the Continental Congress*, qtd. in Elkins and McKitrick 31).

Although it is useful and important to discuss with students the narrowly political motivations for abandoning the Articles of Confederation, such an approach fails to account for the larger, and perhaps more telling, ideological transformations that were guiding the country toward a stronger national government. Most important, there was a growing sense that political powers actually lie with the "people" rather than with their representatives. Now, as Gordon Wood, Stanley Elkins and Eric McKitrick, and others have pointed out, the "sovereignty of the people was not in itself a new idea. [. . .] But it had always been something of a platitude, conveying little practical meaning" (Elkins and McKitrick 11). During the 1780s, however, a growing number of social and political developments — such as mob action, the rise of organizations working outside established laws (including constitutional conventions), and increasing constitutional restraints on legislative authority—combined to make clear the general claims of the people that the power to create laws and implement them ought not to be in a particular body of men but in the people at large (Wood, *Creation* 363). Such changes signaled not only a crisis of confidence in representation but also a larger crisis of authority that threatened to undermine all the benefits of the Revolution. For Federalists, especially, who were obsessed "with disorder," most of the "evils of American society," such as "the breakdown of authority, the increase of debt, the depravity of manners, and the decline of virtue" were solvable only through a rearrangement of the social order. Many Federalists conceived "of the Constitution as a political device designed to control the social forces the Revolution had released" (Wood, *Creation* 476). By examining the specific problems as well as the broader cultural and social transformations that prepared the way for the Constitution, teachers can encourage students to consider more fully the multilayered arguments for and against the Constitution, thus deflecting students' inclination to idealize the era of the early Republic.

After having reviewed with students some of the specific social, political, and cultural problems of the 1780s, I turn to philosophic similarities between Federalists and Anti-Federalists. For instance, they shared assumptions about the legitimacy of natural law. It could be argued that such assumptions were so deeply embedded in Anglo culture that they were infrequently argued explicitly in debates over the Constitution (White 25–37), yet a tacit acknowledgment of this belief lay behind most arguments for or against the Constitution.

One specific strategy for highlighting such an abstract concept as natural law is to begin with students' own brief consideration of the source of legitimacy of laws. I often ask them to take a few moments to write down the originating authority behind a law, such as a law protecting free speech. Inevitably, their responses are varied, some locating such authority in the government (the government gives us this right rather than protects it for us), specific historical figures (the concept of free speech was first conceived by certain thinkers who popularized it), to God (free speech is a God-given right). Beginning with these differing responses, we talk about which theories tend to assume that laws are constructed (they are not natural and timeless but human constructs) and which tend to assume that laws are natural (they do not need to be constructed because they exist in nature or in God's nature).

After this exercise students are usually better able to "read into" assumptions about natural rights and natural law in the Federalist and Anti-Federalist writings, such as Madison's comment in *The Federalist* number 43 about "the transcendent law of nature and nature's God, which declares that the safety and happiness of society are the objects at which all political institutions aim" (279). Likewise, Anti-Federalist writer Brutus notes that governments are obligated to reserve "to the people such of their essential natural rights, as are not necessary to be parted with" (Storing 2: 373).

Another feature common to Federalist and Anti-Federalist writings that students often note and question is frequent references to "the people." Before discussing how the groups conceived of and represented "the people" differently, it is useful, if possible, to discuss eighteenth-century conceptions of "virtue" or "public good." Some teachers in upper-level or graduate courses might want to expose students to the long and complex debate between scholars who emphasized "classical republicanism" (which emphasized virtue) and those who emphasized "liberalism" (which emphasized individualism and materialism), but for the purposes of studying Federalist and Anti-Federalist writings, a brief discussion of the concept of virtue is generally enough (see Shalhope). It often helps students untangle the various references to "the people" by noting how, despite their differences, Federalists and Anti-Federalists both conceived of a republic (at least in their public writings) as a place composed of virtuous citizens; that is, citizens willing to sacrifice "individual interests to the greater good of the whole" (Wood, *Creation* 53). Although the extent to which virtue was actually felt or even achieved is of course endlessly debatable, a brief discussion of the word *virtue* helps students account for passages such as one from *The Federalist* number 10, in which Madison defends the notion of a republic as opposed to a democracy by noting that through representative government "the public voice, pronounced by the representatives of the people, will be more consonant to the public good than if pronounced by the people themselves" (82). With a greater understanding of the extent to which appeals to the public good informed both Federalist and Anti-Federalist rhetoric, students are in a better position to appreciate later differences in how these two groups conceived of the public.

Finally, I have found that some background in the rise of the party system helps students understand the often bitter and disdainful language both groups used to characterize parties. As one historian puts it, the "fathers hoped to create not a system of party government under a constitution but rather a constitutional government that would check and control parties" (Hofstadter 53). Or as Kenyon observes, "the contemporary opponents of the Constitution feared parties or factions in the Madisonian sense just as much as did Madison, and they [. . .] feared parties in the modern sense even more than Madison did" ("Political Thought" cx). Thus, Anti-Federalist writers such as Hampden can worry that parties might arise "to the great injury of the general government" (Storing 4: 201) while Federalist writers like Hamilton can write of the "intolerant spirit" that characterizes political parties (34). So despite real differences between the groups, in the late 1780s neither were arguing for a formal party system to help provide the kinds of checks and balances that eventually became such an important — almost mythic — component of the American political system. Teachers might find it useful to examine eighteenth-century prejudices against party, because through such a discussion students are less likely to read back current associations about the legitimacy of the party system into the arguments of the 1780s.

Conflict

After exploring important assumptions Federalist and Anti-Federalist writers shared, students are better prepared to look closely at some of the ideological differences — many of them significant — between the groups. Indeed, as Lance Banning has observed, the quarrel over the Constitution was one of great ideological depth (236). Although there are several ways to approach the substance and importance of such differences, I have found that students react more favorably to strategies that emphasize power, identity, and difference so that specific issues such as faction, majority rule versus minority rights, representation, and so forth are examined in relation to a larger ideological struggle rather than as isolated legal and political terms. It is impossible to cover every facet of the debate over the Constitution, so I offer several questions to help frame discussion. Whose voices count in the new republic? Who gets listened to? Who doesn't? How is the new government going to ensure that the people are represented in the political process? Who, precisely, are "the people?" Who decides what is a faction and what is not? How is the new republic going to account for difference? When encouraged to think of the Federalist and Anti-Federalist writings in the light of these questions and others, students express interest in the debates, perhaps because many of these issues are relevant to familiar contemporary political, social, and cultural issues.

The ways in which the Federalists and Anti-Federalists answered these questions reveals often sharp distinctions between them and thus make a good beginning for discussion of different versions of America. One successful strategy for introducing students to such conflicts is to give them issues to look for as they read *The Federalist* number 10 (Madison's famous discussion of faction) and an Anti-Federalist essay (the letters of Brutus or the Federal Farmer are useful for this exercise). As they read, I ask them to list (1) definitions of and assumptions about what constitutes a "faction" from both sets of writings (factions can be compared with today's "special interest groups") and (2) solutions that the writings offer for handling "problems" factions pose. Such narrow examinations of the arguments encourage students to see how, for most Federalists, difference or diversity is something to be controlled (in number 10 Madison speaks of "controlling its *effects*" [80]), while for most Anti-Federalists difference is so basic to human experience that attempts to represent or control it are doomed.

Students can more clearly detect such conflicts when asked to examine closely how the vocabularies of Federalists and Anti-Federalists portray those who are "different" enough to be considered minorities or factions. While Federalists usually write of difference or diversity in generalized language (as faction, party, or interest), Anti-Federalists are more apt to refer specifically to "laws," "customs," or "climates" as the basis of different interests. Brutus, for example, uses such language in an essay from November 1787 in which he questions whether the proposed Constitution's scheme of representation is adequate:

> I will venture to affirm that number cannot be found in the state, who will bear a just resemblance to the several classes of people who compose it. In this assembly, the farmer, the merchant, mecanick, and other various orders of people, ought to be represented according to their respective weight and numbers; and the representatives ought to be intimately acquainted with the wants, understand the interests of the several orders of society, and feel a proper sense and becoming zeal to promote their prosperity. (Storing 2: 380)

For Brutus, difference arises not so much from clashing ideas as from the diverse cultural and occupational situations that give rise to various and conflicting ideas. His comment later in the same essay that the "well born, and highest orders in life, as they term themselves, will be ignorant of the sentiments of the middling class of citizens" (381) suggests that class issues are more important than acknowledged by Federalists, who de-emphasized class by departicularizing various competing interests and instead referring to them in a more abstract vocabulary.

Yet what truly differentiates Anti-Federalist rhetoric from Federalist rhetoric is again its conception and representation of difference. The Federal Farmer notes the significance of the different "opinions, customs, and views" of people from different regions. "These difference are not so perceivable among the members of congress," he notes. "The Eastern states are very democratic," the Southern states "are composed chiefly of rich planters and slaves," while the middle states "partake partly of the Eastern, and partly of the Southern character" (Storing 2: 236). Unlike Hamilton, who conceived of different interests derived solely from vocation, the Federal Farmer conceives of difference as arising from "opinions, customs, and views," which are much more difficult to represent, even virtually, on a national level. "It is deceiving a people to tell them they are electors, and can chuse their legislators," the Federal Farmer continues, "if they cannot, in the nature of things, chuse men from among themselves, and genuinely like themselves" (266). This is a significant distinction, and it has implications for the varying ways in which both sides imagined order and disorder rhetorically. For Anti-Federalists the distinctiveness of various differences and the chaos of diversity could not be managed by the proposed Constitution, as Samuel Adams suggests in a letter to Richard Henry Lee:

> And can this National Legislature be competent to make Laws for the *free* internal Government of one People, living in Climates so remote and whose 'Habits & particular Interests' are and probably always will be so different. [. . .] It appears to me difficult if practicable. Hence then may we not look for Discontent, Mistrust, Disaffection to Government and frequent Insurrections[. . .]. (Bailyn 446)

Whereas Federalists imagined civil chaos would result from free and unrestrained formation of factions and affiliations, Anti-Federalists imagined chaos resulting from impractical efforts to create a national representative political structure reflecting the various interests of the people. This difference, again, rests on conflicting representations of just who the potentially rebellious people are: broad, economically oriented interest groups as in much Federalist rhetoric or specific members of various geographies and classes (or "orders") as in Anti-Federalist rhetoric. By exploring with students the subtle but important differences between Federalist and Anti-Federalist conceptions of order and disorder, teachers can help students see the debate over the Constitution not just as a dry legal one but rather as one that also reflected — and shaped — broader cultural and social tensions and fears.

Although some scholars, especially Charles A. Beard and Jackson Turner Main, have read the Federalist and Anti-Federalist debate as an essentially economic and social one that pitted wealthier, urban Federalists against middle-class, agrarian Anti-Federalists (Main xi–20; 249–81), clear evidence for such generalizations has always been shaky (Kenyon, "Political Thought" xxxvi–vii). However, whether the basis of the differences is economic or not, the notion that there were drastically different ideological assumptions underlying the rhetoric of both camps is still widely held (see, e.g., Duncan xxiv). To move the class from broad comments about ideological assumptions to a more concrete, text-oriented discussion of real differences between both groups, I sometimes ask students to make a chart with the word "People" across the top, the heading "Federalist comments" on the left side, and "Anti-Federalist comments" on the right. Students then simply record instances where either group invokes or mentions the people. In class, students share their lists and try to find patterns: Are "the people" represented positively or negatively? Are they assumed to have authority? Does the writer argue that the proposed federal government control the people or be controlled by them? Of course, every class does not answer these questions and others the same way. But the questions encourage students to read critically and purposefully as well as to think about how language reflects and shapes assumptions about power.

The debate about whether the proposed Constitution should include a formal bill of rights represents more clearly than any other single example the profound differences between Federalist and Anti-Federalist visions of the new republic. I generally cover the Bill of Rights in class not only because of its continuing tremendous importance as a legal and cultural document but also because it reveals Anti-Federalists as ideologically modern in their desire for a specific, contractual enumeration of the peoples' rights. That is, while Federalists are often portrayed as the more progressive, forward-looking group (after all, they "won" the debate, as Appleby reminds us), perhaps the most culturally sacred features of the Constitution are embodied in the Bill of Rights, a negatively expressed ("Congress shall make no law [. . .]") contractual list of checks on the federal government largely — perhaps completely — the result of Anti-Federalist pressure.

The debate over including a bill of rights provides students the opportunity to study the conflict from the related angles of language and power. First, Anti-Federalist arguments for such a bill stem in large part from their general mistrust of vague language, particularly the Constitution's. "Cato," for instance, argues that "inexplicitness seems to pervade this whole political fabric" (Storing 2:117), while "A Bostonian" suggests that many lawyers and judges support the Constitution because their "fortune and dependence depend principally on its inaccuracy, its vague and ambiguous terms, its incomprehensibleness" (Storing 4: 229). Many Anti-Federalists interpreted such vague language as deliberate Federalist preparation to dilute states' rights in favor of an overly strong federal government. A bill of rights would theoretically protect citizens from interpretations that could be constructed out of "ambiguous" and imprecise language. Writers of *The Federalist*, however, contended that the very arbitrariness of language itself made it a necessarily inadequate system of representation. In number 37 Madison indirectly takes up the Constitution's vague language by arguing that not only the objects that we consider obscure (such as laws) but also our faculties for understanding them are imperfect, as is the language we use to describe them. "The use of words is to express ideas," Madison writes. "Perspicuity, therefore, requires not only that the ideas should be distinctly formed, but that they should be expressed by words distinctively and exclusively appropriate to them. But no language is so copious as to supply words and phrases for every complex idea, or so correct as not to include many equivocally denoting different ideas" (229). Thus, in a few sentences, Madison undercuts Anti-Federalist charges about the Constitution's linguistic vagueness, suggesting that language itself is inadequate to capture fully the complexities of political discourse.

Yet after the Constitution was submitted to the states for ratification, Anti-Federalists continued to demand a more precise enumeration of the peoples' rights. Students are sometimes surprised to learn that the drafters of the Constitution did not really even consider a bill of rights until the issue was raised by the document's opponents (Wood, *Creation* 536). Federalist arguments against such a bill were also predicated on assumptions about the power of language, albeit for different reasons from those in Anti-Federalist arguments. For instance, many Federalists believed that a bill of rights would incorrectly imply that any right not explicitly mentioned was not protected. More important, however, their opposition rested on the fundamental assumption that since the people and the government were basically the same, protection was not needed — and indeed would be redundant. Under pressure, however, Madison and others began preparing a bill of rights. I generally spend time in class discussing the process that led to the Bill of Rights in order to encourage students to think of the document — and by extension other political and literary works — as the product of a process. That is, thinking of the Bill of Rights as a kind of inevitable predetermined document that appeared on the scene ready-made suggests a false sense of like-mindedness between Federalists and Anti-Federalists. To encourage students to think about the Bill of Rights as the product of wrangling and debate rather than as an "official" text handed down by our "Founding Fathers," it is worth noting that, during state ratification debates, roughly 210 amendments were submitted and that after duplications were removed, eighty amendments remained, from which Madison drafted the first eight amendments. In the fall of 1789 Congress submitted twelve amendments to the states and by December 1791 the states had accepted the ten that became the Bill of Rights (Sharp 29; Elkins and McKitrick 60–61).

———

I have generally found that, when approached as a series of writings important not only for their immediate and specific historical and philosophical significance but also for their larger cultural import, the Federalist and Anti-Federalist writings can engage students just as other writings, more traditionally thought of as "literary," from that period. I sometimes speak of the debate as a part of a broader cultural narrative about what kind of place the new country should be. While it would be disingenuous to speak of the Federalist and Anti-Federalist conflict as a mere narrative — it would risk taking the debate "out of history" and minimizing its very real social context — I do try to open certain doors and let students decide to enter or not. Through one such door lies a way of thinking about the conflict as part of an emerging "national" narrative. We sometimes examine Hamilton's awareness in *The Federalist* number 34 that the framers have drafted a Constitution that will have implications for "remote futurity" (207), in one sense the students themselves. In short, Federalists and Anti-Federalists alike seemed to be acutely aware that their arguments looked beyond their immediate historical moments and were part of an emerging American narrative, one still open to interpretation, although they could not have known how. What I sometimes refer to in class as the "anxiety" embedded in the debate (such as the worry over disorder or chaos) is very much a part of this narrative.

An approach to Federalist and Anti-Federalist writings that moves from discussions of consensus to discussions of conflict helps students think of the debate as part of a larger discursive legacy still relevant today. By focusing on ideas and concepts such as virtue, natural law, party, faction, and representation not just as separate topics but also as part of a larger debate about power and difference, students are better able to see the conflict surrounding the ratification of the Constitution as something that mattered and, just as important, something that still matters.

Works Cited

Primary Works

Bailyn, Bernard. *The Debate on the Constitution*. New York: Lib. of America, 1995.

Hamilton, Alexander, John Jay, and James Madison. *The Federalist Papers*. Ed. Clinton Rossitter. New York: Mentor, 1961.

Lewis, John D., ed. *Anti-Federalists versus Federalists: Selected Documents*. San Francisco: Chandler, 1967.

Storing, Herbert J. *The Complete Anti-Federalist*. 7 vols. Chicago: U of Chicago P, 1981.

Secondary Works

Appleby, Joyce. "The American Heritage — The Heirs and the Disinherited." *Liberalism and Republicanism in the Historical Imagination*. Cambridge: Harvard UP, 1992. 210–31.

Banning, Lance. "Republican Ideology and the Triumph of the Constitution, 1789–1793." *William and Mary Quarterly* 3rd ser. 31 (1974): 167–88. Rpt. in *After the Constitution: Party Conflict in the New Republic*. Ed. Banning. Belmont: Wadsworth, 1989. 233–53.

Beard, Charles A. *An Economic Interpretation of the Constitution of the United States*. New York: Macmillan, 1913.

Duncan, Christopher M. *The Anti-Federalists and Early American Political Thought*. De Kalb: Northern Illinois UP, 1995.

Elkins, Stanley, and Eric McKitrick. *The Age of Federalism: The Early American Republic, 1788–1800*. New York: Oxford UP, 1993.

Hofstadter, Richard. *The Idea of a Party System: The Rise of Legitimate Opposition in the United States, 1780–1840*. Berkeley: U of California P, 1969.

Kenyon, Cecelia, ed. *The Antifederalists*. Boston: Northeastern UP, 1985.

———. "The Political Thought of the Antifederalists." Kenyon, *Antifederalists* 54–82.

Main, Jackson Turner. *The Anti-Federalists: Critics of the Constitution, 1781–1788*. Chapel Hill: U of North Carolina P, 1961.

Shalhope, Robert E. "Republicanism, Liberalism, and Democracy: Political Culture in the Early Republic." *The Republican Synthesis Revisited: Essays in Honor of George Athan Billias*. Ed. Milton M. Klein et al. Worcester: Amer. Antiquarian Soc., 1992. 37–53.

Sharp, James Roger. *American Politics in the Early Republic: The New Nation in Crisis*. New Haven: Yale UP, 1993.

White, Morton. *Philosophy,* The Federalist, *and the Constitution*. New York: Oxford UP, 1987.

Wood, Gordon S. *The Creation of the American Republic, 1776–1787*. Chapel Hill: U of North Carolina P, 1969.

———. Introduction. Kenyon, *Antifederalists* ix–xxiv.

Genre Studies

William J. Scheick

Early Anglo-American Poetry: Genre, Voice, Art, and Representation

The subject and cultural matter of British American poetry from Anne Bradstreet's *The Tenth Muse* (1650) to Phillis Wheatley's *Poems on Various Subjects, Religious and Moral* (1773) is diverse. This matter, ranging from late-Renaissance and Reformed traditions to Neoclassical standards, necessitates attention to historical context and such notions as the chain of being, universal order, sin, common sense, and reason. Brief books by E. M. W. Tillyard and Peter Gay are helpful in introducing students to this pertinent information. Of course, even as a pedagogical prop any historical approach is at best contingent, one version among alternatives (White). So from time to time I mention problems inherent in all acts of historicizing, including several indeterminacies in my own approach to early Anglo-American poetry.

I present these poems in terms of a tiered axis of chronological perspectives, including genre, voice, art, and representation, capped with some poststructural considerations. The order of these perspectives is not crucial to my goal of incrementally deepening my students' perspectives on this verse, except for representation, which I position last because it provides a cautionary counterbalance to the other three.

Genre

That many students can identify various genres is one advantage to the literary-model approach. Selecting a representative type of early American verse is difficult, and the choice is often determined by what has previously succeeded with students. Since I have found the elegy, a complex form rich for pedagogical purposes, to be unappealing even to graduate students, I tend to prefer the meditative poem. Meditative verse does not evince a single pattern, for its European antecedents are many; but in general, and as practiced by the Puritans, it focuses on a religious topic germane to the interior spiritual drama of the poet (Martz).

The richest examples of early colonial meditative poetry show the influence of the emblem tradition, such as exhibited in the English verse of Francis Quarles and George Herbert. Images (candles, wings, skulls, hearts, children) from Quarles's seventeenth-century bestseller *Emblems* and from a hieroglyphic poem such as Herbert's "Easter-Wings" (which visually converts the fallen-over hourglass of mortality into a butterfly of redemptive ascent) show that meditative verse often expresses religious concepts through verbal pictures. Such a poem may focus on the sea to represent humanity's helplessness in a turbulent world, as in Philip Pain's *Daily Meditations*, or on trees and rivers to represent, respectively, humanity's former Edenic posture and present temporal condition, as in Anne Bradstreet's frequently reprinted "Contemplations." In the unusual instance of "Meditation 2.3" Edward Taylor presents his own face as an emblem of mortality; students, urged to discern the fifty-one-year-old poet's facial features as well as the significance of these features in the poem, detect such details as his hirsute cheeks, blemished skin, and graying blond hair. This poem, related to early Puritan emblematic interpretations of human names and bodies, dramatizes how intensely personal meditative verse is.

Emblems such as these are concrete instances of how Puritans read nature as *liber mundi* (creation as a divinely inspired text that reiterates Scripture). Emblems tend to have layers of signification, and so students with some knowledge of the Bible might be encouraged to think further about verticality (the trees) and horizontalness (the river) in "Contemplations." In this poem, with the same number of stanzas as Christ's age at his crucifixion, the two natural types of river and trees emblematically suggest the intersection of the divine (eternal) and the human (temporal) on Christ's cross (Scheick). Similarly, Taylor's often anthologized "Meditation 1.8" offers such emblems as a caged bird, which represents, at the microcosmic level, the famished soul confined within the body and, at the macrocosmic level, inept humanity confined beneath the dome of nature. The proliferation of natural and domestic types in Taylor's poem — horizon, cage, barrel, bread loaf, inverted bowl — at first seems free-associative; but all share the emblematic shape of the half circle. After students recall the traditional symbolism of the circle (unity, perfection) and its religious significance, I ask them to consider the value of the half circle for the poet, who laments that he can only write crookedly (produce marred meditations) because he is in the dark while the sun (Son, i.e., Christ) is beyond the arched horizon. Exemplifying how Puritans viewed nature emblematically, the half-circle natural types in Taylor's late-seventeenth-century meditation intimate the scriptural prophecy of Christ's second coming.

If such types give Taylor hope rather than assurance concerning his own personal redemption, a century later similar images usually convey a far more secular and presumptive prophecy. During the eighteenth century's revival of classical aesthetic models meditation lost its status as a predominant cultural art form. The epic, narrative verse in elevated style celebrating episodes historically and prophetically important to a people, became a popular classical mode in the new republic, dating from such early epic gestures as *A Poem, on the Rising Glory of America* by Philip Freneau and Hugh Henry Brackenridge. The epic traces in this work refer to Columbus's discovery of America, the settlers' feats, and the heroes' sacrifices during the French and Indian War — each embedded in another classical type, the dialogic pastoral mode celebrating agriculture.

As students contrast the imagery of this 1772 poem with the late-seventeenth-century emblems in Bradstreet's "Contemplations" and

Taylor's "Meditation 1.8," they can be directed toward the following observations. Rather than symbolize scriptural meanings in the Christian *liber mundi* tradition, the natural types in *Rising Glory* reinforce historical meanings in the British imperial tradition. Whereas the meditative poets a century earlier rehearse the scriptural version of human events in the hope that the divine prophecies include them as individuals, Freneau and Brackenridge collapse the millennial prediction of the Book of Revelation into a rehearsal of Western history and recent New World settlement. They announce, at least in this youthful phase of their careers, that America, the "final stage" of empire, is destined to fulfill Old World history. In *Rising Glory* nature symbolizes not spiritual admonition but secular fulfillment, specifically fortune through commodification: "Much wealth and pleasure agriculture brings"; "Nor less from golden commerce flow the streams / Of richest plenty on our smiling land" (lines 356, 374–75).

When concluding the comparison I ask students whether a Puritan meditator would likely have written in the manner of the later poem. Most say no, but several indicate that certain images and the sentiment of the 1772 poem could have been meditatively applied to the imagined regenerative state of the elect in heaven. This point reminds students that the religious energy of the Puritan meditation and the secular energy of the later dialogic pastoral are subtly related despite evident generic differences.

Voice

In contrasting the seventeenth-century meditation and the eighteenth-century epic-pastoral, including their nature imagery, my students are often quick to notice a related difference concerning voice. They are struck by the apparent loneliness of the Calvinistic meditative authors, who write as if no fellow human being could help them satisfy their primary spiritual desires. They detect Bradstreet's attraction to the beauty of nature in "Contemplations" and her affection for her spouse and children in such poems as "A Letter to Her Husband" and "Upon My Son Samuel." But they also acknowledge her isolation as "[s]ilent alone" her life follows "pathless paths" in a world that is at best a "lonely place, with pleasures dignifi'd" (lines

50–51, 144). Students likewise observe that in "Meditation 1.8" Taylor stands alone beneath the night sky, which is as beautiful to him as are the woods to Bradstreet and as insufficient to meet his spiritual needs. Like Bradstreet, Taylor presents nature, however much its splendor and plenitude fill his eyes, as "[a]n Empty Barrell": the "Creatures field" (nature) provides "no food for Souls" (14–16).

For meditative poets like Bradstreet and Taylor the beauty of nature does not invite proto-Romantic sentiment. This beauty, instead, is a divine goad indicting them as fallen descendants of Adam and Eve. Musing on the grandeur of nature as the artwork of the Logos, Bradstreet is struck "mute," her poem virtually discontinued after stanza 9; and Taylor, dizzy from starvation (the lack of Eucharistic manna), struggles with "puzzled thoughts" virtually depleted, "pore[d]" out, in the first stanza of his poor and porous poem (line 5). At such points, typical of Puritan meditative manner, both poets turn away from the book of nature, which only reminds them of what humanity has lost, and toward Holy Writ, as collective Christian memory, to recall the Old Testament account of the fall from grace and the New Testament gospel of redemption. Taylor's meditation ends with an authorized fantasy of his conceivable election to salvation; and Bradstreet's meditation ends with *memento mori* devices, including an allusion to the heavenly antithesis of the gravestone, designed to counter her vanity, a personal proclivity she confesses in "To My Dear Children." Neither meditator presumes redemption; indicted by nature, each remains a humble voice actively disposed to wait passively for the revelation of divine will after death.

Transatlantic comparisons may help students understand this unfamiliar attitude toward voice. While the meditative poem reveals a Renaissance ancestry, especially in its display of verbal agility, the Reformed version practiced by the Puritans downplays the value of the self, especially in typological terms. Typology, the correspondence between foreshadowing Old Testament matter and consummating New Testament matter, might or might not include the meditator, and that has considerable consequences concerning a poet's voice. When, for example, Herbert's Low Anglican "Aaron" is matched with Taylor's Congregationalist "Meditation 2.23," some students notice that the English poet concludes with a confident and affirmative sense of his share in the Old Testament high priest's fulfillment in Christ, whereas the New England poet (who occasionally alludes to Herbert's verse) finds no comfort in the Aaron type and instead only hopes that he might somehow be found worthy of redemption as one of the high priest's cups. Similar comparisons can be made between Herbert's "Affliction V" (on Noah's ark) and "The Altar" (on the Hebrew sacrificial table) and Taylor's "Meditation 2.29" and "Meditation 2.82." Here my students have seen, without much prompting, that Herbert's orderliness and neat resolution are in distinct contrast to Taylor's apparent disorder and irresolution.

Nearly a century later the swains in *Rising Glory* provide an even greater contrast. Their dialogic exchange and celebration of the common good (at least as they understood it) demonstrate an appreciation of community not evident in the meditative monologues. The voices of these country youths convey self-possession, not helplessness, and in nature they find incentive to speak rather than indictment and curtailment of speech. They share the meditators' regard for the rich plenitude of nature, but they do not draw biblical parallels from natural signs. They express a millennial and utilitarian vision of a "Paradise a new" where the commodification of natural riches fulfills human aspirations (line 754).

Sometimes a few students seem supportive of this essentially Deistic, exuberant voice prophesying the domination of nature for human benefit. I ask them to compare the sentiment of *Rising Glory* and Gaspar Pérez de Villagrá's seventeenth-century epic *Historia de la Nueva México*, which the class sampled earlier in the semester. Since students usually criticize Villagrá's celebration of unmitigated conquest, the comparison encourages a fuller awareness of the social and environmental implications of the 1772 poem.

My students even more often prefer the optimism of *Rising Glory* over the self-deprecation of Calvinistic meditations. On such occasions I ask them to determine which voice exhibits a greater appreciation of beauty. The ensuing debate touches on the question of what we mean by beauty, but finally students delve again into the poems. I consider the debate particularly successful if certain subtleties emerge — when, say, someone argues that the meditators' sense of dispossession increased their valuation of nature's beauty whereas the pastoralists' relentless stress on utilization and commodification may have blinded them to that perception.

However, this differentiation of voice risks the suggestion that seventeenth- and eighteenth-century authors were either strict Calvinists or implicit Deists. Phillis Wheatley's late-eighteenth-century verse, especially the widely available "On Being Brought from Africa to America," counters this misperception effectively because it mingles a Congregationalist sensitivity to the Bible and an Enlightenment awareness of politics. To highlight Wheatley's regard for personal liberty and her esteem for Holy Writ, I ask students to interpret the elliptical last two lines: "Remember, *Christians*, *Negroes*, black as *Cain* / May be refin'd, and join th' Angelic train" (lines 7–8). Some read the lines as "Remember, *Christians*, [that] *Negroes*," whereas others read them as "Remember [that] *Christians*, [and] *Negroes*." Does the final line refer only to intellectual and aesthetic refinement, such as the poet's careful management of metrics and rhyme, or does it also possibly refer to the management of the ambiguous syntax of the preceding line to imply the equality of both races as mutually "benighted soul[s]" (line 2)? To ask these related questions is to inquire into Wheatley's religiopolitical voice, which performs and proves her argument that an African American can be taught to understand the refinements of both religion and art. Advanced students might further be asked to consider whether the final line tactfully alludes to images from Isaiah, the poet's favorite prophetic scriptural book, specifically Isaiah 6.1 and 48.10. If so, then her voice simultaneously defers to scriptural authority (like the seventeenth-century meditative poets) while it subtly asserts its authority (like the eighteenth-century epic-pastoral poets) by making an unprecedented racial application of two biblical passages.

Art

Wheatley's poem is basically an encomium, the classical verse of praise revived by the eighteenth-century English authors she admired. In typical neoclassical manner, her poem is presented in rhymed couplets of nearly perfect iambic pentameter. In comparison to such model precision, the slight irregularities of the last two lines, including the ambiguous syntax and possible truncated allusions, appear to draw attention to themselves, particularly since they are emphatically introduced by the direct address "Remember." Are these irregularities the product of the young author's cunning or her lack of skill? Students who see these effects as intentional tend to value the poet's voice as empowered in its Enlightenment insistence on social revision. Students who see these effects as unintentional tend to assess her voice as inherently alienated from the religious and cultural paradigms it unsuccessfully attempts to assimilate and mimic.

Questions concerning intention apply as well to Puritan meditative verse. Bradstreet's "Contemplations," for instance, breaks into uneven units: stanzas 1–9 (on the book of nature), stanzas 10–20 (on biblical history), 21–23 (on human life in New Testament terms), 24–28 (on emblematic birds and fish), and 29–33 (on the mariner soul in the prone vessel of the body). Oddities occur, such as the echo of the first unit at the start of the third; and the fourth unit is structurally more a lateral swelling than a linear development of the gist of the poem, which is perhaps why some anthologists delete it. Is such fragmentation the product of Bradstreet's amateurishness or of her humility? Does it express her artistic refusal to vainly construct a poetic monument to herself in a world defined by time's "fatal wrack," which (as the poet observes) crumbles "into th' dust" all "sumptuous monuments" (lines 225, 229)?

Taylor's meditations, seemingly so free-associative and nonsequential, are likewise open to questions concerning intention. Does Taylor consciously revise the patterns of such metaphysical poets as Herbert, or is he a pale, inept version of them? Possibly Taylor practices a "decorum of imperfection," a poetic mode that recognizes the depravity of art, the impropriety of celebrating human life, and the human inability to glorify God (Mignon). As we saw in "Meditation 1.8," beneath the surface chaos of a poetic voice that presents itself as benighted, malnourished, feverish, sick, and maladroit, there is a semicircle emblem that engenders hope by intimating a divine order potentially encompassing and redeeming the poet's temporal disorder. Taylor's concern with salvation affects his art in another manner: he vacillates between despair and presumption just as the soulbird in "Meditation 1.8" is depicted in various postures of fall and ascent. The Puritan meditative poet usually tries neither to presume nor to despair but to await disclosure of divine will; hence the series of poem-suspending questions in the penultimate stanzas of "Meditation 1.8" and "Meditation 2.3," which both end with a hope for redemption rather than with an optimistic personal redress typical of, say, Herbert's poetry.

For Wheatley, as students should see by now, salvation is far more imminent, not only spiritually but politically, especially regarding abolition. For Freneau and Brackenridge, personal salvation lies in the utilization of natural and human resources, in the temporal and secular fulfillment of American millennial prospects, "richly stor'd with all / The luxuries of life" (line 787). *Rising Glory* includes religious tradition and imagery, such as the poets' wish for Isaiah's power of prophecy and their claim that the star of Bethlehem now shines on America. But in contrast to Wheatley's presentation of religious and historical matters as integral concerns, Freneau and Brackenridge's religious allusions are hollow reeds, mere stage properties, in an ebullient secular forecast. Students readily sense that *Rising Glory*, unlike Puritan meditative verse and Wheatley's poetry, emphasizes the surfaces of life, at least overtly. If the 1772 poem does not quite replicate the catalogs of earlier New World advertisements (Richard Rich's poem *Newes from Virginia*, for example), it delights in the material world as commodity. Even the pronunciation of the names of things is delightful, as if artfully fashioned words were physical objects rather than representations.

Representation

At this point I urge my class to delve beneath the surface representations and the design of *Rising Glory* to discover less evident features of the poem and the colonial enterprise it celebrates. If time permits, the sanguine vision of this poem can be instructively compared with the jaundiced satire of Ebenezer Cook(e)'s *The Sot-Weed Factor*. Or students can focus on the admission in *Rising Glory* that "the mysteries of future days" are unknowable, which remark may stimulate class scrutiny of the limitations in the author's awareness (line 594). My students, many of them Hispanic, notice the poem's chauvinism, including its anti-Spanish sentiment. Some notice that the iterated claim that "merciful" Britain did not, like "cruel Spain," shed "seas of Indian blood" is challenged when the poem elsewhere mentions "heroes" "from Canada / To Georgia" who slew "Indian hosts" (lines 51–52, 259–60). I then ask whether the poem's silence about the future presence of Native Americans implicitly participates in the racial displacement and extermination overtly depicted in Villagrá's epic. Some hesitate to make that indictment, but others sense how cultural oversights and silence can also be powerful instruments of suppression.

Students may need more help detecting still other problems in these poems, such as how the derivativeness of *Rising Glory* undermines its authors' claims for a new American art or how the diffusion of its focus — it nervously flits from one thing to another as if fearful of looking too closely — fails to impart a substantial identity to the colonies. In this poem America seems more a reification of abundant energy than the momentous culmination of history. In short, the poem accidentally somewhat reflects the instability of the polymorphous society of late-eighteenth-century America. *Rising Glory* omits more than a future for Native Americans; it is also silent about slaves, who Wheatley knew were not "by freedom blest" (line 787). But is Wheatley's nuanced representation of herself as a religiously and spiritually refined person who politely raises Cain similarly compromised? I urge students to consider the potential cost of the poet's burying the resistant aesthetics of "Being Brought" — its possible appropriation of ministerial authority in suggesting unprecedented racial readings of Isaiah's prophesies — beneath an outward acquiescence to conventional religious and literary authorization. Even if Wheatley hoped to instill her revisionary message deep within the reader's mind, does her positioning of her resistance below the conventional surface merely reenact the slave's daily experience of oppression? Class responses tend to be sharply divided.

Some students argue that the Puritan meditative poets were reenacting a form of enslavement too, particularly through an early Calvinistic devaluation of human capability, the very capacity Freneau and Brackenridge later exalt. Although, as I said, my students prefer the optimism of *Rising Glory* to the self-deprecation of Calvinistic meditations, they tend to distrust as exaggeration Freneau and Brackenridge's representation of "America" and to trust as genuine the Puritans' representation of their humble submission to divine authority. When they do I ask them to differentiate between the preoccupation with the personal fulfillment that is prophesied in *Rising Glory* and the preoccupation with personal salvation featured in the Puritan meditations.

I also remind students that the meditators assumed personae in a culturally authorized sinner-saint drama, not only by envisaging redemption but also by addressing specific audiences (Hammond). Moreover, if Bradstreet and Taylor practiced a decorum of imperfection, then they composed and evaluated their verse in relation to a humanly constructed paradigm. Therefore they valued their art, even if only as an expression of their incapability, potentially blurring the boundary between humility and pride.

In, say, Bradstreet's 1666 poem on the burning of her house and in Taylor's 1683 poem on a sweeping flood, both of which seesaw between resentment toward and acceptance of divine will, my students encounter other indications that submission to divine authority might not have been easy for Puritans. Bradstreet interrupts the recollection of lost prized material possessions with "Adieu, Adieu; All's Vanity" (line 36), a safe, conventional ventriloquising of Ecclesiastes 1.14. I ask my students, Since there is no personal poetry in this formulaic line, no detail, does Bradstreet's declaration inhabit the same emotion-laden, well-furnished house as the previous lines of the poem? Does the disruptiveness of this line signal her flight from a potentially rebellious sentiment, as if the house of her emotion-filled verse were also dangerously on fire? Here, as throughout my effort, I am content if students plumb such questions from various angles and discover diverse, even antithetical, grids of *represented* meanings.

Although my approach privileges depth over breadth of perception, it is designed to enlarge student appreciation of contextual implications, artistic techniques, subtextual subtleties, and finally conceptual limitations. This last goal — acknowledging the enigmatic elusiveness of certainty and hence viewing resolute determination skeptically — is personally important to me. To appreciate the persistence of mystery at the edge of human understanding is implicitly to urge a profound communal humility and tolerance.

Works Cited

Primary Works

Bradstreet, Anne. *The Works of Anne Bradstreet*. Ed. Jeannine Hensley. Cambridge: Harvard UP, 1967.

Cook(e), Ebenezer. *The Sot-Weed Factor*. 1708. *Colonial American Poetry*. Ed. Kenneth Silverman. New York: Hafner, 1968. 282–301.

Freneau, Philip, and Hugh Henry Brackenridge. *A Poem, on the Rising Glory of America*. 1772. *Colonial American Poetry*. Ed. Kenneth Silverman. New York: Hafner, 1968. 423–43.

Herbert, George. *The Works of George Herbert*. Ed. F. E. Hutchinson. Oxford: Clarendon, 1941.

Pain, Philip. *Daily Meditations*. 1668. Excerpted in *American Poetry of the Seventeenth Century*. Ed. Harrison T. Meserole. University Park: Pennsylvania State UP, 1985. 287–91.

Quarles, Francis. *The Complete Works of Francis Quarles*. Ed. A. B. Grosart. 3 vols. New York: AMS, 1967.

Rich, Richard. *Newes from Virginia*. 1610. *American Garland*. Ed. Charles A. Firth. Oxford: Clarendon, 1915. 9–16.

Taylor, Edward. *The Poems of Edward Taylor*. Ed. Donald E. Stanford. New Haven: Yale UP, 1960.

Wheatley, Phillis. *Phillis Wheatley and Her Writings*. Ed. William H. Robinson. New York: Garland, 1984.

Villagrá, Gaspar Pérez de. *Historia de la Nueva México*. 1610. Excerpted in *The Heath Anthology of American Literature*. Ed. Paul Lauter. Vol. 1. Lexington: Heath, 1998. 163–72.

Secondary Works

Gay, Peter. *The Age of Enlightenment*. New York: Time-Life, 1966.

Hammond, Jeffrey A. *Sinful Self, Saintly Self: The Puritan Experience of Poetry*. Athens: U of Georgia P, 1993.

Martz, Louis. *The Poetry of Meditation: A Study of English Literature in the Seventeenth Century*. New Haven: Yale UP, 1962.

Mignon, Charles W. "Edward Taylor's *Preparatory Meditations*: A Decorum of Imperfection." *PMLA* 83 (1968): 1423–28.

Scheick, William J. *Design in Puritan American Literature*. Lexington: UP of Kentucky, 1992.

Tillyard, E. M. W. *The Elizabethan World Picture*. London: Chatto, 1943.

White, Hayden. *Metahistory: The Historical Imagination in Nineteenth-Century Europe*. Baltimore: Johns Hopkins UP, 1973.

Joseph Fichtelberg

Early American Prose Fiction and the Anxieties of Affluence

Early American prose fiction presents a special challenge to under-graduates. While the genre is more recognizable than sermons, tracts, and other colonial documents, it uses familiar novelistic materials in often unfamiliar ways. In my teaching I try to resolve this uncanny reading experience by considering the rapidly changing cultural scene in the early republic. I use what Gordon Wood calls the essential difference of the eighteenth century (181) to recapture the shifts in ideological orientation and economic practice, in definitions of gender, and in self-fashioning so crucial to the new nation.

Since I treat prose fiction in the second half of a survey of early American literature, I begin with texts that express many critical issues of the period. Franklin's *Autobiography* lays the groundwork by underscoring republican conflicts over the proper balance between self-interest and public service, a problem nicely captured in the distinctions between parts 1 and 3 of the text. The crucial mediator is Franklin's "Art of Virtue" (59). This key term in eighteenth-century culture is often difficult to convey: students readily grasp the moral dimension of virtue, reflected in Franklin's confession of errata, but they must work harder to see its civic dimensions — the notion that Franklin's economic success may threaten republican order. That civic dimension gives the *Autobiography* its dramatic force and allows me to point toward issues that novelists will endlessly explore.

James Madison and Alexander Hamilton in *The Federalist Papers* help to underscore many problems that Franklin announced. The tensions in the work between elite and popular rule seem to come alive in Hamilton's assertion (no. 35) that merchants are the natural spokesmen for laborers — a view that students find suspiciously elitist. I use their suspicion to foreground one of Madison's most startling appeals, in number 14, that Americans, "knit together as they are by so many chords of affection," might still live "as members of the same family" (66). This political use of sentiment, echoing John Winthrop's plea to be "knitt more nearly together in the Bond of brotherly affeccion" (2: 283), allows me to establish a context for one of the era's dominant literary themes, the social uses of sentiment. Sentiment here is a conservative force, a means of imagining a national family impervious to the erosions of faction and interest. But sentiment, in the form of active benevolence, was also a means to envision a new liberal order, reflected in Adam Smith's notion of sympathy (*Theory* 23) and the humanitarian claims of English capitalists (Haskell 151). In short, sentiment, and the novels that exploit it, exposes the strains of a deferential culture coming to terms with an emerging market.

One of the most useful texts for studying those strains is J. Hector St. John de Crèvecoeur's *Letters from an American Farmer* (1782). Like all important ideological fictions, the work attempts to elide central contradictions, exemplified in three cardinal points. I ask students first to consider the caged-slave episode of Letter IX, the discussion of the three regions of settlement in Letter III, and James's flight to the frontier in Letter XII. Although students are horrified by the depiction of the tortured slave, they also frequently express skepticism about James's emotional posturing and dining with the slave's tormentor. Much of his passionate outburst in the earlier part of the letter thus seems bad conscience, whose very excess clashes sharply with the balanced geography of Letter III — where the middle, farming regions in which James lives moderate the extremities of maritime enterprise and frontier violence. But if James so extravagantly values moderation in Letter III, why does he appear to embrace the frontier in Letter XII, even referring to himself as a "frontier inhabitant" (205)?

In answer, I ask students to look closely at the text's structure. In Letter II, for example, James's effusiveness on the farm seems to be associated with extravagance and waste. He longs to wander far away but feels bound by his father's bequest; he longs to express his profound emotions but finds no language equal to the task. On an annual pigeon shoot he can hardly count the victims, all attracted to the caged, blinded pigeon each farmer retains — a striking anticipation of the caged slave. Such conflicts point to the much more elaborate tensions of the Nantucket letters, in which the enormous profits of whaling are counterbalanced only by the high cost of living on the island and the inhabitants' frugality. Students then see that Crèvecoeur's *Letters* does indeed have a dramatic structure and purpose, one that projects a nightmare violation of republican restraint. What James intends on the frontier — the abode of excess — however, is by no means clear. Some students accept his utopian dreams of simplicity and his desire to escape the rapacious British. Others are disturbed by his subtle assertion of cultural superiority to the Native Americans to whom he will flee, a superiority echoed in James's slaveholding and in his imagining the colonies a preserve for Europeans alone. In any case, the text lays bare the strains experienced by many of Crèvecoeur's contemporaries as they tried to imagine the instabilities of an emerging liberal order.

When we take up the novels themselves, beginning with William Hill Brown's *The Power of Sympathy* (1789), I present students with yet another anomaly: the apparent regressiveness of early republican literary tastes. While English readers had largely abandoned the novel of seduction for subtler explorations of social manners in the work of Fanny Burney, Charlotte Smith, and, later, Jane Austen, American readers remained engrossed in tales of fallen women and imperiled virtue. Several plausible explanations have been offered for the disparity, including anxiety over republican virtue (Mulford xiv–vii; Kerber

199–200; Lewis 699–703), concern over threats to republican resolve (Fliegelman 235–45; Barnes 9–11), and conflicts between republican ideals and political or social realities (Davidson 110–40; Stern 5–6). I call on all these approaches in class and attempt to link them with a yet wider problem discussed by Steven Watts: the psychological and social crises imposed by a rapidly expanding market (*Republic* 14).

Despite its austere moralism *The Power of Sympathy* captures many of these concerns. Students are often puzzled by this book, which resembles less a novel than a series of anticipatory gestures toward a novel. Discussing the succession of scandals in the text — the accounts of Elizabeth Whitman, Fanny Apthorp, the mad Fidelia, and the unfortunate Harringtons — we become aware not only of the novel's contrapuntal rhythm of error and admonition but also of the excessive posturing of its characters. The widespread hostility toward novels among moral censors of the day may account for the rhythm: Brown seems painfully aware of the need to be factual, instructive, and proper yet also stimulating and slightly scandalous. But when students scoff at Fidelia's mannered grief or Harrington's effusive sympathy with the slave mother of letter 36, I use their skepticism to lead us toward the text's central contradiction — the possibility that virtue itself may be insufficient. Mrs. Holmes, in letter 7, properly asserts, "A great proportion of our happiness depends on our own choice" (15). Yet when the rakish Harrington genuinely reforms and falls for the virtuous Harriot, he is thrust into an incestuous relationship with his illegitimate sister, precipitating his suicide. My students rightly ask why, in republican America, where stubborn patriarchs were everywhere yielding to energetic youth, the sins of fathers should be visited on their dutiful sons.

In answer, I explore the possibility that the younger Harrington may himself be guilty of a crime — the inability to keep diverse influences within bounds. In a discourse on reading in letter 11, Reverend Holmes claims that the literary marketplace presents a flood of books that the judicious reader ought to channel. The claim echoes Madison's fear in *Federalist* 37 that it was an "arduous" task to mark "the line of partition" between objects "extensive and complicated in their nature" (178). Although Madison here addresses distinctions between federal and state power, his larger concern involves adapting elite authority to what the historian J. G. A. Pocock has called a world of "moving objects" (qtd. in Agnew 175) — the exuberance and excess of a liberal society. When the younger Harrington, in a moment of supreme moral insight, praises sensibility as the "inexhaustible spring of love supreme" from which flows a "tide of affection and SYMPATHY" (62), he expresses the novel's deepest social contradiction, that the expansive energies of the new republic might also shake it to pieces. Brown's text thus shows the indispensable but frightening power of republican sympathy.

What is most striking about Charles Brockden Brown's two most readily available Gothic fictions, *Wieland* (1798) and *Edgar Huntly* (1799), is how placid, even prosperous, social settings can quickly disintegrate into chaos. Students respond most readily to the incommensurabilities in *Wieland*: the gap between Theodore Wieland's rational behavior and his eventual madness; the irresoluteness of Carwin compared with his fearsome Gothic attributes; the laughable mildness of his terrible ventriloquism; the labored mentations of Clara Wieland as she struggles to unravel the simplest ruses. Such discrepancies, however, are critical to Brown's social concerns. English practitioners like Anne Radcliffe and Monk Lewis used the Gothic novel to explore anxieties over the authority of reason, religion, and social rule. For Brown, who notoriously disavowed European trappings, the American Gothic exposed other fears — the political anxieties of a young republic beset throughout the 1790s by internal factions and the menace of world war. I help students see those anxieties by asking them to find references to light: beams, rays, glimmerings, gleams. When students find and analyze the light imagery, it becomes clear that the boundaries separating benign from hostile perceptions, the light of reason from spontaneous combustion, are all too permeable, precisely as Madison had argued in *Federalist* 37. Another useful strategy is to discuss the novel's interior spaces. Brown's careful structure reveals that houses, closets, diaries, even minds offer no sanctuary from violators natural or supernatural, a paranoia I also note in late-Federalist political rhetoric. When we turn to Clara Wieland, one of the more resolute of the era's female narrators, I ask students to find passages depicting her as either a vigorous, independent spirit or the dupe of her passions and fears. That it is difficult to characterize her suggests a larger conflict in the text and the times, a desire to control social forces too urgent to contain.

The sense of violated interiority reappears in *Edgar Huntly*, which draws on the captivity narratives with which my students are familiar. I ask them to take a stand on what motivates Huntly: Is he a benevolent youth trying to extend his sympathy to strangers, or is he a savage fighter learning harsh truths about the frontier? Most readers find it hard to decide. If Edgar attempts to lay bare the secrets of Waldegrave's murder or Clithero's guilt, he must also learn the difference between benevolence and impotence. If he roves the wilderness, penetrating caverns in his eagerness to aid Clithero, he must also kill "savages" and become savage himself. In trying to do right, he is overborne by his unconscious impulses, signified by the frequent references to caves, pits, shattered containers, and lost or stolen manuscripts. The novel's power lies in these suggestive conflicts — conflicts that recall the murderous struggles to subdue the frontier (Slotkin 384–90) and the equally vicious struggles to protect the republic from Jacobins, aliens, and other demons of the Federalist imaginary. Brown's Gothic terrors thus disclose all too frightening social prospects.

Novels by women in the 1790s reflect a similar distrust of unrestrained passion but in ways that suggest the special problems raised by gender. I occasionally find it useful to pair two of the decade's best-sellers, Susanna Rowson's *Charlotte Temple* (1791) and Hannah Webster Foster's *The Coquette* (1797), to explore such themes. *Charlotte Temple* strikes most students as a fairly conventional and obvious tale counseling young readers in prudence; the challenge is to give the text urgency. I ask students first to compare its plot to that of a novel like *Edgar Huntly*. Whatever their differences, the novels share one feature: like the prodigal sons of popular contemporary fiction (Fliegelman), Charlotte is a wanderer, a social atom detached from family and friends. What distinguishes Charlotte is not only her more limited autonomy but also the greater anxieties attending it — anxieties that point to the revolutionary nature of republicanism. At home, republican wives must "by constant assiduity and unremitted attention" recall wandering husbands (66; Lewis 713–15). But once in circulation themselves, wanderers like Charlotte become the focus of contradictory tendencies. As a fallen woman, betrayed by her own naive passions, Charlotte is a warning against the passionate self-interest that threatens all republics. As an object of benevolence, though, the occasion of sympathy, she stimulates the redemptive feeling that transforms societies. So that students will appreciate that power, I ask them to note the number of times in the novel that class boundaries are violated. From Mr. Temple's defiance of his own aristocratic father in marrying the daughter of a benevolent but ruined merchant, to the fortune-hunting Mlle La Rue's marriage to a wealthy New Yorker, to Montraville's treacherous marriage to the fashionable Julia Franklin, the novel's social relations fluctuate as constantly as Charlotte's palpitating heart. And therein lies Rowson's dilemma: she warns that prudence must direct youthful passion, but she also knows that passions have become the indispensable currency of a new, more fluid, social order, much like the passionate wandering of Edgar Huntly. Charlotte is an object lesson in the perils of republican sensibility.

In *The Coquette*, by contrast, a bright, gay, and volatile protagonist circulates in a more assertive, even aggressive, manner. At the outset, I ask students to consider the text's odd extremes—the assertion by Mrs. Richman and Eliza, in letter 23, that women should be allowed a vigorous, if tempered, political expression, and Eliza's late self-condemnation as "the disgrace of my family, and a dishonor to virtue and my sex!" (159). Foster shows enough sympathy with both positions to make it easy for students to take sides: Is Eliza a cultural rebel or, as one student put it, "a crybaby who gets what she deserves"? Certainly the latter sentiment captures the text's moral purpose. But if Eliza is a chastened rebel, she is not quite the moral object lesson that Elizabeth Whitman was in *The Power of Sympathy*. To point up the difference, we discuss how the text appeals to various cultural models of conduct, from handbooks of female decorum like John Gregory's *A Father's Legacy to His Daughters* to male exemplars such as Chesterfield and Franklin. Like Franklin, Eliza attempts to rise in the world, and the novel is never entirely certain how to treat that desire (Smith-Rosenberg 178). Although Foster seems to condemn Eliza's rejection of Reverend Boyer's "elegant sufficiency" (47) for a chance at Major Sanford's fortune, she takes pains *not* to restrict money-mindedness to the novel's suspect characters. Boyer himself warns Eliza that her virtue may "depreciate" (84), and even Mrs. Richman discusses child-rearing in terms of payment and "ample reward" (97). A more telling ambiguity involves the novel's three dead babies, a detail that never fails to disturb even Eliza's sternest critics. Foster was historically bound to kill off Eliza's son and perhaps morally bound to kill off Sanford's. But why would Foster destroy the "reward" of the upright Mrs. Richman, if not to challenge the harsh decree that delivering a male heir was a woman's only means of economic productiveness? Eliza's rebelliousness could not be allowed to triumph in *The Coquette*, but neither would her spirit rest easily.

Foster's ambivalence suggests wider tensions in the cultural position of early American novelists. While they felt called on to combat the luxuries and seductions that republican moralists linked to the market, they were equally dependent on that market. For novels were also commodities, vendible private property that received constitutional endorsement, and thus were tied to an expanding world of market relations (Breen) rapidly transforming Federalist America into what the historian Robert Wiebe calls a new "open society." I often use two early-nineteenth-century novels by women, Tabitha Gilman Tenney's *Female Quixotism* (1801) and Rebecca Rush's *Kelroy* (1812), to suggest the strains involved in reconciling the early American novel's essentially conservative appeal with its radical potential.

Tenney's novel, one of the most accomplished of the period, is a self-conscious satire that not only condemns the romantic theatricality of its protagonist, Dorcasina Sheldon, but also questions the theatrical expectations of her audience. As a distillation of the fears expressed by contemporary opponents of the novel, Dorcasina provides a useful counterpoint to the tragic victims of seduction. Because her foibles are obvious, I ask my students to observe how the novel develops wider cultural issues. Tenney, the wife of a Federalist congressman elected in 1800, is troubled by the Jeffersonian revolution.

Her frequent mockery of gazing, for example — Dorcasina's love-smitten glances at O'Connor and Captain Barry and the soulful looks of her feigned suitors — suggests the preoccupation with mutual spectatorship that Jean-Christophe Agnew associates with eighteenth-century representations of the market (170). The disguises and elaborate ruses adopted by all characters in the novel point to a society still struggling to reconcile the mutual suspicion of unrestrained competition with the affective, often capricious ties uniting competitors. And as we consider the novel in this light, a provocative possibility develops: that Dorcasina, the butt of all the text's cruel jokes, is also the guardian of its most privileged values.

I develop this theme by asking students to make a moral diagram of the novel's characters, ranged around Dorcasina. On her dark side are impostors and rogues; on her bright side are guardians of common sense, including Scipio and the Stanlys. But do the bright characters remain bright or do they change? What distinguishes them from their darker counterparts? Like Seymore, Scipio plays tricks; like O'Connor, Barry is drawn to the Sheldons' wealth. If Dorcasina's fantasies confirm her foolishness, what distinguishes her role-playing from the elaborate ruses of those around her? Even the loyal Stanly, who promised to care for Dorcasina after her father's death, kidnaps her in a romantic charade that turns her into a mouthpiece for republican principle. "And now, I entreat you, sir," she appeals, "to grant me my liberty, and suffer me to return where I alone can be happy, to my dear native village; [and] to my home [. . .]" (296). Indeed, the Stanlys' resort to imposture exposes Tenney's widest social criticism, that all moral types are infected by what Agnew calls a threshold mentality (4), the market-driven expectation that any encounter promises infinite satisfaction. While O'Connor finds Dorcasina "a thousand times more charming" (31) than he foresaw, the upright Barry imagines the wealthy heiress to "possess a thousand attractions" (156). And while Dorcasina frets over which fashionable dress to wear, her servant John Brown revels in her late father's superfine coats and holland shirts, spreading them out on the bed like some nineteenth-century Gatsby. Even the humble farmhouse to which Dorcasina is led after being kidnapped has its teatime, and there seems to be little difference between the fantasies of commoners and those of their betters. All are caught in a dizzying web of commodities, ever threatening to spiral out of control. If Dorcasina gets the hard knocks she deserves, it may be only because she is less elusive than those who surround her.

Rush's *Kelroy* addresses the same problem from an opposite perspective, asking readers to imagine a world so rationalized that it lacks a moral center. I often begin by comparing Rush's mockery of Dr. Blake and the Gurnets with Jane Austen's treatment of John Dashwood and Lucy Steele in *Sense and Sensibility* (1811). Although the satire in the two works is structurally similar, their resolutions are not. In Austen, the standard of rational and cultivated behavior, embodied by Elinor Dashwood, is never in doubt. Even when she discovers Edward Ferrars's secret engagement to the "illiterate, artful and selfish" Lucy, Elinor is still able to "we[ep] for him more than for herself" (160), suggesting a refined and rational sensibility. For Rush, by contrast, social propriety seems poised over a vacuum. Her readers know they must spurn boorishness, but they are far less certain what the novel opposes to it. Neither the lovesick Walsingham nor the impoverished Kelroy nor even the virtuous Emily Hammond herself can ultimately stand up to Mrs. Hammond, the text's evil genius, whose force of character obliterates all resistance. What is most striking about Mrs. Hammond, though, is the banality of her evil. After we finish the novel I ask students to explain her vindictiveness toward Emily: Why would a mother so torment a dutiful daughter? The only clue the novel gives is that Mrs. Hammond has been possessed by the market, her soul displaced by the spirit of rational calculation. How and why does that happen?

In answer, I point to cultural and generic conditions. Since the first Congress, Americans had been whipsawed by economic booms and busts, erratic markets made more uncertain by French seizures, English blockades, and American embargoes. Such conditions approximated those that Thomas Kavanagh describes for eighteenth-century France, in which unprecedented economic uncertainty and social upheaval gave rise to cultural reflections on chance: gambling, statistics, and the novel. Mrs. Hammond is Rush's portrait of a character so overcome by the erratic logic of such markets that she can no longer distinguish her motives from the brutal behavior of fortune. From the outset she manages risk in her life, adapting to hostile conditions, retreating when she must, striking when she can. Her overwrought responses to the fire that destroys her house and to her subsequent lottery winning are of a piece with her response to the courtship of her two daughters: all involve a ruthless pragmatism that makes moral reflection impossible. Indeed the ubiquitous gambling in the novel provides the most arresting link between the behavior of markets and that of individuals. For Mrs. Hammond is a nightmare version of Franklin, honing the mere appearance of propriety until the effort finally paralyzes her. And the most frightening aspect of the nightmare is that no one she touches survives.

Although the texts I discuss here generally suggest a conservative sensibility, they clearly were also the midwives of liberalism. By presenting characters impelled by passion, such fictions explore in rigorous detail the commercial society envisioned by Francis Hutcheson, David Hume, Adam Smith, and others — one in which affections rather than deference bind individuals. When in the antebellum period social affections turned inward to the domestic economies of sentimental fiction, the work of the early novels was complete. Market relations had at last come to seem natural, intimate, and comforting.

Works Cited

Primary Works
Austen, Jane. *Sense and Sensibility*. Ed. Tony Tanner. Harmondsworth: Penguin, 1986.
Brown, Charles Brockden. *Edgar Huntly; or, Memoirs of a Sleep-Walker*. Ed. Norman S. Grabo. Harmondsworth: Penguin, 1988.
———. Wieland *and* Memoirs of Carwin the Biloquist. Ed. Jay Fliegelman. Harmondsworth: Penguin, 1991.
Brown, William Hill. *The Power of Sympathy*. Ed. Carla Mulford. Harmondsworth: Penguin, 1996.
Crèvecoeur, J. Hector St. John de. Letters from an American Farmer *and* Sketches of Eighteenth-Century America. Ed. Albert Stone. Harmondsworth: Penguin, 1987.
The Federalist Papers. Ed. Garry Wills. New York: Bantam, 1982.

Foster, Hannah Webster. *The Coquette*. Ed. Cathy N. Davidson. New York: Cambridge UP, 1986.

Franklin, Benjamin. *Benjamin Franklin's* Autobiography. Ed. J. A. Leo Lemay and P. M. Zall. New York: Norton, 1986.

Gregory, John. *A Father's Legacy to His Daughters*. Worcester: Thomas, 1795.

Rowson, Susanna. *Charlotte Temple*. Ed. Cathy N. Davidson. New York: Oxford UP, 1986.

Rush, Rebecca. *Kelroy*. Ed. Dana D. Nelson. New York: Oxford UP, 1992.

Smith, Adam. *The Theory of Moral Sentiments*. New York: Kelley, 1966.

Tenney, Tabitha Gilman. *Female Quixotism, Exhibited in the Romantic Opinions and Extravagant Adventures of Dorcasina Sheldon*. Ed. Jean Nienkamp and Andrea Collins. New York: Oxford UP, 1992.

Winthrop, John. "A Modell of Christian Charity." *Winthrop Papers*. Ed. Stewart Mitchell. 5 vols. Boston: Massachusetts Historical Soc., 1927–49.

Secondary Works

Agnew, Jean-Christophe. *Worlds Apart: The Market and the Theater in Anglo-American Thought, 1550–1750*. Cambridge: Cambridge UP, 1986.

Barnes, Elizabeth. *States of Sympathy: Seduction and Democracy in the American Novel*. New York: Columbia UP, 1997.

Breen, T. H. "'Baubles of Britain': The American and Consumer Revolutions of the Eighteenth Century." *Past and Present* 119 (1988): 73–104.

———. "An Empire of Goods: The Anglicization of Colonial America, 1690–1776." *Journal of British Studies* 25 (1986): 467–99.

Davidson, Cathy N. *Revolution and the Word: The Rise of the Novel in America*. New York: Oxford UP, 1986.

Fliegelman, Jay. *Prodigals and Pilgrims: The American Revolution against Patriarchal Authority, 1750–1800*. Cambridge: Cambridge UP, 1982.

Haskell, Thomas L. "Capitalism and the Origins of the Humanitarian Sensibility, Part 2." *The Antislavery Debate: Capitalism and Abolitionism as a Problem in Historical Interpretation*. Ed. Thomas Bender. Berkeley: U of California P, 1992. 136–60.

Kavanagh, Thomas. *Enlightenment and the Shadows of Chance: The Novel and the Culture of Gambling in Eighteenth-Century France*. Baltimore: Johns Hopkins UP, 1993.

Kerber, Linda K. *Women of the Republic: Intellect and Ideology in Revolutionary America*. Chapel Hill: U of North Carolina P, 1980.

Lewis, Jan. "The Republican Wife: Virtue and Seduction in the Early Republic." *William and Mary Quarterly* 3rd ser. 44 (1987): 689–721.

Mulford, Carla. Introduction. The Power of Sympathy *and* The Coquette. Harmondsworth: Penguin, 1996. ix–li.

Slotkin, Richard. *Regeneration through Violence: The Mythology of the American Frontier, 1600–1860*. New York: Harper, 1996.

Smith-Rosenberg, Carroll. "Domesticating 'Virtue': Coquettes and Revolutionaries in Young America." *Literature and the Body: Essays on Populations and Persons*. Ed. Elaine Scarry. Baltimore: Johns Hopkins UP, 1988. 160–84.

Stern, Julia. *The Plight of Feeling: Sympathy and Dissent in the Early American Novel*. Chicago: U of Chicago P, 1997.

Watts, Steven. *The Republic Reborn: War and the Making of Liberal America, 1790–1820*. Baltimore: Johns Hopkins UP, 1987.

———. *The Romance of Real Life: Charles Brockden Brown and the Origins of American Culture*. Baltimore: Johns Hopkins UP, 1994.

Wiebe, Robert H. *The Opening of American Society: From the Adoption of the Constitution to the Eve of Disunion*. New York: Knopf, 1984.

Wood, Gordon S. *The Radicalism of the American Revolution*. New York: Knopf, 1992.

Jeffrey H. Richards

Early American Drama and Theater

Recently, scholars have called for new thinking on early American drama and theater (Avery; Mulford, "Re-presenting"; Richards, *Theater*). While some newer approaches will likely be suitable only for specialists, the study of drama in the undergraduate classroom can enrich the experience of students and provide useful ways of thinking about literature and culture during the period to 1800. Many early English colonists — even immigrants who opposed the development of the stage in the New World — brought some familiarity with drama as a literary form and with the theater as a cultural institution. A number of texts not normally taught as drama — Bradstreet's poem "The Flesh and the Spirit," for example — can be reconsidered as a particular form of play. Other texts, written primarily for reading alone rather than for acting, offer commentary on the politics, customs, and myths of the period. Plays from the late eighteenth century, meant to be acted, can illustrate emerging forms of mass culture and popular attitudes toward art. Examining the place of the playwright in the

early theater may further illuminate the problem of literary authorship in the early republic. Finally, including plays in classes on early
American literature provides a link from developing traditions back
to Elizabethan and medieval English drama and forward to melo-
drama, stage realism, film, and television.

One can teach a number of plays in classes on early American literature. Most of the earliest plays serve political and satiric ends and
can be used to highlight Anglo-American and other conflicts. Plays
written after the Revolutionary War, particularly, seek to entertain on
stage as well as instruct in print and can foster discussions of the place
of the stage in culture (see Strand). Women authors are a significant
presence among early dramatists, with Mercy Otis Warren, Susanna
Rowson, and Judith Sargent Murray dominating. No African American author of a play before 1800 is known, but some plays include references to or even feature black characters, notably John Leacock's
The Fall of British Tyranny and Royall Tyler's *The Contrast*. Other plays
have been alleged to include African American characters, including
Thomas Forrest's *Disappointment* (Mays) and Robert Munford's *Candidates*, but as David Mays and Rodney Baine point out, that is by no
means certain. Yet the plays raise many significant themes, including
the roles of women in society, the meaning of the term *slavery*, the
function of dramatic satire as political protest, the theater as a site of
or escape from controversy, and the formation of American national
culture. By recognizing that citizens of colonial and republican
America read, wrote, saw, and protested for and against plays, students encounter a broader context for all literature from the period.

When I teach early American drama, I like to present theater as a
cultural force, something that includes the institution of the stage but
is larger than that. A good example of how drama and what I call the
theatrics of culture intersect is Munford's *The Candidates* (see Baine).
Because the play — probably never acted — depicts a specific election
in colonial Virginia (for 1770), I use that satiric comedy to draw connections to elections in general. Thus students can see not only how
vote buying, special interests, political speechifying, and overall
election-year foolery parallel their understanding of political contests
over two hundred years later but also how Munford captures the

theatricality of elections themselves. Students find in Munford a ready entrance into what might first seem a remote past and into larger issues of drama and of its relation to cultural practices.

The Puritan rejection of the stage, styled an "antitheatrical prejudice" by Jonas Barish, is a common explanation for the lack of plays from the seventeenth and early eighteenth centuries. The fear of acting (a form of hypocrisy, as ministers pointed out) and of actors (as criminals and vagabonds) may have produced a legal and social climate that was certain to keep out "The Players" (Crashaw), but it cannot explain the complex attitudes of early colonists. I like to note to students that there was, after all, a nonconformist, even Puritan dramatic tradition that included everything from transcripts of ecclesiastical trials of the Lollards in the late 1300s to the religious plays of John Foxe in the 1550s (Kendall; Richards, *Theater* 61–84). John Calvin and other dissenting theologians often used theatrical tropes in the vein of *theatrum mundi*. Such Massachusetts luminaries as Increase Mather and Samuel Sewall read or owned plays, including those by ancient Greek dramatists, Ben Jonson, and John Dryden, even though they criticized the mounting of shows. Not surprisingly, the more secular-minded Virginians had direct experience with the stage. Captain John Smith knew London playwrights and must have frequented the theater enough to see his adventures in Virginia mocked on stage (Barbour). William Byrd II, who spent nearly half his life in England, noted in his diary his regular attendance at London playhouses (Lockridge). Thus although there were few places to put on plays, people in northern and southern colonies held dramatic or theatrical thinking — not always the same thing — to be acceptable forms of rendering experience.

One way of observing this resistance to the "antitheatrical prejudice" is to consider some early American texts as plays. Asking students to visualize the speakers, stages, and actions in these texts enables them to experience more directly material that might first appear distant or abstract. Bradstreet's dialogue between Flesh and Spirit, a deft poem of statement and reversal, is part of a long tradition of dialogue literature that has origins in pastoral debates of classical writing and continues through the eighteenth century in American colleges as a formal exercise, as in Francis Hopkinson's 1762 piece, "An Exercise Containing a Dialogue and Ode." Smith's *Generall Historie of Virginia* (1624) exhibits a similar dialogue-debate structure, especially in the scenes where Smith and Powhatan match contrasting worldviews. More overtly, Michael Wigglesworth's dream-vision poem *Day of Doom* (1662), includes virtual stage directions in the margins and a preponderance of dialogue as sinners are brought before the bar to discourse with the judging Christ. In Wigglesworth's *God's Controversy with New England* (1662), God speaks in a dramatic monologue. An even better example of dramatic construction of material is Edward Taylor's *God's Determinations*, a poem that includes dialogues and a narrative of redemption, putting the drama of salvation into a form approximating a literary drama (387–459). In short, having students conceive these works as drama allows them to think in new ways about accepted generic categories.

After considering with students the cultural landscape of seventeenth-century Anglo-America, I introduce specific dramatic and theatrical history. While colonial Americans by the eighteenth century were reading Shakespeare, Dryden, Congreve, and Farquhar, few Anglo-Americans before 1716 would have had an opportunity to see a play in an actual theater. Court records in Accomac County, Virginia, allege a performance of something called "The Bear and the Cub" in 1665, probably in a tavern on the outskirts of Pungoteague (Meserve 16), but no other written record is known of a public performance of a play before theaters were constructed in Williamsburg, New York, and Charleston in the second, third, and fourth decades of the eighteenth century (McNamara 6–27). From this history, students comprehend quickly that colonial writers had little incentive to write for the stage.

Many students who take my American drama course are theater majors; they are particularly interested in the moment the stage became its own force beyond the cultural events such as elections or trials that illustrate the theatricality of social life. I focus on the period in theatrical history when traveling groups of actors come from England to put on plays. The Murray-Kean company made a brief appearance in the late 1740s, but the more significant troupe was the

Hallam family, who inaugurated their American seasons in Williamsburg in 1752. For the next two decades the Hallams, David Douglass, and other itinerants appeared in cities and towns along the eastern seaboard. English-language theater came to Charleston, Savannah, Norfolk, Baltimore, Philadelphia, and New York at various times during the eighteenth century. Students are often amused to learn that because of skepticism over the appropriateness of theatrical entertainments, some performances were billed as "lectures," in which scenes from a well-known play (such as *Othello*) would illustrate a talk (on, e.g., jealousy). Eventually, the Hallams were able to construct theaters in Philadelphia and New York and drop the ruse of the lecture (Highfill; Silverman 60–61, 64–69). Nevertheless, theater remained very much tied to local custom and attitude; Boston, for example, a stronghold of opposition to the stage, had no professional theater season until 1794. These details help illuminate for students the frequent presence of the justifying prologue, best represented by Tyler in *The Contrast*. At the same time, explaining that theaters rarely if ever employed black actors helps students understand why African American characters were rarely represented beyond crude types (see Ashby).

I also like to introduce early the material conditions of acting and watching drama. Plays look different when one takes into account certain aspects of the eighteenth-century stage. For instance, most staged plays were accompanied by music and billed with a musically oriented second feature (Porter). One might ask students, then, how it affects interpretation to imagine the virtuous Maria singing the "Song of Alknomook" in *The Contrast* rather than merely reciting a poem. Students often feel singing gives the play an artificiality that works against the more "natural" gossip between Charlotte and Letitia. Another critical problem arises when one considers that most leading actors in America before 1800 were British-born and were trained either in England or in Jamaica. Thus, in teaching *The Contrast*, I raise the complication that Tyler wrote the part of the backwoods Yankee Jonathan for a British-born actor, Thomas Wignell, who fled to Jamaica during the Revolution (Hill; Wright). The Yankee colonel, Manly, was played by Lewis Hallam, Jr., another British actor who spent most of his career in the American colonies and Jamaica. Critically, the performance history illuminates the literary text, as students see the nationalism in Tyler's play as contingent on the attitudes of an American audience watching British actors playing Americans.

One can show how theater and drama interact in the eighteenth century by pairing two of the first plays written by Anglo-Americans: Thomas Godfrey, Jr.'s *The Prince of Parthia* and Forrest's *The Disappointment* (Mays). By contrasting Godfrey's high-flown and unrelieved blank verse with Forrest's American dialects and spicy humor and by framing the discussion as a choice that theater managers actually had to make, an instructor can illustrate several long-standing conflicts: between the apostles of art drama and the advocates for an entertaining stage, between Europeanized and distinctly American works, and between the belief that the stage should avoid controversy and the belief that the stage is a place to air controversies. Forrest's play, a satire on local figures, was originally scheduled to be produced in Philadelphia by the American Company in 1767, the year of its composition. However, complaints from some of those Forrest pilloried led to the play's being withdrawn in favor of a verse tragedy written in 1759 by Godfrey, a writer from Philadelphia and Wilmington, North Carolina, who had died in 1763. The theater managers' choice of a Shakespeareanized drama about fraternal and filial conflicts in ancient Parthia over a localized, satiric, ethnic-humor play that was sure to stir controversy reveals a great deal about the workings of drama and theater in early America. Although a few eighteenth-century American playwrights attempted to capture something like the peculiar flavor and mores of contemporary society—Munford, Jonathan Sewall, and Tyler, for instance—not many such works made it to the stage. Most playwrights before 1787, whether using local or distant history and settings, wrote for readers, not playgoers, often for satiric effect (Hunter). Thus students recognize that stage realism, much prized in the twentieth century, was not especially welcome in the playhouses of eighteenth-century Anglo-America.

The era of the American Revolution produced many plays that can be used as springboards to discussion about political representations in drama. Munford's *The Patriots* and *The Candidates* give glimpses into prewar Virginia political life. As in politics, so in art; many of the plays divide quite neatly into Whig and Tory. Two of the Tory works stand out for potential classroom use. *The Battle of Brooklyn*, an anonymous play published by the loyalist printer in New York, Rivington, ridicules the flight of Washington's troops from Long Island in August 1776. As a topical, history-in-the-making drama, it illustrates for students not only that drama was then a form of news but also that many Americans in 1776 believed that the patriots were fumbling rabble who would be quickly dispatched and Washington no more than a "little minded barbarian" (90). Another Tory play, and one of the most intriguing, is Crèvecoeur's "Landscapes." First published in 1925 as one of the cast-off "sketches" that did not get printed with *Letters from an American Farmer*, "Landscapes" is in essence a closet drama of an overly zealous Committee of Safety who uses its power during wartime to persecute Tories. Students find the satire in the play especially biting in its scorn for revolutionary behavior. Because of the complexity of the issues and the relation of the piece to Crèvecoeur's other work, the play would probably work best with upper-level students who can be presumed to know *Letters*.

Two of the patriot plays available can be taught as contrasts to the Tory dramas. Mercy Otis Warren's *The Group* works well against "Landscapes" as fanatical loyalists in the one and fanatical patriots in the other try to justify their positions. Warren wrote two other political satires, *The Adulateur* and *The Defeat*; but *The Group* exists in a more satisfactory textual state and is the most interesting of the three. *The Group* examines the loyalist officials left in Boston after the villain of the previous two Warren plays, Governor Thomas Hutchinson, has fled to London. While clearly excoriating the Tory line and promoting Whig ideology and patriot action, Warren also allows a few loyalist and British characters to reflect on the difficulty of their situation (Richards, *Mercy Otis Warren* 84–102). Students can see that life unfolded on both sides as a drama, each side using play form to condemn the opposition and give sympathy to victims.

John Leacock's patriot play *The Fall of British Tyranny*, although quite long, works well for showing students how drama could be developed both as propaganda and as a source for ongoing news. Like Warren's, Leacock's play intends each character to be read as reflecting a living person and it ranges over many venues and events from 1775 to early 1776. Unlike in *The Battle of Brooklyn*, the play's logical classroom mate, the patriot fighters and Washington are heroes in *Fall*. If I could only use one play before *The Contrast*, I would choose *Fall* because it has so many uses. As one of the first plays to depict African American characters, it shows the complexity of racial issues during the Revolution. The enemy governor, Lord Dunmore, offers slaves their freedom, while the patriots fight to keep the slave system intact. The play is also full of allusions to the world as a stage, showing how theater functions as a significant metaphor for revolutionary rhetoric. As with *The Group*, some historicizing, including identifying who characters represent, helps students, but it should not be the main focus. Instead, I use *Fall* to demonstrate how rival concepts of theater — the world as a stage versus the stage as a world — mirror political and cultural divisions in the Revolution (Richards, *Theater* 249–51).

To show the full variety of early drama, I like to include at least one blank-verse play. Godfrey's *Prince* illustrates the form, but I prefer to use Warren's *The Ladies of Castile* as an example of postrevolutionary drama. Both Godfrey and Warren used blank verse and distant events in time and place to elevate their works into art. Warren's work in particular looks forward to a trend among nineteenth-century playwrights to evoke contemporary themes through work set in other times. In *Ladies* and another blank-verse play, *The Sack of Rome*, both written in the 1780s and published in 1790, Warren features strong female characters whose strength and political conviction appear at moments of national crisis. In *Ladies* Donna Maria, married to the Spanish republican hero, Don Juan, stands up to the imperial forces that threaten to crush an incipient democratic rebellion. Of all plays before 1800 *Ladies* best exemplifies the doctrine of republican motherhood, but as a blank-verse tragedy, it works to demonstrate for students how the form is used to enhance and enlarge the importance of a subject (Kerber 269–71; Oreovicz; Richards, *Mercy Otis Warren* 107–20; Watts 40–42).

I have found in my drama class that, to keep student interest, it is best to follow a blank-verse tragedy from the period with a social comedy. Tyler's *The Contrast* is the best-known of all early plays, and justifiably so. I use it to illustrate acting techniques of the period, from Charlotte's well-staged ankle revelation in act 1 (a class favorite) to Manly's appeal for applause at the conclusion of act 5, which, if I play it and time it right for the end of the class, usually will generate a clap or two. Like Leacock's *Fall, The Contrast* shows how differing conceptions of theater — stage as place of instruction versus playhouse as site of entertainment — inform Tyler's entire conception of his drama. Adapting the mode of a Sheridan comedy to the American — specifically, New York — scene, the playwright manages to capture not only some types that would long inhabit the stage, such as the Yankee and the stiff romantic hero, but also themes connected to an emerging republic. Filled with references to the existing New York stage and to the issue of the appropriateness of the theater in the new polity, Tyler's comedy enables readers to laugh at several sides of the debate. Jonathan imagines the stage literally as a living room; Dimple considers the theater merely a stage at which to exhibit his rakish social persona. It is Manly who speaks the position maintained by the action of the play: that the theater has a place in culture as long as it encourages virtue, not vice (see Evelev). Thus the question of whether theater must be responsible for the civic education of a society grows naturally out of the play's action and humor.

Through recent republication, Judith Sargent Murray's play *The Traveller Returned* has been rescued from the obscurity in which it lay since it was mounted in Boston in 1796 (see Kritzer 14–15; Meserve 155; Harris). I have taught it only twice, but students seem to enjoy discovering a woman author who wrote for the stage rather than the closet. Murray, who had seen *The Contrast* and written a prologue for it, borrows some of the same conventions; therefore, I find it interesting when students remark that Murray shows a greater variety of characters than Tyler does. Her plot resurrects the tension between Whig and Tory, particularly at the end of the war, a tension I connect to the earlier political propaganda plays. At last unveiling his identity, the traveler reconciles with his wife, and in the various restorations that result, Murray demonstrates that political bygones need to be bygones. Like Tyler she articulates the Federalist view that theater and social distinction still have their place in the republic, and that playwrights can satirize foibles gently, safely, and responsibly.

While both Murray's and Tyler's plays are examples of American comedies that incorporate current or recent events, one postwar play, William Dunlap's *André*, shows the dangers of representing American history as tragedy. Filled with father-son, British-American, loyalist-patriot, and other such tensions (Fliegelman 216–19; Philbrick, "Spy"), *André* demonstrates how issues left from the Revolution affected the serious drama. Its author was the most prolific of early American playwrights, and he also wrote the comic *Darby's Return* about an Irishman's American experiences. The story is based on the controversial hanging, ordered by George Washington, of Major John André, a British officer captured and tried as a spy for his role in the treachery of Benedict Arnold. Dunlap's drama, like earlier history plays by Brackenridge and Burk, uses poetry to elevate the action. However, Dunlap's attitude is far less overtly patriotic than the other playwrights'. As a youth, Dunlap spent the war in New York with his Tory parents. His play reflects his deep ambivalence — and perhaps his audience's — over the interpretation of the Revolution. Few literary works from the period work as well to demonstrate the agonizing in the 1790s over the nation's direction. Students find the young American officer, Bland, who identifies strongly with the British prisoner and nearly renounces his allegiance to his cause, both an attractive and a dangerous figure.

One other play from the 1790s incorporates several trends from the period, Rowson's *Slaves of Algiers*. Indeed, in a class covering several of the plays discussed above, *Slaves* can bring together a number of issues from other works. Although the plot has standard late-century familial revelations (making it quite similar to *The Traveller Returned*), a theme of American nationalism (like *The Contrast*), and conflicts over loyalty (like *André*), Rowson generates particular interest by figuring a seraglio and the sexual slavery of women. Intrigues and counterintrigues abound, along with cross-dressing, but at the end the children of Columbia, as the Americans are styled, are free. Nevertheless, as with Warren's *Ladies*, the exotic setting masks a number of issues in American culture; indeed, the class can use the drama to look at such issues as gender construction, slavery, and the creation of an "American character" in the early republic. When Rebecca says at the end, "By the Christian law, no man should be a slave" (92), students discover the enormous implications of her remark for patriarchal, slaveholding America.

I conclude with a note on sources. One problem in teaching early American drama has to do with representation. For example, only one surviving play from before 1800 includes significant mention of Native Americans (Rogers). A greater problem for teachers is access. Only a few general American literature anthologies available include a play—usually, just *The Contrast*—from the eighteenth century. The more specialized drama anthologies in paperback usually have at most three plays from before 1800. Therefore, to teach more than a few dramas from the period, one must rely on photoreprints or books on reserve. (Among older or out-of-print anthologies with early plays and good introductions, the best are Clark; Halline; Moody; Moses; Philbrick, *Trumpets*; Quinn, *Representative American Plays*.) Plays printed in the eighteenth century can be accessed through Early American Imprints, but it is difficult to teach the works on the microcard version. Even so, with a combination of currently available paperback collections and older anthologies on reserve or coursepacks, a number of plays can be taught profitably.

The scholarship on theater history is relatively extensive (a few examples include Dunlap, *History*; Hill; Hornblow; Seilhamer; Wilmeth; Wright); Hugh F. Rankin and Jared Brown focus exclusively on material in this period. However, many of the older works, and even more recent ones, have numerous errors of fact, and teachers should use them with caution, cross-checking them against other works. Indeed, even Jared Brown missed the point that John Leacock wrote *The Fall of British Tyranny* (Brown 74) as shown by Francis James Dallett and Carla Mulford (Introduction) some time ago. Local histories abound, many published in the earlier years of the twentieth century and before (Larson); some of the most useful are those by

William W. Clapp, George C. D. Odell, Thomas Clark Pollock, and Martin Staples Shockley. But relatively little critical work integrates the conditions of performance with the plays being mounted or pursues the influence of theater on actual playwriting in America. Perhaps the best such work remains the theater portion of Kenneth Silverman's *Cultural History*.

Some responses to early theater have been collected (Moses and Brown; Wolter); Jürgen C. Wolter provides an extensive, if not exhaustive, bibliography of early criticism aimed specifically at American plays. Several serviceable histories of American drama do provide links to the theater of the day, most notably those by Walter J. Meserve, Arthur Hobson Quinn, Gary A. Richardson, Jack A. Vaughan, Garff B. Wilson, and Calhoun Winton. Most anthologies have some bibliographic references, at least to the plays they contain; Mulford ("Re-presenting") contains an extensive bibliography useful for scholars of the pre-1800 period.

For teachers of *The Contrast*, there is, fortunately, substantial but not yet overwhelming literature on the playwright and the play. G. Thomas Tanselle's book is the best basic introduction to Tyler, supplemented by Ada Lou Carson and Herbert L. Carson and by chapters in Daniel F. Havens (8–51) and Silverman (536–67). Among articles or chapters on the play, Donald T. Seibert helps place it in the tradition of the comedy of manners; Lucy Rinehart and Richards (*Theater* 265–79), point out one theme that is especially useful in a classroom situation: the metatheatrical dimension of *The Contrast*. However, much work on Tyler's play can also be applied to other works before 1800; the relative paucity of critical articles on drama before 1800 should not deter teachers from introducing it to undergraduate students.

Works Cited

Primary Works

The Battle of Brooklyn: A Farce in Two Acts. 1776. Meserve and Reardon 81–102.

Brackenridge, Hugh Henry. *The Battle of Bunkers-Hill*. Moses 233–76.

Bradstreet, Anne. "The Flesh and the Spirit." Lauter et al. 302–05.

Burk, John Daly. *Bunker Hill; or, The Death of General Warren*. 1797. Moody 61–86.

Clapp, William W., Jr. *A Record of the Boston Stage*. 1853. New York: Greenwood, 1969.

Clark, Barrett H., ed. *America's Lost Plays*. 1940. 20 vols. in 10. Bloomington: Indiana UP, 1963–65.

Crashaw, William. "A Sermon." 1610. *The Genesis of the United States [. . .] 1605–1616*. Ed. Alexander Brown. Vol. 1. Boston: Houghton, 1891. 366.

Crèvecoeur, Michel-Guillaume-Jean de (J. Hector St. John). "Landscapes." *Letters from an American Farmer and Sketches of Eighteenth-Century America*. Ed. Albert E. Stone. New York: Viking, 1981. 414–89. Rpt. as *Landskapes. More Letters from the American Farmer: An Edition of the Essays in English Left Unpublished by Crèvecoeur*. Ed. Dennis D. Moore. Athens: U of Georgia P, 1995. 230–93.

Dunlap, William. *André*. 1798. Moses 499–654. Also in Richards.

———. *Darby's Return: A Comic Sketch*. 1789. Meserve and Reardon. 103–13.

———. *History of the American Theatre*. 2 vols. 1832. London: Bentley, 1833.

Franklin, Benjamin, V, ed. *The Plays and Poems of Mercy Otis Warren*. Delmar: Scholars' Facsimiles, 1980. N. pag.

Godfrey, Thomas, Jr. *The Prince of Parthia*. 1765. Quinn 1–42.

Halline, Allan Gates, ed. *American Plays*. New York: American Book, 1935.

Harris, Sharon M., ed. *Selected Writings of Judith Sargent Murray*. New York: Oxford UP, 1995.

Hopkinson, Francis. "An Exercise Containing a Dialogue and Ode." 1762. Moody 5–6.

Hunter, Robert. *Androboros, A Biographical Farce in Three Acts*. 1714. Meserve and Reardon 1–40.

Kritzer, Amelia Howe, ed. *Plays by Early American Women, 1775–1850*. Ann Arbor: U of Michigan P, 1995.

Lauter, Paul, et al., eds. *The Heath Anthology of American Literature*. 2nd ed. Vol. 1. Lexington: Heath, 1994.

Leacock, John. *The Fall of British Tyranny*. 1776. Moses 277–350.

Mays, David, ed. *The Disappointment; or, The Force of Credulity*. By Thomas Forrest ["Andrew Barton"]. Gainesville: UP of Florida, 1976.

Meserve, Walter J., and William R. Reardon, eds. *Satiric Comedies*. Bloomington: Indiana UP, 1969. Vol. 21 of *America's Lost Plays*.

Moody, Richard, ed. *Dramas from the American Theatre, 1762–1909*. Cleveland: World, 1966.

Moses, Montrose J., ed. *Representative Plays by American Dramatists*. Vol. 1: 1765–1819. 1918. New York: Blom, 1964.

Moses, Montrose J., and John Mason Brown, eds. *The American Theatre As Seen by Its Critics, 1752–1934*. New York: Norton, 1934.

Munford, Robert. *The Candidates; or, The Humours of a Virginia Election*. 1798. Moody 11–26.

————. *The Patriots. A Collection of Plays and Poems*. Petersburg, 1798. 53–132.

Murray, Judith Sargent. *The Traveller Returned*. 1798. Kritzer 97–136. Also in Harris.

Odell, George C. D. *Annals of the New York Stage*. 15 vols. New York: Columbia UP, 1927–49.

Philbrick, Norman, ed. *Trumpets Sounding: Propaganda Plays of the American Revolution*. New York: Blom, 1972.

Quinn, Arthur Hobson, ed. *Representative American Plays, 1767–1923*. Rev. 3rd ed. New York: Century, 1925.

Richards, Jeffrey H., ed. *Early American Drama*. New York: Viking, 1997.

Rogers, Robert. *Ponteach; or, The Savages of America*. Moses 109–208.

Rowson, Susanna. *Slaves in Algiers; or, A Struggle for Freedom*. 1794. Kritzer 55–95.

Sewall, Jonathan. *A Cure for the Spleen; or, Amusement for a Winter's Evening*. Boston, 1775.

Smith, John. *The Generall History of Virginia, New-England, and the Summer Isles*. 1624. Vol. 2 of *The Complete Works of Captain John Smith*. Ed. Philip L. Barbour. 3 vols. Chapel Hill: U of North Carolina P, 1986. 25–488.

Taylor, Edward. *Poems*. Ed. Donald E. Stanford. New Haven: Yale UP, 1960.

Tyler, Royall. *The Contrast*. 1790. Watt and Richardson 19–51. Also in Halline; Moody; Moses; Quinn; Richards.

Warren, Mercy Otis. *The Adulateur*. 1772. Franklin.

————. *The Defeat*. 1773. Franklin.

————. *The Group*. 1775. Kritzer 29–53.

————. *The Ladies of Castile*. 1790. Franklin.

————. *The Sack of Rome*. 1790. Franklin.

Watt, Stephen, and Gary A. Richardson, eds. *American Drama, Colonial to Contemporary*. Fort Worth: Harcourt, 1995.

Wigglesworth, Michael. *The Day of Doom; or, A Poetical Description of the Great and Last Judgment, with Other Poems*. Ed. Kenneth B. Murdock. 1929. New York: Russell, 1966.

————. *God's Controversy with New England*. 1873. Lauter et al. 284–95.

Wolter, Jürgen C., ed. *The Dawning of American Drama: American Dramatic Criticism, 1746–1915*. Westport: Greenwood, 1993.

Secondary Works

Ashby, Clifford. "A Black Actor on the Eighteenth-Century Boston Stage?" *Theatre Survey* 28.2 (1987): 101–02.

Avery, Laurence G. "A Proposal Concerning the Study of Early American Drama." *Educational Theatre Journal* 29 (1977): 243–50.

Baine, Rodney M. *Robert Munford: America's First Comic Dramatist*. Athens: U of Georgia P, 1967.

Barbour, Philip L. "Captain John Smith and the London Theater." *Virginia Magazine of History and Biography* 83 (1975): 277–79.

Barish, Jonas. *The Antitheatrical Prejudice*. Berkeley: U of California P, 1981.

Brown, Jared. *The Theatre in America during the Revolution*. Cambridge: Cambridge UP, 1995.

Carson, Ada Lou, and Herbert L. Carson. *Royall Tyler*. Boston: Twayne, 1979.

Dallett, Francis James, Jr., "John Leacock and *The Fall of British Tyranny*." *Pennsylvania Magazine of History and Biography* 78 (1954): 456–75.

Evelev, John. "*The Contrast*: The Problem of Theatricality and Political and Social Crisis in Postrevolutionary America." *Early American Literature* 31 (1996): 74–97.

Fliegelman, Jay. *Prodigals and Pilgrims: The American Revolution against Patriarchal Authority*. Cambridge: Cambridge UP, 1982.

Havens, Daniel F. *The Columbian Muse of Comedy: The Development of a Native Tradition in Early American Social Comedy, 1787–1845*. Carbondale: Southern Illinois UP, 1973.

Highfill, Philip, Jr. "The British Background of the American Hallams." *Theatre Survey* 11 (1970): 1–35.

Hill, Errol. *The Jamaican Stage, 1655–1900: Profile of a Colonial Theatre*. Amherst: U of Massachusetts P, 1992.

Hornblow, Arthur. *A History of the Theatre in America from Its Beginnings to the Present Time*. 2 vols. Philadelphia: Lippincott, 1919.

Kendall, Ritchie D. *The Drama of Dissent: The Radical Poetics of Nonconformity, 1380–1590*. Chapel Hill: U of North Carolina P, 1986.

Kerber, Linda K. *Women of the Republic: Intellect and Ideology in Revolutionary America*. Chapel Hill: U of North Carolina P, 1980.

Larson, Carl F. W. *American Regional Theatre History to 1900: A Bibliography*. Metuchen: Scarecrow, 1979.

Lockridge, Kenneth A. *The Diary, and Life, of William Byrd II of Virginia, 1674–1744*. Chapel Hill: U of North Carolina P, 1987.

McNamara, Brooks. *The American Playhouse in the Eighteenth Century*. Cambridge: Harvard UP, 1969.

Meserve, Walter J. *An Emerging Entertainment: The Drama of the American People to 1828*. Bloomington: Indiana UP, 1977.

Mulford, Carla. Introduction. *John Leacock's First Book of the American Chronicles of the Times, 1774–75*. Newark: U of Delaware P, 1987. 11–48.

———. "Re-presenting Early American Drama and Theatre." *Resources for American Literary Study* 17 (1990): 1–24.

Oreovicz, Cheryl Z. "Heroic Drama for an Uncertain Age: The Plays of Mercy Warren." *Early American Literature and Culture: Essays Honoring Harrison T. Meserole*. Ed. Kathryn Zabelle Derounian-Stodola. Newark: U of Delaware P, 1992. 192–210.

Philbrick, Norman. "The Spy as Hero: An Examination of *André* by William Dunlap." *Studies in Theatre and Drama: Essays in Honor of Hubert C. Heffner*. Ed. Oscar G. Brockett. The Hague: Mouton, 1972. 97–119.

Pollock, Thomas Clark. *The Philadelphia Theatre in the Eighteenth Century*. Philadelphia: U of Pennsylvania P, 1933.

Porter, Susan L. *With an Air Debonair: Musical Theatre in America, 1785–1815.* Washington: Smithsonian, 1991.

Quinn, Arthur Hobson. *A History of the American Drama from the Beginning to the Civil War.* New York: Appleton, 1943.

Rankin, Hugh F. *The Theater in Colonial America.* Chapel Hill: U of North Carolina P, 1965.

Richards, Jeffrey H. *Mercy Otis Warren.* New York: Twayne, 1995.

———. *Theater Enough: American Culture and the Metaphor of the World Stage, 1607–1789.* Durham: Duke UP, 1991.

Richardson, Gary A. *American Drama from the Colonial Period through World War I: A Critical History.* New York: Twayne, 1993.

Rinehart, Lucy. "A Nation's 'Noble Spectacle': Royall Tyler's *The Contrast* as Metatheatrical Commentary." *American Drama* 3.2 (1994): 29–52.

Seibert, Donald T., Jr. "Royall Tyler's 'Bold Example': *The Contrast* and the English Comedy of Manners." *Early American Literature* 13 (1978): 3–11.

Seilhamer, George O. *History of the American Theatre.* 3 vols. Philadelphia: Globe, 1889.

Shockley, Martin Staples. *The Richmond Stage, 1784–1812.* Charlottesville: UP of Virginia, 1977.

Silverman, Kenneth. *A Cultural History of the American Revolution [. . .] 1763–1789.* 1976. New York: Columbia UP, 1987.

Strand, Ginger. "The Many Deaths of Montgomery: Audiences and Pamphlet Plays of the Revolution." *American Literary History* 9.1 (1997): 1–20.

Tanselle, G. Thomas. *Royall Tyler.* Cambridge: Harvard UP, 1967.

Vaughan, Jack A. *Early American Dramatists from the Beginnings to 1900.* New York: Ungar, 1981.

Watts, Emily Stipes. *The Poetry of American Women from 1632 to 1945.* Austin: U of Texas P, 1977.

Wilmeth, Don B. *The American Stage to World War I: A Guide to Information Sources.* Detroit: Gale, 1978.

Wilson, Garff B. *Three Hundred Years of American Drama and Theatre.* 2nd ed. Englewood Cliffs: Prentice, 1982.

Winton, Calhoun. "The Theatre and Drama." *American Literature, 1764–1789: The Revolutionary Years.* Ed. Everett Emerson. Madison: U of Wisconsin P, 1977. 87–104.

Wright, Richardson. *Revels in Jamaica, 1682–1838.* 1937. New York: Blom, 1969.

Gregory Eiselein

American Self-Fashioning and the Problems of Autobiography

The difficulties of teaching autobiography are different from the challenges of teaching, say, poetry. When I teach Edward Taylor or Philip Freneau, students tell me they don't get it. When we read autobiographies, students find the form easy, familiar. This isn't surprising, of course. Autobiographical forms are found everywhere from television talk shows to criticism. Beginning by examining this initial comfort or engagement with autobiography generates lively discussion and prepares the way for problematizing and defamiliarizing autobiography. Questioning the simplicity and transparency of autobiography encourages dialogue and careful, critical reading. Moreover, approaches to autobiography that seek to defamiliarize its conventions and complicate its truths can allow students to grapple with questions about the relation of nation and self to writing and literary form.

Problematizing America

A diverse reading schedule presents students with competing definitions of what "America" is and what it means to be "American," just

229

as it converts "early America" into an elusive notion or problem for discussion. Rather than settling these issues for students, I challenge them with open-ended questions about "early America." How should the fact that "America" (as in the United States) didn't officially exist until 1776 shape the field "early American literature"? How does the transatlantic scope of some stories (Ashbridge, Equiano, many Puritan texts) make them less or more "American"? Thus, teaching autobiography can highlight the diversity of writings and cultures in America before 1800. In my descriptions of my early American courses, I tell students they will study writings by women, men, Africans, Europeans, Native peoples, Puritans, Quakers, Catholics, deists, criminals, explorers, slaves, pirates, rural people, scientists, rich folks and poor, among others. The Whitmanesque catalog dispels the notion that early American literature means Puritan literature plus "the founding fathers." I emphasize geographic diversity by teaching New England literature alongside texts from the mid-Atlantic region, Virginia, the backcountry South, and the Southwest as well as texts by nomadic or multiregional autobiographers (like Equiano).

While no course can fully represent the diversity of early America, teaching autobiography can make it more feasible to teach an inclusive multicultural course. Many who did not or could not write drama or poetry sometimes told a life story. The stories of African Americans like Jacob Francis and Belinda exist because each narrated events from their lives for a deposition or petition. Rachel Wall and Samuel Frost would probably not have composed autobiographies had they not been convicted of crimes and urged to relate their ignominious stories to an eager public. Others wrote life stories unintentionally (Alvar Núñez Cabeza de Vaca's story is a report) or as private records. These accidental autobiographers usually did not intend to produce public memoirs or consider themselves authors; yet their life stories now provide early American literature teachers texts by people besides the usually white, usually privileged authors of poetry or fiction. Moreover, many early American autobiographies (like Samson Occom's "A Short Narrative of My Life" or John Winthrop's "Christian Experience") are brief, so that classes can cover several in one semester.

Once we've read several different texts and talked about the heterogeneity of early America, I invite students to make connections among these diverse "American" autobiographies by placing texts in dialogue. I ask students to compare, for instance, Cabeza de Vaca's narrative with Mary Rowlandson's account of her captivity among Algonkian Indians. Both autobiographers are European-born Christians who (following disasters in which European protection schemes utterly fail) find themselves living among Native peoples whose radically non-European languages, customs, and beliefs the narrators do not always understand. Both provide specific, detailed descriptions, especially of food. Why do Rowlandson and Cabeza de Vaca spend time describing food? Students tell me the food is so different and the narrators so hungry that eating leaves an impression. We follow through by comparing the food passages to more abstract passages and talking about the differences in style. Both narrators are resourceful characters who find hybridized (partly European, partly Indian) ways of adapting themselves to Indian life: Rowlandson knits stockings, hats, handkerchiefs, and shifts for the Indians; Cabeza de Vaca acts as a healer, trader, and mediator. Both texts are spiritual autobiographies — first-person accounts of God's providence, grace, and miraculous intervention in their lives.

To get at differences between the two, I ask students to describe the narrators' attitudes toward Native peoples and the language with which they convey those attitudes. Occasionally discussion starts with a comparison of Rowlandson's graphic and sensational style and Cabeza de Vaca's plain, understated description (as rendered in the spare, modernized Covey translation we use). Discussion usually starts, however, with accounts of how objective and understanding Cabeza de Vaca is compared with the ethnocentric, intolerant Rowlandson. Pressed to support their views, students rush to Rowlandson's narrative and read passages where she calls Native Americans "cruel and barbarous Salvages" (28), "merciless Heathen" (32), and "hell-hounds" (33). Students cite Cabeza de Vaca's description of Indian hospitality and generosity (56–58) as an example of his openmindedness. Other students will often question, complicate, or take apart the dichotomy of tolerant Cabeza de Vaca versus intolerant Rowlandson. These students point out that Rowlandson describes

Indians sharing food with her and giving her a Bible (56, 37–38). Some note the limits of Cabeza de Vaca's cultural relativism: he wants to convert the Indians; he calls the Yguaces "great thieves," "great liars," and "great drunkards" (80); he's a Spanish explorer-adventurer.

Comparing Rowlandson's and Cabeza de Vaca's stories enables the class to discuss the role cultural differences like gender, religion, ethnicity, and region play in the constitution of a self. How is Rowlandson's response to captivity different (if at all) because she's a woman? How (if at all) does Cabeza de Vaca's Catholicism shape his perspective of Native peoples? I never ask students to consider Cabeza de Vaca the typical Spanish explorer or Rowlandson the representative Puritan woman, just as I expect neither autobiographer to define what it means to be American. But I do want students to think about how these differing social identities shape the life stories, how religious beliefs influence the tropes and plots used to tell a story, how gender enables certain narrative roles for the autobiographer and forbids others.

Problematizing the Self

When I teach poetry, I ask my students to distinguish between the author and the poem's speaker. When I teach fiction, we talk about narrative stances. When I teach autobiography, I use both approaches. Although autobiography deliberately conflates author and protagonist, I encourage my students to treat the speaking "I" as a persona, a not-always-reliable speaking voice the author invents to tell a story. Approaching autobiographical personas as characters — not exactly deceptions, but certainly fictions — makes analysis of autobiographies as literary texts more expedient. To make the speaking "I" a focus for discussion, I ask students where the self in the autobiography comes from. Wary students usually respond, What do you mean by "self"? Sometimes I provide an ordinary definition: the self is that combination of thoughts, feelings, sensations, perceptions, memories, identifications, and corporeality that makes up the individuality and identity of a person. Other times I start a discussion about theories of identity formation. There are a variety of contested views about the location or origin of the self, I suggest. Some theorists emphasize identification, others stress differentiation, writing, language, knowledge, discourse, or imitation. If students express interest in a particular theory, I might briefly sketch Lacan's thoughts about the subject as a product of language, Foucault's ideas about the constitutive role of discourse in identity formation, or Kristeva's theory of abjection (a kind of differentiation). Students join in by talking about the role of the family, the influence of one's beliefs on personality, and even Freud. After such a discussion, what the self is seems less self-evident, and students have often become interested in the processes by which a self becomes a self. These conversations about where selves come from turn the self into an issue or a problem and prepare the way for further questions. To what extent is this self a product of this text? How does the autobiographer literally write herself or himself into an identity?

Into this discussion I sometimes introduce this sweeping generalization: autobiography is a movement between concealment and revelation, deceiving and confessing to readers in a self-reflexive way. Autobiographers hide things they don't want you to see, and they reveal things they never intended to show you. I start discussion using this hiding-revealing binary by asking, Why did the author write this autobiography? Students in early American classes can be quick with responses. Anne Bradstreet and Benjamin Franklin use autobiography to pass along moral and practical lessons to their children. Spiritual autobiographies are religious lessons about God's grace. I press the discussion by wondering aloud, How does a didactic purpose shape what is hidden and what revealed? How does the autobiographer shape a particular kind of self for this audience or purpose? I might also ask students how they adapt stories about themselves for different audiences; I follow up with, Do the facts change or just your presentation of them?

Certain autobiographical genres raise their own problems about intent. Captivity narratives, for example, usually have a didactic function similar to spiritual autobiographies. Yet if I ask about multiple purposes or cross-purposes, students point out that other agendas shape these narratives. For many students, the violence toward sleeping Indians in Hannah Dustan's narrative and John Williams's anti-Catholic rhetoric seem inappropriate for lessons about God's deliverance and mercy: other-hating political agendas contradict the Christian message and reveal a divided self. Other students conclude Puritans always set themselves apart from "savages" (Dustan 163), scheming "papists" (J. Williams 198), and others they didn't like: Indian hating and messages of God's sweet deliverance go together in Puritan writing. We also talk about the tensions between religious purposes and entertainment. Despite their religious messages, criminal narratives, like captivity narratives, were popular entertainment. So, I ask, do the entertaining elements (the presentation of captivity and escape as an adventure story, the emphasis on shocking details of murder, bestiality, and highway robbery) thwart, contradict, or overwhelm the religious purposes? Often students make analogies to the present: television preachers use lurid details about sin to capture the audience's attention; the news sensationalizes crime, blurring the difference between journalism and entertainment. These "digressions" are superb opportunities to discuss the historicity of the union between entertainment and moral lesson, and I'll ask students to compare, say, *The Confession, &c. of Thomas Mount* with some recent well-publicized trial or crime story in the news. Such comparisons encourage students to think about the historically specific ways criminality is constructed and the connection of the present to the past.

While discussing autobiographers' purposes, I ask students to look for revelations the autobiographer doesn't intend. What in this text doesn't fit with the autobiographer's expressed or secretly intended purpose? Bradstreet writes so that her children "may gain some spiritual advantage" by reading about her trials and the ways God uses "affliction" to strengthen faith (240, 241). So what in "To My Dear Children" doesn't quite fit with this avowed purpose? When I last taught this piece, students told me the autobiography was full of uncertainty. Instead of providing reassurances about God's mercy and love, Bradstreet raises questions that suggest doubt about her Puritan beliefs (Is there a God? How can I know? How can I know the Puritan God is the true God? [243–44]) and that are unanswered or answered in not quite satisfying ways. Asking students to find moments where the language or images fail to match intentions encourages careful analytical examination of texts, just as it provides a complex perspective on the self in the text. Moreover, when students discover or articulate these problems in class, they seem to feel an ownership of the problem, which motivates them to seek a resolution or way of understanding the contradictions.

I follow up these class discussions with a writing assignment that allows students to discover hands-on how discourses construct the self in the text. I ask students to write a chapter of their own autobiography, a narrative about some aspect of their personal history. In preparation we consider that autobiographies are not simple, boring transcriptions of remembered events; like other literary texts, they use language to create meaning in figurative or symbolic ways. Begin with a striking memory, I suggest, and shape it into an imaginative self-representation. Think about what you want your narrative to do and be creative.

Although one could use this exercise in any course on autobiography, I adapt it to the study of early American literature by encouraging students to write in modes we study during the semester — conversion stories, travel narratives, confessions, and Franklinian self-made-man tales. Students also keep journals, write autobiographical poems, and model their autobiographies on criminal narrative formulas. While many early Americans wrote private life stories, I discourage students from doing so. I really don't want them to tell me their secrets. The focus of this assignment is not their lives but their writing. (This brings sighs of relief from most students.) And students workshop their stories publicly in peer groups. I don't want students to exempt themselves because their pieces are "too personal." Students read each other's work and provide the kind of balanced, specific, constructive advice they might find useful in revising their own writing.

Following workshops, students revise and hand in their autobiographies. When I return their work, I ask them to write third-person analyses of their papers and consider questions like those we applied to early American texts. What does the autobiography reveal about its narrator? What does it hide? What is its purpose? What does it tell us about the narrator's culture and historical moment? How does the language fit or not fit the autobiography's purpose? What are the text's themes? The aim is to encourage students to think critically about their own work and see autobiography as a process of constructing a self with words. Students are then much better poised to understand how Sarah Kemble Knight's and Franklin's selves are not exactly reflections of an authentic interiority but products of language. Moreover, such writing exercises encourage students to think about how the self in the text cannot precisely coincide with the self who writes and to recognize how early American autobiographers use shared conventions and narrative structures to create a self. This assignment asks students to see themselves as socially constructed, which, as Carla Mulford points out, can make them uneasy (343); but it also invites them to participate actively in constructing their (own?) textual selves — which, as writing assignments go, can be pretty fun.

Problematizing the Genre

What *is* autobiography anyway? According to Gertrude Stein, "Anything is an autobiography" (5). College students, however, will probably give you a more specific answer, for example, autobiography is nonfictional text someone wrote about herself or himself. Many titles of early American autobiography support this view: *Some Account of the Fore Part of the Life of Elizabeth Ashbridge [. . .] Written by Her Own Hand*, for example. But then, especially after a student slips and calls an autobiography a "novel," which almost always happens, I wonder, What's the difference between narrative fiction and autobiography? Students may assert a distinction: fiction is made up, autobiography is true. Charles Brockden Brown's *Wieland* is fictional, Samuel Sewall's *Diary* autobiographical. Other students might note that the categories are not mutually exclusive. Fiction can have autobiographical elements, and certain kinds of fiction (epistolary novel, first-person narrative) resemble autobiographical forms. We might also talk about how elements of fiction (plot, character) and its conventions (use of suspense, happy or tragic endings, and so on) shape how autobiographers present their lives.

But, I ask, what if an autobiographer deliberately makes up events? Is the work still autobiography or has it become fiction? What if someone narrates a life story to someone else who writes it down, as with John Marrant or Hannah Dustan? Are these as-told-to narratives autobiographies? Why or why not? What if the autobiographer is, well, untrustworthy, like Stephen Burroughs? What if the writer creates a persona to express personal experiences and feelings? To what extent, for example, should we consider Crèvecoeur's *Letters from an American Farmer* fiction? In what ways is it autobiography? If it's not exactly either, how would you classify it, and why? Why does it matter how you classify a text? Why do we have to worry about genre? Why can't we treat texts in their idiosyncratic individuality?

I sometimes take the opposite approach and introduce students to rigid or precise definitions of autobiography, which emphasize publication, unity, length, introspection, factualness, and the author's individuality (Harmon and Holman 46; Gusdorf). According to these definitions, autobiographies are meant for the public; they are highly self-conscious and carefully structured (like a literary text); they provide an extended treatment of a life. During the semester someone may observe how diaries, life histories (dictated, ghostwritten, or rewritten life stories), and other texts are not, according to the definitions, autobiographies. Students also point out how these definitions exclude many of their favorite texts, such as *The Book of Abigail and John* (Adams and Adams), the criminal narratives, *The Travel Diary of Elizabeth House Trist*, and James Albert Ukawsaw Gronniosaw's *Narrative*. Because the narrower definitions ignore texts students find interesting and valuable, as well as almost all life writings by women and non-Westerners (see Friedman), students may consider them invalid or not useful. Even the most famous autobiographies from early America fall short of the more rigid definitions in certain respects. Jonathan Edwards's "Personal Narrative" is certainly introspective, but it is also short and only posthumously published. Franklin referred to his narrative as a "History," an "Account of my Life," and, in his letters, his "memoirs," although it is now called *The Autobiography* and represents for many the archetypal American autobiography (Lemay and Zall xviin1); the last of these designations suggests not the unity of the text, but its fragmentation, its "irreducible plurality" (Looby 135). Sometimes I mention to the class that the word *autobiography* didn't exist until 1797 and didn't become common until the nineteenth century, after our course's chronological end point (Cooley 1; "Autobiography"). Hence, it can start to appear that there are no early American "autobiographies."

Of course, other perspectives on the term *autobiography* emphasize the impossibility of defining the term (Olney, "Some Versions" 237), its ubiquity (Sayre), or its multiple possibilities (Stein). Daniel Shea, for instance, suggests that "Indian stories of origins are the type of all autobiography" ("Prehistory" 27). After proposing this notion as a hypothesis, I ask students to read an origin narrative (like "Talk concerning the First Beginning") and to think about it as an autobiography. Student responses vary. Although they like reading origin and emergence stories, many students reject Shea's hypothesis, saying it distorts the term *autobiography* or misunderstands creation narratives. Other students begin talking about autobiography as a subgenre of the origin story that focuses on the creation of the self (a European emphasis) rather than the land or the people.

Using another approach that tests definitions of autobiography, a teacher might assign a narrative from Hakluyt's *Principall Navigations*, one of Columbus's letters, or a selection by John Smith (*The Generall Historie of Virginia*) or William Bradford (*Of Plymouth Plantation*). Are these explorers' and historians' accounts autobiographical? The central, dramatic roles that Smith gives himself make his histories seem like autobiographies; but students find Bradford so absent from the events he narrates that they don't really see how *Of Plymouth Plantation* can be autobiographical. I tell them Robert Sayre, a respected scholar of American autobiography, considers it autobiographical; they don't change their minds. What about an autobiography of a group? Well, students reply, shouldn't a group autobiography be written by the group?

Another way to approach genre issues is to talk about the kinds of autobiographical forms available to early American storytellers: diary, confession, journal, travel narrative, memoir, letters, slave narrative, jeremiad, captivity narrative, history, and so on. What kinds of stories or lives appear in what kind of autobiographical genre? Who keeps diaries? Who has time to keep a diary? Who writes slave narratives? Captivity narratives? Memoirs? What kind of distinctions would you make among captivity narratives, rogues' histories, and spiritual autobiographies? What does a journal hide or reveal that is different from what a letter, memoir, instructional guide, or dictated autobiography might hide or reveal?

I usually spend a significant amount of time talking about spiritual autobiography, for example. It is an important genre for Puritans and Quakers, and it can include many texts outside the Quaker and Puritan traditions (Franklin's *Autobiography* or Cabeza de Vaca's *Adventures*, e.g.). Moreover, in early American courses that cover about three centuries, issues that link very different texts are useful. Religion, treated in a comparative, historical manner, seems to encourage an array of connections among diverse texts. I might start the discussion with a definition: "The spiritual autobiographer is primarily concerned with the question of grace: whether or not the individual has been accepted into divine life, an acceptance signified by psychological and moral changes which the autobiographer comes to discern in his past experience" (Shea, *Spiritual Autobiography* xi). Then I ask how well this sentence describes the concerns of the early American autobiographers we've encountered. To what extent does Equiano's account of God's miraculous interventions make his *Interesting Narrative* a spiritual autobiography? Are criminal narratives, focused on the teller's sin and conversion, a kind of spiritual autobiography? What does it do to our conception of the genre to think of criminals (like Esther Rodgers) or deists (like Franklin) as spiritual autobiographers? What if a text, though religious, is not exactly focused on the teller's spiritual grace but rather, as in Charles Woodmason's *Journal*, the bad behavior of others? Is it a spiritual autobiography or an autobiographical text with spiritual elements? Why or when would such distinctions matter?

Discussions about various definitions of autobiography can further students' inquiries into the process of making literary-critical definitions. Conversations about autobiography and genre lead to discussions about what literature is. Even the most "literary" of early

American autobiographies (Knight, Edwards, Franklin) can seem hurried, fragmentary, even careless. Whose aesthetic values should we use to judge the literariness of early American life stories? Hence, questions about "literature" often take us back to examinations of cultural contexts and of differing cultural values (see Mulford). If a text is not intended to be literary but rather seems just an account of a life, should we call it "literature" and study it in a literature course? Students usually seem to think so. These stories, "literary" or not, reveal how language was used to (re)create a time, a culture, an ethos, a self; they tell us much about past cultures and the role of language in identity formation. Autobiographies also tell us something, students insist, about ourselves.

Works Cited

Primary Works

Adams, Abigail, and John Adams. *The Book of Abigail and John: Selected Letters of the Adams Family, 1762–1784*. Ed. L. H. Butterfield et al. Cambridge: Belknap–Harvard UP, 1975.

Andrews, William L., ed. *Journeys in New Worlds: Early American Women's Narratives*. Madison: U of Wisconsin P, 1990.

Ashbridge, Elizabeth. *Some Account of the Fore Part of the Life of Elizabeth Ashbridge*. Ed. and introd. Daniel B. Shea. Andrews 117–80.

Belinda. "Petition of an African Slave." *American Women Writers to 1800*. Ed. Sharon M. Harris. New York: Oxford UP, 1996. 253–55.

Bradford, William. *Of Plymouth Plantation, 1620–1647*. Introd. Francis Murphy. New York: Mod. Lib., 1981.

Bradstreet, Anne. "To My Dear Children." *The Works of Anne Bradstreet*. Ed. Jeannine Hensley. Cambridge: Belknap–Harvard UP, 1967. 240–45.

Brown, Charles Brockden. *Weiland; or, The Transformation: An American Tale*. Garden City: Anchor-Doubleday, 1973.

Burroughs, Stephen. *Memoirs of Stephen Burroughs*. Boston: Northeastern UP, 1988.

Cabeza de Vaca, Alvar Núñez. *Adventures in the Unknown Interior of America*. Trans. and ed. Cyclone Covey. Albuquerque: U of New Mexico P, 1983.

Columbus, Christopher, et al. *The Four Voyages of Columbus*. Trans. and ed. Cecil Jane. New York: Dover, 1988.

Crèvecoeur, J. Hector St. John de. Letters from an American Farmer *and* Sketches of Eighteenth-Century America. Ed. and introd. Albert Stone. New York: Penguin, 1981.

Dustan, Hannah. "A Narrative of Hannah Dustan's Notable Deliverance from Captivity." Vaughan and Clark 159–64.

Edwards, Jonathan. "Personal Narrative." Lauter 581–92.

Equiano, Olaudah. *The Interesting Narrative of the Life of Olaudah Equiano. The Classic Slave Narratives.* Ed. and introd. Henry Louis Gates, Jr. New York: Mentor, 1987. 1–182.

Francis, Jacob. Deposition. *The Revolution Remembered: Eyewitness Accounts of the War for Independence.* Ed. John C. Dann. Chicago: U of Chicago P, 1980, 390–99.

Franklin, Benjamin. *Benjamin Franklin's* Autobiography. Ed. J. A. Leo Lemay and P. M. Zall. New York: Norton, 1986.

Frost, Samuel. *The Confession and Dying Words of Samuel Frost.* D. Williams 282–87.

Gronniosaw, (James Albert) Ukawsaw. *A Narrative of the Most Remarkable Particulars in the Life of James Albert Ukawsaw Gronniosaw, an African Prince.* Jehlen and Warner 719–25.

Hakluyt, Richard. *Voyages and Discoveries: The Principal Navigations, Voyages, Traffiques, and Discoveries of the English Nation.* Ed., abr., and introd. Jack Beeching. Harmondsworth: Penguin, 1972.

Jehlen, Myra, and Michael Warner, eds. *The English Literatures of America, 1500–1800.* New York: Routledge, 1997.

Knight, Sarah Kemble. *The Journal of Madam Knight.* Ed. and introd. Sargent Bush, Jr. Andrews 67–116.

Lauter, Paul, et al., eds. *The Heath Anthology of American Literature.* 3rd ed. Vol. 1. Boston: Houghton, 1998.

Marrant, John. *A Narrative of the Lord's Wonderful Dealings with John Marrant, a Black.* Ed. Rev. W. Aldridge. London: Gilbert, 1785.

Mount, Thomas. *The Confession, &c. of Thomas Mount.* D. Williams 336–41.

Occom, Samson. "A Short Narrative of My Life." Lauter 981–86.

Rodgers, Esther. *The Declaration and Confession of Esther Rodgers.* D. Williams 94–109.

Rowlandson, Mary. *A True History of the Captivity and Restoration of Mrs. Mary Rowlandson.* Ed. and introd. Amy Schrager Lang. Andrews 11–65.

Sewall, Samuel. *The Diary of Samuel Sewall.* Lauter 410–13.

Smith, John. *The Generall Historie of Virginia, New-England, and the Summer Isles.* Lauter 186–91.

Stein, Gertrude. *Everybody's Autobiography.* New York: Random, 1937.

"Talk concerning the First Beginning (Zuni)." Lauter 27–41.

Trist, Elizabeth House. *The Travel Diary of Elizabeth House Trist: Philadelphia to Natchez, 1783–84.* Ed. and introd. Annette Kolodny. Andrews 181–232.

Vaughan, Alden T., and Edward W. Clark, eds. *Puritans among the Indians: Accounts of Captivity and Redemption, 1676–1724.* Cambridge: Belknap–Harvard UP, 1981.

Wall, Rachel. *Life, Last Words, and Dying Confession of Rachel Wall.* D. Williams 336–41.

Williams, Daniel E., ed. *Pillars of Salt: An Anthology of Early American Criminal Narratives.* Madison: Madison House, 1993.

Williams, John. *The Redeemed Captive Returning to Zion*. Vaughan and Clark 165–226.

Winthrop, John. "John Winthrop's Christian Experience." Lauter 234–38.

Woodmason, Charles. *The Carolina Backcountry on the Eve of the Revolution: The Journal and Other Writings of Charles Woodmason, Anglican Itinerant*. Ed. and introd. Richard J. Hooker. Chapel Hill: U of North Carolina P, 1953.

Secondary Works

"Autobiography." *Oxford English Dictionary*. 2nd ed. 1989.

Cooley, Thomas. *Educated Lives: The Rise of Modern Autobiography in America*. Columbus: Ohio State UP, 1976.

Friedman, Susan Stanford. "Women's Autobiographical Selves: Theory and Practice." *The Private Self: Theory and Practice of Women's Autobiographical Writings*. Ed. Shari Benstock. Chapel Hill: U of North Carolina P, 1988. 34–62.

Gusdorf, Georges. "Conditions and Limits of Autobiography." Olney, *Autobiography* 28–48.

Harmon, William, and C. Hugh Holman. *A Handbook to Literature*. 7th ed. Upper Saddle River: Prentice, 1996.

Lemay, J. A. Leo, and P. M. Zall. Introduction. The Autobiography of Benjamin Franklin: *A Genetic Text*. Knoxville: U of Tennessee P, 1981. xv–lviii.

Looby, Christopher. *Voicing America: Language, Literary Form, and the Origins of the United States*. Chicago: U of Chicago P, 1996.

Mulford, Carla. "Seated amid the Rainbow: On Teaching American Writings to 1800." *American Literature* 65 (1993): 342–48.

Olney, James, ed. *Autobiography: Essays Theoretical and Critical*. Princeton: Princeton UP, 1980.

———. "Some Versions of Memory / Some Versions of *Bios*: The Ontology of Autobiography." Olney, *Autobiography* 236–67.

Sayre, Robert F. Introduction. *American Lives: An Anthology of Autobiographical Writing*. Ed. Robert F. Sayre. Madison: U of Wisconsin P, 1994. 3–17.

Shea, Daniel B. "The Prehistory of American Autobiography." *American Autobiography: Retrospect and Prospect*. Ed. Paul John Eakin. Madison: U of Wisconsin P, 1991. 25–46.

———. *Spiritual Autobiography in Early America*. Princeton: Princeton UP, 1968.

Kathryn Zabelle Derounian-Stodola

Captivity Narratives

The term *captivity narrative* refers to a literal or symbolic, factual or fictional story in which a captor takes a hostage, usually a member of another group. Most early American captivity narratives concern European settlers captured by Native Americans, although a few treat African American hostages or even Native Americans captured by other Native Americans.[1] Some scholars see the Indian captivity narrative as a discrete — and perhaps America's earliest indigenous — literary genre. Other scholars hold that the captivity narrative includes not just the Indian captivity narrative but also the slave narrative, the spiritual autobiography, and many other cognate forms that provide its genealogy (for example, the hostage account and the UFO abduction story). Whether one teaches captivity narratives generally or Indian captivity narratives specifically will, of course, affect choice of texts and teaching orientation. But either way, asking students what the basic element of any captivity narrative is usually generates the response that it requires a captor and a captive, and the discussion can proceed from there.

Contexts

Once students grasp the captor-captive dynamic, the instructor can invite them to consider a number of issues before or during analysis of a text. Students' familiarity with cowboys-and-Indians stories — which frequently involve elements of the Indian captivity narrative — can provide a transition to these issues. The first question, which tends to surface spontaneously, is why Native Americans took captives. The class quickly guesses the motives of trade, enslavement, and revenge but may need help with the other two, ransom and adoption. Students are intrigued that contrary to popular mythology, captives were taken for reasons besides revenge and were not necessarily harmed beyond the trauma of the initial attack, especially if they were to be ransomed or adopted into a tribe to replace lost family members. On the subject of adoption, instructors might explain that many Native Americans did not have the same cultural constructs of "racial purity" that Europeans had and accepted many different ethnic varieties into tribes.

Students often want to know how many captives were taken. The available statistics are at best imprecise; we can never know how many hostages died or disappeared, especially in the seventeenth and eighteenth centuries when recordkeeping was patchy, and even into the nineteenth century, when white-Indian contact and conflict continued on new frontiers. But since students crave numbers, it is worth noting that an estimated 1,641 New Englanders were captured between 1675 and 1763 alone (Vaughan and Richter 53). Indian captivity was both a real and a vividly imagined possibility for many of the early white settlers. To dramatize this psychology, I ask students to consider a current account of hostage taking so that they can better understand how even one incident can empower the captor and terrorize the group from which the captive was targeted.

A class can readily take up the issue of gender regarding the fate(s) of captives by comparing the frequently anthologized Puritan accounts by Mary Rowlandson and John Williams. Although Native Americans captured both males and females, men and very young children were more likely than women or preadolescents to be killed in the initial attack. Other captives — especially pregnant women or recently delivered mothers — might die in the harsh conditions of a forced march, as Williams's wife did. Traditional happy endings included escape or ransom (Mary Rowlandson was eventually ransomed for twenty pounds), though the captive's reintegration to his or her original culture might be difficult.

Finally, students are interested to learn that a considerable number of captives either acculturated (temporarily accepted cultural differences and tried to adapt to their new lives) or transculturated (permanently crossed cultures, usually by remaining with the American Indians). Again, the Rowlandson and Williams texts can illustrate this distinction. Rowlandson began to become acculturated during her three-month captivity, as seen in her changing attitudes toward food; but Eunice Williams, John Williams's daughter, transculturated to Kahnawake life in Canada, married, had children, and had no interest in returning to the Puritan community despite repeated inducements to do so (Demos). Significantly, the "prime candidate for transculturation was a girl aged seven through fifteen" (Vaughan and Richter 64), since she was likely to be more pliable and passive than a boy of the same age. I encourage students to ponder whether cultural identity is fixed or whether, under certain circumstances and over time, it is variable. Those who believe it is fixed can understand why the captives' original families and communities continued to think of and refer to them as such and tried to "redeem" them, sometimes for decades. Students who decide identity is variable can see that the designation *captive* is no longer appropriate. Does Eunice Williams remain a Puritan throughout her life, or does she become a Kahnawake Indian who took the Catholic Christian name Marguerite as well as the Kahnawake names A'ongote and Gannenstenhawi (Demos 141–63)? Or does she integrate both identities?

From here, the class might speculate on how duration of captivity and gender of captive affect literary treatment. It is hard to determine whether there really are more captivity narratives by and about women than men, but certainly many of the best-known focus on women. In a traditional interpretation, the accounts by or about men highlight action, escape, or adventure, whereas those by or about women emphasize passivity and distress. One of the strongest narrative patterns — though by no means the only one — involves a victimized girl or woman overpowered by male Indians. Asked for examples from Rowlandson's captivity narrative, students might mention the initial attack on the garrison, in which her sister dies; the death of her six-year-old daughter, Sarah; and the killing of Goodwife Joslin.

Such archetypes served a strong propagandist purpose by inciting white America's hatred for Native peoples. This is especially true where male editors — often ministers — recast the stories of semiliterate female captives. In the seventeenth and early eighteenth centuries, for example, Cotton Mather edited and propagandized the stories of many women captives including Hannah Dustan and Hannah Bradley (who was captured *twice* within eight years). But recent commentary complicates the dominant image of the victimized woman by suggesting that going through captivity, then publishing her story, paradoxically gave the ex-captive an agency she did not possess before. It could allow her to reverse ethnic and gender stereotypes in criticizing her own culture and showing that Native American men could be sympathetic, not savage, and that white women could be empowered and articulate storytellers, not passive pawns (Castiglia; Fitzpatrick; Namias). If time allows, it is best to use a variety of texts to suggest the complex gender roles of men and women (for many examples see Burnham; Castiglia; Derounian-Stodola; Derounian-Stodola and Levernier; Ebersole; Namias).

Students sometimes wonder how so many Indian captivity narratives came to be printed. Early captives themselves gave various reasons for publishing. Some had political or spiritual agendas, and indeed their texts appeared as broadsides, almanacs, or pamphlets as well as books. Captivity accounts, including Rowlandson's and Williams's, were among America's first best-sellers (see Mott; Vail). Sometimes, as with Rowlandson, returned captives claimed that they wrote because their family and community urged them to do so or so that they would not be destitute. Others wanted to raise money to ransom remaining relatives or friends. Students enjoy speculating on why today's hostages publish their stories, why the accounts are popular, and why — since hostages are usually ordinary people — they might require the services of ghostwriters.

Subtexts

Two exercises that use short, complete texts can help students gain perspective on the mythic and cultural reworkings of the same basic story, that is, how successive generations reinvent and reinterpret texts for their own ends. The activities can be oral or written and can involve individual students or groups.

The first exercise focuses on Pocahontas (c. 1595–1617) and uses John Smith's account from the *Generall Historie* of his rescue by Pocahontas, which appears in many American literature anthologies. Students encountering this text for the first time are astounded by the flimsy basis of the Pocahontas industry that has subsequently evolved in print and nonprint culture. The class can consider the propaganda value of the 1616 engraving of Pocahontas reproduced in Smith's *Generall Historie*, then think about other manifestations of Pocahontas, culminating — so to speak — in the Disney version (Larkins; Tilton; Young). Students can discuss, give oral reports on, or analyze in writing these cultural reworkings of the Pocahontas myth. Incidentally, students should be told that the name Pocahontas, popularized by Smith, was a nickname; Matoaka was her formal Native American name; and Rebecka was her Christian name and the name by which she was married to John Rolfe — *not* John Smith — in 1614. Students can draw their own conclusions about why Smith chose to use her nickname rather than her other names and why we continue to use it today. The instructor can also note the irony that while John Smith's capture in 1608 by Powhatan, Pocahontas's father, is well known, Pocahontas's capture in 1613 by Captain Samuel Argall is not so well known.

The second exercise focuses on Hannah Dustan (1657–1736; spelled variously as *Dustan*, *Dustin*, or *Duston*), a Puritan woman captured in 1697 in Haverhill, Massachusetts, just after she had given birth to a child who was killed in the initial attack. After a forced march, Dustan masterminded and carried out, with two accomplices, the slaying and scalping of the ten Indians who had taken her. Cotton Mather published three versions of this story in 1697, 1699, and 1702, all glorifying Dustan's act. Grappling with the question to what extent — if any — Dustan was justified in killing the killers of her child, scalping them, and then seeking and obtaining a bounty usually generates a great deal of class discussion. Some students defend Dustan as a vigilante (and, of course, the class can discuss contemporary vigilantes as cult heroes), while others condemn her as a criminal for taking such a grisly revenge. The nineteenth-century retellings of this story by Hawthorne and Thoreau — among others — cast a darker, Romantic shadow, vilifying Dustan (Arner; Franklin; Levernier and Cohen; Ulrich; Whitford). Students shown the reworkings of the same seventeenth-century captivity come to understand the fluidity of narrative and of cultural and individual interpretations.

A Case Study: Mary Rowlandson's Captivity Narrative

Instructors of American literature survey courses who have time to teach only one Indian captivity narrative are likely to select the most anthologized example, Mary Rowlandson's.[2] The narrative is important because many critical issues intersect there: it is representative as a woman's text, a Puritan text, a spiritual autobiography, and an editorialized text; it is distinctive in that it is structurally and stylistically satisfying, sophisticated, and, for many reasons, complex. The account has the added bonus that students at different levels relate to it emotionally and intellectually and identify it as one of the few early texts they really enjoy reading, pointing to its drama, poignancy, and discursive power.

To contextualize the narrative, teachers might wish to address Rowlandson's life story. Brought up in an affluent, literate household, Mary (White) Rowlandson married Rev. Joseph Rowlandson around 1656. She was captured by an alliance of Narragansetts, Nipmucks, and Wampanoags and held from February to May 1675/76. Joseph Rowlandson died suddenly in 1678, and his widow married Samuel Talcott, a community leader, in 1679. She died in 1711 (Greene;

Salisbury). Providing some background on a captive's pre- and post-captivity life helps students avoid the tendency to see that person in a "captivity vacuum" or to draw only on the narrative for what is often incomplete and inaccurate information.

Like all life writings, Rowlandson's text is multilayered and multivocal because its author is also its main character. The major ambiguity in Rowlandson's characterization is whether she fashions herself as a victimized, spiritually fallen woman who regains her sense of devotional direction by submitting to a trial of faith and then writing a spiritual autobiography or whether she reveals herself as a tough, victorious survivor, and thereby a chosen child of God, who adapts to her situation by using strategies including barter, manipulation, and even theft. To reveal this strain, I usually begin by asking students whether they think they would be passive or active if they were taken hostage. Then, if the class is small enough, I might arbitrarily divide it and ask one group to look closely at the narrative for evidence of the "victim" interpretation and the other for evidence of the "victor" interpretation. From this exercise, students realize that there is ample support for either reading. Then I complicate matters and move beyond easy polarization by referring to recent scholarship on Rowlandson that examines her "liminal" state between two cultures and the difficulty she had when released in reintegrating and revalidating herself within the dominant white culture (Burnham; Toulouse).

Rowlandson gives extended textual attention to herself as protagonist and to her antagonists, the Native Americans. The instructor might ask, "What does Rowlandson think of American Indians and how does she present them?" Initially, students point to her stereotyping, evident in phrases such as "hell-hounds" and "merciless heathen." But they soon indicate that her attitudes fluctuate toward individuals such as her master, the Narragansett sachem (chief) Quanopin, and her mistress, Weetamoo, sachem of the Pocassets. When asked to compare Rowlandson's commentaries on Quanopin and on Weetamoo, students cannot fail to note her rapport with her master, whom she calls "the best Friend that I had of an *Indian*" (Twelfth Remove), and her clashes with her mistress, a "Severe and proud Dame" (Nineteenth Remove), as Rowlandson describes her.

These interactions magnify the ethnohistorical value of Rowland-son's account.

To introduce the issue of the several sometimes distinct, some-times overlapping, voices in Rowlandson's text, instructors can show the sections in which she participates in the action and the biblical and psychological parts in which she interprets events. Teachers can also tell students that one minister or more may have edited the text, though that cannot be proved: Joseph Rowlandson, whose last ser-mon was often appended to early editions of the narrative, and In-crease Mather, who almost certainly wrote a preface that appeared in early editions. Editorial intervention may explain why a strong narra-tive foreground is constantly interrupted by spiritual, political, and psychological reflections designed to relegate the action to the back-ground. In this way, the story becomes what the Puritans referred to as "a providence," in which something literal is rendered symbolic.

Because many captivity narratives were written by hacks and pub-lished hurriedly to enhance their sales potential, they are not always aesthetically valuable. However, students often volunteer that Row-landson's narrative shows considerable literary expertise and is aes-thetically and emotionally satisfying. It blends lucid, biblically inspired prose with biblical references and quotations. This narrative texture in which Rowlandson retells her experiences — real or cre-ated — and quotes from the Bible defines her own individual style, and it prevails over the mediated anti-Indian, pro-Puritan editorializ-ing. Undergraduates especially recall the vivid descriptions of the ini-tial attack; the constant search for food and spiritual solace; the death of Goodwife Joslin; Rowlandson's theft of food from an English child captive; and the haunting final paragraphs where she lies awake at night, unable to forget her experiences.

To teach students a little more about Puritan publishing practices and the precarious role of a woman author, I like to discuss intertextu-ality. The seventeenth-century editions of Rowlandson's narrative of-ten had a three-part structure: the inflammatory "Preface to the Reader," which was probably by Increase Mather but was simply signed *Per Amicum* ("By a Friend"); the narrative itself; and finally Jo-seph Rowlandson's last sermon, which he preached on 21 November

1678 (see Derounian). Framing a Puritan woman's work between commentaries by two men contemporaries validated her work—in Puritan, communal, terms—but also diminished and patronized it. Other information on the narrative's publication history indicates that it was one of the earliest American best-sellers and that by the eighteenth century it was already considered a classic—information teachers can use to discuss best-sellers then and now and to explore the issue of popular and elite texts.

Other Pedagogical Considerations

Teaching an entire course on captivity narratives can reveal to students the dynamic interaction of rhetoric, politics, literature, gender, and popular culture. Instructors might begin with wide theoretical issues such as mythic-archetypal schemas and with historical and political contexts. They can move to a more or less chronological consideration of specific texts—extracted or whole—including Rowlandson's. Other topics for consideration include gender issues, the discursive treatment of Native Americans, and the captivity narrative's cultural work, especially its propagandist uses. Later, the course may progress to fictional applications such as James Fenimore Cooper's *The Last of the Mohicans* (1826), as well as more recently recovered early women's texts such as Ann Eliza Bleecker's *The History of Maria Kittle* (1797), Lydia Maria Child's *Hobomok* (1824), and Catharine Maria Sedgwick's *Hope Leslie* (1827)—written in response to *Mohicans*—and end with countless twentieth-century examples (see Castiglia; Derounian-Stodola). For a postmodern perspective on early captivity narratives, students can read British writer Angela Carter's poignant short story "Our Lady of the Massacre." Finally, to illustrate that the Indian captivity narrative finds expression in media other than print culture, the class can view film versions, including *Little Big Man* (1964), *Blackrobe* (1991), *Dances with Wolves* (1991), and *Thunderheart* (1992). The course could end with one special celluloid gem, *Susannah of the Mounties*, an Indian captivity narrative starring Shirley Temple! (Burnham; Castiglia; Derounian-Stodola and Levernier; Ebersole; Namias).

Three student-paper topics from a course I taught on Indian captivity narratives took a wide definition of the form and applied its characteristics in innovative ways; they offer a sense of other student outcomes in this type of curriculum. One student considered the motifs of "baby-bashing" and cannibalism and tied them into a "demonology" of propaganda against all out groups (Ramsey); another student, whose ancestors were among the founding families of Texas, took her great-grandmother's pioneer diary and analyzed the wilderness fantasy themes there having to do with white–Native American interactions, both real and imagined; and a third considered the theory of propaganda and then looked at similar rhetorical and pictorial applications in Nazi anti-Semitic texts and anti-Indian accounts published in and sanctioned by white America.

Instructors who teach entire courses on captivity narratives or incorporate only a narrative or two into the curriculum might try to keep the following points in mind. A chronological, cultural, and geographical variety of texts gives students a broader sense of the form's scope. To counteract the prevailing tendency to define the early captivity narrative as exclusively Puritan, teachers can specify that other Christian denominations told and used captivity texts for their own spiritual and secular purposes. *The Jesuit Relations*, published yearly in Europe from 1632 to 1673, told of Catholic missionaries captured in New France; and Jonathan Dickinson's *God's Protecting Providence*, published in 1699, is one of the best-known Quaker examples of the captivity experience. Since captivity accounts were often published with propagandist and racist agendas — mostly anti-Indian, but also, in the late eighteenth century, for example, anti-British and anti-French — it is helpful to consider the texts within their cultural contexts rather than in isolation. A multicultural approach would point out that Native Americans captured African Americans, other Native Americans, and Hispanics as well as Anglo-Americans and that captivity narratives were published in Europe and the Americas in languages other than English. Instructors might clarify that the Indian captivity narrative form refers to accounts embedded within longer works — for example, the Pocahontas episode in Smith's *Generall Historie* — in addition to separately published texts, including those by Rowlandson and Williams. And finally, instructors might indicate that the published accounts are frequently mediated by an editor, making issues of truth and authority difficult or impossible to assess.

Captivity narratives are valuable documents charting our literary and cultural history. Yet they also force us to consider how apparent oppositions such as power and powerlessness, victory and victimization, freedom and captivity, self and other, civilization and savagery, writer and reader are instead part of a much more complicated continuum bound by texts and revealed by textual analysis.

Notes

1. The best-known early captivity narrative with an African American main character is John Marrant's (1788).
2. Rowlandson's narrative is extensively anthologized, and any version is acceptable to use at the undergraduate level. However, knowing more about the early imprints will help the instructor make a better informed choice from the available editions. Four editions of Rowlandson's narrative appeared in 1682: the first was published in Boston, but only a few leaves of it have survived; the "second addition" (sic), titled *The Sovereignty and Goodness of God*, was published in Cambridge and was set from the now-lost first edition, though, as the misspelling "addition" suggests, it contained many errors; the third edition, also published in Cambridge with the same title, set out to correct the errors, though apparently with minimal success; the fourth, titled *A True History* and published in London, was set at least from the first edition and possibly from the manuscript. I recommend the versions in Vaughan and Clark and in Salisbury, which follow the second or third editions, and the version in Andrews and in Derounian-Stodola, which follows the fourth edition (Derounian).

Works Cited

Primary Works

Andrews, William L., ed. *Journeys in New Worlds: Early American Women's Narratives*. Madison: U of Wisconsin P, 1990.

Derounian-Stodola, Kathryn Zabelle, ed. *Women's Indian Captivity Narratives*. New York: Penguin, 1998.

Franklin, Wayne, ed. *American Voices, American Lives: A Documentary Reader*. New York: Norton, 1997.

Marrant, John. *A Narrative of the Lord's Wonderful Dealings with John Marrant*. London, 1788.

Salisbury, Neal, ed. *The Sovereignty and Goodness of God*. Boston: Bedford, 1997.

Vaughan, Alden T., and Edward W. Clark, eds. *Puritans among the Indians: Accounts of Captivity and Redemption, 1676–1724*. Cambridge: Harvard UP, 1981.

Secondary Works

Arner, Robert D. "The Story of Hannah Dustan: Cotton Mather to Thoreau." *American Transcendental Quarterly* 18 (1973): 19–23.

Burnham, Michelle. *Captivity and Sentiment: Cultural Exchange in American Literature, 1682–1861*. Hanover: UP of New England, 1997.

Castiglia, Christopher. *Bound and Determined: Captivity, Culture-Crossing, and White Womanhood from Mary Rowlandson to Patty Hearst*. Chicago: U of Chicago P, 1996.

Demos, John. *The Unredeemed Captive: A Family Story from Early America*. New York: Knopf, 1994.

Derounian, Kathryn Zabelle. "The Publication, Promotion, and Distribution of Mary Rowlandson's Indian Captivity Narrative in the Seventeenth Century." *Early American Literature* 23 (1988): 239–61.

Derounian-Stodola, Kathryn Zabelle. "The Gendering of American Fiction: Susanna Rowson to Catharine Sedgwick." *Making America, Making American Literature*. Ed. A. Robert Lee and W. M. Verhoeven. Amsterdam: Rodopi, 1995. 165–81.

Derounian-Stodola, Kathryn Zabelle, and James A. Levernier. *The Indian Captivity Narrative, 1550–1900*. New York: Twayne, 1993.

Ebersole, Gary. *Captured by Texts: Puritan to Post-modern Images of Indian Captivity*. Charlottesville: UP of Virginia, 1995.

Fitzpatrick, Tara. "The Figure of Captivity: The Cultural Work of the Puritan Captivity Narrative." *American Literary History* 3 (1991): 1–26.

Greene, David L. "New Light on Mary Rowlandson." *Early American Literature* 20 (1985): 24–38.

Larkins, Sharon. "Using Trade Books to Teach about Pocahontas." *Georgia Social Sciences Journal* 19 (1988): 21–25.

Levernier, James A., and Hennig Cohen, eds. *The Indians and Their Captives*. Westport: Greenwood, 1977.

Mott, Frank Luther. *Golden Multitudes: The Story of Best Sellers in the United States*. New York: Bowker, 1947.

Namias, June. *White Captives: Gender and Ethnicity on the American Frontier*. Chapel Hill: U of North Carolina P, 1993.

Ramsey, Colin. "Cannibalism and Infant Killing: A System of 'Demonizing' Motifs in Indian Captivity Narratives." *CLIO: A Journal of History, Literature, and the Philosophy of History* 37 (1994): 55–68.

Tilton, Robert. *Pocahontas: The Evolution of an American Narrative*. New York: Cambridge UP, 1994.

Toulouse, Teresa. "'My Own Credit': Strategies of (E)Valuation in Mary

Rowlandson's Captivity Narrative." *American Literature* 64 (1992): 655–76.

Ulrich, Laurel Thatcher. *Good Wives: Image and Reality in the Lives of Women in Northern New England, 1650–1750.* New York: Random, 1982.

Vail, R. W. G. *The Voice of the Old Frontier.* 1949. New York: Octagon, 1970.

Vaughan, Alden T., and Daniel K. Richter. "Crossing the Cultural Divide: Indians and New Englanders, 1605–1763." *Proceedings of the American Antiquarian Society* 90 (1980): 23–99.

Whitford, Kathryn. "Hannah Dustin: The Judgement of History." *Essex Institute Historical Collections* 108 (1972): 304–25.

Young, Philip. "The Mother of Us All: Pocahontas Reconsidered." *Kenyon Review* 24 (1962): 391–415.

Part II

Selected Courses

Russell Reising

The Early American Literature Survey

The good news for teachers of early American literature is that publishers are expanding their offerings in our field. Probably in response to the Heath anthology's expanded sampling of writers and texts not included in most previous collections, most two-volume anthologies have beefed up their pre-1800 selections to the point that a survey of early American literature can be taught with an anthology and two or three additional texts. In addition to this trend, the proliferation of affordable editions of early novels, travel writings, captivity narratives, poetry, and theological tracts provides a rich variety of primary materials available for classroom use.

This richness offers us new challenges and opportunities for our syllabi, enabling a variety of approaches to the colonial and early republican American literary landscape. Like anyone teaching a periodized approach to a national literature, the teacher of early American literature needs to make some complicated initial decisions. Do we want a thesis-driven course to highlight a particular take on our earliest literature? Do we introduce our students to as broad and representative a selection of available materials as possible? Or do we want the course to lead into whatever we do with courses in the "American Renaissance" or other configurations of nineteenth-century American literary production? Do we take on the richness and variety of colonial genres (the lyric, the elegy, the sermon, historical writing, spiritual autobiography, personal narrative, nature observation, and so forth)? Do we highlight the "Puritan origins" of later American writing; the heterogeneous admixture of various ethnic, racial, geographic, religious, and ideological traditions; the centrality of nature in the "American experience"; constructions of the self, or gender relations in early America? These are only a few possibilities confronting us in the wilderness of early American writing.

I propose a model for a survey in early American literature responsive to many of these options, one that begins with an investigation of American Puritanism and then demonstrates the persistence of some of its most important issues, ideas, themes, styles, and metaphors throughout the eighteenth century and into the earliest decades of the nineteenth.[1] The course works by placing the early Protestant tradition (which many cultural and literary historians believe was still powerfully alive for Emily Dickinson) into a dialogue with many other voices and emergent traditions — antinomian, Native American, Quaker, Anglican, atheist, Deist, and others. Easily adjustable to fit either a quarter or a semester schedule, the approach introduces students to the breadth and depth of literary production in the colonies and the early republic, focusing on such key topics as the understanding of the human self, views of nature, gender issues, and questions of religious design and duty. Such an approach not only provides a coherent framework but also investigates an important cultural tradition without assuming it was the only way that early Americans experienced and articulated their world.

To suggest the varieties of religious experience commonly lumped together as "Puritan," I highlight the diversity, even incoherence, rather than monolithic uniformity of early Calvinist materials.[2] Perhaps most important, one should outline some central tenets of Calvinism and Puritanism by explaining in detail the so-called TULIP of Calvinist theology, an acronym first codified at the Synod of Dort

(1618–19). *T*otal depravity is that state of utter fallenness and spiritual desolation afflicting humankind as a result of original sin. *U*nconditional salvation reflects the belief that there are literally no conditions that human beings can fulfill in order to earn heavenly grace, a doctrine that is often referred to as "salvation by faith [as opposed to good works] alone" and that lies at the heart of numerous controversies within New England. *L*imited elect signifies that only a very few people were likely to be chosen for salvation (election) by even the most merciful God. *I*rresistible grace indicates the overpowering influence of God's saving energies on those chosen for redemption. *P*erseverance in the path is a doctrine that both describes the way that saints live and requires all Puritans to conduct their lives *as though* every act they perform *does* either influence or indicate their spiritual states.

Establishing these tenets of faith from the outset is of immense help in addressing student questions about the strangeness and seeming incoherence of Puritan theology. They also provide interesting angles on many Puritan elegies and pseudo elegies, such as Bradstreet's "To My Dear and Loving Husband" and "Before the Birth of One of Her Children" and Taylor's "Upon Wedlock and Death of Children," in which the poets express bizarre optimism about their and their loved ones' likely spiritual destinies. A few other concepts help explain and situate Puritanism. Puritan historiography, for example, anticipated the doctrine of manifest destiny in its vision of the Puritans as God's chosen people blazing a path through time into the apocalypse. The rigid hierarchies definitive of Puritan family structures recast all interpersonal pairings (husband and wife; parent and child; master and servant) as sublunar versions of the dominant God-human relationship. In a problematic extension of these hierarchies, Puritan beliefs commonly scorned intellectual and cultural ambition among women, frequently defining intellectual women as freaks or mentally ill. Various cultural concerns (prohibitions against novel reading, dancing, stage plays, the celebration of holidays like Christmas and Easter, the adornment of churches, and ministerial garb) can be communicated through lectures and references to passages in the reading materials. Literary and stylistic concerns such as the so-called "plaine stile" and typology and such recurring motifs as the suddenness and unexpectedness of death and the "gracious afflictions" characterize the journals of John Winthrop and Samuel Sewall and the transcripts of the trial of Anne Hutchinson, while most Puritan materials in any anthology demonstrate the significance and conventions of such genres as the elegy, the long didactic poem, the millennial speculation, and historical narratives.

The first section of the course can be arranged by the following concepts: orthodoxy, orthodoxy and its others (alternatives or resistance to orthodox Puritan beliefs and practices), and the inner lives of early Americans (diaries, journals, personal narratives, poetry). The purpose of such an arrangement is to suggest both Puritanism as a theoretical construct and the ways people actually experienced and responded to their "official" culture. Regardless of which anthology or text you have chosen, materials such as William Bradford's *Of Plymouth Plantation*; John Winthrop's "A Model of Christian Charity" and "Journals"; theological writings by Thomas Hooker, John Cotton, and either Increase or Cotton Mather; Michael Wigglesworth's *The Day of Doom*; Jonathan Edwards's "Sinners in the Hands of an Angry God"; and perhaps selections from Edwards's typological tour de force *Images or Shadows of Divine Things* constitute a useful set of initial readings that suggest the evolution of American Puritanism from the early-seventeenth through mid-eighteenth centuries. Many anthologies also include excerpts from the trial of Anne Hutchinson, which highlight in dramatic terms both hyperorthodox visions and Hutchinson's powerful gendered opposition to them. In these readings there is ample material to foreground such issues as Puritan exceptionalism (Winthrop's "city upon a hill," and Mather's preface to *Wonders of the Invisible World*), Puritan views of nature (Bradford; Edwards), typological metaphoricity (Winthrop, Edwards), human vulnerability to sudden and unexpected destruction (Winthrop, Wigglesworth, Edwards), various articulations of facets of Puritan beliefs, and Puritan literary sensibilities and conventions. By taking three or four sermons—from Winthrop's lay text usually called "A Model of Christian Charity" to Hooker's "A True Sight of Sin" to Edwards's famous "Sinners in the Hands of an Angry God"—we can trace the mutations of *official* doctrine. Each text assumes and addresses different audiences, deploys different rhetorical strategies, and suggests widely different theological and cultural perspectives; each represents, in other words, almost a different Puritanism.

Lest this model be confused as *the* model for the study of early colonial literature, we can now examine some alternative visions, such as early promotional poetry; Native American writings on nature; Thomas Morton's *New English Canaan*; Roger Williams on church government and language; writings from the Spanish settlement of Central America, the Floridas, and the Southwest; and French literature from the Canadas, among others. By articulating different theological, social, and cultural values, these alternative texts challenge the notion of a dominant, let alone autonomous, Puritan tradition.

From readings in orthodox and alternative positions, the survey can then move to journal selections, personal narratives, and other potentially more private and introspective documents. Selections from Winthrop's journal can be effectively juxtaposed with Sewall's diary, John Woolman's journal, Jonathan Edwards's "personal narrative," William Byrd's "secret" diary, and maybe even Anne Bradstreet's anecdotal advice to her children. The subjectivities exposed and examined in these works provide personal examples of the colonial ideologies surveyed earlier, while demonstrating that modes of subjectivity and levels of introspection differ within any movement or moment and also change over time. Examined together, these texts also suggest various possibilities for exploring generic differences and audience awareness, as some (Winthrop and Woolman) were written as public documents, while others (Edwards) were unpublished but probably circulated among friends and associates, and still others (Sewall and Byrd) were obviously never intended for a reading audience. These documents of orthodoxy, its alternatives, and more private significance demonstrate that Hester Prynne's advice to Pearl that "we must not always talk in the market-place [or in public documents] of what happens to us in the forest" (185; ch. 22) holds true even for cultures and beliefs often regarded as stable and unified. Puritan culture did not exhibit only one-dimensional piety and citizenship, and there was certainly not one Puritanism, Puritan self, or

Puritan discourse; even the most publicly sanctioned rhetorical certainty and bravado in early colonial cultures coexisted with and was marked by unevenness, dissent, questionings, and self-doubt.

The survey course's turn to poetry reinforces the cultural dynamism and density suggested by these early units of study. In addition to sampling verses from the *New England Primer* and, more recently, some Native American chants or prayers, most anthologies include poetry by Bradstreet, Wigglesworth, and Taylor, all of which can be examined in the light of *both* their aesthetic *and* their cultural significance. Anne Bradstreet's poetry ("The Author to Her Book," "The Prologue," "Before the Birth of One of Her Children," and the letter poems to her absent husband, for example) dramatizes the gender issues revealed in Winthrop's journal or Wigglesworth's *Day of Doom*. In other poems ("The Flesh and the Spirit," the poem on the burning of her house, and most of her many elegies) Bradstreet's poetry wages a struggle between intellectual adherence to Puritanism and emotional revulsion at many of its demands, a struggle evident at every poetic level, from overt themes and content to the subtlest poetic nuances of style, rhyme, stanzaic divisions, and line (note, for example, the brilliant syntactic inversions and the cry of "but why" in the very center of her elegy for her infant grandson, Simon Bradstreet). Whether we focus on the occasional poems or on the preparatory meditations, resources for studying Edward Taylor's work grow richer by the day. Taylor's poetry can, of course, be studied primarily for its rhetorical and stylistic complexity or for its resemblances to English metaphysical poetics, but virtually any theme one highlights in the survey can apply productively to him, including the gracious affliction poem, typological thinking, the ceaseless vacillations of Puritan interiority, and the dialectic of Puritan spiritual certainty and doubt. As a minister, Taylor can be compared with Hooker, Mather, and Edwards; as a poet, with Bradstreet and Wigglesworth; and as a human being, with any writer read so far in the course.

Having worked well into the eighteenth century with various Puritan texts, you can move stylistically and historically to writings of the Enlightenment and the late eighteenth century. William Byrd II's *History of the Dividing Line betwixt Virginia and North Carolina* and the *Secret History*, J. Hector St. John de Crèvecoeur's *Letters from an American Farmer*, Benjamin Franklin's *Autobiography*, Thomas Paine's *The Age of Reason*, Thomas Jefferson's *Notes on the State of Virginia*, and, in some collections, even scientific writings by Benjamin Rush provide representative samples of late colonial and early republican ideas, styles, and concerns in genres such as autobiography, nature and travel writing, and political tracts. In comparison with earlier Protestant writers, Byrd, Franklin, Paine, and Rush advocate decidedly new and emergent understandings of the viability of the individual self, more or less freed from restrictive Protestant notions of human fallibility and sin, and experiment with the newly valued powers of human agency, rational thinking, scientific objectivity, and both domestic and cosmic optimism. Their views of the natural world depart greatly from the suspicion always lurking behind Puritan writings, which struggled, usually unsuccessfully, to perceive North American nature as something other than a "howling wilderness." They also anticipate the poetic and novelistic concerns of the earliest years of the republic. We can, for example, stress the revolutionary influence of Enlightenment discourses. Franklin's sense of the self as an ongoing construction project differs greatly from the teleology imposed by a rigid scheme of salvation or damnation that has no room for nuance or gradation. Paine's aggressive unbelief and Byrd's, Franklin's, Jefferson's, and Rush's utilitarian and pragmatic views of nature all reimagine the centrality of human reason to the evolution of the species. Similarly, the evolution of a literary and political discursive style of shrewdly pragmatic and instrumental utility can be seen as continuing some elements of the "plaine stile" while announcing a powerful and competing worldview. Byrd's histories and secret diary and Franklin's *Autobiography* can also be read against earlier Puritan spiritual autobiographies and compared with the varieties of subjectivity articulated in journals, diaries, and occasional writings and an earlier theological positioning of human life in general.

Late-century poetry, also, can be read as continuing earlier ideological and stylistic notions while anticipating nineteenth-century concerns and strategies. Phillis Wheatley, for example, borrows forms from New England Protestantism — her elegiac practices and her apparent adherence to Puritan notions of salvation — while also introducing the possibilities of political struggle and thus formulating many priorities and complexities that will come to be codified as the discourse of slave narratives. Her most famous and most frequently anthologized poem, "On Being Brought from Africa to America," for example, can be read in the tradition of the "gracious affliction" poem, which would posit that the physical tragedy of her being abducted, sold, and enslaved is actually a spiritual boon, introducing her into the glorious scheme of Christian salvation. Like the burning of Anne Bradstreet's house and the deaths of Edward Taylor's children, Wheatley's enslavement can be reprocessed to reveal spiritual meaning inherent in the social and physical world. Wheatley's "On Imagination" can similarly be read in the context of other poems on fancy, imagination, or poetry, such as Bradstreet's "The Prologue" and "The Author to Her Book," Freneau's "To an Author," and Bryant's "The Power of Fancy," which can be discussed with regard to the Puritan "plaine stile." Samuel Sewall's *The Selling of Joseph* (1700) and John Woolman's *Some Considerations on the Keeping of Negroes* (1754), two of the first abolitionist writings in the colonies, make an exciting supplement to Wheatley's work.

The poetry of Philip Freneau and William Cullen Bryant similarly responds both to contemporary political and cultural struggles (Freneau's "To an Author," for example) while also staking out territory for nature poetry later extended by Cooper and some Transcendentalists (Freneau's "The Wild Honey-Suckle" and Bryant's "Thanatopsis," "To a Water Fowl," and "Inscription on the Entrance to a Wood," for example). Comic poems such as Ebenezer Cook's *The Sot-Weed Factor* and Joel Barlow's "The Hasty Pudding" and political verse such as Barlow's *The Vision of Columbus* and Timothy Dwight's "Columbia" can fill out a sense of eighteenth-century poetry by presenting both parodic critiques of colonial provincialism and serious political visions. Both approaches represent poetic versions of the discursive ranges found in Franklin's *Autobiography*.

The final week(s) of the early American survey can address early fictional narratives, many of which can be connected thematically to much of the earlier work. Charles Brockden Brown's *Wieland* or

Edgar Huntly, Hannah W. Foster's *The Coquette*, Susanna Rowson's *Charlotte Temple*, and slightly later narratives such as Catharine Maria Sedgwick's *Hope Leslie*, Rebecca Rush's *Kelroy*, and Lydia Maria Child's *Hobomok* can all be studied for their referential or allusive relation with earlier New England culture, their explorations of colonial subjectivity and gender relations, their responses to the founding of the United States of America, or their roles in founding a new fictional practice capable, at once, of breaking away from the various prohibitions against fiction writing common in American culture and of reading and articulating the challenges and possibilities of the new republic. For example, we can study the examination in *Wieland*, *Charlotte Temple*, and *The Coquette* of how young adults negotiate their freedoms, their futures, and their options for worldly happiness once liberated from traditional authority figures and social structures. The protagonists are test cases for the efficacy of proper upbringing and moral training (*Charlotte Temple*), seriousness of purpose (*Wieland*), and the possibilities of freedom in a new republic (*The Coquette*). All have dense settings that locate them within the history of American ideas, and all press their narratives to remorselessly tragic conclusions, as if to demonstrate that no religious or political ideology can prepare an emerging American citizenry for all its challenges. Whether they intend to or not, they all come close to verifying the Puritan vision of a remote and angry deity whose operations repeatedly frustrate human understanding, however pure one's motives and however moral and loving one's family or community.

I try to focus on the richness of stylistic, ideological, and cultural content in the first two centuries of literary production in the colonies and early republic. However, this approach can also introduce students to the kinds of issues and themes that preoccupied American writers throughout much of the nineteenth century. A teacher might even choose to conclude the course with a writer whose major output falls between the first two decades of the nineteenth century and the period of literary production commonly called the American Renaissance. Many works by Washington Irving and James Fenimore Cooper, to cite just two examples, possess a Janus-faced relation to their precursors and successors, returning to and commenting on particulars of colonial life with the advantage of historical distance but without the stylistic and thematic complexity we usually associate with writers like Nathaniel Hawthorne. Even one of Hawthorne's so-called Puritan tales or two not only can suggest the endurance of some of the issues and personages studied in the early American survey but also can offer a latter-day literary meditation on the earliest days of colonial literature. In any event, courses in early American literature have come a long way since the ones I took, in which, as I recall, we were studying Edgar Allan Poe by the fourth week.

Notes

1. Throughout this essay, references to writers and to works not specifically listed in Works Cited are from the *Macmillan Anthology of American Literature*, volume 1, *Colonial through Romantic*, edited by George McMichael.

2. There are many excellent resources for the teacher confronting these texts and this period for the first time. For general background, I recommend that teachers and potential teachers of early American literature surveys consult the works by the following literary scholars and historians: Bercovitch, Erikson, Hall, Morgan, Parrington, and Ziff. All these studies are rich in historical information, anecdotal observations, pertinent primary materials, and literary insights. For commentaries on primary texts and colonial writers, the essays in journals such as *Early American Literature*, *New England Quarterly*, and *American Literature* can be of great use. All help flesh out a more thorough sense of early colonial culture and enable us to bring the literary texts we teach to life.

Abbreviated Syllabus
The Early American Literature Survey

Week 1   Introduction and Business
Lecture on key concepts and cultural contexts of Puritanism

Week 2   Orthodoxy
John Winthrop, "A Model of Christian Charity"
Thomas Shepard, "The Covenant of Grace"
Samuel Danforth, "A Brief Recognition of New England's Errand into the Wilderness"

Week 3   Orthodoxy, cont.
Thomas Hooker, "A True Sight of Sin"
Michael Wigglesworth, *The Day of Doom*
Jonathan Edwards, "Sinners in the Hands of an Angry God," *Images or Shadows of Divine Things* (selections)

Week 4   Opposition
Roger Williams, "The Bloudy Tenant of Persecution"
Thomas Morton, *The New English Canaan*
John Woolman, *Some Considerations on the Keeping of Negroes*
Anne Hutchinson, "The Examination of Mrs. Anne Hutchinson at the Court of Newtown"

Week 5   Journals and Diaries
John Winthrop, Anne Bradstreet, Mary Rowlandson, Samuel Sewall, William Byrd, John Woolman

Week 6   Poetry
Anne Bradstreet, "The Prologue," "The Author to Her Book," "Before the Birth of One of Her Children," "A Letter to Her Husband, Absent upon Publick Employment," "Here Follow Some Verses upon the Burning of Our House (July 10, 1666)"

Week 7   Poetry, cont.
Edward Taylor, selections from *Preparatory Meditations*, "Upon a Spider Catching a Fly," "Upon a Wasp Chilled with Cold," "The Ebb and the Flow," "Upon Wedlock and the Death of Children"

Week 8   Eighteenth-Century Poetry
Phillis Wheatley, "On Imagination," "On Being Brought from Africa to America," "An Hymn to the Morning," "An Hymn to the Evening," "On Virtue," "To S. M., A Young African Painter, on Seeing His Works"

Week 9   Eighteenth-Century Poetry, cont.
Philip Freneau, "To Sir Toby," "The Wild Honey-Suckle," "The Indian Burying Ground," "On Mr. Paine's Rights of Man"
Joel Barlow, "The Hasty Pudding"
Ebenezer Cook, *The Sot-Weed Factor*

Week 10 Eighteenth-Century Prose
        Benjamin Franklin, *The Autobiography*
Week 11 Prose, cont.
        Franklin, cont.
        Thomas Paine, from *The Age of Reason*
        Thomas Jefferson, from *Notes on the State of Virginia*
Week 12 Fiction
        Hannah Foster, *The Coquette*
Week 13 Fiction
        Susanna Rowson, *Charlotte Temple*
Week 14 Fiction
        Charles Brockden Brown, *Wieland*
Week 15 Fiction
        Brown, cont.

Works Cited

Primary Works

Baym, Nina, et al., eds. *The Norton Anthology of American Literature*. Vol. 1. New York: Norton, 1997.

Bradstreet, Anne. *The Works of Anne Bradstreet*. Ed. Jeannine Healey. Cambridge: Harvard UP, 1967.

Brown, Charles Brockden. *Edgar Huntly; or, Memoirs of a Sleep-walker*. New York: Penguin, 1988.

———. *Wieland; or, The Transformation*. New York: Harcourt, 1926.

Child, Lydia Maria. Hobomok *and Other Writings on Indians*. New Brunswick: Rutgers UP, 1986.

Foster, Hannah W. *The Coquette*. New York: Penguin, 1996.

Gunn, Giles, ed. *Early American Writing*. New York: Penguin, 1994.

Hawthorne, Nathaniel. *The Scarlet Letter*. Ed. Ross C. Murfin. Boston: St. Martin's, 1991.

Heimert, Alan, and Andrew Delbanco, eds. *The Puritans in America: A Narrative*. Cambridge: Harvard UP, 1985.

Jehlen, Myra, and Michael Warner, eds. *The English Literatures of America, 1500–1800*. New York: Routledge, 1997.

Lauter, Paul, et al., eds. *The Heath Anthology of American Literature*. 3rd ed. Vol. 1. Boston: Houghton, 1997.

Martin, Wendy, ed. *Colonial American Travel Narratives*. New York: Penguin, 1994.

McMichael, George, ed. *Anthology of American Literature*. 5th ed. Vol. 1. New York: Macmillan, 1996.

McQuade, Donald, ed. *The Harper American Literature*. Vol. 1. New York: Harper, 1994.

Miller, Perry, ed. *The American Puritans*. New York: Columbia UP, 1956.

Rowson, Susanna. *Charlotte Temple*. New York: Oxford UP, 1986.

Rush, Rebecca. *Kelroy*. New York: Oxford UP, 1992.

Sedgwick, Catharine Maria. *Hope Leslie*. New Brunswick: Rutgers UP, 1991.

Taylor, Edward. *The Poetical Works of Edward Taylor*. Ed. Thomas H. Johnson. Princeton: Princeton UP, 1966.

Wheatley, Phillis. *The Collected Works of Phillis Wheatley*. Ed. John Shields. New York: Oxford UP, 1988.

Secondary Works

Bercovitch, Sacvan. *The American Jeremiad*. Madison: U of Wisconsin P, 1978.

———. *The Puritan Origins of the American Self*. New Haven: Yale UP, 1975.

Erikson, Kai T. *Wayward Puritans: A Study in the Sociology of Deviant Behavior*. New York: Wiley, 1966.

Hall, David D. *Worlds of Wonder, Days of Judgment: Puritan Religious Beliefs in Early New England*. Cambridge: Harvard UP, 1989.

Morgan, Edmund. *The Puritan Dilemma: The Story of John Winthrop*. Boston: Little, 1958.

———. *The Puritan Family: Religion and Domestic Relations in Seventeenth-Century New England*. New York: Harper, 1966.

Parrington, V. L. *The Colonial Mind, 1620–1800*. Vol. 1 of *Main Currents in American Thought*. Norman: U of Oklahoma P, 1927.

Ziff, Larzer. *Puritanism in America: New Culture in a New World*. New York: Vintage, 1973.

Karen E. Rowe

Gender, Genre, and Culture: A Two-Quarter Graduate Seminar

Writing on 31 March 1776 to her husband, John, then in attendance at the Second Continental Congress, which would promulgate the Declaration of Independence, with characteristic wit Abigail Adams petitioned her spouse "in the new Code of Laws [. . . to] Remember the Ladies," while cautioning him that "all Men would be tyrants if they could" and threatening that "if perticular care and attention is not paid to the Laidies, we are determined to foment a Rebelion" (Adams and Adams 121). Following hard upon the publication of Thomas Paine's famous manifesto, Abigail's wifely advice might be considered mere common sense, that women should be as liberated from their status as "vassals" of the "Naturally Tyrannical" male sex as Americans from British monarchical rule (121). In early American literary studies the overwhelming attention paid to the founding fathers has often obliterated the voices of women writers, Bradstreet, Rowlandson, and Wheatley excepted, and ignored the complicated gender relations that emerge as graphically from accounts of early colonizations by Columbus and Cortés as they do, even more provocatively, from later eighteenth-century proclamations of a new republic built upon Enlightenment ideals of rationalism, democracy, and individual rights. "Remember[ing] the Ladies," however, is a far harder task than reconstituting a cultural and political history of the Americas from primarily male-authored texts. Perhaps more aptly subtitled "How to Foment Abigail's Rebellion," my two-quarter sequence of graduate seminars is designed not only to make more accessible men's private and public discourses about women, which often mingle adoration with stern instructions about the proper conduct of the female life, but also to recuperate texts written by women who spoke with their own voices, whether they conformed with the spiritual ideals of a virtuous wife and mother or claimed a political and intellectual equality by defying social norms and subversively manipulating literary genres (Davidson).

Because they require an ability to undertake independent research, the seminars Gender, Genre, and Culture I and II: Women in Early American Literature presume a population of graduate students in early modern British and American studies likely to be conversant with new historicism, feminist theory, and cultural or postcolonial studies. Selected from readily purchasable paperback editions and anthologies, the readings may also be adapted for an upper-division survey, an undergraduate seminar, or a full-semester offering. Although materials are rapidly becoming available, for advanced seminars it may be necessary to place on library reserve or to photocopy primary documents that are hard to obtain, such as Grace Smith's *The Dying Mother's Legacy* (1712) and Sarah Wentworth Morton's *Ouabi* (1790), or those, such as Benjamin Rush's "Thoughts upon Female Education" (1787), that are published only in expensive hardback editions of collected essays. Instructors can also draw upon excellent collections, including Meserole's *American Poetry of the Seventeenth Century*, Silverman's *Colonial American Poetry*, Cowell's *Women Poets in Pre-Revolutionary America, 1650–1775*, and Harris's *American Women Writers to 1800*, and upon facsimile editions, such as the *Poems of Jane Turell and Martha Brewster*, *The Colonial American Family*, or *The Posthumous Works of Ann Eliza Bleecker*. For Gender, Genre, and Culture I, I created two collections, reproduced by our campus-based

Academic Publishing Service (APS), of colonial poems on women, love, children, religion, and death (by Saffin, Davies, Tompson, Warren, Evans, and Ladd, among others) and of prose writings such as Cotton Mather's *Elizabeth in Her Holy Retirement* and Benjamin Wadsworth's *The Well-Ordered Family*. For Gender, Genre, and Culture II two new APS booklets assembled a variety of late-eighteenth-century documents: poems, southern women's wartime accounts (*Letters of Eliza Wilkinson*; "A Dialogue between a Southern Delegate and His Spouse"), lyrics on the "noble savage" from Ann Hatton's opera *Tammany*, and the less-easily obtainable captivity narratives "The History of Maria Kittle," by Ann Eliza Bleecker, and "A True Narrative of the Sufferings of Mary Kinnan." Hannah Foster's *The Boarding School* (1798), Susanna Rowson's *Mentoria; or, The Young Lady's Friend* (1794), and *The Female Advocate* (1801) are not available in modern editions, but they can be reproduced from microfilm sources. The act of reconstruction itself challenges our preconceptions about the paucity of colonial writings by and about women and launches many students on their own journeys of discovery in rare-book libraries, microfilm collections, and genealogical and historical society archives.

By bringing newer theoretical models to bear on materials often relegated to musty archives and by grounding studies of later American literature on a firmer base of historical and cultural knowledge, both seminars seek by example and impetus to push forward research on women in early American writing, history, and society and to stimulate graduate students to undertake dissertations. Although my preset syllabi establish the primary readings and frameworks for our collaborative explorations of gender, genre, and culture, the students' self-generated weekly research presentations (20–30 minutes) set the agenda for the three-hour sessions and often for their subsequent prospectuses (1–2 pages), annotated bibliographies (10 items), and critical essays (20–25 pages). Whether the students choose to build upon recent criticism, analyze themes and authorial voice within lesser-known texts, or apply theoretical concepts to canonical readings, the seminar participants initiate daily topics for discussion—with a little help from their friends and their faculty facilitator.

In the genuine sense of a colloquium led by different participants, these seminars become conversations that refine students' critical judgments, generate ongoing comparisons among texts, and
reconceptualize how gendered ideologies shaped the early American
cultures within which women were situated and constructed. In such
a colloquy, the professor functions less as an authority than as a director who sets out problems to be interrogated, weaves together loose
threads of ideas, teases out relationships among writers, entertains
varying interpretations, fleshes out little-known historical events and
beliefs, marks shifts of literary genre, and maps out the overall progress. But the seminar's framework should remain sufficiently flexible
in order to accommodate alternative topics, such as women's participation in Revolutionary theater or in literary salons; to promote un-
fettered exchange of students' interpretive readings, essay proposals,
and bibliographic materials; to keep the research questions fresh and
open-ended; and to stimulate revisionist thinking about recurrent as
well as emergent issues, theories, and texts. In each colloquium, therefore, the class participants create a course together and test out cultural
and literary hypotheses to see whether they have viability. The archi-
tectural design may be mine, but the vibrant collaborations (in what
one student called a "feminist workspace") are born of students'
imaginations and investigations.

Organized chronologically and thematically, both seminars focus
on three overarching inquiries. First, how is gender — specifically "the
feminine" and "woman" — constructed within different early American contexts, at critical historical moments, and in tandem with shifting political ideologies? Women, in this sense, are defined by
normative behaviors and roles as much as by that which is labeled deviant or different. How then are women represented in texts, recon-
figured by ruptures in the social fabric, read as cultural signs, and
displayed through iconographies of the Americas? Second, how do
women become "speaking subjects," often through a struggle to discover the self (a slippery term) in relation to predetermined sociocultural and religious dictates? The trace evidence is both veiled by and
revealed through the double-telling, self-questioning, and strategic
displacements of voice in texts. Third, do men and women writers

variously adopt and transform literary conventions and genres? If so, how? In sermons, treatises, love lyrics, and elegies by men, a presumptive narrator often subjects a woman to the authoritative male gaze of a husband, father, minister, or God, thereby praising her as a mirror for or enhancement of the masculine self. By contrast, epistles, poems, essays, conduct guides, captivity narratives, romances, and autobiographies by women seek to create a self-authorizing voice and vision or to explore the complex cultural dynamics that make it nearly impossible for women to wield the pen at all, since the "carping tongue," as Bradstreet attests, proclaims "my hand a needle better fits" ("The Prologue" 27, 28). To what extent, then, does Hannah Foster bow to literary and cultural conventions when she condemns Eliza Wharton to death for female excesses (novel reading and romantic fancies among them), even while Foster herself uses the sentimental subgenre to invite female readers to resist such an entrapment within gender inequalities that limit a woman's liberty to choose — a husband, a life, a literary mode.

Gender, Genre, and Culture I opens with Native American and Spanish legends of womanhood, including Iroquois creation myths, Cochiti and Laguna Yellow Woman stories, and representations of La Malinche in accounts by Cortés and Bernal Díaz and in pictoglyphs from Aztec codices, in part to disrupt the Puritan hegemony in colonial American studies and in part because of the fluent Spanish of a new subset of American comparativists. Entitled Originating Visions, this section also juxtaposes the exploration narratives that imagine Native women according to imperialist models of the "exotic" and the mythologizing accounts of La Malinche, La Llorona, and the Virgen de Guadalupe with canonically familiar sermons by New England ministers who draw upon Genesis, Proverbs, and 1 Corinthians to situate women within the Puritan community. Homiletic treatises prescribe female virtues and roles, as in Cotton Mather's *Ornaments for the Daughters of Zion* and Wadsworth's *The Well-Ordered Family; or, Relative Duties*, but Ivy Schweitzer argues that the very premises of Puritan theology create a more pervasive "gynesis" of "redeemed subjectivity" that makes all elect church members into feminine Brides of Christ (32, 34), a process that Edward Taylor enacts in his *Preparatory*

Meditations on Canticles. By dislocating our sense of what constitutes a text as well as our Protestant-centered vision of what civilization and conquest mean for women, these selections establish the seminar's methods and matter. Through a study of many different genres — story, myth, travel accounts, elegies, sermons, histories, captivity narratives, trial records, journals, poetry, romances, autobiographies — we can explore how cultural constructions positioned "colonial" and "colonized" women within the family, church, and society or, alternatively, outside communal boundaries as exiles, witches, betrayers, captives, apostates, and independent spirits.

Although cultural ideologies may determine women's expected roles as dutiful (virtually asexual) wives, mothers, or nuns, writings by women betray far less acquiescence and far more rebellious struggle as well as ardent passion expressed in spiritual meditations, love poems, and elegies. How, for example, does Sor Juana Inés de la Cruz (1648?–95) speak from behind the veil in her 1691 *La Respuesta* (*The Answer*) to defend her "reasonable" pursuit of knowledge and literary art in seventeenth-century New Spain and in her famous baroque poems, such as "Primero sueño," to reclaim her voice from the silence of a Catholic nunnery? Sor Juana's reflections on God, nature, passion, and reason usefully complement Bradstreet's similarly intense religious doubts, her struggles to find a poetic voice within a Puritan culture that privileges domesticity over authorship, and her seeking, as in her poem "Contemplations," of God's revelations in nature as much as within Scripture. Writing also of wilderness hardships, Bradstreet frequently grieves for deceased or distant loved ones in poems that exemplify her meditative self-examination and reluctant acquiescence to God's will. In contrast to the emphasis on women as "speaking subjects," this section also elaborates on our notions of gendering by examining representations of the feminine subject by men writers, such as Samuel Sewall in his *Diary,* Ebenezer Turell in his *Memoirs of the Life and Death of the Pious and Ingenious Mrs. Jane Turell* (1735), and the poets Thomas Thatcher, John Saffin, Benjamin Tompson, Samuel Davies, and Nathaniel Evans. In lovers' dialogues, memoirs, elegies, or funeral orations, men writers often draw upon formulaic eulogizings of feminine virtues, yet they may also reveal unsuspected depths of passion and loss, thereby complicating the questions of how public utterances register private sentiment and whether women remain unalterably the creations of masculine discourse.

If "woman" is constructed within dominant Anglo-American society by both cultural ideologies and literary representations, how, we ask in the course's third section, do women express "resistances from the margins," often by daring to speak out as "captives, exiles, and revolutionaries"? In Mary Rowlandson's captivity narrative *The Soveraignty and the Goodness of God* and in the accounts of "Hannah Duston" by Cotton Mather, Nathaniel Hawthorne, and Henry David Thoreau, women become doubly symbolic. As persecuted victims of "heathen tribes" who return to the Puritan community or execute a just vengeance, these women (and their stories) justify a belief in God's providential redemption of virtuous saints. Tainted, however, by their wilderness sojourn among "pagan" Indians, female captives also elicit fears of women's susceptibility to "natural" and "native" desires, precisely those which the Christian soul, reason, and church must seek to suppress. Rowlandson's marginal status, neither of the tribe nor securely within the Puritan fold, heightens the reader's consciousness of the female as "other" in both cultures, yet paradoxically offers Rowlandson an ideal position as ethnographic observer and narrator. In trial records of Anne Hutchinson's antinomianism we find also the origins of a countermythology of the "American Jezebel" (as Cotton Mather stigmatizes her), the rebellious woman whose outspokenness threatens a patriarchal ministry that values cultural hegemony. By ending with Quakerism in Jane Hoskens's *The Life and Spiritual Sufferings of That Faithful Servant of Christ* (1771) and Elizabeth Ashbridge's *Some Account of the Fore Part of the Life of Elizabeth Ashbridge* (written 1750–55; pub. 1774), the course seeks the beginnings of what might be called modern American women's autobiography in accounts that embrace religious paradigms yet curiously foreshadow women's contemporary struggles toward selfhood in reaction against male abuse and domination. But the seminar might also study the Salem witchcraft trials or culminate with the rise of religious enthusiasm and affections during the Great Awakening and the consequent redefining of women's spirituality that set the stage for later American assertions of female independence and subjectivity. Reading from Mather ("Hannah Duston," "Hydra Decapitata," "Ignes Fatui") and Hawthorne ("The Duston Family," "Mrs. Hutchinson," "The Gentle Boy") to accompany the accounts of Rowlandson, Hutchinson, and Ashbridge, we retrace literary redactions of what become early American myths of womanhood as powerful as those that link La Llorona and La Malinche to writings by contemporary Chicanas, such as Sandra Cisneros and Helena María Viramontes, or the Yellow Woman stories to those of Leslie Marmon Silko. Throughout Gender, Genre, and Culture I, therefore, we read texts as malleable and dynamic expressions of cultural beliefs, voiced selves, and shifting concepts of the "feminine" subject.

Gender, Genre, and Culture II, subtitled more aptly, American Women and the Age of Revolution, plunges us into a radically different world, in which women emerge as "revolutionary subjects" who adopt Enlightenment principles of reason, democratic philosophies of government, the rhetoric of individual rights, and a reconfiguration of community to forward political and personal aims, whether as citizen mothers in the new republican family, as self-fashioners who enact independent choices, or as educated women with innate rationality and sensibilities. Launched by a study of poems by William Boyd, Elizabeth Graeme Fergusson, Juba, Judith Sargent Murray, Sarah Wentworth Morton, Annis Boudinot Stockton, and of prose writings, such as Thomas Paine's "Occasional Letter on the Female Sex," Murray's provocative essays "On the Equality of the Sexes" and "Observations on Female Abilities," and Charles Brockden Brown's *Alcuin*, this seminar poses the "woman question." If political equality, then why not gender equality and egalitarian marriages? If freedom from monarchical rule, then why not freedom from tyrannical husbands? What are women's inalienable rights?

Women, we cannot forget, also create America's history, whether through epistles, emblemized by Abigail Adams's brilliant correspondence or by Mary V. V.'s "Dialogue between a Southern Delegate and His Spouse" (1774; Anonymous); wartime journals (*Letters of Eliza Wilkinson* [1781–82] or *Sally Wister's Journal* [. . .] *1777–1778*); or compendious annals, such as Mercy Otis Warren's *History of the Rise,*

Progress, and Termination of the American Revolution (1805). Useful throughout the section Cultural Constructions of the Female Sex and the section Women and the Making of American History is Linda Kerber's *Women of the Republic: Intellect and Ideology in Revolutionary America*, which is replete with pictorial representations that display the gendered iconographies of Britannia (negligent mother and whore) as opposed to America, Columbia, and Liberty (virtuous Roman matrons and fecund Natives), images that Warren, for one, deploys in her poetic satires. Women's entry into the public (and published) domain is sanctioned too by the advent of heroic verse, in which female writers eulogize famous American leaders, as Wheatley, Stockton, and Warren do by glorifying George Washington — thereby crafting their own visions as makers and transmitters of an American heroic destiny, not simply its puppets.

Despite the rhetoric of democracy, race and class as well as sexual mores continue to determine a woman's position and perspective, often resituating her outside "civilized" society as gender revisionist, captive, or critic. Aphra Behn's *Oroonoko* (1688), for instance, violates social norms of reticent modesty by portraying a white woman's sexual obsession with an ennobled black male body, yet it also reinscribes a colonialist racial superiority by violently killing off the fertile black female. Similar fascinations with the "noble savage" — whether in Ann Hatton's opera *Tammany; or, The Indian Chief* (1774), or Morton's *Ouabi* (1790) — complement the complex fictionalizations in "The History of Maria Kittle" (1793) and in Kinnan's "A True Narrative" (1795), in which captive women identify with Native otherness. The poet Phillis Wheatley, self-styled the "Ethiop," uses her marginal status as a slave (and creates literary personas) to lay claim to Enlightenment reason *and* religious authority, thereby subtly challenging the exclusivity of a book-learned Harvard elite and ministry.

The seminar continues with the section Age of Education and the Rise of Women's Literate Culture, a culture that blurs once clear-cut distinctions between didactic manuals and fictional romances. Foster's *The Boarding School* (1798) and Rowson's *Mentoria* (1794), together with the anonymous *Female Advocate* (1801) and essays by Murray, Rush, and Noah Webster, set the terms of debate about educating women. Is learning enlightening or debilitating? Does rational study (and literacy) nurture or corrupt female virtue, promote women's mobility from private domestic spaces into the public sphere, or foster the republican mother's responsibility to inculcate national civic values? When women are educated to make their individual choices in the new world marriage market, the "W(rites) of Courtship and Marriage" (in the words of my title for the class session of week 8) become as much the topic of conduct guides as of correspondence, whether in the Adamses' private letters, in *Robert Bolling Woos Anne Miller* (unsuccessfully), or in Murray's 1796 drama, *The Traveller Returned*. Simultaneously, the eighteenth-century rise of a print culture enables women to write themselves into the public domain by adopting more varied literary genres — from histories to romances, celebratory odes and poetic epistles to patriotic and love dramas.

The emphasis throughout the course on the constructions of a female culture, on the new freedoms that women exercise as speaking subjects, and on the diverse genres adopted as modes of self-expression culminates with the first novels written by and about American women — Rowson's *Charlotte Temple* (1791), Foster's *The Coquette* (1797), and Murray's *The Story of Margaretta* (1798). Although quarrels rage about the deleterious effects of novel reading, such popular fictions cultivate a taste for sentiment and sentimentality, create new images of the female body as a displayed object, and redefine standards by which to judge female morality according to prescribed religious virtues, a conformity with social proprieties, and a rational exercise of individual autonomy. Romance conventions — seduction and betrayal; a "captivity" of the affections; a heroine's conflict between reason and passion; epistolary confessions; a female community united by virtuous friendships; the perils of "dangerous" (sexual) knowledge, reading, and fancy; and a morally redemptive death — take shape in these earliest American novels, whose popularity unleashes a literary deluge of women's fiction in the nineteenth century.

Although Abigail Adams petitions men to relinquish the "harsh title of Master for the more tender and endearing one of Friend"

(121), her epistolary art claims equality without apology or permission, since she has already inscribed herself as a speaking subject through the act of writing. Gender, Genre, and Culture I and II provide models of how we who teach early American literatures might trace the historical, cultural, and literary progress of women, how they evolve from silent servants into revolutionary selves, and how representations shift from woman imagined as the "other" by the masculine gaze to women as "subjects," created by self-authorizing, multiplicitous, and unique voices. Each instructor will recraft the exploration differently, by bringing to bear new theoretical approaches from Julia Kristeva to Stephen Greenblatt, Carol Gilligan to Cathy Davidson, and by collaborating with the students who will become the next generation of early Americanists.

Syllabus
Gender, Genre, and Culture I:
Women in Early American Literature

Originating Visions: Cultural Constructions through Story, Myth,
and Legend

Week 1   Introduction: "Creating" Women: Biblical and Indian Narratives
Genesis.
"The Iroquois Creation Story," *Norton Anthology* 1: 53–57.
"Cochiti and Laguna Pueblo Traditional Yellow Woman Stories,"
Allen, *Spider Woman's Granddaughters* 181–88.
"Sh-ah-cock and Miochin or the Battle of the Seasons," Allen, *Sacred
Hoop* 222–44; rpt. *Leslie Marmon Silko: "Yellow Woman"* 83–111.

Week 2   Mothers in Zion, According to the Fathers: Woman as Signi-
f(y)cant Other
A. The Sociocultural Role of Women in New England: Sermons
Cotton Mather (1663–1728), *Ornaments for the Daughters of
Zion* (1692). [APS]*
Cotton Mather, *Elizabeth in Her Holy Retirement* (1710). [APS]
Benjamin Wadsworth, *The Well-Ordered Family; or, Relative Du-
ties* (1712). [APS]
Excerpts from Leviticus, Proverbs, Ruth, 1 Corinthians.
B. The Gynesis of Redeemed Subjectivity: Meditations
Ivy Schweitzer, "Introduction: Gendering the Universal," *Work
of Self-Representation* 1–39.
The Song of Solomon.
Edward Taylor (1642?–1729), selected *Preparatory Meditations*
on Canticles, from *The Poems of Edward Taylor* (ed. Stanford).

Week 3   Conquest and the Construction of Female Myths: La Malinche, the
Virgen de Guadalupe, and La Llorona
Hernán Cortés (1485–1547), "Excerpts" from *Letters from Mexico*
72–75, 374–77, 464–65. Video available.
Bernal Díaz del Castillo (1492–1584), "Excerpts" from *Conquest of
New Spain* (1517–21) 85–87, 146–54, 189–204, 245–51.
Diego Muñoz Camargo (15??–1612/14), "Pictographs of Women
and La Malinche," from *Lienzo de Tlaxcala*, selected plates 1–156.
"History of the Miraculous Apparition of the Virgin of Guadalupe
in 1531" (1649), *Heath* 1: 474–82.
"La Llorona, Malinche, and the Unfaithful Maria," *Heath* 1:
1328–31.
Joe Hayes, *La Llorona — The Weeping Woman: An Hispanic Legend
Told in Spanish and English* (1987).

---

*APS stands for UCLA's Academic Publishing Service, which reproduced materials for
Rowe's seminar.

Gloria Anzaldúa (1942–), "Excerpts" from *Borderlands/La Front-era: The New Mestiza* (1987) 1–51.

Sandra Cisneros (1954–), "Woman Hollering Creek," *"Woman Hollering Creek" and Other Stories* 43–56.

Speaking Subjects: Constructing a Feminine Self in Colonial Literature

Week 4   Pious Nuns and Spanish Catholicism in Colonial Mexico
Sor Juana Inés de la Cruz (1648?–95), *A Woman of Genius* (1691).
————, *Sor Juana Inés de la Cruz: Poems.*

Week 5   Pious Matrons in Puritan New England: Meditations in God's Service
Anne Bradstreet (1612–72), *Tenth Muse* (1650), in *The Works of Anne Bradstreet.*
Ivy Schweitzer, "Anne Bradstreet: 'In the Place God Had Set Her,'" *Work of Self-Representation* 127–80.
(Optional) John Berryman (1914–72), "Homage to Mistress Bradstreet," *Collected Poems* 10–32.

Week 6   Courtship and Marriage in New England: Diaries and Love Poetry
Samuel Sewall (1652–1730), "The Courtship of Mrs. Winthrop," from *The Diary of Samuel Sewall (1674–1729)*. [APS]
Selected poems from *Women in Colonial American Poetry, 1620–1800*. [APS]

Week 7   Death of Mothers in Our Israel: Funeral Sermons and Elegies
Cotton Mather, *Maternal Consolations* (1714). [APS]
Grace Smith (n.d.–1712), *The Dying Mother's Legacy; or, The Good and Heavenly Counsel of That Eminent and Pious Matron* (1712). [APS]
Ebenezer Turell (1702–78), *Memoirs of the Life and Death of the Pious and Ingenious Mrs. Jane Turell (1708–1735)*, pub. 1735. [APS]
Selected elegies from *Women in Colonial American Poetry, 1620–1800*. [APS]

Resistances from the Margins: Speaking Captives, Exiles, and Revolutionaries

Week 8   Hazards in the Wilderness: Captivity Narratives
Mary Rowlandson (c. 1635–c. 1678), *The Sovereignty and the Goodness of God* (1682), in Andrews, ed. *Journeys in New Worlds* 11–65.
Cotton Mather, "A Notable Exploit; Wherein, Dux Faemina Facti," *Magnalia Christi Americana* (1702), bk. 7, 90–91.
Nathaniel Hawthorne (1804–64), "The Duston Family," *Miscellanies* (1876) 229–38.
Henry David Thoreau (1817–62), "Hannah Duston," *A Week on the Concord and Merrimack Rivers* (1849).

Week 9   The Making of an American Jezebel: When Testimony Becomes Myth

"The Examination of Mrs. Ann Hutchinson at the Court at Newtown," from *The History of the Province of Massachusets-Bay* (1767), and "A Report of the Trial of Mrs. Ann Hutchinson before the Church in Boston, March, 1638," in Hall, ed., *The Antinomian Controversy, 1636–1638* 311–48, 349–95.

Cotton Mather, "Hydra Decapitata; or, The First Synod of New-England, Quelling a Storm of Antinomian Opinions," *Magnalia Christi Americana* (1702), bk. 7, 14–21. [APS]

Nathaniel Hawthorne, "Mrs. Hutchinson," *Tales, Sketches, and Other Papers* (1878) 217–26.

Week 10 Seeking the Self, Seeing the Light: Quaker Women

Elizabeth Ashbridge (1713–55), *Some Account of the Fore Part of the Life of Elizabeth Ashbridge* (written c. 1750–55, 1st pub. ed. 1774), in Andrews, ed., *Journeys in New Worlds* 117–80.

Nathaniel Hawthorne, "The Gentle Boy" (1832), *Tales and Sketches* 108–38.

Jane Hoskens (1693/4–1760?), *The Life and Spiritual Sufferings of That Faithful Servant of Christ, Jane Hoskens, A Public Preacher among the People Called Quakers* (1771; 2nd ed. 1810).

Cotton Mather, "Ignes Fatui; or, The Molestation Given to the Churches of New-England by That Odd Sect of People Called Quakers," *Magnalia Christi Americana* (1702), bk. 7, 21–29. [APS]

Gender, Genre, and Culture II:
American Women and the Age of Revolution

Age of Enlightenment: Cultural Constructions of the Female Sex

Week 1   Introduction: Revolutionary Subjects
William Boyd (1777–1800), "Woman," *Specimens of American Poetry* 83–86.
Elizabeth Graeme Fergusson (1737–1801), "On the Mind's Being Engrossed by One Subject," *Heath* 1: 691.
Juba, "To the Ladies of Maryland," in Silverman, ed., *Colonial American Poetry* 324–25.
Judith Sargent Murray (1751–1820), poems from *Selected Writings* "On the Equality of the Sexes" 3–4.
"Observations on Female Abilities" 15.
"Desultory Thoughts upon the Utility of Encouraging a Degree of Self-Complacency, Especially in Female Bosoms" 44–45.
Sarah Wentworth Morton (1759–1846), "Ode Inscribed to Mrs. M. Warren," *Heath* 1: 708–09.
Annis Boudinot Stockton (1736–1801), "To Miss Mary Stockton[,] an epistle upon some gentleman refusing to admit ladies of their circle [. . .]," in *Only for the Eye of a Friend* 176–77.
Mercy Otis Warren (1728–1814)
"A Thought on the Inestimable Blessing of Reason," Cowell, *Women Poets* 77–78.
"To Mr Adams," Cowell, *Women Poets* 78–79.
"To Mrs. Montague," Cowell, *Women Poets* 86. [APS]
Susanna Wright (1697–1784), "To Eliz Norris — at Fairhill," Cowell, "Womankind" 799–800. [APS]

Week 2   Rhetoric of Enlightenment: Women in the Age of Reason
Charles Brockden Brown (1771–1810), *Alcuin* (1798). [APS]
Constantia [Judith Sargent Murray (1751–1820)], "On the Equality of the Sexes" (Mar. and Apr. 1790), *Heath* 1: 1058–64; or *Selected Writings* 3–14. Drafted 1779.
————, "Desultory Thoughts upon the Utility of Encouraging a Degree of Self-Complacency, Especially in Female Bosoms" (Oct. 1784), *Heath* 1: 1052–55; or *Selected Writings* 44–48.
————, "Observations on Female Abilities" (1788), in *The Gleaner* (1798) 3: 88–91; ed. Baym 702–31; or *Selected Writings* 15–43.
Sarah Wentworth Morton (1759–1846), Introduction, "The Sexes," and "Apology," *My Mind and Its Thoughts* (1823) xv–xvii, 219–21, 287–88.
Thomas Paine (1737–1809), "An Occasional Letter on the Female Sex," (Aug. 1775), in *Life and Works of Thomas Paine* 2: 85–92. [APS]
Alexis de Tocqueville (1805–59), selections from *Democracy in America* (1835).

Week 3 Claiming Rights, Claiming Citizenship: Women in the New Republic

Abigail (1744–1818) and John (1735–1826) Adams, "Sections II and III," *The Book of Abigail and John*.

Anonymous [Mary V. V.], "A Dialogue between a Southern Delegate and His Spouse on His Return from the Grand Continental Congress. A Fragment Inscribed to the Married Ladies of *America*" (1774). [APS]

Judith Sargent Murray (1751–1820), "Sketches of the Present Situation of America," in *The Gleaner* (1798) 1: 26–27; ed. Baym 206–22; or *Selected Writings* 49–68.

Mercy Otis Warren (1728–1814), "An Address to the Inhabitants of the United States of America," in *History of the Rise, Progress and Termination of the American Revolution* (1805) iii–viii. [APS]

———, from *Poems, Dramatic and Miscellaneous* (1790):
"A Political Reverie" 188–94.
"The Squabble of the Sea Nymphs" 202–05.
"To the Hon. J. Winthrop, Esq." 208–12.
"The Genius of America Weeping the Absurd Follies of the Day. — October 10, 1778" 246–52.

Eliza Wilkinson (n.d.), *Letters of Eliza Wilkinson, during the Invasion and Possession of Charlestown, S.C., by the British in the Revolutionary War* (1839) (written c. 1781–82). [APS]

Sarah Wister (1761–1804), *Sally Wister's Journal [. . .] Being a Quaker Maiden's Account of Her Experiences with Officers of the Continental Army, 1777–1778*. [Optional]

Week 4 When the Other Speaks: Is Slavery the Price of Freedom?

Aphra Behn (1640–89), *Oroonoko; or, The Royal Slave. A True History* (1688).

Phillis Wheatley (1753?–84), selections from *Poems on Various Subjects, Religious and Moral* (1773) and *Poems of Phillis Wheatley*.

———"Letter to Samson Occom" (1774), excerpt from *Heath* 1: 1112.

Jupiter Hammon (1711–1806?), "An Address to Miss Phillis Wheatly [sic], Ethiopian Poetess" (1778), *Heath* 1: 976–79.

Sarah Wentworth Morton (1759–1846), "The African Chief," from *My Mind and Its Thoughts* (1823) 201–03; or *Heath* 1: 706–07.

Read selectively from

Margaretta V. Faugeres (1771–1801), "Fine Feelings Exemplified in the Conduct of a Negro Slave," from *A Collection of Essays, Prose and Poetical* (1793) 268–70. [APS]

Essays on slavery by J. Hector Crèvecoeur, Olaudah Equiano, Benjamin Franklin, Philip Freneau, Thomas Jefferson, Prince Hall, Jupiter Hammon, Lemuel Haynes, excerpted in the *Heath Anthology*.

Maria Stewart (1803–79), *Religion and the Pure Principles of Morality* (1831). [APS]

Age of Revolution: Women and the Making of American History

Week 5   The Mourning/Making of American Heroes: Fathers of the Nation, according to the Mothers
Selections from
Annis Boudinot Stockton (1736–1801), *Only for the Eye of a Friend: The Poems of Annis Boudinot Stockton.*
Phillis Wheatley (1753?–84), *The Poems of Phillis Wheatley.*
The Heath Anthology of American Literature, volume 1.
Women in Eighteenth-Century American Poetry.

Week 6   Revolutionary Mythographies: Columbia and the Noble Savage; or, How to Capture a Woman
Ann Julia Kemble Hatton (1764–1838), *The Songs of Tammany; or, The Indian Chief. A Serious Opera* (John Street, New York, 3 Mar. 1794). [APS]
Sarah Wentworth Morton (1759–1846), *Ouabi; or, The Virtues of Nature: An Indian Tale in Four Cantos* (1790). [APS]
Ann Eliza Bleecker (1752–83), "The History of Maria Kittle," in *The Posthumous Works* (1793) 19–87. See also the "Memoirs of Mrs. Ann Eliza Bleecker" i–xviii. [APS]
Mary Kinnan (1763–1848), *A True Narrative of the Sufferings of Mary Kinnan,* in *Held Captive by Indians* 319–32. [APS]
Literary and Pictorial Representations of Columbia.
Read selectively from writings, excerpted in the *Heath Anthology,* by Hendrick Aupaumut (Mahican), Timothy Dwight, Benjamin Franklin, Philip Freneau, Thomas Jefferson, Samson Occom (Mohegan), and Jane Johnston Schoolcraft (Ojibwa).

Age of Education and the Rise of Women's Literate Culture: The Feminine Self as Speaking Subject in Republican Literature

Week 7   Educating Republican Women
Hannah Foster (1758–1840), selections from *The Boarding School; or, Lessons of a Preceptress to Her Pupils* (1798). [APS]
Judith Sargent Murray (1751–1820), "On the Domestic Education of Children" (May 1790), in *Heath* 1: 1055–57.
Susanna Rowson (1762–1824), selections from *Mentoria; or, The Young Lady's Friend* (1794). [APS]
Benjamin Rush (1745–1813), "Thoughts upon Female Education" (1787), in *Essays: Literary, Moral and Philosophical* 44–54. [APS]
Read selectively from
The Female Advocate. Written by a Lady (1801). [APS]
Hannah Mather Crocker (1752–1829), *Observations on the Real Rights of Women* (1818). [APS]
Noah Webster (1758–1843), "On the Education of Youth in

America," *A Collection of Essays and Fugitiv[e] Writings on Moral, Political and Literary Subjects* (1790). [APS]

Week 8 The Epistolary Moment: The W(rites) of Courtship and Marriage
Abigail (1744–1818) and John Adams (1735–1826), "Sections I and IV," *The Book of Abigail and John*.
Bolling, Robert (1738–75), *Robert Bolling Woos Anne Miller: Love and Courtship in Colonial Virginia, 1760* (Miller b. 13 Mar. 1742/43, d. 14 Sept. 1779).
Judith Sargent Murray (1751–1820), *The Traveller Returned* (1796), in *The Gleaner* (1798) 3: 116–63; ed. Baym 638–82; or *Selected Writings*, 103–52.
Annis Boudinot Stockton (1736–1801), selections from *Only for the Eye of a Friend: The Poems of Annis Boudinot Stockton*.
Selected poems from *The Heath Anthology of American Literature*.
Selections from *Women in Eighteenth-Century American Poetry*. [APS]

Age of Romance: Women in the Literary Marketplace

Week 9 When Reason Fails: Female Flirtation and Dangerous Liaisons
Hannah W. Foster (1758–1840), *The Coquette; or, The History of Eliza Wharton; a Novel; Founded on Fact* (1797).
Royall Tyler (1757–1826), Introduction. *Algerine Captive* (1797).
Optional readings from
William Hill Brown, *The Power of Sympathy* (1789).
Judith Sargent Murray (1751–1820), *Virtue Triumphant* (1795), in *The Gleaner* (1798) 3: 15–87; ed. Baym 543–614.
———, "Occasional Epilogue to the *Contrast*," *Heath* 1: 1065–67.
Royall Tyler (1757–1826), *The Contrast* (1790), *Heath* 1: 1147–88.

Week 10 Seducing the Female Reader: The Romance of Betrayal
Susanna Haswell Rowson (1762–1824), *Charlotte, a Tale of Truth* (1791)
Judith Sargent Murray (1751–1820), "The Story of Margaretta," from *The Gleaner* (1798), in *Selected Writings* 153–272.

Works Cited

Gender, Genre, and Culture I: Women in Early American Literature
Primary Works

Allen, Paula Gunn, ed. *Spider Woman's Granddaughters: Traditional Tales and Contemporary Writing by Native American Women*. Boston: Beacon, 1989.
American Poems, Selected and Original. Ed. Elihu Hubbard Smith. Litchfield: Collier and Buel, 1793. Rpt. *American Poems (1793)*. Ed. William K. Bottorff. Gainesville: Scholars', 1966.

Andrews, William A., ed. *Journeys in New Worlds: Early American Women's Narratives*. Madison: U of Wisconsin P, 1990.

Anzaldúa, Gloria. *Borderlands/La Frontera: The New Mestiza*. San Francisco: Aunt Lute, 1987.

Ashbridge, Elizabeth. *Some Account of the Fore Part of the Life of Elizabeth Ashbridge*. Nantwich, Eng.: By the [Sampson] family, 1774. Andrews 117–80.

Berryman, John. "Homage to Mistress Bradstreet." *Collected Poems, 1937–1971*. Ed. Charles Thornbury. New York: Farrar, 1989. 10–32.

Bosco, Ronald A., ed. *New England Funeral Sermons*. Vol. 4 of *The Puritan Sermon in America, 1630–1750*. Delmar: Scholars', 1978.

Bradstreet, Anne. *The Works of Anne Bradstreet*. Ed. Jeannine Hensley. Cambridge: Belknap–Harvard UP, 1967.

Brewster, Martha. *Poems on Divers Subjects*. New-London: Edes and Gill, 1757. Rpt. in *Poems of Jane Turell and Martha Brewster*. Ed. Kenneth A. Requa. Delmar: Scholars', 1979.

Camargo, Diego Muñoz. *Lienzo de Tlaxcala*. In *Descripción de la ciudad y provincia de Tlaxcala de la Indias y del mar océano para el buen gobierno y ennoblecimiento dellas*. Ed. René Acuña. Mexico: U Nacional Autonoma de Mexico, 1981.

Cisneros, Sandra. *"Woman Hollering Creek" and Other Stories*. New York: Random, 1991.

Colman, Benjamin. *A Devout Contemplation on the Meaning of Divine Providence, in the Early Death of Pious and Lovely Children*. Boston: Allen for Perry, 1714. Rpt. in Bosco 21–50.

———. *Reliquiae Turellae, et Lachrymae Paternae. The Father's Tears over His Daughter's Remains. Two Sermons [. . .] to Which Are Added, Some Large Memoirs of Her Life and Death by Her Consort, the Reverend Mr. Ebenezer Turell*. Boston, 1735.

Columbus, Christopher. *The Four Voyages of Christopher Columbus*. Ed. and trans. J. M. Cohen. Harmondsworth: Penguin, 1969.

Columbus, Christopher, with Bartolomé de las Casas. *The Diario of Christopher Columbus's First Voyage to America, 1492–1493, Abstracted by Bartolomé de las Casas*. Ed. and trans. Oliver Dunn and James E. Kelley, Jr. Norman: U of Oklahoma P, 1989.

———. *Personal Narrative of the First Voyage of Columbus to America from a Manuscript Recently Discovered in Spain*. Trans. Samuel Kettell. Boston: Wait, 1827. Microbook Lib. of American Civilization, LAC no. 12283.

Cortés, Hernán. *Hernan Cortes: Letters from Mexico*. Trans. A. R. Pagden. New York: Grossman, 1971.

Cruz, Sor Juana Inés de la. *Sor Juana Inés de la Cruz: Poems. A Bilingual Anthology*. Trans. Margaret Sayers Peden. Binghamton: Bilingual, 1985.

———. *A Woman of Genius: The Intellectual Biography of Sor Juana Inés de la Cruz*. Salisbury: Lime Rock, 1982.

Davies, Samuel. *Miscellaneous Poems, Chiefly on Divine Subjects*. Williamsburg: Hunter, 1752. Rpt. in *Collected Poems of Samuel Davies, 1723–1761*. Ed. Richard Beale Davis. Gainesville: Scholars', 1968.

Díaz del Castillo, Bernal. *Historia verdadura de la conquista de la Nueva España*. Madrid, 1632. *The Conquest of New Spain*. Trans. J. M. Cohen. Harmondsworth: Penguin, 1963.

Hall, David D., ed. *The Antinomian Controversy, 1636–1638: A Documentary History*. 2nd ed. Durham: Duke UP, 1990.

Hawthorne, Nathaniel. "The Duston Family." *Miscellanies: Biographical and Other Sketches and Letters*. Boston: Osgood, 1876. Boston: Houghton, 1883. 229–38.

———. "The Gentle Boy." *Nathaniel Hawthorne:* Tales and Sketches, A Wonder Book for Girls and Boys, *and* Tanglewood Tales for Girls and Boys. New York: Lib. of Amer., 1982. 108–38.

———. "Mrs. Hutchinson." *Tales, Sketches, and Other Papers by Nathaniel Hawthorne*. Ed. George Parsons Lathrop. Boston: Houghton, 1878. 217–26.

Hayes, Joe. *La Llorona — The Weeping Woman: An Hispanic Legend Told in Spanish and English by Joe Hayes*. El Paso: Cinco Puntos, 1987.

The Heath Anthology of American Literature. Ed. Paul Lauter et al. 3rd ed. 2 vols. Boston: Houghton, 1998.

Hoskens, Jane. *The Life and Spiritual Sufferings of That Faithful Servant of Christ, Jane Hoskens, a Public Preacher among the People Called Quakers*. Philadelphia: Evitt, 1771. 2nd ed. Stanford: Laurence, 1810. Early American Imprints, 2nd ser., no. 20387.

Hutchinson, Ann[e], "The Examination of Mrs. Ann Hutchinson at the Court at Newtown." In *The History of the Province of Massachusets-Bay*. By Thomas Hutchinson. Vol. 2. Boston: Fleet, 1767. Hall 311–48.

———. "A Report of the Trial of Mrs. Ann Hutchinson before the Church in Boston, March, 1638." *Proceedings of the Massachusetts Historical Society* 2nd ser. 4 (Oct. 1888): 161–91. Hall 349–95.

Ladd, Joseph Brown. *The Literary Remains of Joseph Brown Ladd*. New York: Sleight, 1832.

Mather, Cotton. *Elizabeth in Her Holy Retirement*. Boston: Green, 1710. Rpt. in Rothman and Rothman.

———. *Magnalia Christi Americana*. London: Parkhurst, 1702. Rpt. New York: Arno, 1972.

———. *Maternal Consolations*. Boston: Fleet, 1714. Rpt. in Bosco 51–94.

———. *Ornaments for the Daughters of Zion*. Cambridge: S. G. and B. G. for Phillips at Boston, 1692. 3rd ed. Boston: Kneeland and Green, 1741. Rpt. Introd. Pattie Cowell. Delmar: Scholars', 1970.

Meserole, Harrison T., ed. *Seventeenth-Century American Poetry*. New York: New York UP, 1968. Rpt. *American Poetry of the Seventeenth Century*. University Park: Pennsylvania State UP, 1985.

Murdock, Kenneth B., ed. *Handkerchiefs from Paul*. Cambridge: Harvard UP, 1927. Rpt. New York: Garrett, 1970.

The New Scofield Reference Bible. Authorized King James Version. Ed. C. I. Scofield et al. New York: Oxford UP, 1967.

The Norton Anthology of American Literature. Ed. Nina Baym et al. 5th ed. 2 vols. New York: Norton, 1998.

Rothman, David J., and Sheila M. Rothman, eds. *The Colonial American Family: Collected Essays*. New York: Arno, 1972.

Rowlandson, Mary. *The Soveraignty and the Goodness of God, Together with the Faithfulness of His Promises Displayed; Being a Narrative of the Captivity and Restauration of Mrs. Mary Rowlandson*. Cambridge, 1682. Rpt. *A True History of the Captivity and Restoration of Mrs. Mary Rowlandson*. London: Poole, 1682. Andrews 11–65.

Saffin, John. *John Saffin His Book: A Collection of Various Matters of Divinity Law and State Affairs Epitomiz'd in Verse and Prose*. Introd. Caroline Hazard. New York: Harbor, 1928.

Sewall, Samuel. *The Diary of Samuel Sewall*. In *Collections of the Massachusetts Historical Society*. 5th ser. Vol. 7. Boston: Mass. Historical Soc., 1882. Ed. M. Halsey Thomas. 2 vols. New York: Farrar, 1973.

Silko, Leslie Marmon. *Leslie Marmon Silko: "Yellow Woman."* Ed. Melody Graulich. New Brunswick: Rutgers UP, 1993.

Silverman, Kenneth, ed. *Colonial American Poetry*. New York: Hafner, 1968.

Smith, Grace. *The Dying Mother's Legacy; or, The Good and Heavenly Counsel of That Eminent and Pious Matron*. Boston: Green, 1712.

Taylor, Edward. *The Poems of Edward Taylor*. Ed. Donald E. Stanford. New Haven: Yale UP, 1960. Abr. ed. New Haven: Yale UP, 1963. Rpt. Chapel Hill: U of North Carolina P, 1989.

Thoreau, Henry David. "Hannah Duston." *A Week on the Concord and Merrimack Rivers*. Boston: Munroe, 1849. *The Concord and Merrimack*. Ed. Dudley C. Lunt. Boston: Little, 1954. 231–37.

Tompson, Benjamin. *Benjamin Tompson, Colonial Bard: A Critical Edition*. Ed. Peter White. University Park: Pennsylvania State UP, 1979.

———. *Benjamin Tompson, 1642–1714*. Ed. Howard Judson Hall. Boston: Houghton, 1924.

Turell, Ebenezer. *Memoirs of the Life and Death of the Pious and Ingenious Mrs. Jane Turell*. Boston: Kneeland and Green for Edwards and Foster, 1735. Rpt. in *Poems of Jane Turell and Martha Brewster*. Ed. Kenneth A. Requa. Delmar: Scholars', 1979.

Viramontes, Helena María. *"The Moths" and Other Stories*. Houston: Arte Público, 1985.

Wadsworth, Benjamin. *The Well-Ordered Family; or, Relative Duties*. Boston: Green, 1712. Rpt. in Rothman and Rothman.

Women in Colonial American Poetry, 1620–1800. Comp. Karen E. Rowe. Los Angeles: Assoc. Students UCLA, Academic Publishing Service, 1994.

Women in Colonial American Prose, 1620–1800. Comp. Karen E. Rowe. Los Angeles: Assoc. Students UCLA, Academic Publishing Service, 1994.

Secondary Works

Allen, Paula Gunn. *The Sacred Hoop: Recovering the Feminine in American Indian Traditions*. Boston: Beacon, 1986.

Koehler, Lyle. *A Search for Power: The "Weaker Sex" in Seventeenth-Century New England*. Urbana: U of Illinois P, 1980.

Merrim, Stephanie, ed. *Feminist Perspectives on Sor Juana Inés de la Cruz*. Detroit: Wayne State UP, 1991.

Norton, Mary Beth. *Founding Mothers and Fathers: Gendered Power and the Formation of American Society*. New York: Knopf, 1996.

Schweitzer, Ivy. *The Work of Self-Representation: Lyric Poetry in Colonial New England*. Chapel Hill: U of North Carolina P, 1991.

Gender, Genre, and Culture II: American Women and the Age of Revolution

Primary Works

Adams, Abigail, and John Adams. *The Book of Abigail and John: Selected Letters of the Adams Family, 1762–1784*. Cambridge: Harvard UP, 1975.

Anonymous [Mary V. V.]. "A Dialogue between a Southern Delegate and His Spouse on His Return from the Grand Continental Congress. A Fragment Inscribed to the Married Ladies of *America*." New York: Rivington, 1774. Rpt. in *Magazine of History with Notes and Queries* 18.4 (1921): 287–97.

Anonymous. *Joanna; or, The Female Slave: A West Indian Tale*. London: Bentley for Relfe, 1824. Goldsmiths'-Kress Lib. of Economic Literature, no. 24322.

Behn, Aphra. *Oroonoko; or, The Royal Slave: A True History*. London: Canning, 1688. Introd. Lore Metzger. New York: Norton, 1973. Ed. Joanna Lipking. New York: Norton, 1997.

Bleecker, Ann Eliza. "The History of Maria Kittle." *Posthumous Works* 19–87.

———. "Memoirs of Mrs. Ann Eliza Bleecker." *Posthumous Works* i–xviii.

———. *The Posthumous Works of Ann Eliza Bleecker, in Prose and Verse. To Which Is Added, a Collection of Essays, Prose and Poetical by Margaretta V. Faugeres*. New York: Swords, 1793. Rpt. Upper Saddle River: Literature House/Gregg, 1970. History of Women, reel 15, no. 79.

Bolling, Robert. *Robert Bolling Woos Anne Miller: Love and Courtship in Colonial Virginia, 1760*. Ed. J. A. Leo Lemay. Charlottesville: UP of Virginia, 1990.

Brown, Charles Brockden. *Alcuin: A Dialogue*. New York: Swords, 1798. Ed. Lee R. Edwards. New York: Grossman, 1971. History of Women, reel 17, no. 96.

———. *Alcuin: A Dialogue; Memoirs of Stephen Calvert*. Bicentennial ed. Kent: Kent State UP, 1987. Vol. 6 of *The Novels and Related Works of Charles Brockden Brown*. Ed. Sydney J. Krause et al. 6 vols. 1977–87.

Brown, William Hill. *The Power of Sympathy*. Boston: Thomas, 1789. Ed. William S. Osborne. New Haven: Coll. and Univ. P, 1970.

[Child, Lydia Maria, ed.]. "Joanna; or, The Female Slave." *The Oasis*. Ed. Lydia Maria Child. Boston: Bacon, 1834. 65–105. History of Women, reel 159, no. 1014.

Cowell, Pattie. "'Womankind Call Reason to Their Aid': Susanna Wright's

Verse Epistle on the Status of Women in Eighteenth-Century America." *Signs* 6 (1981): 795–800.

———. *Women Poets in Pre-Revolutionary America, 1650–1775: An Anthology.* Troy: Whitson, 1981.

Crocker, Hannah Mather. *Observations on the Real Rights of Woman, with Their Appropriate Duties, Agreeable to Scripture, Reason and Common Sense.* Boston: For the author, 1818. Rpt. in *Sex and Equality.* Ed. Annette K. Baxter. New York: Arno, 1974.

Evans, Nathaniel. *Poems on Several Occasions, with Some Other Compositions.* Philadelphia: Dunlap, 1772. Rpt. *George Washington's Copy of Poems on Several Occasions.* Introd. Andrew Breen Myers. New York: Fordham UP, 1976.

Faugeres, Margaretta V. *A Collection of Essays, Prose and Poetical, by Margaretta V. Faugeres.* Bleecker, *Posthumous Works* 263–375.

The Female Advocate. Written by a Lady. New Haven: Green, 1801. Early American Imprints, 2nd ser., no. 487.

Foster, Hannah W. *The Boarding School; or, Lessons of a Preceptress to Her Pupils.* Boston: Thomas and Andrews, 1798. History of Women, reel 34, no. 221.

———. *The Coquette; or, The History of Eliza Wharton; A Novel; Founded on Fact.* Boston: Etheridge for Larkin, 1797. Ed. and introd. Cathy N. Davidson. New York: Oxford UP, 1986.

Harris, Sharon M., ed. *American Women Writers to 1800.* New York: Oxford UP, 1996.

Hatton, Ann Julia Kemble. *The Songs of Tammany; or, The Indian Chief: A Serious Opera.* New York: Harrison and Faulkner, 1794. Early American Imprints, 1st ser., no. 27100.

The Heath Anthology of American Literature. Ed. Paul Lauter et al. 3rd ed. 2 vols. Boston: Houghton, 1998.

Held Captive by Indians: Selected Narratives, 1642–1836. Ed. Richard VanDer-Beets. Knoxville: U of Tennessee P, 1973.

Kinnan, Mary. *A True Narrative of the Sufferings of Mary Kinnan, Who Was Taken Prisoner by the Shawnee Indians on the Thirteenth Day of March, 1791, and Remained with Them till the Sixteenth of August, 1794.* Elizabethtown: Kollock, 1795. *Held Captive by Indians* 319–32.

Kritzer, Amelia Howe, ed. *Plays by Early American Women, 1775–1850.* Ann Arbor: U of Michigan P, 1995.

Morton, Sarah Wentworth. *My Mind and Its Thoughts in Sketches, Fragments, and Essays.* Boston: Wells and Lilly, 1823. Rpt. Introd. William K. Bottorff. Delmar: Scholars', 1975.

———. *Ouabi; or, The Virtues of Nature: An Indian Tale in Four Cantos. By Philenia, a Lady of Boston.* Boston: Thomas and Andrews, 1790. Early American Imprints, 1st ser., no. 25848.

Murray, Judith Sargent. *The Gleaner. A Miscellaneous Production. By Constantia.* 3 vols. Boston: Thomas and Andrews, 1798. Introd. Nina Baym. Schenectady: Union Coll. P, 1992.

————. *Selected Writings of Judith Sargent Murray*. Ed. Sharon M. Harris. New York: Oxford UP, 1995.

Paine, Thomas. *The Life and Works of Thomas Paine*. Ed. William M. Van der Weyde. 2 vols. New Rochelle: Thomas Paine Natl. Historical Assn., 1925.

Rowson, Susanna. *Charlotte, a Tale of Truth*. London: Lane at Minerva, 1791. 1st Amer. ed. Philadelphia: Carey, 1794. *Charlotte Temple*. Ed. Cathy N. Davidson. New York: Oxford UP, 1986.

————. *Mentoria; or, The Young Lady's Friend. In Two Volumes*. Philadelphia: Smith for Campbell, 1794. Early American Imprints, 1st ser., no. 27654.

Rush, Benjamin. "Thoughts upon Female Education." *Essays, Literary, Moral and Philosophical*. 2nd ed. Philadelphia: Bradford, 1806. 75–92. Ed. Michael Meranze. Schenectady: Union Coll. P, 1988. 44–54.

Specimens of American Poetry with Critical and Biographical Notes. Ed. Samuel Kettell. 3 vols. Boston: Goodrich, 1829.

Stedman, Gabriel. *Narrative of a Five Years Expedition against the Revolted Negroes of Surinam, in Guiana, on the Wild Coast of South America*. London, 1796. Rpt. 2 vols. Barre: Imprint Soc., 1971. Ed. Richard Price and Sally Price. Baltimore: Johns Hopkins UP, 1988.

Stewart, Maria. *Religion and the Pure Principles of Morality*. Pamphlets on Slavery 18. Boston: Garrison and Knapp, 1831. *Maria W. Stewart, America's First Black Woman Political Writer: Essays and Speeches*. Ed. Marilyn Richardson. Bloomington: Indiana UP, 1987. 28–43.

Stockton, Annis Boudinot. *Only for the Eye of a Friend: The Poetry of Annis Boudinot Stockton*. Ed. Carla Mulford. Charlottesville: UP of Virginia, 1995.

Tocqueville, Alexis de. *Democracy in America*. London: Saunders and Otley, 1835. Ed. J. P. Mayer and Max Lerner. New York: Harper, 1966.

Tyler, Royall. *The Algerine Captive; or, The Life and Adventures of Doctor Updike Underhill, Six Years a Prisoner among the Algerines*. Hartford: Gleason, 1816.

Warren, Mercy Otis. *History of the Rise, Progress, and Termination of the American Revolution*. 3 vols. Boston: Manning and Loring for Larkin, 1805. Rpt. New York: AMS, 1970.

————. *Poems, Dramatic and Miscellaneous by Mrs. M. Warren*. Boston: Thomas and Andrews, 1790. Rpt. in *The Plays and Poems of Mercy Otis Warren*. Introd. Benjamin Franklin V. Delmar: Scholars', 1980.

Webster, Noah. "An Address to Yung [sic] Ladies." *Collection* 406–14.

————. *A Collection of Essays and Fugitiv[e] Writings on Moral, Political and Literary Subjects*. Boston: Thomas and Andrews, 1790.

————. "On the Education of Youth in America." *Collection* 1–37.

Wheatley, Phillis. *The Poems of Phillis Wheatley*. Ed. Julian D. Mason, Jr. Rev. and enl. ed. Chapel Hill: U of North Carolina P, 1989.

Wilkinson, Eliza. *Letters of Eliza Wilkinson, during the Invasion and Possession of Charlestown, S.C., by the British in the Revolutionary War*. Ed. Caroline Gilman. New York: Colman, 1839. Rpt. New York: Arno, 1969.

Wister, Sarah. *Sally Wister's Journal [. . .] Being a Quaker Maiden's Account of Her Experiences with Officers of the Continental Army, 1777–1778*. Philadelphia: Ferris and Leach, 1902.

Women in Eighteenth-Century American Poetry. Comp. Karen E. Rowe. Los Angeles: Assoc. Students UCLA, Academic Publishing Service, 1996.

Women in Eighteenth-Century American Prose Writings. Comp. Karen E. Rowe. Los Angeles: Assoc. Students UCLA, Academic Publishing Service, 1996.

Secondary Works

Cott, Nancy. *The Bonds of Womanhood*. New Haven: Yale UP, 1977.

Davidson, Cathy. *Revolution and the Word: The Rise of the Novel in America*. New York: Oxford UP, 1986.

Gilligan, Carol. *In a Different Voice: Psychological Theory and Women's Development*. Cambridge: Harvard UP, 1982.

Greenblatt, Stephen J. *Marvelous Possessions: The Wonder of the New World*. Chicago: U of Chicago P, 1991.

———. *Renaissance Self-Fashioning: From More to Shakespeare*. Chicago: U of Chicago P, 1980.

Hoffman, Ronald, and Peter J. Albert. *Women in the Age of the American Revolution*. Charlottesville: UP of Virginia, 1989.

Kerber, Linda K. *Women of the Republic: Intellect and Ideology in Revolutionary America*. Chapel Hill: U of North Carolina P for Inst. of Early Amer. History and Culture, 1980. Chapel Hill: U of North Carolina P, 1997.

Kristeva, Julia. *Desire in Language: A Semiotic Approach to Literature and Art*. Ed. Leon S. Roudiez. Trans. Thomas Gora, Alice Jardine, and Leon Roudiez. New York: Columbia UP, 1980.

———. *The Kristeva Reader*. Ed. Toril Moi. New York: Columbia UP, 1986.

Norton, Mary Beth. *Liberty's Daughters: The Revolutionary Experience of American Women, 1750–1800*. Boston: Little, 1980. Ithaca: Cornell UP, 1996.

José F. Aranda, Jr.

Common Ground on Different Borders: A Comparative Study of Chicano/a and Puritan Writers

I'm sitting in my history class,
The instructor commences rapping
I'm in my U.S. History class,
And I'm on the verge of napping.

The Mayflower landed on Plymouth Rock.
Tell me more! Tell me more!
Thirteen colonies were settled.
I've heard it all before.

What did he say?
Dare I ask him to reiterate?
Oh why bother
It sounded like he said,
George Washington's my father.

I'm reluctant to believe it,
I suddenly raise my mano
If George Washington's my father,
Why wasn't he Chicano?

— Richard Olivas

The course I describe below was first taught in 1995 at Rice University as an upper-level seminar. Putting this course together was the culmination of years of my contemplation about two key issues: first, how to present early American literature differently to undergraduates, who are otherwise ill-prepared to take on the more substantive matters in this colonial period, from the English Civil War and typological exegesis to the poetics of "plain speech" and biblical tropes; and, second, how to connect early American literature with minority discourses. The latter concern troubled me even more than the first. In fact, I was truly disquieted until I recognized for myself what Richard Olivas's parody of Poe's "The Raven" so clearly reminds us: the twentieth-century classroom has facilitated the education (indoctrination) of Chicano and Chicana students into the histories and literatures of a Puritan Anglo America.

Olivas's poem alerts his readers that minorities have a complicated relation to a Puritan past, especially since we have not taught viable alternatives like pre-Columbian history or even Spanish colonialism. For better or worse, schooling and cultural norms have made the Puritans theirs. But what about them? Is the reverse also true? Are they latter-day Puritans? These questions are the philosophical basis of my course and the inquiries it encourages. Seeking no "either-or solution" to study of the Puritans or to the ways in which the Puritan past is still used to create "our" past, I decided to chart out "an errand in the wilderness" worthy of our postmodern age and of the students we are fortunate enough to teach.

What follows is an exploration of what happens when you take the middle road, a comparative perspective, with these materials. Let me begin, however, by describing what I had been trained to know. During my graduate studies, I discovered that scholars conferred on Puritan writers from this period a mythic and national literary status. From Sacvan Bercovitch, I learned that the United States had had a rhetorical and mythic investment in reinventing New England as the birthplace of democracy, nationalism, a national literature. Yet I came also to understand from Nina Baym that what had seemed a "natural" progression of history in Manifest Destiny was in fact due to nineteenth-century Whig party politics. These politicians, along with educators, historians, and writers, constructed a collective past based on New England history in order to justify territorial expansion. On a parallel course, nineteenth-century American publishers searched and found able spokespersons for New England (hence, "the nation") in Ralph Waldo Emerson, Nathaniel Hawthorne, and several other New Englanders.

These historic reinventions prefigured New England's rise in academic circles in the 1930s. Once again, the Puritans came into prominence to fulfill a national agenda. The Puritan historians of the 1930s discovered a "usable past" to counter the national disillusionment during the Great Depression and to defend against the threat of fascism in Europe. Furthermore, the literary canon that emerged after World War II portrayed American writers as champions of literary, social, and political dissent. As scholars merged modernist values with political resolve, Puritan and nineteenth-century writers gained national preeminence. F. O. Matthiessen's *American Renaissance* perhaps did more than any other book to solidify the alignment of American writers with political dissent, through a broad definition of democratic values.

Yet by the 1960s it was clear that the canon had fostered a tradition of dissent in American letters that left many women and minority writers unrepresented. Only in the light of the civil rights and feminist movements — and the alternative presses and scholars they produced — could separate literary histories and canons be created. Nevertheless, though the 1990s saw the canon expand to include women and ethnic writers in numbers larger than ever, its simple inclusiveness has not succeeded in ameliorating its traditional reception by readers. "American literature" is still primarily received and identified as male, white, and Anglo-Protestant. This traditionalism, I argue, is the result of Puritan studies' early relation to canon formation, in which critics constructed a literary history that favored authors who identified with a national identity based on New England history.

As part of the continuing effort to revise the canon, my course proposes a broad integration of canonical and noncanonical figures in American literature. I first note that the dominant trend of twentieth-century American literary criticism identifies American literary history with a Puritan past. In Puritan writings early scholars found the origins of an American literature. This narrative of origins has served a broad spectrum of positivist purposes from the cultural to political. It has also served to misrepresent competing colonial histories in North America and to ignore the relations of non-Puritans and non-Anglos to this myth of origins. How, I thus ask, did that myth affect Chicano and Chicana literature and criticism in the twentieth century? How are we to make sense of Chicano and Chicana literature's alternative origin myth of Aztlán? What role does a search for literary origins play in the constructions of canons, countercanons, and literary nationalisms?

To answer such questions, part 1 of the course, Contemporary Views on American Literary History, seeks to problematize and historicize what is taken as American literary history. By reviewing the intense debate among prominent scholars, students quickly come to understand how a literary history is constructed to reflect the historical and cultural practices that produced it. This is an important recognition, because discourses involving literary origins have periodically shaped critical discussions of literary history, aesthetic criteria, canon formation, and national politics in this century. Without an increased sensitivity to questions of literary origins, a Puritan past will continue to frustrate efforts to revise the canon.

Part 2, Theories of Origins, Theories of Continuity in Practice, is devoted to rereading early critical introductions to both Puritan studies and Chicano studies. Read against each other, these critical texts reveal instantly the essential differences between them: Anglo-Saxon versus Native American and mestizo, English versus Spanish, Puritan versus Catholic, colonizer versus colonized, and so forth. Yet a more careful reading also reveals their shared consistency in framing literary history through a myth of origins, such as the Puritan exodus to America, as exemplified in Winthrop's city on a hill, versus the pre-Columbian myth of Aztlán, as portrayed in Chicano protest poetry. With myths of origins in place, both cultural texts interpret literary history as verifying their community's perceived privileged role in the evolving history of the Americas. Both cultures are surprisingly on common ground in nationalizing literature and in claiming a regional voice as the basis of cultural identity. Yet the critics of Chicano studies, unlike most Puritan scholars, are poignantly aware of the vast power differential that exists between the myth of Aztlán and Winthrop's city on a hill.

This comparison of critical approaches to literary history demonstrates how the rise of a singular national myth in literary studies affected the evolution of attitudes about women and ethnic writers in the twentieth century. It also alerts us to the literary status that Puritan writers accrued during the twentieth century within the scholarship that "rediscovered" them. In turn, this scholarship inspired a new audience to read the Puritans as the first ideal immigrant community of the United States. More important, the comparison helps us measure the response of ethnic writers likely to be disaffected by the politics and aesthetic values assigned to a Puritan literary tradition, and ultimately it subtly indicates the intercultural dynamism that can be found when questions of national origins, colonial history, and cultural identity are foregrounded and problematized.

Because of the scholarly contributions of feminist and ethnic scholars since the 1960s, it now appears that American criticism is entering a new phase. Paul Lauter's editorship of *The Heath Anthology of American Literature* (1990) — now in its third edition — serves notice that many of the reforms envisioned for two decades are finally realized. Annette Kolodny's recent call for a literary history that accounts for non-Puritan colonial histories of North America and Ramón Gutiérrez's recovery of just such a history, taken together with the *Heath Anthology*, begin the necessary process of broadening knowledge of the various origins of American literary history. And they do so, it should be stressed, by relying on an interdisciplinary methodology. It now seems possible to value alternative writers and criticism while drawing out broader synthetic trends in American literature.

With a similar interdisciplinary effort in mind, part 3, History as Communal Narratives, proposes that students consider literary origins and theories of continuity as attempts by different communities to write themselves into history. By reading Américo Paredes one week and William Bradford the next (or, similarly, Mary Rowlandson and Cherríe Moraga), the section exposes students to different histories deployed in the name of community. The combination of texts requires students to entertain the viability of noncanonical narratives that compete for the same regional or national privileged status that canonical texts are often assumed to symbolize. In addition to supplying competing narratives of literary origins, this section also helps draw out the discursive markers that link ethnic literatures to the mainstream canon: millennialism, the centrality of the poet to narratives of the nation-state, claims on "America" as homeland, immigration, citizenship, patriarchy, gender roles, and issues of sexuality. Finally, this section clarifies for students the binational character of Chicano and Chicana literature, a crucial matter as more and more Chicano and Chicana writers find their way to mainstream markets and reading communities and redefine what we think of when we think of "American" literature.

In this regard this section — with its comparative approach — fosters the sense that a more culturally and racially dynamic national literature, not exclusively dependent on a single collective literary history based on seventeenth-century New England writers, is in reach. Apart from revising the canon's exclusionary practices, a comparative approach would broaden our understanding of writers and readers as they interact across gender politics, racial categories, and class lines and on the subject of writing "American" literature. And it would keep "alternative theorists" honest too, permitting them not to take for granted that, say, the "native" voice is the authentic voice of Chicano and Chicana identity. It too is constructed. Thus the goal of the course is not to reify a hegemonic influence of Puritan myth and history over all literary history, but to emphasize the need to understand the effects and countereffects — along with the affects and counter-affects — of a New England legacy on ethnic writers in the twentieth century.

The final section, part 4, Comparative Readings: Acts of Disruptions, Acts of Inventions, proposes a direct comparison between contemporary Chicano and Chicana authors and Puritan writers from seventeenth-century colonial New England. The central question for the section might be phrased thus: How does one make sense of a canon that stretches from Anne Bradstreet to Sandra Cisneros without sacrificing history and all common sense and theoretical notions of "difference"? The goal of the section is to juxtapose canonical poets like Edward Taylor with Chicano poets like Gary Soto to illustrate how the discourses of literary origins, dissent, and literary nationalism have shaped postmodern American poetry and the reception of these poets in the late twentieth century.

Although different from each other, each set of compared readings (Chicano and Puritan) intervenes on the unquestioned preeminence of Anglo-Puritan texts in literary history. These combinations begin on some common ground. Thus Cotton Mather's and Pat Mora's focus on "America" as landscape allows a glimpse into the Puritan construction of the New World as empty, without people, whereas Mora's poetry clearly peoples her landscape with Native American ancestors and their displaced voices. Michael Wigglesworth's jeremiad is compared with Lorna Dee Cervantes's own Chicana jeremiad on the hellish entrapment of women in a patriarchal society. Finally, a comparison of Gary Soto with Edward Taylor lends itself to gender analysis. Despite their obvious differences, both poets draw from masculine discourses transformative metaphors that verify for them the existence of a transcendent universe.

These are just some ways that a comparative approach can open up our teaching of early American literature. While highly speculative, the final section nevertheless encourages students to trust their creative minds to make connections heretofore unthinkable. Having said that, it is incumbent on students (and the teacher) to remind one another about the limits of transhistorical, transcultural analysis, such as the essentializing of cultural traits or myths for rhetorical purposes, the eliding of ethnic diversity and conflict in favor of cultural nationalism, or even the subsuming of "sexual difference" under "nation" or "race." Yet these limits also serve to encourage students to read multiple colonial histories as a way to contextualize their thoughts and avoid easy reductive reasoning. Without a doubt, this section, like the course, requires a suspension of the traditional methods of teaching and thinking about early American literature, yielding heightened curiosity among students, challenging classroom discussions, and creative writing assignments. My only disappointment has been the lack of time to do more.

Since I last taught the course, there has been an explosion of materials that would make courses like this even more interesting and viable in a chronological format. Most of these new materials are directly from the ten-year project known as Recovering the US Hispanic Literary Heritage Project, funded by several of the nation's most prestigious foundations and businesses, AT&T, Ford, the Andrew W. Mellon foundation, and the National Endowment for the Humanities. The project has as its mandate the location, preservation, and publication of literary sources by Hispanic writers from the colonial period to 1960. The project, directed by Nicolás Kanellos, of the University of Houston, has been busily assembling an unparalleled bibliography of Hispanic authors and their works that in the end will also include hundreds of newspaper entries. Its work on nineteenth-century Spanish-language newspapers from New York and Philadelphia to San Antonio and Los Angeles (and many other locales) alone is reconfiguring traditional notions of literacy and writing in the Hispanic community after 1848. In addition, the project has funded scores of scholars to carry out research on forgotten authors and texts or manuscripts never before read by the public, the fruits of which will surely direct further research for years to come.

Indeed, the project has already recovered and republished María Amparo Ruiz de Burton, a California writer of novels and plays. Her first novel, *Who Would Have Thought It?* (1872) is especially important to a course like this, because it is a biting satire and critique of New England society and culture — the perfect text to evaluate the ongoing nineteenth-century reinvention of a Puritan past. Also available is Alvar Núñez Cabeza de Vaca's account of his disastrous expedition into North America in 1528. His cautionary tale as colonizer is revealing, especially when compared to Anglo tracts that promoted immigration to the New World. Finally, a new English translation of Mexico's colonial poet Sor Juana Inés de la Cruz facilitates a comparison with Anne Bradstreet. A comparative colonial history of the Americas is taking shape because of these and similar recovery efforts.

Syllabus
Common Ground on Different Borders:
A Comparative Study of Chicano/a and Puritan Writers

This course is organized around an examination and critique of traditional concepts of American literature, like a Puritan myth of origins,
theories of continuity, and the American Renaissance. We deconstruct
the nationalist definitions of American literature that have excluded
and marginalized Chicano and Chicana writers by denaturalizing Puritan writers as the progenitors of American literature. Puritan writers
are important not because they represent quintessential American "origins" but because they were constructed as semiotically important to
contemporary literature. By positing Puritan writers as "other," this
course places Chicano and Chicana authors closer to the center of cultural issues and debates that have shaped American literature broadly
in the twentieth century. Guiding our discussion will be such themes
as dissent, immigration, millennialism, "America" as the promised
land, and community identity. Writers include Gary Soto, Edward
Taylor, Pat Mora, Cotton Mather, Américo Paredes, William Bradford,
Cherríe Moraga, Mary Rowlandson, Lorna Dee Cervantes, and
Michael Wigglesworth.

Required Texts
Lorna Dee Cervantes, *Emplumada*
William Bradford, *Of Plymouth Plantation*
Pat Mora, *Chants and Borders*
Cherríe Moraga, *Loving in the War Years*
Américo Paredes, *With His Pistol in His Hand*
Mary Rowlandson, "The Sovereignty and Goodness of God"
Gary Soto, *New and Selected Poems*
Edward Taylor, *The Poetical Works of Edward Taylor*
Roger Williams, *A Key into the Language of America*

Course Packets
The Third Woman (Chicana poetry)
Critical essays on American literary history
Aztlán

Part I: Contemporary Views on American Literary History
Week 1   A round of introductions
           Rediscovering colonial history
Week 2   Annette Kolodny's "Letting Go Our Grand Obsessions: Notes to-
           wards a New Literary History of the American Frontiers."
           María Herrera-Sobek's "Canon Formation and Chicano Literature"

Sau-ling Cynthia Wong's introduction, "Constructing an Asian American Textual Coalition"

Week 3   Sacvan Bercovitch's "The Problem of Ideology in American Literary History"
Ramón Saldívar's "Race, Class, and Gender in the Southwest: Foundations of an American Resistance Literature and Its Literary History"
R. C. De Prospo's "Marginalizing Early American Literature"
Writing assignment: three pages

Part 2: Theories of Origins, Theories of Continuity in Practice

Week 4   Perry Miller and Thomas H. Johnson's introduction to *The Puritans*
Giles Gunn's introduction to *Early American Writing*
W. C. Spengemann's "Early American Literature as a Period of Literary History"

Week 5   Luis Valdez's introduction to *Aztlán*
Selections from *Aztlán*: "La Causa: In the Beginning," "The Children of the Aztec"; selection from *Readings on La Raza*: "Mecha"
Poetry selection from *Aztlán*: "Voices of the Chicanos"

Week 6   Chicana poetry selections from *The Third Woman*

Week 7   Roger Williams's *A Key into the Language of America*
Writing assignment: five pages

Part 3: History as Communal Narratives

Week 8   Américo Paredes's *With His Pistol in His Hand*

Week 9   William Bradford's *Of Plymouth Plantation, 1620–1647*

Week 10   Cherríe Moraga's *Loving in the War Years*

Week 11   Mary Rowlandson's "The Sovereignty and Goodness of God"
Writing assignment: five pages

Part 4: Comparative Readings: Acts of Disruptions, Acts of Inventions

Week 12   Selections from Cotton Mather's *Magnalia Christi Americana* and Pat Mora's *Chants* and *Borders*

Week 13   Selections from Michael Wigglesworth's *Day of Doom* and Lorna Dee Cervantes's *Emplumada*

Week 14   Selections from Edward Taylor's *Poetical Works* and Gary Soto's *Elements of San Joaquin* and *Black Hair*
Final paper assignment, eight to ten pages. Topic to be announced.

Works Cited

Primary Works

Aztlán: An Anthology of Mexican American Literature. Ed. Luis Valdez and Stan Steiner. New York: Knopf, 1972.

Cabeza de Vaca, Alvar Núñez. *The Account.* Ed. and trans. Martin A. Favata and José B. Fernández. Houston: Arte Público, 1993 (1542).

Bradford, William. *Of Plymouth Plantation, 1620–1647.* New York: Modern Library, 1981.

Cervantes, Lorna Dee. *Emplumada.* Pittsburgh: U of Pittsburgh P, 1981.

Inés de la Cruz, Sor Juana. *Poems, Protest, and a Dream.* Trans. Margaret Sayers Peden. New York: Penguin, 1996.

Lauter, Paul, et al., eds. *The Heath Anthology of American Literature.* 2nd ed. 2 vols. Lexington: Heath, 1994.

Mather, Cotton. *Magnalia Christi Americana.* Vol. 1. Hartford: Silus Andrus, 1855 [1702].

Mora, Pat. *Borders.* Houston: Arte Público, 1986.

———.*Chants.* Houston: Arte Público, 1985.

Moraga, Cherríe. *Loving in the War Years: lo que nunca pasó por sus labios.* Boston: South End, 1983.

Olivas, Richard. Untitled poem. *El Espejo — The Mirror: Selected Chicano Literature.* Ed. Octavio Ignacio Romano-V and Herminio Ríos C. Berkeley: Quinto Sol, 1972.

Paredes, Américo. *With His Pistol in His Hand.* Austin: U of Texas P, 1958.

Readings on La Raza: The Twentieth Century. Ed. Matt S. Meier and Feliciano Rivera. New York: Hill, 1974.

Rowlandson, Mary. "The Sovereignty and Goodness of God." *Puritans among the Indians: Accounts of Captivity and Redemption, 1676–1724.* Ed. Alden T. Vaughan and Edward W. Clark. Cambridge: Belknap–Harvard UP, 1981. 27–75.

Ruiz de Burton, María Amparo. *Who Would Have Thought It?* 1872. Ed. Rosaura Sánchez and Beatrice Pita. Houston: Arte Público, 1995.

Soto, Gary. *Black Hair.* Pittsburgh: U of Pittsburgh P, 1985.

———. *The Elements of San Joaquin.* Pittsburgh: U of Pittsburgh P, 1997.

———. *New and Selected Poems.* San Francisco: Chronicle, 1995.

Taylor, Edward. *The Poetical Works of Edward Taylor.* Ed. and introd. Thomas H. Johnson. Princeton: Princeton UP, 1974.

The Third Woman. Ed. Dexter Fisher. Boston: Houghton, 1980.

Wigglesworth, Michael. *Day of Doom. The Puritans.* Rev. ed. Vol. 2. Ed. Perry Miller and Thomas A. Johnson. New York: Harper, 1963. 587–606.

Williams, Roger. *A Key into the Language of America.* Ed. and introd. John J. Teunissen and Evelyn J. Hinz. Detroit: Wayne State UP, 1973.

Secondary Works

Baym, Nina. "Early Histories of American Literature: A Chapter in the Institution of New England." *American Literary History* 1 (1989): 459–88.

Bercovitch, Sacvan. "The Ends of American Puritan Rhetoric." *The Ends of Rhetoric: History, Theory, Practice.* Ed. John Bender and David E. Wellbery. Stanford: Stanford UP, 1990. 171–91.

———. "The Problems of Ideology in American Literary History." *Critical Inquiry* 12.4 (1986): 631–53.

De Prospo, R. C. "Marginalizing Early American Literature." *New Literary History* 23.2 (1992): 233–65.

Gunn, Giles, ed. *Early American Writing*. New York: Penguin, 1994.

Gutiérrez, Ramón A. *When Jesus Came, the Corn Mothers Went Away: Marriage, Sexuality and Power in New Mexico, 1500–1846*. Stanford: Stanford UP, 1991.

Herrera-Sobek, María. "Canon Formation and Chicano Literature." *Recovering the U.S. Hispanic Literary Heritage*. Ed. Ramón Gutiérrez and Genaro Padilla. Houston: Arte Público, 1993. 209–219.

Kolodny, Annette. "Letting Go Our Grand Obsessions: Notes towards a New Literary History of the American Frontiers." *American Literature* 64 (1992): 1–18.

Lauter, Paul. "The Literatures of America: A Comparative Discipline." *Redefining American Literary History*. Ed. A. La Vonne Brown Ruoff and Jerry W. Ward, Jr. New York: MLA, 1990. 10–34.

Matthiessen, F. O. *American Renaissance: Art and Expression in the Age of Emerson and Whitman*. London: Oxford UP, 1941.

Miller, Perry, and Thomas A. Johnson, eds. *The Puritans*. Rev. ed. Vol. 1. New York: Harper, 1963.

Saldívar, Ramón. "Race, Class, and Gender in the Southwest: Foundations of an American Resistance Literature and Its Literary History." *Chicano Narrative: The Dialectics of Difference*. Madison: U of Wisconsin P, 1990. 10–25.

Spengemann, W. C. "Early American Literature as a Period of Literary History." *A New World of Words: Redefining Early American Literature*. New Haven: Yale UP, 1994. 1–50.

Wong, Sau-ling Cynthia. "Constructing an Asian American Textual Coalition." *Reading Asian American Literature: From Necessity to Extravagance*. Princeton: Princeton UP, 1993. 3–17.

Dennis D. Moore

From "The Melting Pot"
to Multiculturalism

"It is part of the American character," if we are to believe Thomas Jefferson, writing to his daughter Patsy in 1787, "to consider nothing as desperate; to surmount every difficulty by resolution and by contrivance" (qtd. in Ferguson 495). Five years earlier, a book of essays that appeared in London had raised — and answered — the seemingly simple question, "What, then, is the American, this new man?" Farmer James, the fictional narrator of most of J. Hector St. John de Crèvecoeur's 1782 *Letters from an American Farmer*, answers his own question with a metaphor that seems steeped in simplicity and optimism: "Here individuals of all nations are melted into a new race [. . .]" (70). These comments by two late-eighteenth-century patriarchs help illustrate two closely related elements of any substantive discussion of the elusive quality "Americanness": American identity and American exceptionalism. The former emphasizes qualities that Americans all supposedly share, as in Jefferson's assertion about industriousness; the latter emphasizes qualities that distinguish Americans from everyone else, as in Farmer James's question and answer.

Efforts at defining Americanness have continued up to the present, in spite of recent changes in emphasis. Addressing such changes is part of the idea behind my course From "The Melting Pot" to Multiculturalism, offered as part of Florida State's American studies course Changing Concepts of the American Character.

Since the 1960s American studies has been coming to terms with the kind of fundamental epistemological change that the late historian of science Thomas Kuhn described as a "paradigm shift." While the expression is now more widespread, Kuhn used it to describe not only changes in the ways scientists explain phenomena—for example, on the basis of new discoveries and the rethinking of earlier assumptions—but also the concomitant questioning of scientific structures per se (Aronowitz 524–30).[1] Indeed, writing in *American Quarterly* in 1979, Gene Wise applies the Kuhnesque expression "paradigm dramas" to the shifts that had characterized the middle half of the twentieth century (293–95).[2] More recently, Philip Fisher describes the central shift as one away from discussing myth (which "is always singular") and toward analyzing rhetorics ("always plural"). The latter, he writes in his introduction to the collection *The New American Studies*, "is the place where language is engaged in cultural work, and such work can be done on, with, or in spite of one or another social group" (vii). References to "cultural work" evoke not only Jane Tompkins's revisionist readings of the American Renaissance but also the broader shift, of which her scholarship is a part, toward a more self-consciously ideological stance, be it one of feminism, Marxist or materialist criticism, poststructuralism, new historicism, or postcolonial or cultural studies. As frequently and as sharply as these positions can conflict with one another, together they help distinguish the current emphasis of American studies from that in the mid–twentieth century.

It is precisely that earlier perspective out of which the course I describe originated. At mid-century, the expression "the American character" referred specifically to one of two basic ways of making sense of Americanness. Books by Constance Rourke and David Potter, whose subtitles are *A Study of the National Character* and *Economic Abundance and the American Character*, respectively, exemplify this "national character" approach. By the time those books appeared, many scholars were distancing themselves from the approach, recognizing the inherent risk that it would essentialize people, lumping everyone together into one supposedly homogenous category. The other approach that was dominant at mid-century, the "myth and symbol school," was in its way equally concerned with totalizing: with the help of such books as Henry Nash Smith's *Virgin Land: The American West as Symbol and Myth* and Alan Trachtenberg's *Brooklyn Bridge: Fact and Symbol*, readers could trace recurring patterns of imagery in our culture and argue that they were fundamental, that is, part of the foundation of Americanness. To the extent that both approaches helped explain what it meant for practically anyone to be an American, both fit under the rubric of "myth" that Fisher's introductory essay discusses. Neither one has totally disappeared, either in the theory or the practice of American studies, any more than the melting-pot ideology has been totally subsumed by multiculturalism.

In comparing notes on the first day about "the national character" — Does it mean the same thing to everyone? Has it always? Does gender enter into it? Do class and race? Is it the same for an immigrant as for the children of immigrants? — two patterns quickly become clear: everyone brings numerous stereotypes to such a discussion, and there is much more to it than first meets the eye. From the beginning I ask the students to picture a continuum from the melting pot to multiculturalism, two ideas that at first seem mutually exclusive. To avoid a simple dichotomy and work instead toward the notion of a series of possible positions, I build the discussion the first day around two parallel questions, beginning with whether the thirty-five or so of us in the classroom are, ourselves, a microcosm of the melting pot.

By design, the course attracts students in majors ranging from financial management to history to social work to undecided to elementary education to English and, occasionally, American studies; although its course number designates it is as upper-division, a freshman or sophomore might be sitting alongside a graduating senior, given that the three credit hours help satisfy undergraduate requirements in liberal studies. Because the course is the first exposure for almost all these students to American studies, I describe the discipline in the syllabus: "American studies tends to be *interdisciplinary* and *eclectic*, often drawing on the best of history, art history, literature, and such fields as sociology and geography to examine our complex, pluralistic society. Many of the questions it addresses involve the characteristics, if any, that make Americans *exceptional*."

Discussing the abstraction of a melting pot leads to a discussion of melting-pot ideology. Having someone simply take out a nickel can be an effective way to remind the class of the reassuring motto *e pluribus unum* ("from many, one"), which, like the idea of a melting pot, connotes homogeneity and uniformity. Werner Sollors's *Beyond Ethnicity* conveniently links Crèvecoeur's name with the metaphor and with numerous other texts that use the metaphor, including Israel Zangwill's 1908 play, *The Melting-Pot*. Moreover, having Sollors's book there that first day, along with titles such as Nathan Glazer and Daniel Patrick Moynihan's *Beyond the Melting Pot* and the Library of America edition of Frederick Douglass's *Autobiographies*, helps make the idea of a reserve reading list more concrete.

The second, parallel question I use to focus the opening day's discussion emerges as we talk about stereotypes: considering the many backgrounds and expectations that identify us as individuals, might we, as a class, embody multiculturalism? The connotations of this term can vary dramatically among these undergraduates that first day, as in the larger society. Some will have taken literature courses from professors who use — or sneer at — the various revisionist anthologies of United States literature. Some arrive ready to cite, chapter and verse, Molly Ivins or Michael Kinsley on multiculturalism's virtues — or Dinesh D'Souza on its vices.

The leap from simply talking about two discrete ideas to positing a continuum is crucial. It is important the first day to address, and to refute, the expectation that the two abstractions are mutually exclusive. It is also important to refute the related expectation that the continuum will simply prove to be a timeline, with every early writer advocating something like a "pure" melting pot and every contemporary writer repudiating it in favor of multiculturalism. My objective the first day is to have the class agree to watch for writers and texts whose positions combine elements of both abstractions, enabling students to replace stereotypes with a greater understanding of the ways various cultures have expressed themselves and made their presence felt all along.

Toward that end, I establish throughout the first half of the semester that our society has not always accepted the melting-pot idea unquestioningly and that recent calls for multiculturalism have numerous historical precedents. As early as 1915, according to David Hollinger, the American philosopher Horace Kallen "envisioned the life of the United States as analogous to a symphony orchestra: each instrument was a distinctive group transplanted from the Old World, making harmonious music with other groups" (92).[3] Similarly, at mid-century Glazer and Moynihan were demonstrating how inappropriate the melting-pot metaphor was for American society. To oversimplify the contemporary debate as a "conflict between multiculturalism and the study of Western European culture" makes no sense, as Lawrence W. Levine shows in *The Opening of the American Mind*: the latter "itself is a product of multiculturalism as the various peoples of Western Europe met and interacted on American soil" (160). Such basic background information helps students put our readings and the culture wars into perspective.[4]

As the accompanying abbreviated syllabus shows, the basic movement among assigned readings, after the first week, is chronological and diachronic. Rather than simply having the readings begin with Mary Rowlandson — or a century later with Crèvecoeur, in order to launch right into his melting-pot metaphor — we begin with two contemporary selections. In addition to sounding more familiar, both establish an analogy the students can use as we continue talking about immigrants' experiences. Together, they give everyone practice from the very beginning at *not* blurring cultures. Calvin Trillin's 1994 *New Yorker* reminiscence about his immigrant parents, which he subsequently reworked into a book, provides an accessible, firsthand account of the differences between immigrants' expectations and their children's. The first time I taught the course we began discussing the Trillin piece on the second day, but I immediately realized that it would help to precede his essay with Hisaye Yamamoto's story "Seventeen Syllables," which introduces the terminology *issei* and *nisei*, for the immigrant generation and their children, respectively. The idea is not to call Abe Trillin *issei* or Calvin and his sister Sukie *nisei* or to label Crèvecoeur the immigrant as *issei* in order to distinguish him from Farmer James (this fictional character's father is supposedly the son of an immigrant [*Letters* 92]). Considering such terminology helps students recognize a pattern while reminding them not to impose that pattern on all other immigrants or immigrant groups.

In discussing the Crèvecoeur selections students invariably challenge his having the narrator Farmer James focus his famous question on "the American, this new *man*" (69). Many undergraduates find this gender specificity no more "self-evident" than the statement in the Declaration that "all men are created equal." Similarly, many students arrive knowing to associate Franklin with the notion of the "self-made *man*," an idea that also appears, with similar assumptions about gender, in Crèvecoeur, Douglass, Alger, and Fitzgerald. Such references to men frequently stimulate thoughtful discussions and substantive research topics involving gender stereotyping.

Throughout the semester, I focus class discussions on trying out various ways of talking about the continuum and where various readings fit (or, perhaps, resist fitting) on it. In asking the class to evaluate each selection, I ask whether the writer consistently and predictably takes one position. To avoid implying that the course is finally about taking sides, I have students consider the many contrasting ways a given writer approaches the question of American identity. A convenient example early in the semester involves Crèvecoeur and his narrators' different stances. Farmer James, the narrator of eleven of the twelve selections in *Letters*, waxes self-righteous in Letter IX about southern planters' cruelty to slaves, comparing the opulence of Charleston to the decadence of Lima, the Spanish Empire's viceregal capital in the Americas. In Letter II, however, he refers to the slaves that are part of his own property, situated among the Quakers in supposedly enlightened Pennsylvania. Moreover, the selections published in the 1920s as *Sketches* contain more voices Crèvecoeur creates to express differing positions on slavery (e.g., 235–36; 267; 288; 317–18; 328; and a cluster in "Landscapes," on 439, 472, and 487–

88). There are still more examples of other narrators' stances regarding slavery in Crèvecoeur's essays in *More Letters* (see 6; 71; 87; 88; 107–08; 126–27). Within the first two weeks, students see for themselves that what had *seemed*, when they first encountered Crèvecoeur, simple and optimistic is in fact a conscious oversimplification in order to make a point about the complexity of American identity.

As the syllabus moves toward more recent writings, students recognize similar complexity in how other writers depict various groups. The Alger novel embodies the myth that hard work and determination, the qualities that Jefferson and Crèvecoeur both admired as "industriousness," are the crucial requirements for attaining " 'spectability,'" or acceptance into an American society that presumably cares less about one's origins than about individual merit; Fitzgerald's narrator, Nick Carraway, indulges in a great deal of painful self-scrutiny while questioning just such a myth. Mrs. Turner, an especially vain character in *Their Eyes Were Watching God*, provides another stance relative to the abstraction of a melting pot, advising the protagonist to stay away from darker-skinned blacks ("It's too many black folks already. We oughta lighten up de race" [Hurston 135]). In Willa Cather's "Old Mrs. Harris" interactions among people of different ethnic backgrounds undercut any assumptions that any writer from before the 1980s or 1990s must have preferred the melting pot. Conversely, John Edgar Wideman's "Valaida," with its Josephine Bakeresque title character and its haunted old Mr. Cohen, refuses to align itself neatly with preconceived notions of the positions that writers of color these days will occupy. Richard Rodriguez's elegantly written *Hunger of Memory* also helps undercut such stereotypes.

To help students apply such examples beyond individual class discussions, I develop a variation of this basic writing assignment each time I teach the course:

> Build a research paper around a statement such as "On the continuum we have been discussing that stretches between 'the melting pot' at one end and 'multiculturalism' at the other, I find this very interesting relation between the relative positions of _____ and _____: that [. . .]" Notice that *you*

will be filling in the first two blanks with titles from our assigned readings — and that you will be crafting a thesis statement to follow the colon.

Moreover, the syllabus spells out the following relation: "*Report topics* are specific and finite: you are simply giving your classmates additional information to help them understand our reading. *Paper topics* are also specific, but here the emphasis is on interpreting details and ideas and the ways writers work with them." Having a copy of such basic information on the first day of class helps students begin immediately to focus on the issues at the center of the course. It is also especially helpful to budget some class time, during the first two weeks, for discussing sources of contextual information that students could use for those in-class reports and could consider applying to their research papers. While we read both Douglass and Rowlandson in an inexpensive paperback, for example, I readily refer anyone interested in reporting on Rowlandson to the far more detailed introduction to her narrative in *Journeys in New Worlds* (Andrews). And while most report topics I suggest in this course are not explicitly literary, of course numerous specifically literary approaches fit in well.[5]

In a course that asks students to explore stereotypes there is always the danger that someone will think the only alternative is to lump everyone together into one supposedly homogeneous category — which is precisely the danger I associate above with the national-character approach to American studies. The readings in this course show that the ideology of the melting pot is about just such lumping. Instead of simply substituting a more recent approach, the course encourages students to move beyond stereotyping and settling for either-or choices. They learn, as did Crèvecoeur and his contemporaries, to move beyond the simple answers to the question of what it means to be an American.

Notes

1. In discussing the expression, Stanley Aronowitz places Kuhn's *Structure of Scientific Revolutions* in the perspective of an even broader development, the "throw[ing] into question the status of scientific theory, if not scientific practice, as value neutral" (528).

2. For a more thorough discussion of the relation between the "myth and symbol" and "national character" approaches, see Stannard; Wise. Michael Kammen's essay on American exceptionalism provides particularly helpful background.

3. In 1915 Kallen published a two-part essay in the *Nation*, "Democracy vs. the Melting Pot," challenging the assumption that American society functioned like a melting pot; within a decade, he had expanded his idea of "cultural pluralism" into a book. In the interim Randolph Bourne published "Trans-national America" in the *Atlantic Monthly*, praising the cosmopolitan flavor immigrants infused into America in general and New York City in particular (Hollinger 91–94).

4. As Gregory Jay notes at the beginning of "Taking Multiculturalism Personally," a chapter in *American Literature and the Culture Wars*, "The scholarly and critical literature on the topic [of multiculturalism] continues to expand beyond anyone's capacity to keep up [. . .]" (103). Still, Jay historicizes the culture wars more thoroughly than does Levine.

5. Two helpful resources for students interested in the context of Yamamoto's story "Seventeen Syllables," for example, are the casebook that King-Kok Cheung has compiled and Linda Tamura's recent study, *The Hood River Issei*. A student interested in sociology might do a report on Will Herberg's *Protestant-Catholic-Jew*, which describes a "triple melting pot" — and then incorporate Herberg into a research paper. Instead of expecting to find an undergraduate who will read and report on the Zangwill play, I point students toward Udelson's *Dreamer of the Ghetto*, which contains a helpful chronology (xiii–xv). At the end of the Hurston novel, Henry Louis Gates, Jr., provides a helpful chronology that places Hurston in the context of the Harlem Renaissance (201–07), and his edition of Douglass's autobiographies includes another, more detailed chronology describing abolitionism and slavery and its aftermath (1049–77). For students interested in early attitudes toward the Spanish in general and Spanish-speaking immigrants in particular, I recommend a report on *la leyenda negra*, or the Black Legend, and I refer them to the index of my edition of Crèvecoeur (*More Letters*). Students looking for a more explicitly literary emphasis are often excited to dig up autobiographical connections, in Hemenway's biography, between Verigible "Tea Cake" Woods and the younger man Hurston romanced in the 1930s (231). A student interested in parody might report on Nathanael West's *A Cool Million* vis-à-vis Horatio Alger, and someone who prefers British writers might report on Josiah Bounderby of Coketown, Dickens's blustering parody of a self-made man in *Hard Times*.

Abbreviated Syllabus
From "The Melting Pot" to Multiculturalism

Assigned Texts

Horatio L. Alger, *Ragged Dick*

William Andrews, ed., *Classic American Autobiographies*, which includes Rowlandson, Franklin, Douglass, and Zitkala-Sa

J. Hector St. John de Crèvecoeur, *Letters [. . .] and Sketches [. . .]*

F. Scott Fitzgerald, *The Great Gatsby*

Zora Neale Hurston, *Their Eyes Were Watching God*

Paul Lauter et al., eds. *The Heath Anthology of American Literature*, 3rd ed., vol. 2, which includes selections by Anaya, Bambara, Cather, Cervantes, Jen, Silko, Welch, Wideman, and Yamamoto

Lawrence W. Levine, "From the Melting Pot to the Pluralist Vision." *Opening of the American Mind* 105–20

Richard Rodriguez, *Hunger of Memory*

Calvin Trillin, "Messages from My Father." *New Yorker* (Father's Day issue, 1994)

General Schedule

Week 1   Introductions; Yamamoto story and Trillin

Week 2   Trillin essay, continued; Crèvecoeur, Letter III

Week 3   Rowlandson and Zitkala-Sa (in Andrews)

Week 4   More Crèvecoeur: "History of Mrs. B.," "Frontier Woman," and Letter XII

Week 5   Franklin (in Andrews)

Week 6   Crèvecoeur, Letter IX; first half of Douglass (in Andrews)

Week 7   Remainder of Douglass; first half of Alger

Week 8   Remainder of Alger; Levine

Week 9   Revisiting Trillin essay briefly; Fitzgerald novel

Week 10   Hurston novel

Week 11   First half of Rodriguez

Week 12   Remainder of Rodriguez; Cervantes poem and Wideman story

Week 13   Stories by Cather, Jen, and Silko

Week 14   Stories by Anaya, Welch, Silko, and Bambara

Works Cited

Primary Works

Alger, Horatio. Ragged Dick; *and* Struggling Upward. Ed. Carl Bode. New York: Penguin, 1985.

Andrews, William L., ed. *Classic American Autobiographies*. New York: Mentor, 1992.

————, ed. *Journeys in New Worlds: Early American Women's Narratives*. Wisconsin Studies in Amer. Autobiography. Madison: U of Wisconsin P, 1990.

Cather, Willa. "Old Mrs. Harris." Lauter et al. 1087–1122.

Crèvecoeur, J. Hector St. John de. Letters from an American Farmer *and* Sketches of Eighteenth-Century America. Ed. Albert E. Stone. New York: Penguin, 1986.

————. *More Letters from the American Farmer: An Edition of the Essays in English Left Unpublished by Crèvecoeur*. Ed. Dennis D. Moore. Athens: U of Georgia P, 1995.

Dickens, Charles. *Hard Times*. Ed. Kate Flint. New York: Penguin, 1995.

Douglass, Frederick. *Autobiographies*. Ed. Henry Louis Gates, Jr. New York: Lib. of Amer., 1993.

Fitzgerald, F. Scott. *The Great Gatsby*. New York: Macmillan, 1992.

Hurston, Zora Neale. *Their Eyes Were Watching God*. Fwd. Mary Helen Washington. New York: Harper, 1990.

Lauter, Paul, et al., eds. *The Heath Anthology of American Literature*. 3rd ed. Vol. 2. Boston: Houghton, 1998.

Rodriguez, Richard. *Hunger of Memory: The Education of Richard Rodriguez*. New York: Bantam, 1981.

Tamura, Linda. *The Hood River Issei: An Oral History of Japanese Settlers in Oregon's Hood River Valley*. Urbana: U of Illinois P, 1994.

Trillin, Calvin. "Personal History: Messages from My Father." *New Yorker* 20 June 1994: 56+.

West, Nathanael. *Two Novels:* The Dream Life of Balso Snell *and* A Cool Million. New York: Noonday, 1963.

Wideman, John Edgar. "Valaida." Lauter et al. 2930–37.

Yamamoto, Hisaye. "Seventeen Syllables." Lauter et al. 2611–20.

Zangwill, Israel. *The Melting-Pot*. Vol. 12 of *The Works of Israel Zangwill*. New York: AMS, 1969.

Secondary Works

Aronowitz, Stanley. "The Production of Scientific Knowledge: Science, Ideology, and Marxism." *Marxism and the Interpretation of Culture*. Ed. and introd. Cary Nelson and Lawrence Grossberg. Champaign: U of Illinois P, 1988. 519–41.

Cheung, King-Kok, ed. *"Seventeen Syllables."* Women Writers: Texts and Contexts. New Brunswick: Rutgers UP, 1994.

Ferguson, Robert A. "The American Enlightenment, 1750–1820." *The Cambridge History of American Literature*. Sacvan Bercovitch, gen. ed. Vol. 1: 1590–1820. Cambridge: Cambridge UP, 1994. 345–537.

Fisher, Philip, ed. *The New American Studies: Essays from* Representations. Berkeley: U of California P, 1991.

Glazer, Nathan, and Daniel Patrick Moynihan. *Beyond the Melting Pot: The Negroes, Puerto Ricans, Jews, Italians, and Irish of New York City*. 2nd ed. Cambridge: MIT P, 1970.

Hemenway, Robert E. *Zora Neale Hurston: A Literary Biography.* Fwd. Alice Walker. Urbana: U of Illinois P, 1977.

Herberg, William. *Protestant-Catholic-Jew: An Essay in American Religious Sociology.* Garden City: Doubleday, 1955.

Hollinger, David A. "Pluralism, Cosmopolitanism, and the Diversification of Diversity." *Postethnic America: Beyond Multiculturalism.* New York: Basic, 1995. 79–104.

Jay, Gregory S. *American Literature and the Culture Wars.* Ithaca: Cornell UP, 1997.

Kammen, Michael. "The Problem of American Exceptionalism: A Reconsideration." *American Quarterly* 45.1 (1992): 1–43.

Levine, Lawrence W. *The Opening of the American Mind: Canons, Culture, and History.* Boston: Beacon, 1996.

Potter, David M. *People of Plenty: Economic Abundance and the American Character.* Chicago: U of Chicago P, 1954.

Rourke, Constance. *American Humor: A Study of the National Character.* Rev. ed. Introd. William T. Lhamon, Jr. Tallahassee: UP of Florida, 1986.

Smith, Henry Nash. *Virgin Land: The American West as Symbol and Myth.* Cambridge: Harvard UP, 1950.

Sollors, Werner. *Beyond Ethnicity: Consent and Descent in American Culture.* New York: Oxford UP, 1986.

Stannard, David. "American Historians and the Idea of National Character." *American Quarterly* 23 (1971): 202–20.

Trachtenberg, Alan. *Brooklyn Bridge: Fact and Symbol.* New York: Oxford UP, 1965.

Udelson, Joseph. *Dreamer of the Ghetto: The Life and Works of Israel Zangwill.* Judaic Studies Series. Tuscaloosa: U of Alabama P, 1990.

Wise, Gene. "'Paradigm Dramas' in American Studies." *American Quarterly* 31 (1979): 293–337.

Gary L. Hewitt

New Worlds, 1450–1750: A Historian's Perspective on the Study of Colonial America

Modern students know more than they realize about the history of early America. The luminary figures of the colonial world, like Columbus, Cortés, Pocahontas, and the Pilgrims, are of course familiar to them, and in the Midwest, where I teach, even secondary explorers like Marquette and La Salle are standard fodder in middle-school history courses. Few Americans have not absorbed something of the mythology of pirates or the horrors of African slavery and the Middle Passage. Even more encouragingly, many students have already engaged some of the deeper historical issues of the colonial era, like the demographic catastrophe of epidemics in the New World, the multifaceted possibilities that "America" offered for voluntary immigrants, and the exploitation of Native Americans. And students appear to be truly interested in the central problem of colonial history: the consequences of the encounter of different cultures in the Americas. The possibilities raised by cross-cultural meetings are fascinating in an increasingly multicultural United States.

New Worlds, an intermediate-level history course, attempts to build on this knowledge and interest while moving beyond the dismal facts of encounter, exploitation, and epidemics. Its overarching goal is to give students a window on an early modern colonial order that reached its zenith in the middle of the eighteenth century. Underneath this broad umbrella, the course attempts to complicate and elaborate the process of colonial history in three directions. First, I wish to convey the *diversity* of colonial history in the New World. My course attempts both to show the varied ways that colonies emerged across the Americas and to give a sense of how the experience of the colonies that became the United States was connected to the larger process of colonization. Second, I hope to elucidate the ambiguities of *power* in colonial societies. The course stresses that American colonies were not the expression of European designs but instead developed out of conflict and collaboration among the peoples who came into contact in the geographic area now called America. Finally, I intend to convey how colonial societies emerged as the result of difficult and often extended historical *processes*. Understanding the historical sequences of events, from encounter to conquest to consolidation, is the heart of my task, the unifying theme of the course. The process by which colonial societies developed provides a means for understanding the diversity of life in the New World and making clear the high stakes of colonial power.

Necessarily, this course demands a comparative approach, and one of my intentions is to introduce students to the possibilities (and pitfalls) of comparative history. Certainly, I have not covered every aspect of the history of the New World; instead I have chosen good examples that help convey the diverse experiences of the colonial period and offer interesting possibilities for comparing societies. The course is divided into four units in roughly chronological order: the era of Iberian ascendancy, the seventeenth-century Caribbean, British North America, and imperial reorientations in the eighteenth century. These units in turn contain a series of case studies of colonial ventures. I have tried to assemble the cases into relatively self-contained week-by-week packages, and I include a series of questions on the syllabus that help guide students toward comparative speculations. These comparisons accumulate through the semester, as the students gain familiarity with the material, and they provide an excellent basis for classroom discussions. By the end of the class, I might ask how the Iroquois were similar to Andean peoples or to pirates or slaves. Indeed, just listing the possible similarities on the board both sparks further creative ideas and helps solidify students' understanding of earlier material.

The bulk of learning in the class, as far as I can tell, takes place in the classroom. I occasionally lecture, but at least once a week the class discusses primary documents. I also find analytical discussions of secondary materials, with much use of the chalkboard, to be quite effective in distilling important insights out of complex and detailed reading assignments. My formal assignments — examinations and essays — are intended to help reinforce this classroom learning. The first two exams focus on identifications and broadly comparative essays, while the last exam is an extended exercise in reading a series of primary documents. The exams are quite effective, I believe, in getting students to think broadly about the material while paying close attention to the historical details. The two essay assignments — one a brief explication of a primary document selected by the student, the second a review of a historical study of the colonial period — urge students to apply the lessons of the course to new places. The written work in general is fairly good, though some students, free to choose their own subjects, go a bit too far afield and choose badly, especially in the book review.

Teaching history is different from teaching literature. Historians use different kinds of reading materials — for example, we principally use secondary materials to teach the details of the past. The past is our subject, and we tend to see texts — primary and secondary — as instruments to achieve that end. Yet in early American studies, historians and literary scholars use remarkably similar primary sources: most notably, the narratives of encounter and description that are such interesting windows on the past. In my course I use some of these sources, as well as a lot of secondary material, to teach what I think are the central themes of early American history.

The diversity of colonial experience in the New World is probably the easiest lesson to teach. After all, the course covers three centuries, two continents, and five European and two American empires, along with dozens of African, Native American, and European cultures. Yet this diversity signifies more than simply a happy multiplicity of possibilities — attempting to understand and explain the variations in American experiences is a task in itself. I try to focus my students' attention on how one might organize colonial experiences along a series of axes of differentiation. For instance, the dynamics of encounter itself might be explored. How did the nature of precontact indigenous societies affect the encounter with Europeans? How did the nature of European colonial ventures themselves affect the process of encounter? It appears that Native American societies were far more diverse than their European counterparts and that the shape of the societies already in America more powerfully determined the kind of colony that emerged than the kind of Europeans who colonized it. The differences between the New England colonies and Peru might better be explained by understanding the differences between Algonquians and Incas than those between England and Spain.

The material basis (economic endeavors and labor forms) and relationships between New and Old World peoples probably serve as the two most important axes on which to array the diversity of New World societies. Most colonies were based on exploitation — an important commonality to stress — yet that exploitation varied tremendously over space and time. For instance, New England settlers became subsistence farmers, with limited economic and social connections with their Native neighbors. In contrast, the settlers of early São Paulo, Brazil, intermarried extensively with Native Americans while developing an economy based primarily on subsistence and slave raiding. Spanish American colonies were different from both: in Peru, for example, Spanish and Native worlds were legally distinct, yet the Spanish economy depended utterly on extracting labor power from Native American communities. Finally, the sugar colonies of the Caribbean were based on plantation slavery, where the slave owner served as the focus of economic and social life (and Native Americans were largely displaced by 1525). By asking the same sort of questions of each colonial society — what was its material basis? how did indigenous and European peoples interact? what forms of labor were employed? — some order can be imposed on the diversity, while maintaining a sense of how different New World societies in fact were.

It is all too easy to misunderstand the "New World" as a world that Europeans encountered, conquered, and then remade in their own images and interests. Whether one finally considers this process as providential or horrific, whether one sees Europeans as builders of a New World that was glorious or as exploiters of a New World that was miserable, defining the societies of the New World as the expression of European designs exaggerates their power. Europeans did not have free rein to impose their wills on the lands or the peoples they found in America. Rather, the encounter among American, European, and African peoples in the Western Hemisphere resulted in a complex set of negotiations over the terms of their mutual relationships.

Introducing students to these ambiguities of power in colonial societies is accordingly a central goal of my course. A reading assignment that helps explore this theme and introduce it in a historical as well as a contemporary setting is the prologue to Steve J. Stern's *Peru's Indian Peoples and the Challenge of Spanish Conquest*, "Paradigms of Conquest: History, Historiography, and Politics." Stern discusses how to separate the aftermath of 1492 from the three "utopias" — of gold, God, and glory — that motivated Spanish colonial ventures. Rather than citing the emanation of Spanish will, providence, or hopeless indigenous resistance, Stern argues that the colonial world was the result of politics — power relations among different peoples. Using this intellectual basis, I can bring students to use the representations of the moment of encounter between European explorers and Native Americans to assess the relative power of colonizers and colonized. These representations illustrate a range of mutual responses between Europeans and indigenous peoples. Christopher Columbus, in his diary of the first Spanish encounters with "Indians" in the Caribbean, for instance, depicts the Tainos as helpless and naked, yet Columbus and his crew clearly depend on their Native interlocutors for access to food, shelter, and riches.

Visual imagery too provides a wonderful way to convey these ambiguities. I distribute in class, for instance, a print of John Smith and Opechancanough in early Virginia, in which a very short Smith, armed with a pistol, seizes a very tall and muscular Opechancanough by the hair while a battle between Powhatans and Englishmen rages in the background. The caption reads: "C. Smith taketh the King of Pamaunkee prisoner 1608" (Bridenbaugh 21). The English engraver betrays his own fears of the Indians' power, however, showing Opechancanough looming head and shoulders over Smith and Indians far outnumbering Englishmen in the field. This graphic evidence of indigenous power is a very effective supplement to the historical narrative of Jamestown and the Virginia colony's predicament during its first two decades. Similar interpretations can be gleaned from the wonderful representations of the Spanish conquest reproduced in Miguel León-Portilla's *Broken Spears* and the unique pictorial imagery in Guamán Poma de Ayala's *Letter to a King*.

Once this basic principle is established, the instructor can develop other sorts of ambiguities of power relations across temporal and geographic divides. Stern's wonderful *Peru's Indian Peoples*, for instance, provides an excellent framework for understanding how and why Andean Indians cooperated with Spanish conquerors while maintaining a great degree of autonomy in their day-to-day lives. This historical work can be supplemented with a close reading of petitions from Andean communities about mistreatment from both indigenous leaders and European exploiters, which help highlight the political divisions within both communities. In this way the early efforts of the Spanish to exploit Andean Indian communities can be understood as the work of parasites (Native and European) fattening on and depending on the vitality of their hosts rather than as the work of sword-wielding conquistadors bent on destroying indigenous societies. By the way, the parasite metaphor works quite effectively for students.

The resistance, collaboration, and eventual dependency of Andean Indians serves as an excellent basis for comparisons with other peoples' responses to colonial intrusions—the fate of the Iroquois in North America, for example, or the position of slaves on Brazilian or Caribbean plantations. These comparisons allow complex notions like "resistance" to be introduced to students—for example, by examining a list of demands given by a group of Brazilian runaway slaves as the precondition for their returning to their plantation (Schwartz, *Slaves* 59–63). The slaves demanded better work conditions and more power over their independent production of market commodities. Why would they want to return to slavery when they had independence as runaways? Students strongly resist the idea that there was space for autonomy, if not freedom, within slavery. My hope is that by setting the groundwork for a more complex sense of autonomy in the experiences of Native peoples, the position of slaves will become more clear. In turn, this comparison might begin to evoke a series of comparisons of the experiences of "colonized" peoples in the Americas.

On the first day of class, I inform my students that I will tell the same simple story a bunch of times: that European colonies in America go through, in different ways, a process of contact, conquest, crisis, and consolidation. After an initial period of contact, in which Old and New World peoples tried to figure one another out, Europeans devised ways to conquer (politically, at least) most Native American peoples. The conquest period was violent and offered extraordinary wealth to Europeans willing to exploit American human and physical resources. Yet in the early periods of colonization indigenous peoples also collaborated with the conquerors, usually to try to maintain their autonomy in the face of disease and increasing European demands. Racial identities and definitions were typically fluid in many early colonies. And finally, European colonizers themselves remained highly independent from generally weak and inefficient imperial authorities. Conquest society was ambiguous in its meanings: power relations were unclear despite the high degree of exploitation and violence.

These conquest societies were almost always unstable, and crises followed, usually twenty-five to fifty years after initial colonial efforts. Some of these crises were political, as in Peru, where in 1543 angry Spanish colonizers assassinated the viceroy (and descended into civil war) when he tried to implement reforms, or Virginia, where poor freeholders, servants, and eventually slaves rebelled against a politically and socially dominant master class in 1676. Some crises were economic, as imperial revenues declined because of inefficiencies in early patterns of exploitation. Sometimes military forces from competing imperial powers, neighboring Native American groups, or both in alliance, threatened new colonies, as in Brazil after 1530. Whatever the particulars, the crises tended to have two dimensions: a crisis of authority among the many local political actors and an imperial crisis among the Europeans.

The crises were resolved, in general, by the successful and aggressive assertion of imperial authority into colonial life. The consolidation of imperial authority involved interlocking components: the deployment of the colonial state on behalf of certain European colonial groups, the rationalization of labor forms to streamline the exploitation of American human resources, and the solidification and recapitulation of racial divisions. In Peru, for instance, a strong new viceroy, Don Francisco de Toledo, in the 1560s and 1570s revitalized the *mita*, compulsory Indian draft labor, under the aegis of the colonial state, to tie the interests of the often rebellious *encomendero* elite to the empire. In Virginia after 1676, slaves replaced troublesome English servants as the chief form of labor. The consolidation of systems of exploitation, tied to the assertion of imperial authority, helped define the structure of mature colonial systems across the New World.

By identifying colonialism for students as a three-step process, I am being admittedly schematic and reductive. Yet such an approach serves, paradoxically, as an excellent tool for teaching the ambiguities and diversity of the colonial experience. I try to make the outlines of this colonial story familiar from the outset — I begin the course by tracing it in the Caribbean, where Columbus's encounter and initial conquest was succeeded rapidly by simultaneous revolts by Native peoples and Spaniards, the reinvigoration of imperial authority with the Laws of Burgos (which also define racial relationships in the Caribbean), a series of new labor forms (*encomienda*, African slavery), and finally the introduction of that quintessential American enterprise, sugar cultivation, under the personal subsidy of King Charles. This story can then be told in different ways in the rest of the Americas, with the basic categories of conquest, crisis, and consolidation serving as comfortable starting points for students as they approach new material from Mexico, Peru, Brazil, the Caribbean, Virginia, and even northeastern North America. Stressing the commonalities of the broadest outlines of the process makes the diverse manifestations of that process easier to understand. Instances in which aspects of the colonial experience do not fit the model — Puritan New England, for instance — can be understood as the exceptions they are. Also, attention to process helps ensure that students understand that the social forms of colonial life — slavery, racism, exploitation — did not spring Athena-like from the head of European colonizers, but from a contestation of power over an extended period of time.

Additionally, focusing on the broad outlines of the colonial process allows the course to hang together as more than simply a series of case studies. It could be argued — and indeed, I suggest as much as I teach — that the entire post-Columbus history of the Americas recapitulates on a large scale the theme of a period of violent and exploitative contact in the sixteenth century, crisis in the seventeenth, and imperial consolidation at the beginning of the eighteenth. I present a brief interlude dealing with international competition, warfare, and piracy to highlight how the local political struggles of individual colonies played a part in a larger story. Pirates, corsairs, and buccaneers were at the vanguard of colonial efforts, especially by non-Iberians. Francis Drake and Walter Raleigh are the two most prominent examples of a system of international trade and imperial competition that depended on private enterprise and violence. Not surprisingly, the pirates were often racially mixed, symbolizing the fluidity of early colonial societies, and often slave traders, reminding students of the continuing importance of violence and exploitation in the colonial world. The liabilities of piracy became evident by the end of the seventeenth century, however, and European states consolidated their monopoly on violence while extirpating the pirates. The result was not peace, of course, but chronic warfare as the mature imperial system emerged after 1689. By stressing similarities among the pirates' role in an international system, the runaway slaves' in Jamaica, and the Native peoples', for instance, in British North America, I hope to make tangible the human consequences of these evolving colonial structures.

The broad subject matter and comparative method of this course allows me to move between the particular and the most general fairly easily — to understand human experiences in the colonial world and the structures of individual colonial societies, while tracing out the larger significances of both. John Demos's *Unredeemed Captive*, one of the last books assigned, provides an excellent (and quite literary) model of this kind of historical thinking. Examining the Williams family's story of captivity, Demos powerfully connects the small-scale experiences of a minister whose Puritan faith was redeemed and his daughter, who converted to Catholicism and married a Mohawk, to the larger themes of imperial consolidation and economic expansion in New England. The daughter's story also reminds students, as well as the professor, that despite the strictures of the colonial process, broad and diverse possibilities remained open for the peoples who inhabited the New World.

**Syllabus
New Worlds, 1450–1750**

This semester we will study the history of the Western Hemisphere in the period immediately before, and several centuries after, the arrival of the first Europeans who stayed. For those who experienced the long process of conquest, colonization, adaptation, and resistance, this arrival created a series of "new worlds" for the hemisphere's indigenous peoples and for the millions of Africans brought overseas — not just the Europeans' New World to be conquered, resettled, ignored, or abandoned. The emergence of new societies, new economies, new empires, and new cultures in this encounter of peoples remains one of the most tremendous processes in the history of the modern world.

Class Readings

John Demos, *The Unredeemed Captive*
Richard Dunn, *Sugar and Slaves*
James Lockhart and Stuart Schwartz, *Early Latin America*
Edmund Morgan, *American Slavery, American Freedom*
Daniel Richter, *The Ordeal of the Longhouse*
Robert Ritchie, *Captain Kidd and the War against the Pirates*
Steve Stern, *Peru's Indian Peoples and the Challenge of Spanish Conquest*

> *Unit 1: The Age of Iberian Ascendancy, 1492–1600*

Week 1   Europe, America, and Africa in the Age of "Discovery"

> Questions: What characterized the expansion of Europe in the fifteenth century? Why did it happen? What kinds of patterns of expansion emerged? What kinds of encounters had Europeans already had with non-Europeans? Why were the Iberian powers particularly involved in this expansion? What kinds of precedents did the experience of the fifteenth century offer on the eve of Columbus's voyage in 1492?
>
> Paradigms of colonization and conquest. Reading: *Peru's Indian Peoples*, xxi–liii (prologue to 2nd ed.)
>
> The Mediterranean world expands. Reading: *Early Latin America*, 1–30
>
> Discussion: Considering Christopher Columbus. What did Columbus hope to accomplish in America? Why did he go? What did he find when he got there? How did he represent the people and places that he found? What can we tell about their response to Columbus? Documents: Columbus's diary and letters; Roldán Revolt sources (both in Parry and Keith, vol. 2)

Week 2　Caribbean Models

Questions: What kinds of institutions — political, economic, social — emerged in the Caribbean after Columbus's voyage of 1492? How did the colonizers plan to make colonization pay? What kinds of problems did this pose to the Castilian crown, political and otherwise?

Encounters. Reading: *Early Latin America*, 31–57.

Conquest society: *Encomienda* and exploitation. Reading: *Early Latin America*, 59–85. Why would the Spanish care what happened to the Indians? What was the Spanish crown's response to the reports of brutality and violence coming from the New World? Why did Africans seem to be the answer to the exploitation of Indians? Documents: Bartolomé de Las Casas, *Brief Account of the Destruction of the Indies* (selections); El Requerimiento, 1513; Laws of Burgos, 1511; Sepúlveda and Las Casas on conquest (all three in Parry and Keith, vol. 1)

Week 3　Encounter and Conquest: Mexico and Peru

Questions: What kinds of strategies did the great conquistadores, Cortés and Pizarro, as well as their followers and imitators, adopt in order to defeat large, well-organized empires? How did they succeed, and when did they fail? What kinds of colonial societies did the conquerors erect? How did they make it pay? How did the conquered respond?

The "high civilizations" on the eve of conquest. Reading: *Peru's Indian Peoples*, 3–50.

Conquest and aftermath. Reading: *Early Latin America*, 86–121.

Discussion: The spiritual conquest. Documents: selections from *Broken Spears*

Week 4　The Consolidation of Empire

Questions: What kinds of structural instabilities were part of conquest societies? How did the various members of that society — conquerors, imperial officials, indigenous elites, and indigenous commoners — respond to these instabilities? Why were the stakes seemingly so high? Why did the *mita* appeal to Viceroy Toledo? What stories did the people of Peru tell about the preconquest Incas to explain the postconquest situation?

The Toledan revolution. Reading: *Peru's Indian Peoples*, 51–113; Viceroy Francisco de Toledo's instructions for the *mita*, 1568–71 (*Instruccion*)

Discussion: The Incas, the Pizarros, and the Spanish Empire. Reading: *Peru's Indian Peoples*, finish; *Early Latin America*, 122–80.

The challenge of Spanish conquest. What was the political landscape of mid-sixteenth-century Peru? What was the purpose of each of these narratives? What kinds of attitudes toward royal and local authority does each author express? Documents: Indian justice in Spanish Peru (Parry and Keith, vol. 4)

Week 5 Portuguese Colonization

Questions: What models for colonization did the Portuguese follow in the first century of their involvement in Brazil? What kinds of societies emerged as a result? Why did the effective colonization of Brazil seem so insignificant at first and so important later? What kinds of comparisons can be made between Brazilian society in 1550 and 1580 and its Spanish American counterparts?

Brazil wood and *mamelucos*; Jesuits and aldeias. Reading: *Early Latin America*, 181–201

The Brazilian sugar revolution. Reading: *Early Latin America*, 202–52; Stuart Schwartz, "Indian Labor and New World Plantations"

Unit 2: The Seventeenth-Century Caribbean

Week 6 Pirates, Corsairs, and International Competition

Questions: What happened to the Spanish and Portuguese worlds with the inaugural of imperial competition in the mid-sixteenth century? What attracted the other European powers? How did they plan to tap the wealth of what the French called "Perou"? What role did the settlement of North America play in these plans? What kinds of societies emerged in the context of this competition?

Commercial systems in the New World. Reading: *Captain Kidd*, 1–26

Discussion: Privateers and buccaneers. Reading: *Captain Kidd*, 27–126

Early non-Iberian plans for settlement. Reading: *American Slavery, American Freedom*, 3–43

Week 7 Caribbean Transformations

Questions: Why did the Caribbean emerge as the centerpiece of non-Iberian colonization in the Americas? Why a plantation economy? How did this society emerge from the projects for commerce and piracy that began the process?

The English capture some small islands. Reading: *Sugar and Slaves*, begin

From tobacco to sugar. Reading: *Sugar and Slaves*, continue

Discussion: Why slavery? Reading: *Sugar and Slaves*, finish. Why did slavery eventually emerge as the predominant labor form in the Caribbean? Why did it take a generation or so before it established itself? What precedents did the English build on in introducing slavery? Was slavery primarily an economic decision, or were there other considerations? Why not enslave Europeans?

Unit 3: British North America in Its Context

Week 8   Lessons from Virginia

Questions: Did Virginia face the same basic problems as the Caribbean? What additional factors shaped the emergence of Virginia? What difference did the presence of Indians make? Why did the society flounder so badly for its first two decades, and what made it succeed? Was there a fundamental difference between the use of servants and the use of slaves as laborers? What was that difference?

Pocahontas redux: Indians and settlers in early Virginia. Reading: *American Slavery, American Freedom*, 44–91; Peter Wood, Gregory Merrell, and M. Thomas Hatley, eds., *Powhatan's Mantle* (selections); Carl Bridenbaugh, *Jamestown* (selection)

Tobacco and labor. Reading: *American Slavery, American Freedom*, 92–130; Walsh, "Till Death Us Do Part," or Rutman and Rutman, "Now-Wives and Sons-in-Law" (both in Tate and Ammerman)

Discussion: Indians, colonial rebellion, and slavery. Reading: *American Slavery, American Freedom*, 215–92. Documents: Governor Berkeley on Bacon's Rebellion; Nathaniel Bacon's "Declaration"; Robert Beverley on Bacon's Rebellion (all in Ver Steeg and Hofstader). What was this rebellion all about? Why was it so important? What kinds of tensions did it reflect in colonial society? Why did attacking the Indians seem so important to Bacon and his followers? What did they hope to accomplish?

Week 9   Political Responses

Questions: What was the response of the Virginia elite and imperial officials in London to the disturbances in Virginia? What kinds of policies resulted? How could the empire solve the instability that seemed rampant in Virginia? What kinds of political and cultural forms emerged as a result, according to Morgan?

Toward slavery and racism. Reading: *American Slavery, American Freedom*, 295–337

Discussion: Race, slavery, and democracy. Reading: *American Slavery, American Freedom*, 338–end.

Unit 4: Imperial Reorientations

Week 10 Consolidation in British America

Questions: With the rise of Britain to the status of a world power, what changed in its relation to its colonies? How did the British

Empire include its sometimes wayward colonists? How was slavery and the slave trade related to this process?

The end of piracy? Reading: *Captain Kidd*, 127–82

The new commercial system. Reading: *Captain Kidd*, 183–end. Documents on English mercantilism (Ver Steeg and Hofstader)

The Atlantic slave trade. Reading: John Thornton, *Africa and Africans in the Making of the Atlantic World*, ch. 4 (on reserve)

Week 11 Slavery in the Americas: A Comparative Perspective

Questions: Are there any generalizations that can be made about New World slavery? Any distinctions between different slave societies? How might we characterize relationships between masters and slaves? How might we characterize the relationships among slaves themselves? Why was North American slavery so unusual? What kinds of spaces did slaves have for self-determination or autonomy? And, finally, how is slavery different from freedom?

Slave society and slave resistance. Reading: Ira Berlin, "Atlantic Creoles"; Michael Mullin, *Africa in America*, 77–114. Document: Slave petition from Brazil (Schwartz, *Slaves* 59–63)

Slave community and slave culture. Reading: Sidney Mintz and Richard Price, *Birth of African-American Culture*, 77–114; Mechal Sobel, *The World They Made Together* (selections)

The Iroquois' new world. Reading: *Ordeal of the Longhouse*, 1–74

Week 12 Lessons from Iroquoia

Questions: Were the Iroquois caught in a bad condition, or did they exploit the possibilities of that position? How was their society transformed by European intrusions? Their culture and way of understanding the world? What kinds of conflicts did the presence of Europeans provoke?

Indigenous empires and European empires. Reading: *Ordeal of the Longhouse*, 75–161

Discussion: Life on the margins. Reading: *Ordeal of the Longhouse*, 162–236. Was the position of the Iroquois like that of other "marginal" people in the New World? like that of plantation slaves? runaway slaves? pirates? If so, how so? Were there ways that it was different? Were there other New World peoples in similar situations? What role did race play in making those differences?

Week 13 The Personal Costs of Empire

Questions: What sort of book is *Unredeemed Captive*, anyway? What kinds of historical methods does Demos use? What does the story of the Williams family tell us about the position of French, English, Huron, Abenaki, and Iroquois on the northern frontier?

John Williams: Puritans and Indians. Reading: *Unredeemed Captive*, 1–119

Eunice Williams: Another way. Reading: *Unredeemed Captive*, 120–end

Week 14 New Consolidations

Questions: What happened to American societies as the eighteenth century, a period of rapid international economic expansion, political turmoil, and warfare, progressed? What did empires do in response to these destabilizing forces? What happened to people on the margins of these empires when the empires consolidated?

Maturing societies, maturing empires. Reading: *Ordeal of the Longhouse*, finish

Centrifugal and centripetal forces in New World societies. Reading: *Early Latin America*, 315–68

Works Cited

Primary Works

Guamán Poma de Ayala, Felipe. *Letter to a King: A Peruvian Chief's Account of Life under the Incas and under the Spanish*. Ed. and trans. Christopher Dilke. New York: Dutton, 1978.

Instrucción general sobre minas para el virrey Toledo. Madrid, 8 Dec. 1568. Rpt. in *Anuario de estudios americanos* 46 (1989): 39–68. Ed. Carlos Sempat Assadourian.

Las Casas, Bartolomé de. *The Devastation of the Indies: A Brief Account*. Trans. Herma Briffault. Baltimore: Johns Hopkins UP, 1992.

León-Portilla, Miguel, ed. *The Broken Spears: The Aztec Account of the Conquest of Mexico*. Boston: Beacon, 1992.

Parry, J. H., and Robert G. Keith, eds. *New Iberian World: A Documentary History of the Discovery and Settlement of Latin America to the Early Seventeenth Century*. 5 vols. New York: Times, 1984.

Ver Steeg, Clarence L., and Richard Hofstader, eds. *Great Issues in American History: From Settlement to Revolution, 1584–1776*. New York: Vintage, 1969.

Secondary Works

Berlin, Ira. "From Creole to African: Atlantic Creoles and the Origins of African-American Society in Mainland North America." *William and Mary Quarterly* 3d ser. 53 (1996): 251–88.

Bridenbaugh, Carl. *Jamestown, 1544–1699*. New York: Oxford UP, 1980.

Demos, John. *The Unredeemed Captive: A Family Story from Early America*. New York: Vintage, 1994.

Dunn, Richard. *Sugar and Slaves: The Rise of the Planter Class in the English West Indies, 1623–1714*. New York: Norton, 1972.

Lockhart, James, and Stuart B. Schwartz. *Early Latin America: A History of Colonial Spanish America and Brazil.* Cambridge: Cambridge UP, 1983.

Mintz, Sidney, and Richard Price. *The Birth of African-American Culture: An Anthropological Perspective.* Boston: Beacon, 1992.

Morgan, Edmund. *American Slavery, American Freedom: The Ordeal of Colonial Virginia.* New York: Norton, 1975.

Mullin, Michael. *Africa in America: Slave Acculturation and Resistance in the American South and British Caribbean, 1736–1831.* Urbana: U of Illinois P, 1992.

Richter, Daniel K. *The Ordeal of the Longhouse: The Peoples of the Iroquois League in the Era of European Colonization.* Chapel Hill: U of North Carolina P, 1992.

Ritchie, Robert K. *Captain Kidd and the War against the Pirates.* Cambridge: Harvard UP, 1986.

Schwartz, Stuart B. "Indian Labor and New World Plantations: European Demands and Indian Response in Northeastern Brazil." *American Historical Review* 83 (1978): 42–79.

———. *Slaves, Peasants, and Rebels: Reconsidering Brazilian Slavery.* Urbana: U of Illinois P, 1992.

Sobel, Mechal. *The World They Made Together: Black and White Values in Eighteenth-Century Virginia.* Princeton: Princeton UP, 1987.

Stern, Steve J. *Peru's Indian Peoples and the Challenge of Spanish Conquest: Huamanga to 1640.* 2nd ed. Madison: U of Wisconsin P, 1993.

Tate, Thad W., and David L. Ammerman. *The Chesapeake in the Seventeenth Century: Essays on Anglo-American Society.* New York: Norton, 1979.

Thornton, John K. *Africa and Africans in the Making of the Atlantic World.* Cambridge: Cambridge UP, 1992.

Wood, Peter H., Gregory A. Waselkov, and M. Thomas Hatley, eds. *Powhatan's Mantle: Indians in the Colonial Southeast.* Lincoln: U of Nebraska P, 1989.

Edward J. Gallagher

Resources for Early American Studies: A Selective Guide

The purpose of this guide is both to aid readers who want to go beyond the essays in this volume and to serve as a stand-alone starter
bibliography for early American studies. The guide should be especially useful to nonspecialists, new teachers in the field, and students
at all levels doing research. The guide clusters issues in some of the
ways they have been grouped in this anthology — moving from the
state of the field and general reference works; through geographic,
chronological, generic, and thematic perspectives; into interdisciplinary areas, nonprint materials, and other resources. Necessarily limiting each section to one paragraph, I have tried to include a variety of
approaches to each subject as well as bibliographies or recent critical
works that will naturally lead to further valuable resources that I did
not have space to list. I did not include single-author studies, since
they are relatively easy to find through the print and electronic versions of the *MLA International Bibliography* and other readily accessible means. Works are usually listed under only one heading, so that,
for instance, material on New England women is under women's

studies, not Puritanism. Scholarship in early American studies is vigorously expanding, and a guide like this inevitably begins to date somewhat even before publication. Thus readers will want to build on my work, which was mainly completed in late 1997, by consulting reviews in *Early American Literature*, the MLA bibliography, the recent publications page and "Early American Literature: A Bibliography of Secondary Material" on the Society of Early Americanists' Web site, and the Society of Early Americanists' newsletter.[1]

State of the Field

For the past decade the mission statements in early American literature have set such goals as establishing a unique identity and substituting multiculturalism for a canon based on nationalism, imperialism, Eurocentrism, ethnocentrism, and Puritanism. In "The Study of Colonial American Literature," Philip F. Gura, for instance, calls for deemphasizing New England religious writing (Nina Baym describes how textbooks constructed the New England origin of American history and the Puritan as the "national type") and American exceptionalism (similarly, Joyce Appleby shows historians moving away from patriotic narrative) and for decoupling the early period from the nineteenth century, and Carla Mulford helps provide the means for "expanding the early American canon." For a sense of the passion of this sea change, see Amy Kaplan's perspective on the politics and personal motivation of the highly influential Puritan scholar Perry Miller in "'Left Alone with America.'" Major literary histories edited by Sacvan Bercovitch and by Emory Elliott now proclaim the "virtue of dissensus" but even so do not go far enough according to Peter Carafiol ("America" still provides the locus of coherence), R. C. De Prospo (the "cult of continuity" persists), and Gura (the "new historicism" has not penetrated). Ironically, though, William C. Spengemann's redefinition of the field in *A New World of Words* — based on language, and not just English — seems too radical for many. For his part Jack P. Greene in *The Intellectual Construction of America* finds American exceptionalism rooted in our early writers rather than in the politics of later scholars. Mulford's "Seated amid the Rainbow" describes teaching with the multicultural *Heath Anthology*. Sharon Harris promotes another kind of broadening, that is, more application of feminist, Marxist, postcolonial, and psychoanalytic theories. For a wider context on the history of American literature teaching, see Gerald Graff's *Professing Literature* and David R. Shumway's *Creating American Civilization*.

General Reference

Annual bibliographies include the *MLA International Bibliography* (the CD-ROM starts at 1963), *American Literary Scholarship: An Annual*, *The Eighteenth Century: A Current Bibliography*, *Handbook of Latin American Studies*, and *The Year's Work in Modern Language Studies* (French and Spanish literature). Every issue of the *Journal of American History* lists "Recent Scholarship"; the *Society of Early Americanists Newsletter* regularly includes current bibliography. Lewis Leary's *Articles on American Literature* volumes cover 1900–75. David L. Ammerman and Philip D. Morgan classify 2,001 works in *Books about Early America* according to period, themes, resources, and reference works. The bibliography volume of the Robert Spiller et al. *Literary History* classifies criticism before 1948. Essays on recent scholarship are Gura's "The Study of Colonial American Literature," David D. Hall's "On Common Ground," and those collected in *The Future of Early American History*. Standard literary histories are Bercovitch's *Cambridge History*, Emory Elliott's *Columbia Literary History*, and, for Spanish writers, Leslie Bethell's *Cambridge History of Latin America*. Everett Emerson's collection of essays on nine major writers of early American literature broke new ground. Biocritical author essays with bibliographies can be found in Elliott's Dictionary of Literary Biography volumes, in James Levernier and Douglas R. Wilmes's *American Writers before 1800*, and in Carlos A. Solé and Maria Isabel Abreu's *Latin American Writers*. Mulford, Amy Winans, and Angela Vietto edited *American Women Prose Writers to 1820*. For examples of authors and works currently considered most significant see mass-market general American literature anthologies by such publishers as Harper (McQuade et al.), Norton (Baym et al.), and Heath, whose anthology is now published by Houghton Mifflin

(Lauter et al.). Specifically early American anthologies are Giles Gunn's *Early American Writing* and Myra Jehlen and Michael Warner's *The English Literatures of America, 1500–1800*. Mulford will soon publish a new anthology, *Early American Literatures*. Major journals include *Early American Literature, William and Mary Quarterly* (history), *Journal of the Early Republic* (1789–1848), and *Studies in Puritan American Spirituality*. No journals specialize solely in Spanish or Native American subjects in this period, but consult *The Americas, Colonial Latin American Historical Review, Dispositio, Hispanic American Historical Review, Journal of Latin American Studies, Latin American Research Review, Florida Historical Quarterly, New Mexico Historical Review, American Indian Culture and Research Journal*, and *American Indian Quarterly. De halve maen* focuses on New Netherland.

Exploration and Settlement in General

Surveying travel accounts before Columbus are Loren Baritz's "The Idea of the West" (from Homer on), Mary B. Campbell's *The Witness* (Polo, Mandeville), and Christian K. Zacher's *Curiosity and Pilgrimage* (de Bury, Chaucer, Mandeville). For Norse contacts see Gwyn Jones, *The Norse Atlantic Saga*, and Erik Wahlgren, *The Vikings and America*. A. Bartlett Giamatti and Harry Levin relate America to European paradisaic motifs in *The Earthly Paradise and the Renaissance Epic* and *The Myth of the Golden Age in the Renaissance*, respectively, and Howard Mumford Jones shows greed turn the golden age into the age of gold in *O Strange New World*. In Stephen Greenblatt's *Marvelous Possessions* Renaissance representational practices function as agents of appropriation and enslavement rather than of renunciation as in the medieval period, and the essays in his *New World Encounters* are concerned with "the vision of the vanquished." For Alden T. Vaughan and Virginia Vaughan Shakespeare's Caliban "stands for countless victims" of imperialism, and Eric Cheyfitz reads *The Tempest* as a "prologue to American literature." Louis De Vorsey's *Keys to the Encounter* moves from European and Native worldviews before Columbus through 1580, and D. W. Meinig's *Atlantic America* is a geographic overview to 1800. The ideologies of empire, especially myths and legacies of Rome, are analyzed by David S. Shields

(*Oracles*) and by Anthony Pagden, and Peter C. Mancall offers English colonization plans. Patricia Seed studies such "ceremonies of possession" as planting crosses, building houses, making dictionaries, and processions that created European authority after contact, and Mary C. Fuller sees imperial failures "recuperated by rhetoric." Alden T. Vaughan describes English paradigms for explaining the origins of the Native Americans; Ian K. Steele shows Europeans on warpaths against them. Robert A. Williams, James Muldoon, and L. C. Green and Olive P. Dickason study justifications of conquest. The English "alliance between piety and commerce" is Louis B. Wright's subject. Cannibals, Caliban, and Pocahontas figure in Peter Hulme's study of six "colonial encounters." Donald A. Barclay, James H. Maguire, and Peter Wild edit accounts of explorations of the West to 1805. For Europe registering America, see William Brandon's *New Worlds for Old* (liberty enters conceptions of a golden age or Lotus Land), A. L. Rowse's *The Elizabethans and America*, William M. Hamlin's *The Image of America in Montaigne, Spenser, and Shakespeare*, German Arciniegas's *America in Europe* ("With America [. . .] [s]cientific progress begins, philosophy thrives"), Durand Echeverria's *Mirage in the West* (the French perspective), Jeffrey Knapp's *An Empire Nowhere* (More to Shakespeare), J. H. Elliott's *The Old World and the New* (until 1650, when Europe and America were reasonably integrated), and Karen Ordahl Kupperman's *America in European Consciousness* (until 1750, when *American* was unlikely to mean Native). Wayne Franklin delineates three types of travel writing, and nature is gendered in Annette Kolodny's *The Lay of the Land*. In *Prophetic Waters* John Seelye finds our history from Columbus to Byrd a Conradian imperial fable in which Puritan and Cavalier are complementary. In *Theater Enough* Jeffrey H. Richards examines theatrical figures of speech in the development of national self-identity. William Carlos Williams and D. H. Lawrence both comment on the American grain.

Spanish Colonial Writings

Begin at the beginning: Marvin Lunenfeld's *1492* is an anthology of primary material, and James Axtell's "Columbian Encounters" articles describe the massive quincentenary scholarship. The Columbus legacy is furiously debated: David E. Stannard uses the terms *holocaust* and *genocide*, unlike the moderate language in Axtell's "Moral Reflections." Hans Koning "explodes the myth" of Columbus, John Yewell, Chris Dodge, and Jan DeSirey "confront" it, Robert Royal demanipulates it, and Mary Ellen Jones balances opposing views. Native responses to conquest in Mexico can be found in Miguel León-Portilla's *The Broken Spears* and James Lockhart's *We People Here*, and for the modern Native American perspective see Ray González's *Without Discovery*. David J. Weber and Robert S. Weddle write histories of land (*The Spanish Frontier*) and of sea (*The Spanish Sea*), and James C. Murray surveys the chroniclers from Columbus to Acosta. Analyses of contact in Central America and the Southwest include Inga Clendinnen's *Ambivalent Conquests* (Maya); Ramón A. Gutiérrez, *When Jesus Came* (Pueblo Indians); Andrew L. Knaut, *The Pueblo Revolt of 1680*; J. M. G. Le Clézio, *The Mexican Dream* ("silencing of the Indian world" by the dream of gold); Beatriz Pastor, *The Armature of Conquest* (discourses mythifying and demythifying discovery); José Promis, *The Identity of Hispanoamerica* (a second discovery, that America is *not* Spain); José Rabasa, *Inventing America* (the formation of Eurocentrism); and Tzvetan Todorov, *The Conquest of America* (responses to the Other). For the Southeast see Jerald T. Milanich's primary materials in *Earliest Hispanic / Native American Interactions*, and Milanich and Charles Hudson on de Soto, as well as works in the French section. Anthologies of criticism include those by René Jara and Nicholas Spadaccini, Jerry M. Williams and Robert E. Lewis, María Herrera-Sobek, and Erlinda Gonzales-Berry. Rolena Adorno suggests the direction of Spanish American studies; E. Thomson Shields provides teaching resources.

French Colonial Writings and English Canada

For surveys of the history of the French presence, which is not as well known as the English or perhaps even the Spanish, see W. J. Eccles, *France in America* (1500–1783); Dale Miquelon, *The First Canada* (to 1791); and Charles J. Balesi, *The Time of the French* (1673–1818).

The history of Canada is covered in companion volumes by Marcel Trudel (1524–1663), Eccles (1663–1701), Miquelon (1701–44), and George F. G. Stanley (1744–60). Sequential pictures of history through contemporary documents are presented by Yves F. Zoltvany (1534–1810) and Joseph L. Peyser (1686–1783). Olive Patricia Dickason's *The Myth of the Savage* moves from European images of the Indians in turn to each French settlement in America. Patricia Galloway's collection *La Salle and His Legacy* focuses on the Mississippi region, while Axtell's *The Invasion Within* is "an ethnohistory of the colonial French, English, and Indian efforts to convert each other" in the Northeast. Cornelius J. Jaenen surveys the dual nature of contact with Native Americans; Bruce G. Trigger makes the Natives visible in the development of Canada. Though James T. Moore's Jesuits believed Native culture should be left intact, in contrast, Karen L. Anderson describes the "subjugation of Native women." Confrontations with the Spanish in the Southeast are studied in Paul Quattlebaum's *The Land Called Chicora* (a mythic sylvan utopia), Eugene Lyon's *The Enterprise of Florida* (the expedition of Pedro Menéndez de Avilés), Paul E. Hoffman's *A New Andalucia* (Chicora again), Weddle's *The French Thorn* (rivalry in and around the Gulf of Mexico), and Milanich's *Florida Indians and the Invasion from Europe*. Reuben Gold Thwaites's *The Jesuit Relations* collects primary material. Roberta Hamilton's study of the historiography of New France reveals four conflicting interpretations. W. H. New's *A History of Canadian Literature* and M. Brook Taylor's *Beginnings to Confederation* contain bibliographical essays, and New's *Canadian Writers before 1890* contains essays on authors. On English Canada, see Germaine Warkentin's exploration anthology, D. M. R. Bentley's *Early Long Poems*, the literary history by Carl F. Klinck et al., and the bibliography by R. G. Moyles.

English Puritanism in the Colonies

Founding studies are Perry Miller's *Errand into the Wilderness,* which formulates the Puritan mission to establish a city on a hill, and his synthesis of the "New England mind," which treats all Puritan literature "as if it were the product of a single intelligence," but for debate over

Miller's influence see Francis Butts, Arne Delfs, and Kaplan. Patrick Collinson provides a history of English Puritanism, Larzer Ziff a history of American Puritanism (*Puritanism*). Emerson presents English Puritan writings, while Miller and Thomas H. Johnson and Alan Heimert and Andrew Delbanco present the American Puritans. David Cressy's *Coming Over*, which considers remigration, for instance, and Stephen Foster's *The Long Argument*, which puts the 1630 Great Migration in the "middle" of Puritan history, link Old and New England rather than focusing on American exceptionalism. In *The Puritan Origins of the American Self* and *The American Jeremiad*, Bercovitch examines the Puritan legacy in the rhetoric of American identity. Gura's *A Glimpse of Sion's Glory* (radicals like the Baptists and Quakers), Jon Butler's *Awash in a Sea of Faith* (a complex rather than a one-dimensional religious past), Hall's *Worlds of Wonder, Days of Judgment* (the presence of popular religion), and Janice Knight's *Orthodoxies in Massachusetts* (varieties of religious experience) push beyond what are often felt to be the narrow views of Miller and the Puritan origin of America. Delbanco and Theodore Dwight Bozeman study Puritans as immigrants whose initial intensity is followed by flatness and as traditionalists who were encouraged to lead "ancient lives." Peter N. Carroll and William J. Scheick study Puritanism on the physical frontier and at "logogic" sites, that is, where secular and divine meet. Witchcraft is examined by Carol F. Karlsen, Bernard Rosenthal, and Richard Godbeer (*The Devil's Dominion*). Alfred A. Cave's *The Pequot War* considers bloody contact with the Indians; Norman S. Grabo contrasts English response to the frontier with the Spanish and French. Genre studies include Stephen Carl Arch on the histories, Daniel B. Shea on autobiography (*Spiritual Autobiography*), Patricia Caldwell on the conversion narrative, Harry S. Stout and Emory Elliott on preaching (*Power and the Pulpit*), and Jeffrey A. Hammond and Peter White on poetry. David Hackett Fischer's *Albion's Seed* describes such "folkways" as marriage, sex, work, wealth, and rank.

England's Staple Colonies

Originally, works like Richard Beale Davis's volumes helped shape the concept of "the South," but in "Literature of the Colonial South"

David S. Shields offers an alternative concept, "staple colonies" ("the southern mainland colonies from Maryland to English Florida and the West Indies"), and provides a bibliographical essay on primary material. Lewis P. Simpson and Louis B. Wright analyze the myths of and motivations for colonization in *The Dispossessed Garden* (the "garden of the chattel" not New England's "garden of the covenant") and *The Colonial Search for a Southern Eden* from Raleigh to Montgomery. See Louis D. Rubin's general *History of Southern Literature*. Major historical studies include T. H. Breen's *Tobacco Culture* (Tidewater planters before the Revolution), Rhys Isaac's *The Transformation of Virginia* (traditional ways of life, 1740–90), Allan Kulikoff's *Tobacco and Slaves* (slave society, 1680–1800), and Thad W. Tate and David L. Ammerman's *The Chesapeake in the Seventeenth Century*. In *Pursuits of Happiness* Greene sees the South epitomizing our emerging national culture rather than New England, and Fischer delineates the folkways of Virginia and Appalachia as he did for New England. J. A. Leo Lemay studies the literatures of Virginia and Maryland and suggests the need for like studies of other colonies outside New England. Alan Gallay anthologizes voices of the old South, while George C. Rogers, Anita Rutman, and James P. Whittenburg provide historiography. Moving to the West Indies, in *Main Currents in Caribbean Thought* Gordon K. Lewis studies the evolution from slavery to emancipation to independence between 1492 and 1900. Richard S. Dunn's *Sugar and Slaves* focuses on the rise of the planter class, and Michael Craton's *Testing the Chains* and Mavis C. Campbell's *The Maroons of Jamaica* focus on slave resistance. Angelo Costanzo describes abolitionist slave narratives in "African-Caribbean Narrative."

The Middle Colonies

Pennsylvania, New York, and New Jersey have not received as much attention from literary scholars as other regions. Michael Zuckerman finds that study of the "motley middle" in contrast to New England reconfigures us a plural rather than a singular people, the subject as well of studies by Sally Schwartz and by J. William Frost on toleration and liberty in Pennsylvania and of Joyce D. Goodfriend's study of

New York *Before the Melting Pot*. For Greene in *Pursuits of Happiness*, the middle colonies are one of four regions showing our "considerable diversity," and Patricia U. Bonomi sees this part of the country contributing to "the formation of our political habits." On New York and Dutch America, see Ada van Gastel's "Ethnic Pluralism in Early American Literature," Gerald De Jong's survey of early history and cultural life, Alice P. Kenney's chapter on the image of the Dutch, Ellis Lawrence Raesly's chapter on "the Muse," Roelef van Gelder's survey of Dutch accounts of New Netherland, evocations of the flavor of Dutch culture by Roderic H. Blackburn and Nancy A. Kelley and Blackburn and Ruth Piwonka, primary documents collected by J. Franklin Jameson, historiography by Goodfriend and by Jarvis M. Morse, and other studies cited by Linda Pegman Doezema. On the Quakers, Hugh Barbour and J. William Frost's *The Quakers* and Frost's *The Quaker Family* best introduce this group, which David E. Shi places at the basis of "the simple life," an alternative tradition in American life. Frederick B. Tolles surveys the history and culture of the Quakers, Gary B. Nash their engagement in politics, Jack D. Marietta their withdrawal from politics, Daniel B. Shea their spiritual autobiography, and Richard S. Dunn and Mary Maples Dunn their leader — William Penn — and his world. On Quaker antislavery see studies by Thomas E. Drake and Jean R. Soderlund, historiography by Frost, and anthologies by Frost and by Roger Bruns. Margaret Hope Bacon sees Quaker women as "the mothers of feminism" and presents the journals of three women ministers. C. A. Weslager depicts New Sweden. Albert Cook Myers collects documents about Pennsylvania, New Jersey, and Delaware, and Ammerman and Morgan provide bibliography on New York, New Jersey, and Pennsylvania.

The Enlightenment and Federalism

The republicanism of Bernard Bailyn and the liberalism of Gordon S. Wood provide basic ways to think about the eighteenth century. Roy Porter introduces the European Enlightenment; Henry F. May finds four distinct periods in the American Enlightenment. Robert A.

Ferguson provides the best introduction to the literary history of the Revolution, and Emerson surveys authors, genres, and themes of the Revolutionary years. Heimert argues that religion had more impact on the Revolution than rationality. Carl L. Becker, Garry Wills, and Pauline Maier study the Declaration. Jay Fliegelman shows declaring independence a rhetorical problem and shows the importance of coming-of-age to Revolutionary propaganda in *Prodigals and Pilgrims*. Emory Elliott in *Revolutionary Writers* considers how writers like Barlow, Freneau, Brackenridge, and Brown negotiate the shift from a religious to a nationalist vision of America, while Mark R. Patterson and Christopher Looby both focus on Franklin, Brown, Brackenridge, and the nature of the new nation. Christopher M. Duncan investigates the views of the Anti-Federalists, and Michael Lienesch finds a tension between classical and modern thinking in the formation of our "new order" between 1783 and 1800 that persists today. A special journal issue on the "Iroquois influence" thesis shows that controversy over the origin of our constitution persists too. In *Civil Tongues and Polite Letters in British America*, David S. Shields studies the nature and role of "private society" — coffee houses, clubs, salons, and tea tables. Cathy N. Davidson's *Revolution and the Word* focuses on the novel, and William C. Dowling's *Poetry and Ideology* revives the Connecticut Wits, as does John P. McWilliams's study of the epic. Kenneth Silverman covers painting, music, theater, and literature. Robert Lawson-Peebles shows disappointed nature writers reversing their edenic images, and Pamela Regis treats natural history — the "literature of place" — by Bartram, Jefferson, and Crèvecoeur. J. E. Crowley describes the rhetoric of economic activity, Thomas Gustafson the struggle for a representative language, and Michael Warner the relation between printing and republicanism. Ruth Bloch uses a millennial lens, and Ferguson recovers the law as writers' "lost context." For Ziff writing in the new nation shifts from immanence to representation. Steven Watts finds people like Brackenridge, Freneau, Rush, and Brown concerned with the "culture of capitalism" emerging between 1790 and 1820. Frank Shuffelton's *The American Enlightenment* is a critical anthology divided into the sections "Religion, Science, and the Nature of Man" and "Politics and Nation."

Poetry

León-Portilla presents fifteen poets of the Aztec world, both in English translation and the original Nahuatl; Harrison T. Meserole presents seventeenth-century american poetry; Pattie Cowell collects women poets, 1650–1775. For New England, Hammond focuses on Taylor, Wigglesworth, and Bradstreet in *Sinful Self, Saintly Self*; Peter White's *Puritan Poets and Poetics* collects essays on aesthetics, poets, and genres; and Ivy Schweitzer's *The Work on Self-Representation* is feminist. In *Oracles of Empire* David S. Shields works with British "imperial mythology" from Canada to the Caribbean, and C. D. Mazoff finds "culture shock" in some Canadian poetry. Dowling's *Poetry and Ideology* and McWilliams's *The American Epic* deal with the Connecticut Wits. For oral poetry see Andrew Wiget's *Native American Literature* and other works under the Native American section. James Ruppert's *Guide to American Poetry Explication* and *Seventeenth-Century American Poetry* by Scheick and JoElla Doggett are aids to criticism.

Prose Fiction

Davidson charts "the rise of the novel in America" through such topics as theoretical background, economics, official opposition, literacy, and sentimental, picaresque, and Gothic forms in *Revolution and the Word*. Cynthia S. Jordan finds male writers promoting a patriarchal social order in *Second Stories*. Shirley Samuels treats women, family, and violence. Analyses of Charles Brockden Brown are a substantial part of the canon questioning of Jane Tompkins's *Sensational Designs*. The dialogue between travel writing and later fiction accounts for William C. Spengemann's *The Adventurous Muse*. Jeffrey Rubin-Dorsky finds the early novel unstable and unoriginal. Patricia L. Parker's *Early American Fiction* is a critical bibliography.

Drama

Mulford "re-presents" this field separated from Puritan proscriptions and suggests new approaches. Richards takes new approaches in

Theater Enough. The traditional survey is Arthur Hobson Quinn's *A History of the American Drama*; more recent is Walter J. Meserve's *An Emerging Entertainment*; Jack A. Vaughn provides very brief descriptions of work by Hunter, Lennox, Godfrey, Warren, Leacock, Brackenridge, Tyler, Munford, and Dunlap. Focused studies are Daniel F. Havens, *The Columbian Muse of Comedy*; Jared Brown, *The Theatre in America during the Revolution*; Kent G. Gallagher, *The Foreigner in Early American Drama*; Mary Anne Schofield and Cecilia Macheski, *Curtain Calls* (on women); Eugene H. Jones, *Native Americans As Shown on the Stage*; Hugh F. Rankin, *The Theater in Colonial America* (the *theater*, not the plays); Brooks McNamara, *The American Playhouse in the Eighteenth Century*; Julian Mates, *The American Musical Stage before 1800*; and Susan L. Porter, *With an Air Debonair* (musicals). Jurgen C. Wolter lists periodical criticism from 1746 on. Amelia Howe Kritzer reprints plays by women, Norman Philbrick propaganda plays of the Revolution, and Richards reprints Tyler, Dunlap, and Barker.

Autobiography

Shea's "The Prehistory of American Autobiography" surveys the genre. His *Spiritual Autobiography* focuses on Quakers and Puritans, whereas Dana D. Nelson focuses on Franklin, Occom, Equiano, and Palou/Serra in the late eighteenth century. For Native Americans see H. David Brumble's *American Indian Autobiography*, Hertha Dawn Wong's *Sending My Heart Back across the Years*, and Arnold Krupat's *For Those Who Come After*; for African Americans see William L. Andrews's *To Tell a Free Story*. Caldwell studies the Puritan conversion narrative, G. Thomas Couser finds a "prophetic mode" in Shepard, Woolman, and Franklin; and Joseph Fichtelberg shows unity succumbing to contradiction in the same three authors. Richard D. Brown uses diaries, journals, and letters to examine the diffusion of information between 1700 and 1865. Nellie McKay's "Autobiography and the Early Novel" touches captivity and slave narratives and Native American autobiography. Steven E. Kagle studies *American Diary Literature* to 1799; Margo Culley reprints several eighteenth-century women diarists. Carol Edkins relates spiritual autobiographies by Quaker and Puritan women to the quest for community. Part of Robert F. Sayre's primary anthology, *American Lives*, covers this period. The Ronald Hoffman, Mechal Sobel, and Fredrika J. Teute anthology takes as its theme "reflections on personal identity in early America."

Captivity Narratives

A broad starting point is Kathryn Zabelle Derounian-Stodola and James Arthur Levernier's *The Indian Captivity Narrative, 1550–1900*. Other substantial studies are June Namias's *White Captives* (gender and ethnicity), Gary L. Ebersole's *Captured by Texts* (concluding with film analyses), Christopher Castiglia's *Bound and Determined* (embracing Patty Hearst), and Michelle Burnham's *Captivity and Sentiment* (ambivalent sentimental responses). Richard Slotkin sees the genre shaping the primary American myth. Studies of founding texts are Mitchell Robert Breitwieser's *American Puritanism and the Defense of Mourning* on Mary White Rowlandson and Robert S. Tilton on Pocahontas. Anthologies of primary texts are Alden T. Vaughan and Edward W. Clark's *Puritans among the Indians*, James Levernier and Hennig Cohen's *The Indians and Their Captives*, and Richard VanDer-Beets's *Held Captive by Indians*. John Demos tells the story of a captive who didn't come back.

Other Literary Forms

Daniel A. Cohen's *Pillars of Salt, Monuments of Grace* and Daniel E. Williams's *Pillars of Salt: An Anthology* deal with crime literature, a popular genre in New England. Don L. F. Nilsen's *Humor in American Literature* is a critical bibliography, W. Howland Kenney's *Laughter in the Wilderness* is an anthology of humor to 1783, and Rubin's *The Comic Imagination in American Literature* contains a broad essay on early humor and essays focusing on Franklin and the Connecticut Wits. Bruce Ingham Granger explores the satire of the Revolution, Marcia Miller sees eighteenth-century verse fables as an early but ultimately inadequate attempt to provide a national literature, and Wendy Martin collects four colonial American travel narratives.

Multicultural Studies in General

Russell J. Reising examines schools of criticism (the Puritan origin, the cultural, the self-reflexive) that narrowed the canon and constitute an "unusable past"; Donald Kartiganer and Malcolm A. Griffith provide selections from past critics now often considered negative points of reference. Conversely, Lauter in *Canons and Contexts*, A. LaVonne Brown Ruoff and Jerry W. Ward, Jr. (who "redefine" American literature as a "patchwork quilt created by many hands"), Gregory Jay (who argues for a "multicultural and dialogical paradigm"), and Kolodny (who sees the frontier decenter European design ["Letting Go"]) open the canon. African American, Native American, and Chicano perspectives on expanding the canon can be found, respectively, in Henry Louis Gates's *Loose Canons*, Krupat's *The Voice in the Margin*, and Héctor Calderón and José David Saldívar's *Criticism in the Borderlands*. Earl E. Fitz forges inter-American contexts, for instance, reading the Iroquois *Dekanawida* and Barlow's *Columbiad* in the company of the Chilean *Araucaniad*; Saldívar aims at a "transgeographical conception of American culture," identifying a "distinctive post-colonial, pan-American consciousness"; Carolyn Porter "remaps" our critical terrain to embrace Latin America and Africa. Histories of ethnic groups in America include those by Ronald Takaki and by Leonard Dinnerstein, Roger L. Nichols, and David M. Reimers; a standard reference is Stephan Thernstrom, *Harvard Encyclopedia of American Ethnic Groups*. For Nash North America between 1550 and 1750 is the "interaction" of red, white, and black; Edward Countryman's Americans are a "collision" of the same colors. In *The Word in Black and White* Nelson examines the "oppressive reduction" of diversity before the Civil War. Shuffelton's *A Mixed Race* collects essays on writers, genres, themes; Wiget puts theory into practice, reading Bradford, Pérez de Villagrá, and the Zuni creation myth against the grain. On homosexuality: Jonathan Ned Katz prints documents, Jonathan Goldberg and Richard C. Trexler deal with the Spanish, Walter L. Williams studies the Native American berdache (Will

Roscoe prints origin myths), and Michael Warner and Richard Godbeer focus on the New England "Sodom." Bennett Lovett-Graff reviews the culture wars from Allan Bloom and E. D. Hirsch through
Graff's "teaching the conflicts." Werner Sollors studies ethnicity, David A. Hollinger postethnicity. Arthur M. Schlesinger warns of "the
disuniting of America" if the cult of ethnicity replaces the melting pot
(Philip Gleason charts the evolution of this mythic image), and Hershel Parker questions the "price of diversity." Trevor Burnard points
to indifference to ethnicity in colonial historiography. On teaching
see Mulford's "Recovering the Colonial," John Alberti's *The Canon in
the Classroom*, and Betty E. M. Ch'maj's *Multicultural America*.

Native American Studies

Bruce G. Trigger and Wilcomb E. Washburn's *North America* is a
comprehensive historical survey. Alvin M. Josephy focuses on Native
cultures before Columbus. Pre-Columbian Caribbean cultures are
found in William F. Keegan, *The People Who Discovered Columbus*;
Irving Rouse, *The Tainos*; and Antonio M. Stevens-Arroyo, *Cave of
the Jagua*. Pre-Cortes Aztec and Maya cultures are found in Clendinnen's *Aztecs* and León-Portilla's *The Aztec Image of Self and Society* and
Pre-Columbian Literatures of Mexico. Peggy V. Beck, Anna Lee Walters,
and Nia Francisco present religious beliefs Native Americans hold in
common in *The Sacred*, and Christopher Vecsey studies the life cycle
of myths from emergence through civil society to death, drawing on
a different culture and region for each stage. On oral literature, see
Ruoff's *American Indian Literatures*, which contains an extensive
bibliography, Wiget's *Native American Literature*, Dennis Tedlock's
The Spoken Word, and Paul G. Zolbrod's *Reading the Voice*. Anthologies of primary material include Frederick W. Turner's *The Portable
North American Indian Reader*, Steven Mintz's *Native American Voices*,
Colin G. Calloway's *The World Turned Upside Down*, Richard Erdoes
and Alfonso Ortiz's *American Indian Myths and Legends*, and Brian
Swann's *Coming to Light*. Helen Jaskoski collects criticism on authors
from 1630 to 1940 in *Early Native American Writing*. Native American Donald A. Grinde's "Teaching American Indian History" positions such scholars as Takaki, Kupperman, Francis Jennings, Axtell,

William Cronon, Calvin Martin, Daniel Richter, Grinde himself, and others. Frederick E. Hoxie's *Indians in American History* provides "the Indian side" as well. Influential terms are Roy Harvey Pearce's "savagism and civilization," James Merrell's "New World," and Richard White's "Middle Ground." By region, see Jennings, *The Invasion of America* (New England); Charles Hudson and Carmen Chaves Tesser, *The Forgotten Centuries* (the South); Milanich, *Florida Indians*; Elizabeth A. H. John, *Storms Brewed in Other Men's Worlds* (the Southwest); Dickason, *Canada's First Nations*; and Peter Hulme and Neil L. Whitehead, *Wild Majesty* (the Caribbean). Robert F. Berkhofer's *The White Man's Indian*, Richard Drinnon's *Facing West*, and Benjamin Keen's *The Aztec Image in Western Thought* concern the image of the Native American. Tompkins shows how complicated understanding the term *Indians* is by looking at Native Americans from the differing perspectives of critics like Miller, Jennings, and Axtell, as well as firsthand accounts by Rowlandson and Wood. Jeanne Holland, Wiget, Paula Gunn Allen (*Studies*), and Greg Sarris give teaching suggestions. Richter's "Whose Indian History?" is a bibliographical essay by a historian. Mintz provides an extensive bibliography categorized by period, region, peoples, and topic. Frederick E. Hoxie and Harvey Markowitz's *Native Americans* is an annotated bibliography.

African American Studies

David Brion Davis's books on "the problem of slavery" trace tensions from Old World to New, and Winthrop D. Jordan's *White over Black* sees four racial attitudes in the New World from 1550 to 1812. In *Africa and Africans* John Kelly Thornton looks at Africa's role in trading and contributions to American culture, and regional studies include Edmund S. Morgan's *American Slavery, American Freedom* (Virginia, Jefferson's home) and Peter H. Wood's *Black Majority* (South Carolina, the largest slaveholder by the Civil War). The slaveholder's viewpoint is the subject of Larry E. Tise's *Proslavery* and Eric L. McKitrick's *Slavery Defended*; Frost (*Quaker Origins*) and Bruns collect antislavery materials; and William Dudley's *Slavery* pits voices on both sides. Gerald W. Mullin writes about slave resistance, Mechal Sobel about the world black and white made together. Albert J. Raboteau describes slave religion; James Oliver Horton and Lois E. Horton describe northern blacks building community. The African American is builder not victim in William D. Piersen's history of Spanish, French, and English territory from 1526 to 1790. Early chapters of Blyden Jackson's literary history move from Lucy Terry to David Walker. Jon F. Sensbach's bibliographical essay charts a course forward. The special journal issue on African American culture by Rose Zimbardo and Benilde Montgomery contains Rosalie Murphy Baum's survey essay, "Early-American Literature: Reassessing the Black Contribution." Donald R. Wright's two books provide historical background with, like Peter J. Parish's *Slavery*, extensive bibliography. Adam Potkay and Sandra Burr print four and Vincent Carretta prints sixteen eighteenth-century black writers; Dorothy Porter's large collection *Early Negro Writing* extends into the nineteenth century. In Philip D. Curtin's collection slaves remember Africa.

Women's Studies

Harris's anthology of primary material provides an introductory survey of the "geographic, racial, class, thematic, generic, and aesthetic diversity" of American women writers to 1800. Allen's *The Sacred Hoop* begins in Native American gynocracy. Julie Greer Johnson's *Women in Colonial Spanish American Literature* surveys images by male and female authors; Sandra Messinger Cypess's *La Malinche in Mexican Literature* focuses on the controversial role of Cortés's mistress; Stephanie Merrim's *Feminist Perspectives on Sor Juana* explores this "First Feminist of the New World"; and José E. Limón brings together the three great symbols of Mexican women — Our Lady of Guadalupe, Malinche, and La Llorona. Joyce Marshall edits the letters of New France's Marie de l'Incarnation; Anderson analyzes the fetters on New France's Native women. Laurel Thatcher Ulrich discusses ordinary New England women through biblical images in *Good Wives*, Amanda Porterfield the emergence of religious humanism in *Female Piety in Puritan New England*, Karlsen why most New

England witches were women, Elaine G. Breslaw how an Indian witch fueled Puritan fantasies, and Anne Hutchinson is Amy Schrager Lang's "prophetic woman." Such eighteenth-century constructions as separate spheres, the republican mother, and the republican wife are discussed in Nancy F. Cott's *The Bonds of Womanhood*, Linda Kerber's *Women of the Republic*, Jan Lewis's "The Republican Wife," and Mary Beth Norton's *Liberty's Daughters*. In *Founding Mothers and Fathers* Norton traces the tension between Filmerian and Lockean views of women's power inside and outside of the family. Ronald Hoffman and Peter J. Albert focus on the Revolution, while Larry Eldridge investigates the freedom of women of all colors between 1400 and 1800. Davidson relates the sentimental and picaresque novels especially to women's lives in *Revolution and the Word*. Diaries and letters reveal the frontier potential for "idealized domesticity" to Kolodny in *The Land before Her*. Kathleen M. Brown's "Brave New Worlds" is a bibliographical essay from a historian. Eugenie Andruss Leonard, Sophie Hutchinson Drinker, and Miriam Young Holden cite over one thousand items, broken down into ten major categories and over one hundred subcategories, including "104 Outstanding Colonial Women." William L. Andrews et al. collect the narratives of four women on physical or spiritual journeys. Paula A. Treckel, Carol Berkin, and Joan R. Gundersen describe the lives of seventeenth- and eighteenth-century women, all with bibliographic essays. See also the above section on captivity narratives, a genre especially pertinent to women's studies.

Art

James T. Flexner's *American Painting* is a basic survey of American art; for specific genres see Wayne Craven and Richard H. Saunders and Ellen G. Miles (portraiture) and Edward J. Nygren and Bruce Robertson (landscape). Craven's *American Art* treats painting, sculpture, and architecture together; Charles F. Montgomery and Patricia E. Kane cover art moving "towards independence." For European images of America, see Hugh Honour and Rachel Doggett. Stefan Lorant's *The New World* contains "first pictures" by John White and

Jacques Le Moyne. Paul Hulton presents the complete White. Fredi Chiappelli's *First Images of America* contains essays on images in the arts. Theodore De Bry is the subject of Bernadette Bucher's *Icon and Conquest*, Michael Alexander's *Discovering the New World*, and Tom Conley's "De Bry's Las Casas." Exploration, conquest, and Native American life are well represented in William H. Truettner's collection of nineteenth-century art. For African Americans, see Guy C. McElroy's *Facing History* and Barbara E. Lacey's "Visual Images of Blacks in Early American Imprints." Ellwood Parry deals with both African and Native Americans. Ralph T. Coe presents two thousand years of Native American art. John F. Moffitt and Santiago Sebastián's *O Brave New People* describes "the European invention" of the Indian. See Ammerman and Morgan for bibliography.

Music

Priscilla S. Heard lists all the music books printed in America from 1698 to 1800. General surveys include Charles Hamm, *Music in the New World*; W. Thomas Marrocco and Harold Gleason, *Music in America*; Gilbert Chase, *America's Music*; H. Wiley Hitchcock, *Music in the United States*; Daniel Kingman, *American Music*. Hamm's work is keyed to the *Recorded Anthology of American Music* by New World Records (see also the index by Elizabeth A. Davis), though recordings, now numbering about 250, have been added since publication. Kingman's work has topic bibliographies and is keyed to recordings by New World, the Music in America series of the Society for the Preservation of the American Musical Heritage, Smithsonian/ Folkways, the Library of Congress Archive of American Folk Song, and others. Specific studies include Patricia H. Virga, *The American Opera to 1790*; Dena J. Epstein, *Sinful Tunes and Spirituals* (African American); David P. McAllester, "North American Native Music"; Mates and Susan Porter on musical theater; and Silverman on the Revolutionary period. Jane Girdham describes a course in musical life in the late eighteenth century. For bibliography see Ammerman and Morgan, James R. Heintze's *Early American Music*, David Horn's *The Literature of American Music*, Thomas E. Warner's *Periodical Literature on American Music*, Terry E. Miller's *Folk Music in America*, and D. W. Krummel's *Bibliographical Handbook of American Music*.

History of the Book

Hall's several essays, such as "The Uses of Literacy in New England, 1600–1850" introducing William L. Joyce et al.'s *Printing and Society in Early America*, and his *Cultures of Print* frame the History of the Book project in America. Davidson's *Reading in America* has essays on gender and literacy, chapbooks, and Republican literature, and Peter Dzwonkoski surveys American literary publishing houses. Standard references are Hellmut Lehmann-Haupt, Lawrence C. Wroth, and Rollo G. Silver, *The Book in America*, Joseph Blumenthal, *The Printed Book in America*, and Stephen C. Mohler, "Publishing in Colonial Spanish America." Kevin J. Hayes describes a colonial woman's bookshelf, Leona M. Hudak women printers and publishers. Lawrence A. Cremin and Axtell analyze education, whereas David H. Watters shows the indoctrinating power of *The New-England Primer* and Marion Barber Stowell the combination of useful information and literary entertainment in almanacs. Kenneth A. Lockridge describes literacy in New England, Edwin Wolf II book culture in Philadelphia. Robert D. Arner studies Thomas Dobson, the man "responsible for America's first comprehensive encyclopedia." Ammerman and Morgan provide a bibliography on the book trade and printing.

Material Culture

Thomas J. Schlereth charts the history of this field from 1876 to 1976. *Of Consuming Interest*, by Cary Carson, Ronald Hoffman, and Peter J. Albert, contains essays on such topics as consumer behavior, houses, shopping, advertising, fashion, theater, books, tourism, sport, leisure. See also Ann Smart Martin's special journal issue on material culture in early America. This field ranges from the study of styles of death, such as Allan I. Ludwig's *Graven Images* on New England tombstones, to living in style, such as Richard L. Bushman's discovery that the "refinement of America" began in 1690. See Ammerman and Morgan for bibliography.

Feature Films

The classic Columbus was *Christopher Columbus* (1949) until the quincentennial brought *1492: The Conquest of Paradise* and *Christopher Columbus — The Discovery*. Set in Spanish contact zones are *The Royal Hunt of the Sun* (1969), *Aguirre: The Wrath of God* (1972), *Quilombo* (1986), *The Mission* (1986), and *Cabeza de Vaca* (1993); set in French contact zones are *Ikwe* (1987) and *The Black Robe* (1991). *Forbidden Planet* (1956), *Tempest* (1982), and *Prospero's Books* (1991) are versions of Shakespeare's *The Tempest* (1979). *Squanto* (1994) and *Pocahontas* (1995) re-create our dream of coexistence. *The Plymouth Adventure* (1952) won an Academy Award for best special effects. Hawthorne's anatomy of Puritan New England in *The Scarlet Letter* has versions from Lillian Gish (1926) to Demi Moore (1995). Witchcraft is the subject of *Three Sovereigns for Sarah* (1985), *Love at Stake* (1988), and *The Crucible* (1996). Our pre-Revolutionary and Revolutionary wars are pictured in *America* (1924), *The Last of the Mohicans* (especially 1920 and 1992), *Drums along the Mohawk* (1939), *Allegheny Uprising* (1939), *Northwest Passage* (1940), *Howards of Virginia* (1940), *Johnny Tremaine* (1957), and *Revolution* (1985). *1776* (1972) and *Jefferson in Paris* (1995) portray the founding fathers. *Daniel Boone* (1936) celebrates the hero who opened "the West," and westering is also the subject of *Across the Wide Missouri* (1951). *Captain Blood* (1935) is a classic swashbuckler; *The Sea Hawk* (1940) plays on the "Black Legend." Slavery is the subject of *Roots* (1977), *The Last Supper* (1976), and *Sankofa* (1993). *The Searchers* (1956), *A Man Called Horse* (1970), *Little Big Man* (1970), and *Dances with Wolves* (1990) are captivity narratives.

Film Documentaries and Docudramas

See *The Land of the Eagle* (1991) for the natural world before contact. See *Lost in Time* (1990) for Native Americans in the precontact

Southeast, *The First Frontier* (1989) for the period 1540–1814, *Five Hundred Nations* (1995) for cultures before Columbus, and *Native Americans* (1994) for cultures by region. *Popol Vuh* (1988) is the Mayan creation story, and *Lost Kingdoms of the Maya* (1993) explores history and architecture AD 200–900. *Sacred Ground* (1977) examines Native American attachment to the earth and *More Than Bows and Arrows* (1985) contributions in such areas as mining, irrigation, and medicine. *The Buried Mirror* (1991) is a history of the Spanish in Mexico. *Surviving Columbus* (1990) and *Pueblo Peoples* (1991) describe conquest from the Native American perspective. *Columbus Didn't Discover Us* (1992) is a modern Native American view of continuing negative consequences. *The West* (1996) and *The Journals of Lewis and Clark* (1989), and *Lewis and Clark: The Journey of the Corps of Discovery* (1997) deal with expansion into the American "west." *Roanoak* (1986), *Pocahontas — Her True Story* (1992), *Pocahontas* (1997), and *Thomas Jefferson* (1997) are Virginia-based, *A Midwife's Tale* (1997) New England-based. *Dark Passages* (1990) and *A Son of Africa: The Slave Narrative of Olaudah Equiano* (1996) depict the slave trade, and *Days of Judgment* (1993) explores Salem witchcraft. *Mary Silliman's War* (1994) concerns the Revolutionary War.

CD-ROMS

The *Catalogue of Early American Imprints, 1640–1800* indexes all books printed in America during that time; the *Pennsylvania Gazette* is an eighteenth-century newspaper; *The Performing Arts in Colonial American Newspapers, 1690–1783* indexes and provides full text on thousands of items relating to music, dance, theater, songs, and lyrics. For Native Americans before Columbus, see *Five Hundred Nations* (1995), for witchcraft *The Crucible* (1995), for art *The National Portrait Gallery* and *American Art from the National Gallery*.

Other Resources

Organizations. Perhaps most important for general study are the Society of Early Americanists and the Omohundro Institute of Early

American History and Culture. Other pertinent organizations are the American Society for Eighteenth-Century Studies, the Society of Historians of the Early American Republic (1789–1848), the McNeil Center for Early American Studies, the Roanoke Colonies Research Office, the New Netherland Project, and the Society for the History of Discoveries.

Electronic Discussion Lists. To subscribe, send the following messages without quotation marks: for Earam-L (Society of Early Americanists), "Subscribe Earam-L [your full name]" to listserv@listserv. kent.edu; for H-shear (Society of Historians of the Early American Republic), "Get H-shear apply" to listserv@ksuvm.ksu.edu; for H-oieahcnet (Omohundro Institute of Early American History and Culture), "Sub H-oieahcnet [first name, surname, school]" to listserv @h-net.msu.edu; for Spanbord (Spanish Borders), "Sub Spanbord [your name]" to listserv@asu.edu. Or search the Web for these organizations using your Web browser, and sign up using their home page.

Web Sites. The Society of Early Americanists' Web site (http:// www.hnet.uci.edu/mclark/seapage.htm) maintained by Michael P. Clark is literally the home page for the field at this time. It contains membership information and pages on announcements, events, texts and images, teaching, dissertations, recent and forthcoming publications, journals, and, of significant value, links to many other Web sites where scholars in the field can find useful information on such things as scholarly organizations, museums, historical sites, libraries, online texts, bibliographies, syllabi, and online journals. See also the Web site of the Omohundro Institute of Early American History and Culture (http://www.h-net.msu.edu/~ieahcweb/). Michael Clark's *Cultural Treasures of the Internet* provides information for new users and locates many sites of general interest.

Note

In addition to the contributors to this volume, the following people made helpful suggestions, mainly over Earam-L, the early American internet discussion list, about the contents of this guide: Robert Arner, Martha Bartter, Susan Brill, Michelle Burnham, Sargent Bush, Raoul Camus, William H. Carter, J. Bunker Clark, Michael P. Clark, M. Sam

Cronk, David Curtis, Robert Daly, Thomas M. Davis, Cornelia Dayton, James Dillon, Jane Donahue Eberwein, Charles Gehring, Judith Gray, Edward Griffin, Rosemary Guruswamy, Leah Halper, David Hildebrand, Eric Hinderaker, Jeanne Holland, Myra Jehlen, James C. Keil, Jane Merritt, Tom Nagy, Timothy Nitz, Ron Pen, Arnold Penland, Katherine Preston, John Saillant, James J. Schramer, William Shade, James Sidbury, David Sloan, Jean Soderlund, Timothy Sweet, Angela Vietto, D. E. Vitale, Edward S. Watts, and Larry Worster. Special thanks at Lehigh University to Harold William Halbert for his sharp editing eye and healthy reader instincts, to the librarians Roseann Bowerman and Kathe Morrow, and to the cheerfully indefatigable interlibrary loan staff: William Fincke, Gayle Nemeth, Barbara Parenti, Evelyn Rivas, Jody Schmell, and Patricia Ward.

Works Cited

Adorno, Rolena. "New Perspectives in Colonial Spanish American Literary Studies." *Journal of the Southwest* 32.2 (1990): 173–91.

Alberti, John, ed. *The Canon in the Classroom: The Pedagogical Implications of Canon Revision in American Literature*. New York: Garland, 1995.

Alexander, Michael, ed. *Discovering the New World, Based on the Works of Theodore de Bry*. New York: Harper, 1976.

Allen, Paula Gunn. *The Sacred Hoop: Recovering the Feminine in American Indian Traditions*. Boston: Beacon, 1986.

———, ed. *Studies in American Indian Literature: Critical Essays and Course Designs*. New York: MLA, 1983.

Ammerman, David L., and Philip D. Morgan. *Books about Early America: Two Thousand and One Titles*. Williamsburg: Inst. of Early Amer. History and Culture, 1989.

Anderson, Karen L. *Chain Her by One Foot: The Subjugation of Native Women in Seventeenth-Century New France*. New York: Routledge, 1991.

Andrews, William L. *To Tell a Free Story: The First Century of Afro-American Autobiography, 1760–1865*. Urbana: U of Illinois P, 1986.

Andrews, William L., et al., eds. *Journeys in New Worlds: Early American Women's Narratives*. Madison: U of Wisconsin P, 1990.

Appleby, Joyce. "A Different Kind of Independence: The Postwar Restructuring of the Historical Study of Early America." *William and Mary Quarterly* 50 (1993): 245–67.

Arch, Stephen Carl. *Authorizing the Past: The Rhetoric of History in Seventeenth-Century New England*. De Kalb: Northern Illinois UP, 1994.

Arciniegas, German. *America in Europe: A History of the New World in Reverse*. San Diego: Harcourt, 1986.

Arner, Robert D. *Dobson's Encyclopaedia: The Publisher, Text, and Publication of America's First Britannica, 1789–1803*. Philadelphia: U of Pennsylvania P, 1991.

Axtell, James. *After Columbus: Essays in the Ethnohistory of Colonial North America*. New York: Oxford UP, 1988.

———. "Columbian Encounters: Beyond 1992." *William and Mary Quarterly* 49 (1992): 335–60.

———. "Columbian Encounters: 1992–1995." *William and Mary Quarterly* 52 (1995): 649–96.

———. *The Invasion Within: The Contest of Cultures in Colonial North America*. New York: Oxford UP, 1985.

———. "Moral Reflections on the Columbian Legacy." *Beyond 1492: Encounters in Colonial North America*. New York: Oxford UP, 1992. 241–66.

———. *The School upon a Hill: Education and Society in Colonial New England*. New Haven: Yale UP, 1974.

Bacon, Margaret Hope. *Mothers of Feminism: The Story of Quaker Women in America*. 2nd ed. San Francisco: Harper, 1986.

———, ed. *Wilt Thou Go on My Errand? Three Eighteenth-Century Journals of Quaker Women Ministers*. Wallingford: Pendle Hill, 1994.

Bailyn, Bernard. *The Ideological Origins of the American Revolution*. Cambridge: Harvard UP, 1967.

Balesi, Charles J. *The Time of the French in the Heart of North America, 1673–1818*. Chicago: Alliance Française Chicago, 1992.

Barbour, Hugh, and J. William Frost. *The Quakers*. Westport: Greenwood, 1988.

Barclay, Donald A., James H. Maguire, and Peter Wild, eds. *Into the Wilderness Dream: Exploration Narratives of the American West, 1500–1805*. Salt Lake City: U of Utah P, 1994.

Baritz, Loren. "The Idea of the West." *American Historical Review* 66 (1961): 618–40.

Baum, Rosalie Murphy. "Early-American Literature: Reassessing the Black Contribution." *Eighteenth-Century Studies* 27 (1994): 533–50.

Baym, Nina. "Early Histories of American Literature: A Chapter in the Institution of New England." *American Literary History* 1 (1989): 459–88.

Baym, Nina, et al., eds. *The Norton Anthology of American Literature*. 4th ed. New York: Norton, 1995.

Beck, Peggy V., Anna Lee Walters, and Nia Francisco, eds. *The Sacred: Ways of Knowledge, Sources of Life*. 1977. Tsaile: Navajo Community Coll. P, 1995.

Becker, Carl L. *The Declaration of Independence: A Study in the History of Political Ideas*. New York: Knopf, 1942.

Bentley, D. M. R., ed. *Early Long Poems on Canada*. London, ON: Canadian Poetry, 1993.

Bercovitch, Sacvan. *The American Jeremiad*. Madison: U of Wisconsin P, 1978.

———, gen. ed. *The Cambridge History of American Literature*. Vol. 1: *1590–1820*. New York: Cambridge UP, 1994.

———. *The Puritan Origins of the American Self*. New Haven: Yale UP, 1975.

Berkhofer, Robert F. *The White Man's Indian: Images of the American Indian from Columbus to the Present*. New York: Vintage, 1979.

Berkin, Carol. *First Generations: Women in Colonial America*. New York: Hill, 1996.

Bethell, Leslie, ed. *The Cambridge History of Latin America*. 2nd ed. Cambridge: Cambridge UP, 1995.

Blackburn, Roderic H., and Nancy A. Kelley. *New World Dutch Studies: Dutch Arts and Culture in Colonial America, 1609–1776*. Albany: Albany Inst. of History and Art, 1987.

Blackburn, Roderic H., and Ruth Piwonka. *Remembrance of Patria: Dutch Arts and Culture in Colonial America, 1609–1776*. Albany: Albany Inst. of History and Art, 1988.

Bloch, Ruth. *Visionary Republic: Millennial Themes in American Thought, 1756–1800*. New York: Cambridge UP, 1985.

Blumenthal, Joseph. *The Printed Book in America*. Boston: Godine, 1977.

Bonomi, Patricia U. "The Middle Colonies: Embryo of the New Political Order." *Perspectives on Early American History*. Ed. Alden T. Vaughan and George Athan Billias. New York: Harper, 1973. 63–92.

Bozeman, Theodore Dwight. *To Live Ancient Lives: The Primitivist Dimension in Puritanism*. Chapel Hill: U of North Carolina P, 1988.

Brandon, William. *New Worlds for Old: Reports from the New World and Their Effect on the Development of Social Thought in Europe, 1500–1800*. Athens: Ohio UP, 1986.

Breen, T. H. *Tobacco Culture: The Mentality of the Great Tidewater Planters on the Eve of Revolution*. Princeton: Princeton UP, 1985.

Breitwieser, Mitchell Robert. *American Puritanism and the Defense of Mourning: Religion, Grief, and Ethnology in Mary White Rowlandson's Captivity Narrative*. Madison: U of Wisconsin P, 1990.

Breslaw, Elaine G. *Tituba, Reluctant Witch of Salem: Devilish Indians and Puritan Fantasies*. New York: New York UP, 1996.

Brown, Jared. *The Theatre in America during the Revolution*. New York: Cambridge UP, 1995.

Brown, Kathleen M. "Brave New Worlds: Women's and Gender History." *William and Mary Quarterly* 50 (1993): 311–28.

Brown, Richard D. *Knowledge Is Power: The Diffusion of Information in Early America, 1700–1865*. New York: Oxford UP, 1989.

Brumble, H. David, III. *American Indian Autobiography*. Berkeley: U of California P, 1988.

Bruns, Roger, ed. *Am I Not a Man and a Brother: The Antislavery Crusade of Revolutionary America, 1688–1788*. New York: Chelsea, 1977.

Bucher, Bernadette. *Icon and Conquest: A Structural Analysis of the Illustrations of de Bry's Great Voyages*. Chicago: U of Chicago P, 1981.

Burnard, Trevor. "Ethnicity in Colonial Historiography: A New Organising Principle?" *Australasian Journal of American Studies* 11.1 (1992): 1–14.

Burnham, Michelle. *Captivity and Sentiment: Cultural Exchange in American Literature, 1682–1861*. Hanover: UP of New England, 1997.

Bushman, Richard L. *The Refinement of America: Persons, Houses, Cities.* New York: Knopf, 1992.

Butler, Jon. *Awash in a Sea of Faith: Christianizing the American People.* Cambridge: Harvard UP, 1990.

Butts, Francis. "The Myth of Perry Miller." *American Historical Review* 87 (1982): 665–94.

Calderón, Héctor, and José David Saldívar, eds. *Criticism in the Borderlands: Studies in Chicano Literature, Culture, and Ideology.* Durham: Duke UP, 1991.

Caldwell, Patricia. *The Puritan Conversion Narrative: The Beginnings of American Expression.* New York: Cambridge UP, 1983.

Calloway, Colin G., ed. *The World Turned Upside Down: Indian Voices from Early America.* New York: Bedford–St. Martin's, 1994.

Campbell, Mary B. *The Witness and the Other World: Exotic European Travel Writing, 400–1600.* Ithaca: Cornell UP, 1988.

Campbell, Mavis C. *The Maroons of Jamaica, 1655–1796: A History of Resistance, Collaboration, and Betrayal.* Granby: Bergin, 1988.

Carafiol, Peter. *The American Ideal: Literary History as a Worldly Activity.* New York: Oxford UP, 1991.

Carretta, Vincent, ed. *Unchained Voices: An Anthology of Black Authors in the English-Speaking World of the Eighteenth Century.* Lexington: UP of Kentucky, 1996.

Carroll, Peter N. *Puritanism and the Wilderness: The Intellectual Significance of the New England Frontier, 1629–1700.* New York: Columbia UP, 1969.

Carson, Cary, Ronald Hoffman, and Peter J. Albert, eds. *Of Consuming Interests: The Style of Life in the Eighteenth Century.* Charlottesville: UP of Virginia, 1994.

Castiglia, Christopher. *Bound and Determined: Captivity, Culture-Crossing, and White Womanhood from Mary Rowlandson to Patty Hearst.* Chicago: U of Chicago P, 1996.

Cave, Alfred A. *The Pequot War.* Amherst: U of Massachusetts P, 1996.

Chase, Gilbert. *America's Music: From the Pilgrims to the Present.* New York: McGraw, 1955.

Cheyfitz, Eric. *The Poetics of Imperialism: Translation and Colonization from* The Tempest *to* Tarzan. 2nd ed. New York: Oxford UP, 1997.

Chiappelli, Fredi, ed. *First Images of America: The Impact of the New World on the Old.* Berkeley: U of California P, 1976.

Ch'maj, Betty E. M., ed. *Multicultural America: A Resource Book for Teachers of Humanities and American Studies.* Lanham: UP of America, 1993.

Clark, Michael. *Cultural Treasures of the Internet.* Upper Saddle River: Prentice, 1995.

Clendinnen, Inga. *Ambivalent Conquests: Maya and Spaniard in Yucatan, 1517–1570.* New York: Cambridge UP, 1987.

———. *Aztecs: An Interpretation.* New York: Cambridge UP, 1991.

Coe, Ralph T. *Sacred Circles: Two Thousand Years of North American Indian Art.* London: Arts Council of Great Britain, 1976.

Cohen, Daniel A. *Pillars of Salt, Monuments of Grace: New England Crime Literature and the Origins of American Popular Culture, 1674–1860*. New York: Oxford UP, 1993.

Collinson, Patrick. *The Elizabethan Puritan Movement*. Berkeley: U of California P, 1967.

Conley, Tom. "De Bry's Las Casas." Jara and Spadaccini, *Amerindian Images* 103–31.

Costanzo, Angelo. "African-Caribbean Narrative of British America." *Resources for American Literary Study* 19.2 (1993): 260–74.

Cott, Nancy F. *The Bonds of Womanhood: "Woman's Sphere" in New England, 1780–1835*. New Haven: Yale UP, 1977.

Countryman, Edward. *Americans: A Collision of Histories*. New York: Hill, 1996.

Couser, G. Thomas. *American Autobiography: The Prophetic Mode*. Amherst: U of Massachusetts P, 1979.

Cowell, Pattie, ed. *Women Poets in Pre-Revolutionary America, 1650–1775: An Anthology*. Troy: Whitston, 1981.

Craton, Michael. *Testing the Chains: Resistance to Slavery in the British West Indies*. Ithaca: Cornell UP, 1982.

Craven, Wayne. *American Art: History and Culture*. New York: Abrams, 1994.

———. *Colonial American Portraiture: The Economic, Religious, Social, Philosophical, Scientific, and Aesthetic Foundations*. New York: Cambridge UP, 1986.

Cremin, Lawrence A. *American Education: The Colonial Experience, 1607–1783*. New York: Harper, 1970.

Cressy, David. *Coming Over: Migration and Communication between England and New England in the Seventeenth Century*. New York: Cambridge UP, 1987.

Cronon, William. *Changes in the Land: Indians, Colonists, and the Ecology of New England*. New York: Hill, 1983.

Crowley, J. E. *This Sheba, Self: The Conceptualization of Economic Life in Eighteenth-Century America*. Baltimore: Johns Hopkins UP, 1974.

Culley, Margo, ed. *A Day at a Time: The Diary Literature of American Women from 1764 to the Present*. New York: Feminist, 1985.

Curtin, Philip D., ed. *Africa Remembered: Narratives by West Africans from the Era of the Slave Trade*. Madison: U of Wisconsin P, 1967.

Cypess, Sandra Messinger. *La Malinche in Mexican Literature: From History to Myth*. Austin: U of Texas P, 1991.

Davidson, Cathy N., ed. *Reading in America: Literature and Social History*. Baltimore: Johns Hopkins UP, 1989.

———. *Revolution and the Word: The Rise of the Novel in America*. New York: Oxford UP, 1986.

Davis, David Brion. *The Problem of Slavery in the Age of Revolution, 1770–1823*. Ithaca: Cornell UP, 1975.

———. *The Problem of Slavery in Western Culture*. Ithaca: Cornell UP, 1966.

Davis, Elizabeth A. *Index to the* New World Recorded Anthology of American Music: *A User's Guide to the Initial One Hundred Records.* New York: Norton, 1981.

Davis, Richard Beale. *Intellectual Life in Jefferson's Virginia, 1790–1830.* Chapel Hill: U of North Carolina P, 1964.

———. *Intellectual Life in the Colonial South, 1585–1763.* Knoxville: U of Tennessee P, 1978.

———. *Literature and Society in Early Virginia, 1608–1840.* Baton Rouge: Louisiana State UP, 1973.

De Jong, Gerald F. *The Dutch in America, 1609–1974.* Boston: Twayne, 1975.

Delbanco, Andrew. *The Puritan Ordeal.* Cambridge: Harvard UP, 1989.

Delfs, Arne. "Anxieties of Influence: Perry Miller and Sacvan Bercovitch." *New England Quarterly* 70 (1997): 601–15.

De Prospo, R. C. "Marginalizing Early American Literature." *New Literary History* 23.2 (1992): 233–65.

De Vorsey, Louis, Jr. *Keys to the Encounter: A Library of Congress Resource Guide for the Study of the Age of Discovery.* Washington: Lib. of Congress, 1992.

Demos, John. *The Unredeemed Captive: A Family Story from Early America.* New York: Knopf, 1994.

Derounian-Stodola, Kathryn Zabelle, and James Arthur Levernier. *The Indian Captivity Narrative, 1550–1900.* New York: Twayne, 1993.

Dickason, Olive Patricia. *Canada's First Nations: A History of Founding Peoples from Earliest Times.* Norman: U of Oklahoma P, 1992.

———. *The Myth of the Savage and the Beginnings of French Colonialism in the Americas.* Edmonton: U of Alberta P, 1984.

Dinnerstein, Leonard, Roger L. Nichols, and David M. Reimers. *Natives and Strangers: Ethnic Groups and the Building of America.* 1979. New York: Oxford UP, 1996.

Doezema, Linda Pegman. *Dutch Americans: A Guide to Information Sources.* Detroit: Gale, 1979.

Doggett, Rachel, ed. *New World of Wonders: European Images of the Americas, 1492–1700.* Washington: Folger Shakespeare Lib., 1992.

Dowling, William C. *Poetry and Ideology in Revolutionary Connecticut.* Athens: U of Georgia P, 1990.

Drake, Thomas E. *Quakers and Slavery in America.* New Haven: Yale UP, 1950.

Drinnon, Richard. *Facing West: The Metaphysics of Indian-Hating and Empire-Building.* Minneapolis: U of Minnesota P, 1980.

Dudley, William, ed. *Slavery: Opposing Viewpoints.* San Diego: Greenhaven, 1992.

Duncan, Christopher M. *The Anti-Federalists and Early American Political Thought.* De Kalb: Northern Illinois UP, 1995.

Dunn, Richard S. *Sugar and Slaves: The Rise of the Planter Class in the English West Indies, 1624–1713.* Chapel Hill: U of North Carolina P, 1972.

Dunn, Richard S., and Mary Maples Dunn, eds. *The World of William Penn*. Philadelphia: U of Pennsylvania P, 1986.

Dzwonkoski, Peter, ed. *American Literary Publishing Houses, 1638–1899*. Dictionary of Lit. Biography 49. Detroit: Gale, 1986.

Ebersole, Gary L. *Captured by Texts: Puritan to Postmodern Images of Indian Captivity*. Charlottesville: UP of Virginia, 1995.

Eccles, W. J. *Canada under Louis XIV, 1663–1701*. Canadian Centenary ser. Toronto: McClelland, 1964.

———. *France in America*. 1972. East Lansing: Michigan State UP, 1990.

Echeverria, Durand. *Mirage in the West: A History of the French Image of American Society to 1815*. Princeton: Princeton UP, 1957.

Edkins, Carol. "Quest for Community: Spiritual Autobiographies of Eighteenth-Century Quaker and Puritan Women in America." *Women's Autobiography: Essays in Criticism*. Ed. Estelle C. Jelinek. Bloomington: U of Indiana P, 1980. 39–52.

Eldridge, Larry. *Women and Freedom in Early America*. New York: New York UP, 1997.

Elliott, Emory, ed. *American Colonial Writers, 1735–1781*. Vol. 31 of *Dictionary of Literary Biography*. Detroit: Gale, 1984.

———, ed. *American Colonial Writers, 1606–1734*. Vol. 24 of *Dictionary of Literary Biography*. Detroit: Gale, 1984.

———, ed. *American Writers of the Early Republic*. Vol. 37 of *Dictionary of Literary Biography*. Detroit: Gale, 1985.

———, gen. ed. *Columbia Literary History of the United States*. New York: Columbia UP, 1988.

———. *Power and the Pulpit in Puritan New England*. Princeton: Princeton UP, 1975.

———. *Revolutionary Writers: Literature and Authority in the New Republic, 1725–1810*. New York: Oxford UP, 1982.

Elliott, J. H. *The Old World and the New, 1492–1650*. Cambridge: Cambridge UP, 1970.

Emerson, Everett. *American Literature, 1764–1789: The Revolutionary Years*. Madison: U of Wisconsin P, 1977.

———. *English Puritanism from John Hooper to John Milton*. Durham: Duke UP, 1968.

———. *Major Writers of Early American Literature*. Madison: U of Wisconsin P, 1972.

Epstein, Dena J. *Sinful Tunes and Spirituals: Black Folk Music to the Civil War*. Urbana: U of Illinois P, 1977.

Erdoes, Richard, and Alfonso Ortiz, eds. *American Indian Myths and Legends*. New York: Pantheon, 1984.

Ferguson, Robert A. *The American Enlightenment, 1750–1820*. Cambridge: Harvard UP, 1997.

———. *Law and Letters in American Culture*. Cambridge: Harvard UP, 1984.

Fichtelberg, Joseph. *The Complex Image: Faith and Method in American Autobiography*. Philadelphia: U of Pennsylvania P, 1989.

Fischer, David Hackett. *Albion's Seed: Four British Folkways in America*. New York: Oxford UP, 1989.

Fitz, Earl E. *Rediscovering the New World: Inter-American Literature in a Comparative Context*. Iowa City: U of Iowa P, 1991.

Flexner, James T. *American Painting: The Light of Distant Skies, 1760–1835*. New York: Harcourt, 1954.

Fliegelman, Jay. *Declaring Independence*. Stanford: Stanford UP, 1993.

———. *Prodigals and Pilgrims: The American Revolution against Patriarchal Authority, 1750–1800*. New York: Cambridge UP, 1982.

Foster, Stephen. *The Long Argument: English Puritanism and the Shaping of New England Culture, 1570–1700*. Chapel Hill: U of North Carolina P, 1991.

Franklin, Wayne. *Discoverers, Explorers, Settlers: The Diligent Writers of Early America*. Chicago: U of Chicago P, 1979.

Frost, J. William. "The Origins of the Quaker Crusade against Slavery: A Review of Recent Literature." *Quaker History* 67.1 (1978): 42–58.

———. *A Perfect Freedom: Religious Liberty in Pennsylvania*. New York: Cambridge UP, 1990.

———. *The Quaker Family in Colonial America: A Portrait of the Society of Friends*. New York: St. Martin's, 1973.

———, ed. *Quaker Origins of Antislavery*. Norwood: Norwood, 1980.

Fuller, Mary C. *Voyages in Print: English Travel to America, 1576–1624*. New York: Cambridge UP, 1995.

The Future of Early American History. Spec. issue of *William and Mary Quarterly* 50 (1993): 299–466.

Gallagher, Kent G. *The Foreigner in Early American Drama: A Study in Attitudes*. The Hague: Mouton, 1966.

Gallay, Alan, ed. *Voices of the Old South: Eyewitness Accounts, 1528–1861*. Athens: U of Georgia P, 1994.

Galloway, Patricia K., ed. *La Salle and His Legacy: Frenchmen and Indians in the Lower Mississippi Valley*. Jackson: UP of Mississippi, 1982.

Gates, Henry Louis, Jr. *Loose Canons: Notes on the Culture Wars*. New York: Oxford UP, 1992.

Giamatti, A. Bartlett. *The Earthly Paradise and the Renaissance Epic*. Princeton: Princeton UP, 1966.

Girdham, Jane. "Musical Life in the Eighteenth Century: A Course Description." *Teaching the Eighteenth Century: Three Courses*. Logan: Amer. Soc. for Eighteenth-Century Studies, 1995. 29–42.

Gleason, Philip. "Confusion Confounded: The Melting Pot in the 1960s and 1970s." *Ethnicity* 6.1 (1979): 10–20.

———. "The Melting Pot: Symbol of Fusion or Confusion?" *American Quarterly* 16.1 (1964): 20–46.

Godbeer, Richard. "'The Cry of Sodom': Discourse, Intercourse, and Desire in Colonial New England." *William and Mary Quarterly* 52 (1995): 259–86.

————. *The Devil's Dominion: Magic and Religion in Early New England*. New York: Cambridge UP, 1992.

Goldberg, Jonathan. *Sodometries: Renaissance Texts, Modern Sexualities*. Stanford: Stanford UP, 1992.

Gonzales-Berry, Erlinda, ed. *Pasó por Aquí: Critical Essays on the New Mexican Literary Tradition, 1542–1988*. Albuquerque: U of New Mexico P, 1989.

González, Ray, ed. *Without Discovery: A Native Response to Columbus*. Seattle: Broken Moon, 1992.

Goodfriend, Joyce D. *Before the Melting Pot: Society and Culture in Colonial New York City, 1664–1730*. Princeton: Princeton UP, 1992.

————. "The Historiography of the Dutch in Colonial America." *Colonial Dutch Studies: An Interdisciplinary Approach*. Ed. Eric Nooter and Patricia U. Bonomi. New York: New York UP, 1988. 6–32.

Grabo, Norman S. "Ideology and the Early American Frontier." *Early American Literature* 22.3 (1987): 274–90.

Graff, Gerald. "The Promise of American Literature Studies." *Professing Literature: An Institutional History*. Chicago: U of Chicago P, 1987. 209–25.

Granger, Bruce Ingham. *Political Satire in the American Revolution, 1763–1783*. Ithaca: Cornell UP, 1960.

Green, L. C., and Olive P. Dickason. *The Law of Nations and the New World*. Alberta: U of Alberta P, 1989.

Greenblatt, Stephen. *Marvelous Possessions: The Wonder of the New World*. Chicago: U of Chicago P, 1991.

————, ed. *New World Encounters*. Berkeley: U of California P, 1993.

Greene, Jack P. *The Intellectual Construction of America: Exceptionalism and Identity from 1492 to 1800*. Chapel Hill: U of North Carolina P, 1993.

————. *Pursuits of Happiness: The Social Development of Early Modern British Colonies and the Formation of American Culture*. Chapel Hill: U of North Carolina P, 1988.

Grinde, Donald A., Jr. "Teaching American Indian History: A Native American Voice." *Perspectives* 32.6 (1994): 1+.

Grinde, Donald A., Jr., and Bruce E. Johansen. *Exemplar of Liberty: Native America and the Evolution of Democracy*. Los Angeles: Amer. Indian Studies Center, U of California, Los Angeles, 1991.

Gundersen, Joan R. *To Be Useful to the World: Women in Revolutionary America, 1740–1790*. New York: Twayne, 1996.

Gunn, Giles, ed. *Early American Writing*. New York: Penguin, 1994.

Gura, Philip F. *A Glimpse of Sion's Glory: Puritan Radicalism in New England, 1620–1660*. Middletown: Wesleyan UP, 1984.

————. "The Study of Colonial American Literature, 1966–1987: A Vade Mecum." *William and Mary Quarterly* 45 (1988): 305–41. (See also responses on 342–51.)

————. "Turning Our World Upside Down: Reconceiving Early American Literature." *American Literature* 63.1 (1991): 104–12.

Gustafson, Thomas. *Representative Words: Politics, Literature, and the American Language, 1776–1865*. New York: Cambridge UP, 1992.

Gutiérrez, Ramón A. *When Jesus Came, the Corn Mothers Went Away: Marriage, Sexuality, and Power in New Mexico, 1500–1846*. Stanford: Stanford UP, 1991.

Hall, David D. *Cultures of Print: Essays in the History of the Book*. Amherst: U of Massachusetts P, 1996.

———. "A History of the Book in American Culture." *Book Research Quarterly* 6.2 (1990): 63–69.

———. "On Common Ground: The Coherence of American Puritan Studies." *William and Mary Quarterly* 44 (1987): 193–229.

———. "On Native Ground: From the History of Printing to the History of the Book." *Proceedings of the American Antiquarian Society* 93.2 (1983): 313–36.

———. "The Uses of Literacy in New England, 1600–1850." Joyce et al. 1–47.

———. "The World of Print and Collective Mentality in Seventeenth-Century New England." *New Directions in American Intellectual History*. Ed. John Higham and Paul K. Conkin. Baltimore: Johns Hopkins UP, 1979. 166–80.

———. *Worlds of Wonder, Days of Judgment: Popular Religious Belief in Early New England*. New York: Knopf, 1989.

Hamilton, Roberta. *Feudal Society and Colonization: The Historiography of New France*. Gananoque, ON: Langdale, 1988.

Hamlin, William M. *The Image of America in Montaigne, Spenser, and Shakespeare: Renaissance Ethnography and Literary Reflection*. New York: St. Martin's, 1995.

Hamm, Charles. *Music in the New World*. New York: Norton, 1983.

Hammond, Jeffrey A. *Sinful Self, Saintly Self: The Puritan Experience of Poetry*. Athens: U of Georgia P, 1993.

Harris, Sharon M., ed. *American Women Writers to 1800*. New York: Oxford UP, 1996.

———. "Contemporary Theories and Early American Literature." *Early American Literature* 29.2 (1994): 183–89.

Havens, Daniel F. *The Columbian Muse of Comedy: The Development of a Native Tradition in Early American Social Comedy, 1787–1845*. Carbondale: Southern Illinois UP, 1973.

Hayes, Kevin J. *A Colonial Woman's Bookshelf*. Knoxville: U of Tennessee P, 1996.

Heard, Priscilla S. *American Music, 1698–1800: An Annotated Bibliography*. Waco: Baylor UP, 1975.

Heimert, Alan. *Religion and the American Mind: From the Great Awakening to the Revolution*. Cambridge: Harvard UP, 1966.

Heimert, Alan, and Andrew Delbanco, eds. *The Puritans in America: A Narrative Anthology*. Cambridge: Harvard UP, 1985.

Heintze, James R. *Early American Music: A Research and Information Guide*. New York: Garland, 1990.

Herrera-Sobek, María, ed. *Reconstructing a Chicano/a Literary Heritage: Hispanic Colonial Literature of the Southwest*. Tucson: U of Arizona P, 1993.

Hitchcock, H. Wiley. *Music in the United States: A Historical Introduction*. Englewood Cliffs: Prentice, 1974.

Hoffman, Paul E. *A New Andalucia and a Way to the Orient: The American Southeast during the Sixteenth Century*. Baton Rouge: Louisiana State UP, 1990.

Hoffman, Ronald, and Peter J. Albert, eds. *Women in the Age of the American Revolution*. Charlottesville: UP of Virginia, 1989.

Hoffman, Ronald, Mechal Sobel, and Fredrika J. Teute. *Through a Glass Darkly: Reflections on Personal Identity in Early America*. Chapel Hill: U of North Carolina P, 1997.

Holland, Jeanne. "Problems and Opportunities in Teaching Native American Literature from *The Heath Anthology of American Literature*." Alberti 165–92.

Hollinger, David A. *Postethnic America: Beyond Multiculturalism*. New York: Basic, 1995.

Honour, Hugh. *The New Golden Land: European Images of America from the Discoveries to the Present Time*. New York: Pantheon, 1975.

Horn, David. *The Literature of American Music in Books and Folk Music Collections: A Fully Annotated Bibliography*. Metuchen: Scarecrow, 1977. Supp. 1, with Richard Jackson, 1988.

Horton, James Oliver, and Lois E. Horton. *In Hope of Liberty: Culture, Community, and Protest among Northern Free Blacks, 1700–1860*. New York: Oxford UP, 1997.

Hoxie, Frederick E., ed. *Indians in American History: An Introduction*. Arlington Heights: Davidson, 1988.

Hoxie, Frederick E., and Harvey Markowitz. *Native Americans: An Annotated Bibliography*. Pasadena: Salem, 1991.

Hudak, Leona M. *Early American Women Printers and Publishers, 1639–1820*. Metuchen: Scarecrow, 1978.

Hudson, Charles, and Carmen Chaves Tesser, eds. *The Forgotten Centuries: Indians and Europeans in the American South, 1521–1704*. Athens: U of Georgia P, 1994.

Hulme, Peter. *Colonial Encounters: Europe and the Native Caribbean, 1492–1797*. London: Methuen, 1986.

Hulme, Peter, and Neil L. Whitehead, eds. *Wild Majesty: Encounters with Caribs from Columbus to the Present Day: An Anthology*. New York: Oxford UP, 1992.

Hulton, Paul. America 1585: *The Complete Drawings of John White*. Chapel Hill: U of North Carolina P, 1984.

"The 'Iroquois Influence' Thesis — Con and Pro." *William and Mary Quarterly* 53 (1996): 587–636.

Isaac, Rhys. *The Transformation of Virginia, 1740–1790*. Chapel Hill: U of North Carolina P, 1982.

Jackson, Blyden. *The Long Beginning, 1746–1895.* Vol. 1 of *A History of Afro-American Literature.* Baton Rouge: Louisiana State UP, 1989.

Jaenen, Cornelius J. *Friend and Foe: Aspects of French-Amerindian Cultural Contact in the Sixteenth and Seventeenth Centuries.* New York: Columbia UP, 1976.

Jameson, J. Franklin, ed. *Narratives of New Netherland, 1609–1664.* New York: Scribner's, 1909.

Jara, René, and Nicholas Spadaccini, eds. *Amerindian Images and the Legacy of Columbus.* Minneapolis: U of Minnesota P, 1992.

———, eds. *1492–1992: Re/Discovering Colonial Writing.* Minneapolis: Prisma Inst., 1989.

Jaskoski, Helen, ed. *Early Native American Writing: New Critical Essays.* New York: Cambridge UP, 1996.

Jay, Gregory S. "The End of 'American' Literature: Toward a Multicultural Practice." *College English* 53.3 (1991): 264–81.

Jehlen, Myra, and Michael Warner, eds. *The English Literatures of America, 1500–1800.* New York: Routledge, 1996.

Jennings, Francis. *The Founders of America: How Indians Discovered the Land, Pioneered in It, and Created Great Classical Civilizations; How They Were Plunged into a Dark Age by Invasion and Conquest; and How They Are Reviving.* New York: Norton, 1993.

———. *The Invasion of America: Indians, Colonialism, and the Cant of Conquest.* Chapel Hill: U of North Carolina P, 1975.

John, Elizabeth A. H. *Storms Brewed in Other Men's Worlds: The Confrontation of Indians, Spanish, and French in the Southwest, 1540–1795.* College Station: Texas A&M UP, 1975.

Johnson, Julie Greer. *Women in Colonial Spanish American Literature: Literary Images.* Westport: Greenwood, 1983.

Jones, Eugene H. *Native Americans As Shown on the Stage, 1753–1916.* Metuchen: Scarecrow, 1988.

Jones, Gwyn. *The Norse Atlantic Saga: Being the Norse Voyages of Discovery and Settlement to Iceland, Greenland, and North America.* 2nd ed. New York: Oxford UP, 1986.

Jones, Howard Mumford. *O Strange New World: American Culture, the Formative Years.* New York: Viking, 1964.

Jones, Mary Ellen, ed. *Christopher Columbus and His Legacy: Opposing Viewpoints.* San Diego: Greenhaven, 1992.

Jordan, Cynthia S. *Second Stories: The Politics of Language, Form, and Gender in Early American Fictions.* Chapel Hill: U of North Carolina P, 1989.

Jordan, Winthrop D. *White over Black: American Attitudes toward the Negro, 1550–1812.* Chapel Hill: U of North Carolina P, 1968.

Josephy, Alvin M., ed. *America in 1492: The World of the Indian Peoples before the Arrival of Columbus.* New York: Knopf, 1992.

Joyce, William L., et al., eds. *Printing and Society in Early America.* Worcester: Amer. Antiquarian Soc., 1983.

Kagle, Steven E. *American Diary Literature, 1620–1799*. Boston: Twayne, 1979.

Kaplan, Amy. "'Left Alone with America': The Absence of Empire in the Study of American Culture." *Cultures of United States Imperialism*. Ed. Amy Kaplan and Donald E. Pease. Durham: Duke UP, 1993. 3–21.

Karlsen, Carol F. *The Devil in the Shape of a Woman: Witchcraft in Colonial New England*. New York: Norton, 1987.

Kartiganer, Donald, and Malcolm A. Griffith, eds. *Theories of American Literature*. New York: Macmillan, 1972.

Katz, Jonathan Ned. *Gay American History: Lesbians and Gay Men in the USA: A Documentary History*. New York: Meridian, 1992.

———. *Gay/Lesbian Almanac: A New Documentary*. New York: Harper, 1983.

Keegan, William F. *The People Who Discovered Columbus: The Prehistory of the Bahamas*. Gainesville: UP of Florida, 1992.

Keen, Benjamin. *The Aztec Image in Western Thought*. New Brunswick: Rutgers UP, 1971.

Kenney, Alice P. *Stubborn for Liberty: The Dutch in New York*. Syracuse: Syracuse UP, 1975.

Kenney, W. Howland, ed. *Laughter in the Wilderness: Early American Humor to 1783*. Kent: Kent State UP, 1976.

Kerber, Linda. *Women of the Republic: Intellect and Ideology in Revolutionary America*. Chapel Hill: U of North Carolina P, 1980.

Kingman, Daniel. *American Music: A Panorama*. 2nd ed. New York: Schirmer, 1990.

Klinck, Carl F., et al., eds. *Literary History of Canada: Canadian Literature in English*. 2nd ed. Toronto: U of Toronto P, 1976.

Knapp, Jeffrey. *An Empire Nowhere: England, America, and Literature from Utopia to The Tempest*. Berkeley: U of California P, 1992.

Knaut, Andrew L. *The Pueblo Revolt of 1680: Conquest and Resistance in Seventeenth-Century New Mexico*. Norman: U of Oklahoma P, 1995.

Knight, Janice. *Orthodoxies in Massachusetts: Rereading American Puritanism*. Cambridge: Harvard UP, 1994.

Kolodny, Annette. *The Land before Her: Fantasy and Experience of the American Frontiers, 1630–1860*. Chapel Hill: U of North Carolina P, 1984.

———. *The Lay of the Land: Metaphor as Experience and History in American Life and Letters*. Chapel Hill: U of North Carolina P, 1975.

———. "Letting Go Our Grand Obsessions: Notes toward a New Literary History of the American Frontiers." *American Literature* 64.1 (1992): 1–18.

Koning, Hans. *Columbus: His Enterprise — Exploding the Myth*. New York: Monthly Review, 1991.

Kritzer, Amelia Howe, ed. *Plays by Early American Women, 1775–1850*. Ann Arbor: U of Michigan P, 1995.

Krummel, D. W. *Bibliographical Handbook of American Music*. Urbana: U of Illinois P, 1987.

Krupat, Arnold. *For Those Who Come After: A Study of Native American Auto-biography.* Berkeley: U of California P, 1985.

———. *The Voice in the Margin: Native American Literature and the Canon.* Berkeley: U of California P, 1989.

Kulikoff, Allan. *Tobacco and Slaves: The Development of Southern Cultures in the Chesapeake, 1680–1800.* Chapel Hill: U of North Carolina P, 1986.

Kupperman, Karen Ordahl, ed. *America in European Consciousness, 1493–1750.* Chapel Hill: U of North Carolina P, 1995.

———. *Settling with the Indians: The Meeting of English and Indian Cultures in America, 1580–1640.* London: Dent, 1980.

Lacey, Barbara E. "Visual Images of Blacks in Early American Imprints." *William and Mary Quarterly* 53 (1996): 137–80.

Lang, Amy Schrager. *Prophetic Woman: Anne Hutchinson and the Problem of Dissent in the Literature of New England.* Berkeley: U of California P, 1987.

Lauter, Paul. *Canons and Contexts.* New York: Oxford UP, 1991.

Lauter, Paul, et al., eds. *The Heath Anthology of American Literature.* 3rd ed. Boston: Houghton, 1998.

Lawrence, D. H. *Studies in Classic American Literature.* New York: Seltzer, 1923.

Lawson-Peebles, Robert. *Landscape and Written Expression in Revolutionary America: The World Turned Upside Down.* New York: Cambridge UP, 1988.

Leary, Lewis, comp. *Articles on American Literature: 1950–1967.* Durham: Duke UP, 1970.

———, comp. *Articles on American Literature: 1900–1950.* Durham: Duke UP, 1954.

———, comp. *Articles on American Literature: 1968–1975.* Durham: Duke UP, 1979.

Le Clézio, J. M. G. *The Mexican Dream: or, The Interrupted Thought of Amerindian Civilizations.* Chicago: U of Chicago P, 1993.

Lehmann-Haupt, Hellmut, Lawrence C. Wroth, and Rollo G. Silver. *The Book in America: A History of the Making and Selling of Books in the United States.* 2nd ed. New York: Bowker, 1951.

Lemay, J. A. Leo, ed. *Essays in Early Virginia Literature Honoring Richard Beale Davis.* New York: Franklin, 1977.

———. *Men of Letters in Colonial Maryland.* Knoxville: U of Tennessee P, 1972.

Leonard, Eugenie Andruss, Sophie Hutchinson Drinker, and Miriam Young Holden. *The American Woman in Colonial and Revolutionary Times, 1565–1800: A Syllabus with Bibliography.* Philadelphia: U of Pennsylvania P, 1962.

León-Portilla, Miguel. *The Aztec Image of Self and Society: An Introduction to Nahua Culture.* Salt Lake City: U of Utah P, 1992.

———, ed. *The Broken Spears: The Aztec Account of the Conquest of Mexico.* Boston: Beacon, 1992.

———, ed. *Fifteen Poets of the Aztec World.* Norman: U of Oklahoma P, 1992.

———. *Pre-Columbian Literatures of Mexico*. Norman: U of Oklahoma P, 1969.

Levernier, James, and Douglas R. Wilmes, eds. *American Writers before 1800: A Biographical and Critical Dictionary*. Westport: Greenwood, 1983.

Levernier, James, and Hennig Cohen, eds. *The Indians and Their Captives*. Westport: Greenwood, 1977.

Levin, Harry. *The Myth of the Golden Age in the Renaissance*. Bloomington: Indiana UP, 1969.

Lewis, Gordon K. *Main Currents in Caribbean Thought: The Historical Evolution of Caribbean Society in Its Ideological Aspects, 1492–1900*. Baltimore: Johns Hopkins UP, 1983.

Lewis, Jan. "The Republican Wife: Virtue and Seduction in the Early Republic." *William and Mary Quarterly* 44 (1987): 689–721.

Lienesch, Michael. *New Order of the Ages: Time, the Constitution, and the Making of Modern American Political Thought*. Princeton: Princeton UP, 1988.

Limón, José E. "La Llorona, The Third Legend of Greater Mexico: Cultural Symbols, Women, and the Political Unconscious." *Between Borders: Essays on Mexicana/Chicana History*. Ed. Adelaida R. Del Castillo. Encino: Floricanto, 1990. 399–432.

Lockhart, James, ed. *We People Here: Nahuatl Accounts of the Conquest of Mexico*. Berkeley: U of California P, 1993.

Lockridge, Kenneth A. *Literacy in Colonial New England: An Enquiry into the Social Context of Literacy in the Early Modern West*. New York: Norton, 1974.

Looby, Christopher. *Voicing America: Language, Literary Form, and the Origins of the United States*. Chicago: U of Chicago P, 1996.

Lorant, Stefan, ed. *The New World: The First Pictures of America Made by John White and Jacques Le Moyne and Engraved by Theodore De Bry*. New York: Duell, 1946.

Lovett-Graff, Bennett. "Culture Wars II: A Review Essay." *Modern Language Studies* 25.3 (1995): 99–124.

Ludwig, Allan I. *Graven Images: New England Stonecarving and Its Symbols, 1650–1815*. Middletown: Wesleyan UP, 1966.

Lunenfeld, Marvin, ed. *1492: Discovery, Invasion, Encounter: Sources and Interpretations*. Lexington: Heath, 1991.

Lyon, Eugene. *The Enterprise of Florida: Pedro Menendez de Aviles and the Spanish Conquest of 1565–1568*. Gainesville: UP of Florida, 1976.

Maier, Pauline. *American Scripture: Making the Declaration of Independence*. New York: Knopf, 1997.

Mancall, Peter C., ed. *Envisioning America: English Plans for the Colonization of North America, 1580–1640*. Boston: Bedford, 1995.

Marietta, Jack D. *The Reformation of American Quakerism, 1748–1783*. Philadelphia: U of Pennsylvania P, 1984.

Marrocco, W. Thomas, and Harold Gleason. *Music in America: An Anthology from the Landing of the Pilgrims to the Close of the Civil War, 1620–1865.* New York: Norton, 1964.

Marshall, Joyce, ed. *Word from New France: The Selected Letters of Marie de l'Incarnation.* Toronto: Oxford UP, 1967.

Martin, Ann Smart, ed. *Material Culture in Early America.* Spec. issue of *William and Mary Quarterly* 53 (1996): 3–180.

Martin, Calvin. *The American Indian and the Problem of History.* New York: Oxford UP, 1987.

Martin, Wendy, ed. *Colonial American Travel Narratives.* New York: Penguin, 1994.

Mates, Julian. *The American Musical Stage before 1800.* New Brunswick: Rutgers UP, 1962.

May, Henry F. *The Enlightenment in America.* New York: Oxford UP, 1976.

Mazoff, C. D. "Strategies of Colonial Legitimation in the Early Canadian Long Poem." *Canadian Poetry* 36.1 (1995): 81–113.

McAllester, David P. "North American Native Music." *Musics of Many Cultures: An Introduction.* Ed. Elizabeth May. Berkeley: U of California P, 1980. 307–31.

McElroy, Guy C. *Facing History: The Black Image in American Art, 1710–1940.* San Francisco: Bedford Arts, 1990.

McKay, Nellie. "Autobiography and the Early Novel." *The Columbia History of the American Novel.* Ed. Emory Elliott. New York: Columbia UP, 1991. 26–45.

McKitrick, Eric L. *Slavery Defended: The Views of the Old South.* Englewood Cliffs: Prentice, 1963.

McNamara, Brooks. *The American Playhouse in the Eighteenth Century.* Cambridge: Harvard UP, 1969.

McQuade, Donald, et al., eds. *The Harper American Literature.* 2nd ed. New York: Harper, 1993.

McWilliams, John P. *The American Epic: Transforming a Genre, 1770–1860.* New York: Cambridge UP, 1989.

Meinig, D. W. *Atlantic America, 1492–1800.* 1986. Vol. 1 of *The Shaping of America: A Geographical Perspective on Five Hundred Years of History.* New Haven: Yale UP, 1986–.

Merrell, James H. *The Indians' New World: Catawbas and Their Neighbors from European Contact through the Era of Removal.* Chapel Hill: U of North Carolina P, 1989.

Merrim, Stephanie, ed. *Feminist Perspectives on Sor Juana Inés de la Cruz.* Detroit: Wayne State UP, 1991.

Meserole, Harrison T., ed. *Seventeenth-Century American Poetry.* Garden City: Anchor, 1968.

Meserve, Walter J. *An Emerging Entertainment: The Drama of the American People to 1828.* Bloomington: Indiana UP, 1977.

Milanich, Jerald T., ed. *Earliest Hispanic / Native American Interactions in the American Southeast.* New York: Garland, 1991.

———. *Florida Indians and the Invasion from Europe*. Gainesville: UP of Florida, 1995.

Milanich, Jerald T., and Charles Hudson. *Hernando de Soto and the Indians of Florida*. Gainesville: UP of Florida, 1993.

Miller, Marcia. "Verse Fables in Eighteenth-Century American Newspapers and Magazines." *Resources for American Literary Study* 19.2 (1993): 275–93.

Miller, Perry. *Errand into the Wilderness*. Cambridge: Harvard UP, 1956.

———. *The New England Mind: From Colony to Province*. Cambridge: Harvard UP, 1953.

———. *The New England Mind: The Seventeenth Century*. New York: Macmillan, 1939.

Miller, Perry, and Thomas H. Johnson, eds. *The Puritans: A Sourcebook of Their Writings*. New York: American Book Co., 1938.

Miller, Terry E. *Folk Music in America: A Reference Guide*. New York: Garland, 1986.

Mintz, Steven, ed. *Native American Voices: A History and Anthology*. Saint James: Brandywine, 1995.

Miquelon, Dale. *The First Canada: To 1791*. Toronto: McGraw, 1994.

———. *New France, 1701–1744: "A Supplement to Europe."* Canadian Centenary ser. 4. Toronto: McClelland, 1987.

Moffitt, John F., and Santiago Sebastián. *O Brave New People: The European Invention of the American Indian*. Albuquerque: U of New Mexico P, 1996.

Mohler, Stephen C. "Publishing in Colonial Spanish America: An Overview." *Inter-American Review of Bibliography* 28.3 (1978): 259–73.

Montgomery, Charles F., and Patricia E. Kane. *American Art, 1750–1800: Towards Independence*. Boston: New York Graphic Soc., 1976.

Moore, James T. *Indian and Jesuit: A Seventeenth-Century Encounter*. Chicago: Loyola UP, 1982.

Morgan, Edmund S. *American Slavery, American Freedom: The Ordeal of Colonial Virginia*. New York: Norton, 1975.

Morse, Jarvis M. "Colonial Historians of New York." *New York History* 23.4 (1942): 395–409.

Moyles, R. G. *English-Canadian Literature to 1900: A Guide to Information Resources*. Detroit: Gale, 1976.

Muldoon, James. *The Americas in the Spanish World Order: The Justification for Conquest in the Seventeenth Century*. Philadelphia: U of Pennsylvania P, 1994.

Mulford, Carla, gen. ed. *Early American Literatures*. New York: Oxford UP, forthcoming.

———, ed. *Expanding the Early American Canon*. Spec. issue of *Resources for American Literary Study* 19.2 (1993): 165–308.

———. "Recovering the Colonial, Beginning Again: Toward Multiculturalism in the Teaching of Early American Studies." *Heath Anthology of American Literature Newsletter* 11 (1994): 2–8.

———. "Re-Presenting Early American Drama and Theatre." *Resources for American Literary Study* 17.1 (1990): 1–24.

———. "Seated amid the Rainbow: On Teaching American Writings to 1800." *American Literature* 65.2 (1993): 342–48.

Mulford, Carla, Amy Winans, and Angela Vietto, eds. *American Women Prose Writers to 1820. Dictionary of Literary Biography.* Columbia: Bruccoli, 1998.

Mullin, Gerald W. *Flight and Rebellion: Slave Resistance in Eighteenth-Century Virginia.* New York: Oxford UP, 1972.

Murray, James C. *Spanish Chronicles of the Indies: Sixteenth Century.* New York: Twayne, 1994.

Myers, Albert Cook, ed. *Narratives of Early Pennsylvania, West New Jersey, and Delaware, 1630–1707.* New York: Scribner's, 1912.

Namias, June. *White Captives: Gender and Ethnicity on the American Frontier.* Chapel Hill: U of North Carolina P, 1993.

Nash, Gary B. *Quakers and Politics: Pennsylvania, 1681–1726.* Princeton: Princeton UP, 1968.

———. *Red, White, and Black: The Peoples of Early America.* Englewood Cliffs: Prentice, 1974.

Nelson, Dana D. "Reading the Written Selves of Colonial America: Franklin, Occom, Equiano, and Palou/Serra." *Resources for American Literary Study* 19.2 (1993): 246–59.

———. *The Word in Black and White: Reading "Race" in American Literature, 1638–1867.* New York: Oxford UP, 1992.

New, W. H., ed. *Canadian Writers before 1890.* Dictionary of Literary Biography 99. Detroit: Gale, 1990.

———. *A History of Canadian Literature.* New York: New Amsterdam, 1989.

Nilsen, Don L. F. *Humor in American Literature: A Selected Annotated Bibliography.* New York: Garland, 1992.

Norton, Mary Beth. *Founding Mothers and Fathers: Gendered Power and the Forming of American Society.* New York: Knopf, 1996.

———. *Liberty's Daughters: The Revolutionary Experience of American Women, 1750–1800.* Boston: Little, 1980.

Nygren, Edward J., and Bruce Robertson. *Views and Visions: American Landscape before 1830.* Washington: Corcoran Gallery, 1986.

Pagden, Anthony. *Lords of All the World: Ideologies of Empire in Spain, Britain, and France, c. 1500–c. 1800.* New Haven: Yale UP, 1995.

Parish, Peter J. *Slavery: History and Historians.* New York: Harper, 1989.

Parker, Hershel. "The Price of Diversity: An Ambivalent Minority Report on the American Canon." *College Literature* 18.3 (1991): 15–29.

Parker, Patricia L. *Early American Fiction: A Reference Guide.* Boston: Hall, 1984.

Parry, Ellwood. *The Image of the Indian and the Black Man in American Art, 1590–1900.* New York: Braziller, 1974.

Pastor (Bodmer), Beatriz. *The Armature of Conquest: Spanish Accounts of the Discovery of America, 1492–1589.* Stanford: Stanford UP, 1992.

Patterson, Mark R. *Authority, Autonomy, and Representation in American Literature, 1776–1865.* Princeton: Princeton UP, 1988.

Pearce, Roy Harvey. *Savagism and Civilization: A Study of the Indian and the American Mind.* 1965. Berkeley: U of California P, 1988. Rpt. of *The Savages of America: A Study of the Indian and the Idea of Civilization.* 1953

Peyser, Joseph L., ed. *Letters from New France: The Upper Country, 1686–1783.* Urbana: U of Illinois P, 1992.

Philbrick, Norman, ed. *Trumpets Sounding: Propaganda Plays of the American Revolution.* New York: Blom, 1972.

Piersen, William D. *From Africa to America: African American History from the Colonial Era to the Early Republic, 1526–1790.* New York: Twayne, 1996.

Porter, Carolyn. "What We Know That We Don't Know: Remapping American Literary Studies." *American Literary History* 6.3 (1994): 467–526.

Porter, Dorothy. *Early Negro Writing, 1760–1837.* 1971. Baltimore: Black Classics, 1995.

Porter, Roy. *The Enlightenment.* Atlantic Highlands: Humanities, 1990.

Porter, Susan L. *With an Air Debonair: Musical Theatre in America, 1785–1815.* Washington: Smithsonian, 1991.

Porterfield, Amanda. *Female Piety in Puritan New England: The Emergence of Religious Humanism.* New York: Oxford UP, 1992.

Potkay, Adam, and Sandra Burr, eds. *Black Atlantic Writers of the Eighteenth Century: Living the New Exodus in England and the Americas.* New York: St. Martin's, 1995.

Promis, José. *The Identity of Hispanoamerica: An Interpretation of Colonial Literature.* Tucson: U of Arizona P, 1991.

Quattlebaum, Paul. *The Land Called Chicora: The Carolinas under Spanish Rule with French Intrusions, 1520–1670.* Gainesville: U of Florida P, 1956.

Quinn, Arthur Hobson. *A History of the American Drama: From the Beginning to the Civil War.* 2nd ed. New York: Appleton, 1951.

Rabasa, José. *Inventing America: Spanish Historiography and the Formation of Eurocentrism.* Norman: U of Oklahoma P, 1993.

Raboteau, Albert J. *Slave Religion: The Invisible Institution in the Antebellum South.* New York: Oxford UP, 1971.

Raesly, Ellis Lawrence. *Portrait of New Netherland.* New York: Columbia UP, 1945.

Rankin, Hugh F. *The Theater in Colonial America.* Chapel Hill: U of North Carolina P, 1965.

Regis, Pamela. *Describing Early America: Bartram, Jefferson, Crèvecoeur, and the Rhetoric of Natural History.* De Kalb: Northern Illinois UP, 1992.

Reising, Russell J. *The Unusable Past: Theory and the Study of American Literature.* New York: Methuen, 1986.

Richards, Jeffrey H., ed. *Early American Drama.* New York: Viking-Penguin, 1997.

———. *Theater Enough: American Culture and the Metaphor of the World Stage, 1607–1789.* Durham: Duke UP, 1991.

Richter, Daniel K. *The Ordeal of the Longhouse: The Peoples of the Iroquois*

League in the Era of European Colonization. Chapel Hill: U of North Carolina P, 1992.

———. "Whose Indian History?" *William and Mary Quarterly* 50 (1993): 379–93.

Rogers, George C., Jr. "The South before 1800." *Interpreting Southern History: Historiographical Essays in Honor of Sanford W. Higginbotham*. Ed. John B. Boles and Evelyn Thomas Nolen. Baton Rouge: Louisiana State UP, 1987. 6–47.

Roscoe, Will, ed. *Living the Spirit: A Gay American Indian Anthology*. New York: St. Martin's, 1988.

Rosenthal, Bernard. *Salem Story: Reading the Witch Trials of 1692*. New York: Cambridge UP, 1993.

Rouse, Irving. *The Tainos: Rise and Decline of the People Who Greeted Columbus*. New Haven: Yale UP, 1992.

Rowse, A. L. *The Elizabethans and America*. London: Macmillan, 1959.

Royal, Robert. *1492 and All That: Political Manipulations of History*. Washington: Ethics and Public Policy Center, 1992.

Rubin, Louis D., Jr., ed. *The Comic Imagination in American Literature*. New Brunswick: Rutgers UP, 1973.

———, ed. *The History of Southern Literature*. Baton Rouge: Louisiana State UP, 1985.

Rubin-Dorsky, Jeffrey. "The Early American Novel." *The Columbia History of the American Novel*. Ed. Emory Elliott. New York: Columbia UP, 1991. 6–25.

Ruoff, A. LaVonne Brown. *American Indian Literatures: An Introduction, Bibliographic Review, and Selected Bibliography*. New York: MLA, 1990.

Ruoff, A. LaVonne Brown, and Jerry W. Ward, Jr., eds. *Redefining American Literary History*. New York: MLA, 1990.

Ruppert, James. *Colonial and Nineteenth-Century*. Boston: Hall, 1989. Vol. 1 of *Guide to American Poetry Explication*. 2 vols.

Rutman, Anita. "Still Planting the Seeds of Hope: The Recent Literature of the Early Chesapeake Region." *Virginia Magazine of History and Biography* 95.1 (1987): 3–24.

Saldívar, José David. *The Dialectics of Our America: Genealogy, Cultural Critique, and Literary History*. Durham: Duke UP, 1991.

Samuels, Shirley. *Romances of the Republic: Women, the Family, and Violence in the Literature of the Early American Nation*. New York: Oxford UP, 1996.

Sarris, Greg. *Keeping Slug Woman Alive: A Holistic Approach to American Indian Texts*. Berkeley: U of California P, 1993.

Saunders, Richard H., and Ellen G. Miles. *American Colonial Portraits: 1700–1776*. Washington: Smithsonian, 1987.

Sayre, Robert F., ed. *American Lives: An Anthology of Autobiographical Writing*. Madison: U of Wisconsin P, 1994.

Scheick, William J. *Design in American Puritan Literature*. Lexington: UP of Kentucky, 1992.

Scheick, William J., and JoElla Doggett. *Seventeenth-Century American Poetry: A Reference Guide*. Boston: Hall, 1977.

Schlereth, Thomas J., ed. *Material Culture Studies in America*. Nashville: Amer. Assn. for State and Local History, 1982.

Schlesinger, Arthur M., Jr. *The Disuniting of America*. New York: Norton, 1992.

Schofield, Mary Anne, and Cecilia Macheski, eds. *Curtain Calls: British and American Women and the Theater, 1660–1820*. Athens: Ohio UP, 1991.

Schwartz, Sally. *"A Mixed Multitude": The Struggle for Toleration in Colonial Pennsylvania*. New York: New York UP, 1987.

Schweitzer, Ivy. *The Work of Self-Representation: Lyric Poetry in Colonial New England*. Chapel Hill: U of North Carolina P, 1991.

Seed, Patricia. *Ceremonies of Possession in Europe's Conquest of the New World, 1492–1640*. New York: Cambridge UP, 1995.

Seelye, John. *Prophetic Waters: The River in Early American Life and Literature*. New York: Oxford UP, 1977.

Sensbach, Jon F. "Charting a Course in Early African-American History." *William and Mary Quarterly* 50 (1993): 394–405.

Shea, Daniel B. "The Prehistory of American Autobiography." *American Autobiography: Retrospect and Prospect*. Ed. Paul John Eakin. Madison: U of Wisconsin P, 1991. 25–46.

———. *Spiritual Autobiography in Early America*. 1968. Madison: U of Wisconsin P, 1988.

Shi, David E. *The Simple Life: Plain Living and High Thinking in America Culture*. New York: Oxford UP, 1985.

Shields, David S. *Civil Tongues and Polite Letters in British America*. Chapel Hill: U of North Carolina P, 1997.

———. "Literature of the Colonial South." *Resources for American Literary Study* 19.2 (1993): 174–222.

———. *Oracles of Empire: Poetry, Politics, and Commerce in British America, 1690–1750*. Chicago: U of Chicago P, 1990.

Shields, E. Thomson, Jr. "Beyond the Anthology: Sources for Teaching Sixteenth- and Seventeenth-Century Colonial Spanish Literature of North America." *Heath Anthology of American Literature Newsletter* 12 (1994): 2–3. (See also follow-up articles on 3–11.)

Shuffelton, Frank, ed. *The American Enlightenment*. Rochester: U of Rochester P, 1993.

———, ed. *A Mixed Race: Ethnicity in Early America*. New York: Oxford UP, 1993.

Shumway, David R. *Creating American Civilization: A Genealogy of American Literature as an Academic Discipline*. Minneapolis: U of Minnesota P, 1994.

Silverman, Kenneth. *A Cultural History of the American Revolution: Painting, Music, Literature, and the Theatre in the Colonies and the United States from the Treaty of Paris to the Inauguration of George Washington, 1763–1789*. New York: Crowell, 1976.

Simpson, Lewis P. *The Dispossessed Garden: Pastoral and History in Southern Literature*. Athens: U of Georgia P, 1975.

Slotkin, Richard. *Regeneration through Violence: The Mythology of the American Frontier, 1600–1860*. Middletown: Wesleyan UP, 1973.

Sobel, Mechal. *The World They Made Together: Black and White Values in Eighteenth-Century Virginia*. Princeton: Princeton UP, 1987.

Soderlund, Jean R. *Quakers and Slavery: A Divided Spirit*. Princeton: Princeton UP, 1985.

Solé, Carlos A., and Maria Isabel Abreu, eds. *Latin American Writers*. New York: Scribner's, 1989.

Sollors, Werner. *Beyond Ethnicity: Consent and Descent in American Culture*. New York: Oxford UP, 1986.

Spengemann, William C. *The Adventurous Muse: The Poetics of American Fiction, 1789–1900*. New Haven: Yale UP, 1977.

———. *A New World of Words: Redefining Early American Literature*. New Haven: Yale UP, 1994.

Spiller, Robert, et al., eds. *Literary History of the United States*. 3 vols. New York: Macmillan, 1948.

Stanley, George F. G. *New France: The Last Phase, 1744–1760*. Canadian Centenary ser. 5. Toronto: McClelland, 1968.

Stannard, David E. *American Holocaust: Columbus and the Conquest of the New World*. New York: Oxford UP, 1992.

Steele, Ian K. *Warpaths: Invasions of North America*. New York: Oxford UP, 1994.

Stevens-Arroyo, Antonio M. *Cave of the Jagua: The Mythological World of the Tainos*. Albuquerque: U of New Mexico P, 1988.

Stout, Harry S. *The New England Soul: Preaching and Religious Culture in Colonial New England*. New York: Oxford UP, 1986.

Stowell, Marion Barber. *Early American Almanacs: The Colonial Weekday Bible*. New York: Franklin, 1977.

Swann, Brian, ed. *Coming to Light: Contemporary Translations of the Native Literatures of North America*. New York: Random, 1994.

Takaki, Ronald. *A Different Mirror: A History of Multicultural America*. Boston: Little, 1993.

Tate, Thad W., and David L. Ammerman, eds. *The Chesapeake in the Seventeenth Century: Essays on Anglo-American Society*. Chapel Hill: U of North Carolina P, 1979.

Taylor, M. Brook. *Beginnings to Confederation*. Toronto: U of Toronto P, 1994. Vol. 1 of *Canadian History: A Reader's Guide*. 2 vols.

Tedlock, Dennis. *The Spoken Word and the Work of Interpretation*. Philadelphia: U of Pennsylvania P, 1983.

Thernstrom, Stephan, ed. *Harvard Encyclopedia of American Ethnic Groups*. Cambridge: Harvard UP, 1980.

Thornton, John Kelly. *Africa and Africans in the Making of the Atlantic World, 1400–1680*. New York: Cambridge UP, 1992.

Thwaites, Reuben Gold, ed. *The Jesuit Relations and Allied Documents: Travels and Explorations of the Jesuit Missionaries in New France, 1610–1791*. 73 vols. Cleveland: Burrows, 1896–1901.

Tilton, Robert S. *Pocahontas: The Evolution of an American Narrative*. New York: Cambridge UP, 1994.

Tise, Larry E. *Proslavery: A History of the Defense of Slavery in America, 1701–1840*. Athens: U of Georgia P, 1987.

Todorov, Tzvetan. *The Conquest of America: The Question of the Other*. New York: Harper, 1984.

Tolles, Frederick B. *Meeting House and Counting House: The Quaker Merchants of Colonial Philadelphia, 1682–1763*. Chapel Hill: U of North Carolina P, 1948.

———. *Quakers and the Atlantic Culture*. New York: Macmillan, 1960.

Tompkins, Jane. "'Indians': Textualism, Morality, and the Problem of History." *Critical Inquiry* 13.1 (1986): 101–19.

———. *Sensational Designs: The Cultural Work of American Fiction, 1790–1860*. New York: Oxford UP, 1985.

Treckel, Paula A. *To Comfort the Heart: Women in Seventeenth-Century America*. New York: Twayne, 1996.

Trexler, Richard C. *Sex and Conquest: Gendered Violence, Political Order, and the European Conquest of the Americas*. Ithaca: Cornell UP, 1995.

Trigger, Bruce G. *Natives and Newcomers: Canada's "Heroic Age" Reconsidered*. Kingston: McGill-Queen's UP, 1985.

Trigger, Bruce G., and Wilcomb E. Washburn, eds. *North America*. Cambridge History of the Native Peoples of the Americas 1. New York: Cambridge UP, 1996.

Trudel, Marcel. *The Beginnings of New France, 1524–1663*. Canadian Centenary Ser. 2. Toronto: McClelland, 1973.

Truettner, William H., ed. *The West as America: Reinterpreting Images of the Frontier, 1820–1920*. Washington: Smithsonian, 1991.

Turner, Frederick W., III, ed. *The Portable North American Indian Reader*. New York: Viking, 1974.

Ulrich, Laurel Thatcher. *Good Wives: Image and Reality in the Lives of Women in Northern New England, 1650–1750*. New York: Knopf, 1982.

VanDerBeets, Richard, ed. *Held Captive by Indians: Selected Narratives, 1642–1836*. Knoxville: U of Tennessee P, 1973.

Van Gastel, Ada. "Ethnic Pluralism in Early American Literature: Incorporating Dutch-American Texts into the Canon." *Early American Literature and Culture: Essays Honoring Harrison T. Meserole*. Ed. Kathryn Zabelle Derounian-Stodola. Newark: U of Delaware P, 1992.

Van Gelder, Roelef. "'A Richly Blessed Land Where Milk and Honey Flow': New Netherland Seen by Dutch Eyes." *The Birth of New York: Nieuw Amsterdam, 1624–1664*. New York: New-York Historical Soc., 1982. 26–39.

Vaughan, Alden T. "Early English Paradigms for New World Natives." *Proceedings of the American Antiquarian Society* 102.1 (1992): 33–67.

Vaughan, Alden T., and Edward W. Clark, eds. *Puritans among the Indians: Accounts of Captivity and Redemption, 1676–1724*. Cambridge: Belknap-Harvard UP, 1981.

Vaughan, Alden T., and Virginia Mason Vaughan. *Shakespeare's Caliban: A Cultural History.* New York: Cambridge UP, 1991.

Vaughn, Jack A. *Early American Dramatists: From the Beginnings to 1900.* New York: Ungar, 1981.

Vecsey, Christopher. *Imagine Ourselves Richly: Mythic Narratives of North American Indians.* New York: Crossroad, 1988.

Virga, Patricia H. *The American Opera to 1790.* Ann Arbor: UMI Research, 1982.

Wahlgren, Erik. *The Vikings and America.* London: Thames, 1986.

Warkentin, Germaine. *Canadian Exploration Literature: An Anthology.* Toronto: Oxford UP, 1993.

Warner, Michael. *The Letters of the Republic: Publication and the Public Sphere in Eighteenth-Century America.* Cambridge: Harvard UP, 1990.

———. "New England Sodom." *American Literature* 64.1 (1992): 19–47.

Warner, Thomas E. *Periodical Literature on American Music, 1620–1920: A Classified Bibliography with Annotations.* Warren: Harmonie Park, 1988.

Watters, David H. "'I Spake as a Child': Authority, Metaphor, and *The New-England Primer.*" *Early American Literature* 20.3 (1985–86): 193–213.

Watts, Steven. *The Republic Reborn: War and the Making of Liberal America, 1790–1820.* Baltimore: Johns Hopkins UP, 1987.

Weber, David J. *The Spanish Frontier in North America.* New Haven: Yale UP, 1992.

Weddle, Robert S. *The French Thorn: Rival Explorers in the Spanish Sea, 1682–1762.* College Station: Texas A&M UP, 1991.

———. *The Spanish Sea: The Gulf of Mexico in North American Discovery, 1500–1685.* College Station: Texas A&M UP, 1985.

Weslager, C. A. *The Swedes and Dutch at New Castle.* Wilmington: Middle Atlantic, 1987.

White, Peter, ed. *Puritan Poets and Poetics: Seventeenth-Century American Poetry in Theory and Practice.* University Park: Pennsylvania State UP, 1985.

White, Richard. *The Middle Ground: Indians, Empires, and Republics in the Great Lakes Region, 1650–1815.* New York: Cambridge UP, 1991.

Whittenburg, James P. "Primal Forces: Three Interlocking Themes in the Recent Literature on Eighteenth-Century Virginia." *Virginia Magazine of History and Biography* 104.1 (1996): 113–20.

Wiget, Andrew. *Native American Literature.* Boston: Twayne, 1985.

———. "Reading against the Grain: Origin Stories and American Literary History." *American Literary History* 3.2 (1991): 209–31.

———. "A Talk concerning First Beginnings: Teaching Native American Oral Literature." *Heath Anthology of American Literature Newsletter* 9 (1993): 4–6.

Williams, Daniel E., ed. *Pillars of Salt: An Anthology of Early American Criminal Narratives.* Madison: Madison, 1993.

Williams, Jerry M., and Robert E. Lewis, eds. *Early Images of the Americas: Transfer and Invention.* Tucson: U of Arizona P, 1993.

Williams, Robert A., Jr. *The American Indian in Western Legal Thought: The Discourses of Conquest.* New York: Oxford UP, 1990.

Williams, Walter L. *The Spirit and the Flesh: Sexual Diversity in American Indian Culture*. Boston: Beacon, 1986.

Williams, William Carlos. *In the American Grain*. New York: Boni, 1925.

Wills, Garry. *Inventing America: Jefferson's Declaration of Independence*. Garden City: Doubleday, 1978.

Wolf, Edwin, II. *The Book Culture of a Colonial American City: Philadelphia Books, Bookmen, and Booksellers*. New York: Oxford UP, 1988.

Wolter, Jurgen C. *The Dawning of American Drama: American Dramatic Criticism, 1746–1915*. Westport: Greenwood, 1993.

Wong, Hertha Dawn. *Sending My Heart Back across the Years: Tradition and Innovation in Native American Autobiography*. New York: Oxford UP, 1992.

Wood, Gordon S. *The Creation of the American Republic, 1776–1787*. Chapel Hill: U of North Carolina P, 1969.

———. *The Radicalism of the American Revolution*. New York: Knopf, 1992.

Wood, Peter H. *Black Majority: Negroes in Colonial South Carolina from 1670 through the Stono Rebellion*. New York: Knopf, 1974.

Wright, Donald R. *African Americans in the Colonial Era: From African Origins through the American Revolution*. Arlington Heights: Harlan Davidson, 1990.

———. *African Americans in the Early Republic, 1789–1831*. Arlington Heights: Davidson, 1993.

Wright, Louis B. *The Colonial Search for a Southern Eden*. New York: Haskell, 1973.

———. *Religion and Empire: The Alliance between Piety and Commerce in English Expansion, 1558–1625*. Chapel Hill: U of North Carolina P, 1943.

Yewell, John, Chris Dodge, and Jan DeSirey, eds. *Confronting Columbus: An Anthology*. Jefferson: McFarland, 1992.

Zacher, Christian K. *Curiosity and Pilgrimage: The Literature of Discovery in Fourteenth-Century England*. Baltimore: Johns Hopkins UP, 1976.

Ziff, Larzer. *Puritanism in America: New Culture in a New World*. New York: Viking, 1973.

———. *Writing in the New Nation: Prose, Print, and Politics in the Early United States*. New Haven: Yale UP, 1991.

Zimbardo, Rose, and Benilde Montgomery, eds. *African-American Culture in the Eighteenth Century*. Spec. issue of *Eighteenth-Century Studies* 27.4 (1994): 527–692.

Zolbrod, Paul G. *Reading the Voice: Native American Oral Poetry on the Page*. Salt Lake City: U of Utah P, 1995.

Zoltvany, Yves F., ed. *The French Tradition in America*. Columbia: U of South Carolina P, 1969.

Zuckerman, Michael. "Introduction: Puritans, Cavaliers, and the Motley Middle." *Friends and Neighbors: Group Life in America's First Plural Society*. Philadelphia: Temple UP, 1982. 3–25.

Notes on Contributors

José F. Aranda, Jr., assistant professor of English at Rice University, teaches Chicano and American literature. While working on a book-length manuscript tentatively titled "When We Arrive: Literature, Colonial History, and the Politics of a Chicano Nation," he has had two essays on María Amparo Ruiz de Burton and theories and politics of resistance published, in *American Literature* (1998) and in *Recovering the US Hispanic Literary Heritage*, volume 3 (1999). He plans a book-length cultural biography of Ruiz de Burton that will place her in the context of late-nineteenth-century liberalism and cultural debates.

Rosalie Murphy Baum is associate professor of English at the University of South Florida in Tampa. Editor of the first edition of *Contemporary Poets of the English Language* (1970), she coedited with Seymour Gross the Norton Critical Edition of Nathaniel Hawthorne's *The Blithedale Romance* (1978). She has written numerous essays on American and Canadian literature in journals including *Eighteenth-Century Studies* and *Mosaic*, and her essay on John Williams's captivity narrative was published in *A Mixed Race: Ethnicity in Early America*, edited by Frank Shuffelton (1993). In 1996 she was awarded her university's Krivanek Distinguished Teacher Award.

Pattie Cowell is professor and chair of English at Colorado State University. Her publications include a facsimile edition of Cotton Mather's *Ornaments for the Daughters of Zion* (1978); *Women Poets in Prerevolutionary America, 1650–1775* (1981); *Critical Essays on Anne Bradstreet*, coedited with Anne Stanford (1983); and essays in such journals as *Early American Literature, Signs, Bulletin of Bibliography*, and *American Literary History*. Her current work includes a study of late-eighteenth-century Philadelphia writers' networks.

Kathryn Zabelle Derounian-Stodola, professor of English at the University of Arkansas, Little Rock, co-authored *The Indian Captivity Narrative, 1550–1900* (1993) with her colleague James A. Levernier. She has published a collection, *Women's Indian Captivity Narratives* (1998), and she has edited a collection of essays, *Early American Literature and Culture: Essays Honoring Harrison T. Meserole* (1992), and *The Journal and Occasional Writings of Sarah Wister* (1987). She is at work on a study of the Dakota War of 1862.

Gregory Eiselein is associate professor of English and director of graduate studies at Kansas State University. He is the author of *Literature and Humanitarian Reform in the Civil War* (1996) and of essays in such journals as *Prospects, Clio, Essays in Literature*, and *Texas Studies in Literature and Language*. He is at work on a study of the erotics of literary form in nineteenth-century America and, with Anne K. Phillips, *The Louisa May Alcott Encyclopedia*.

Joseph Fichtelberg is associate professor of English at Hofstra University. He is the author of *The Complex Image: Faith and Method in American Autobiography* (1989) and of many essays on early American literature and culture and the editor, with G. Thomas Couser, of *True Relations: Essays on Autobiography and the Postmodern* (1998). His current project is a book-length study, "Critical Fictions," which treats the relations between early American fictions of sentiment and the rise of liberal society.

Edward J. Gallagher is professor and former chair of English at Lehigh University. He teaches multicultural American literature from colonial times to the present, and his current project involves innovative teaching with electronic resources. He has published essays on John Lloyd Stephens and on the American myth of success, and his current project is a study of John Brougham's mid-nineteenth-century representation of early America. He is the teaching-page coordinator for the Web site of the Society of Early Americanists and coordinator of *SiteScene: A Biweekly Review of New Electronic Resources*, an online publication of the American Studies Crossroads Project.

Philip F. Gura is professor of English and American studies and adjunct professor of religious studies at the University of North Carolina, Chapel Hill. With over thirty-five essays in such journals as *American Literature*, *New England Quarterly*, and the *William and Mary Quarterly*, he has published widely in American literature and culture through the nineteenth century. His books include *The Wisdom of Words: Language, Theology, and Literature in the New England Renaissance* (1981), *A Glimpse of Sion's Glory: Puritan Radicalism in New England, 1620–1660* (1984), and *The Crossroads of American History and Literature* (1996). A skilled "old-time" banjo player, he is the author, with James F. Bollman, of *America's Instrument: The Nineteenth-Century Banjo* (1999).

Sharon M. Harris is professor of English at the University of Nebraska, a founding officer of the Society of Early Americanists, and a coeditor of the journal *Legacy*. She is the author of *Rebecca Harding Davis and American Realism* (1991), along with other titles, including *American Women Writers to 1800: An Anthology* (1995), *Selected Writings of Judith Sargent Murray* (1995), *Redefining the Political Novel: American Women Writers, 1797–1901* (1995), and, with Heidi Jacobs and Jennifer Putzi, *American Women Prose Writers, 1870–1920* (1998). Her current projects include two book-length studies: "Resisting/Colonizers," a study of race, class, and the law in eighteenth-century New England women's writings, and "Doctoring Women," on the role of women physicians in nineteenth-century literature and culture.

Gary L. Hewitt is assistant professor of history at Grinnell College. His areas of expertise — the history of early North America and of plantation societies and slavery — are reflected in recently published work in the *Historical Encyclopedia of World Slavery* (1998) and in his essays "The State in the Planters' Service: Politics and the Emergence of a Plantation Economy in South Carolina" and "Vegetables and Virtue: Eliza Lucas Pinckney, 1722–1795," forthcoming in two collections of essays. He is at work on the book, "Origins of the Old South: The Political Economy of Expansion in South Carolina and Georgia, 1663–1763."

Dennis D. Moore, associate professor of English at Florida State University, received FSU's 1999 University Distinguished Teacher award. He is an active contributor to several professional associations concerned with early American culture. He is the editor of *More Letters from the American Farmer: An Edition of the Essays in English Left Unpublished by Crèvecoeur* (1995), which received the "Approved Edition" citation of the Center for Scholarly Editing. He is completing a readers' edition of Crèvecoeur's unpublished writings and a collection of critical essays about Crèvecoeur.

Carla Mulford, associate professor of English at Pennsylvania State University, was the founding president of the Society of Early Americanists and the editor of colonial materials for the canon-shifting *Heath Anthology of American Literature* (1st ed., 1990). Her publications include over twenty-five essays, as well as *John Leacock's First Book of the American Chronicles of the Times, 1774–1775* (1987); *Only for the Eye of a Friend: The Poems of Annis Boudinot Stockton* (1995); a Penguin Classics edition of W. H. Brown's *The Power of Sympathy* and H. W. Foster's *The Coquette* (1996); and *American Women Prose Writers to 1820*, with Angela Vietto and Amy E. Winans (1998). Her current book project, "Benjamin Franklin and the Discourse of Empire," examines Franklin in the eighteenth-century global imperial marketplace of peoples and ideas.

Dana D. Nelson, professor of English at the University of Kentucky, was guest coeditor of the journal *American Literature* (1998–99). In addition to numerous essays in American literature and cultural studies, her publications include *The Word in Black and White: Reading "Race" in American Literature, 1638–1867* (1991), *National Manhood: Capitalist Citizenship and the Imagined Fraternity of White Men* (1998), and editions of Rebecca Rush's *Kelroy* (1992) and Lydia Maria Child's *Romance of the Republic* (1997). She is writing "Representative/Democracy," a study of the political psychology of representation and democratic practices of the late eighteenth and early nineteenth centuries.

Russell Reising is professor of American literature and chair of the Department of English at the University of Toledo. He is the author of *The Unusable Past: Theory and the Study of American Literature* (1987) and *Loose Ends: Closure and Crisis in the American Social Text* (1997) and numerous articles on American literature in such journals as *American Quarterly, New England Quarterly,* and *Boundary 2.* He is writing two books on LSD, one an analysis of the impact of LSD and psychedelia on Anglo-American culture and the other a collection of interviews.

Jeffrey H. Richards is associate professor and chair of English at Old Dominion University. He is writing a series of essays on early American drama and theater, projects that are outgrowths from his well-known books in the field, including *Theater Enough: American Culture and the Metaphor of the World Stage, 1607–1789* (1991), *Mercy Otis Warren* (1995), and an edition of early plays in the Penguin Classics series, *Early American Drama* (1997).

Nicholas D. Rombes, associate professor of English at the University of Detroit Mercy, recently cofounded the journal *Post Identity*. Currently working on a project on visual culture in the American Enlightenment, he has contributed essays on the Enlightenment and American Federalism to *Studies in American Fiction, Arizona Quarterly*, and *Making America, Making American Literature: Franklin to Cooper* (1996). He is a contributor to *The Heath Anthology of American Literature*, volume 1.

Karen E. Rowe, professor of English at the University of California, Los Angeles, was the 1982 recipient of UCLA's Distinguished Teaching Award. Her areas of expertise include early American studies, women's studies, and multicultural issues in higher education. She has published *Saint and Singer: Edward Taylor's Typology and the Poetics of Meditation* (1986) and articles about early American literature in *Modern Philology* and *Puritan Poets and Poetics* (1985). Her essays on fairy tales, women's literature, and gender and multicultural studies have appeared in journals and critical collections, such as *Fairy Tales and Society* (1986) and *Women of Color and the Multicultural Curriculum* (1994), and teaching anthologies.

James Ruppert, professor of English and Alaska Native studies at the University of Alaska, Fairbanks, is preparing an anthology of Athabaskan oral narratives from Alaska and the Yukon territory. A past president of the Association for the Study of American Indian Literatures, he is the author of *D'arcy McNickle* (1988) and *Mediation in Contemporary Native American Fiction* (1995), in addition to a study guide on poetry, *Guide to Poetry Explication: American Literature, Colonial to Twentieth Century* (1989).

William J. Scheick is J. R. Millikan Centennial Professor of Literature at the University of Texas, Austin. His numerous essays and more than twenty books on British and American literature include the following titles in early American studies: *The Will and the Word: The Poetry of Edward Taylor* (1974); *The Writings of Jonathan Edwards: Theme, Motif, and Style* (1975); *Seventeenth-Century American Poetry: A Reference Guide*, with JoElla Doggett (1977); *Design in Puritan American Literature* (1992); and *Authority and Female Authorship in Colonial America* (1998). He continues to serve as the founding editor of the Society of Early Americanists newsletter.

David S. Shields, professor of English at The Citadel, teaches American literature and culture. Having written numerous works on early American literature and culture, he is writing (with Fredrika Teute) a study of women in the early republican era, "The Republican Court and the Public World of Women." His best-known publications include his long essay on the culture of belles lettres in the *Cambridge History of American Literature*, volume 1 (1994), and his books *Oracles of Empire: Poetry, Politics, and Commerce in British America, 1690–1750* (1990) and *Civil Tongues and Polite Letters in British America* (1997). He is editor of the primary journal in the field, *Early American Literature*.

E. Thomson Shields, Jr., is associate professor of English at East Carolina University, where he directs the Roanoke Colonies Research Office and edits the *Roanoke Colonies Research Newsletter*. Currently at work on a literary history of the colonial Spanish area called la Florida, he has written numerous essays in a variety of journals, including *Early American Literature, Medievalia et Humanistica*, and *Hispanófila*. His two most recent essays are on English and Spanish exploration narratives (Thomas Harriot Seminar Occasional Paper 26, 1998) and on ethnography in Spanish Franciscan writings, in *Recovering the US Hispanic Literary Heritage*, volume 3 (1998).

Frank Shuffelton is professor of English and American literature at the University of Rochester. He has written widely on early American literature and culture. His books include *Thomas Hooker, 1586–1647* (1977) and *Thomas Jefferson, 1981–1990: An Annotated Bibliography* (1992), along with two well-known collections of essays, *The American Enlightenment* (1993) and *A Mixed Race: Ethnicity in Early America* (1993). Currently at work on projects on Mary Rowlandson and Phillis Wheatley, he continues his work on Thomas Jefferson as a man of letters.

Amy E. Winans, assistant professor of English at Susquehanna University, is working on a book-length project tentatively titled "Slaves and Citizens: Early African America and the Discourse of Nations." She has published essays on Anthony Benezet, Olaudah Equiano, and Harriet Jacobs and on slave narratives for the *Reader's Guide to Literature in English* (1996), the *Encyclopedia of American Literature* (1998), and the *American National Biography* (1999). A contributing editor of the Dictionary of Literary Biography volume *American Women Prose Writers to 1820*, she is an associate editor of a forthcoming anthology, *Early American Writings* (gen. ed. Carla Mulford).

Index

The index lists names of persons mentioned in the essays. The appendixes, syllabi, works-cited lists, and Edward Gallagher's bibliographical essay have not been indexed.